3-28.68

ALSO BY CARLO FALCONI

Pope John and His Council

The Popes in the Twentieth Century

CARLO FALCONI

The Popes in the Twentieth Century

From Pius X to John XXIII

Translated from the Italian by Muriel Grindrod

WITH ILLUSTRATIONS

LITTLE, BROWN AND COMPANY   BOSTON   TORONTO

1441387

Contents

Illustrations

Preface

20 July 1903, a little after midday: St Peter's Square, torrid under
the dazzling sun, is completely deserted. At the entrance to the
Piazza Rusticucci, a group of journalists stands about waiting.
Suddenly the rattle of wheels on the paving stones from a *frullone*
travelling at top speed breaks the silence (*frulloni* were the closed
carriages still in use in the Vatican at the beginning of the
century). One of the journalists hurries after the carriage and
manages to catch a glimpse behind its curtains of the stern countenance of Cardinal Serafino Vannutelli. That is enough for him:
he knows what is afoot. The hasty arrival, at so unorthodox an
hour, of the Chief Penitentiary of the Holy Roman Church, whose
office it is to administer the last rites to a dying Pope, speaks more
plainly than any official bulletin issued by the Master of the
Sacred Vatican Palaces: either Leo XIII has just died or his hours
are numbered. Confirmation comes at once from the noisy arrival
of more *frulloni* bringing Cardinals Mathieu, Cassetta, Sanminia-
telli, and others. Soon more prelates arrive from the Vatican or
the various departments of the Curia. By then the group of
journalists has broken up, and a few townspeople begin to appear.
But the siesta hour and the heat still keep the square empty: only
in front of the Arco delle Campane are a few more curious by-
standers beginning to gather. But at two minutes past four, when
Pope Leo breathes his last in his improvised sickroom on the
second floor of the Loggia, no one yet knows of his end.

3 June 1963: for three days and nights St Peter's Square and the
Bernini colonnades and the Piazza Pius XII at the opening to the
Via della Conciliazione have been packed with people. They are
for the most part new to that kind of gathering and in that place,

but most of all new in their silent, sorrowful demeanour. The throng that normally fills the square consists partly of the devout, partly of the curious, equally ready to be astonished or enthusiastic. Some seek inner consolation but the majority are spectators of the dramatic sensations evoked by the folklore of a scenography and choreography handed down for centuries with meticulous fidelity. The throng of these past three days, however, has not been brought here by any festive rite or picturesque ceremony. It knows it will be able to see nothing; it has come not to receive but to give. What has brought it spontaneously here is an invisible rite, carried out without sacred vestments, croziers, or incense, without feathered fans and acolytes. Though celebrated by a Pope, it is a natural rite, the most solemn and august rite in the world, that of the last agony. Between hours of lucidity and unconsciousness, it has been prolonged in uncertainty but now it has reached the limit of hope. Yet among all these people, some of them believers, many of them 'outsiders', there is a deep sense of both emotion and peace, desolation and trust. From time to time, in one corner or another of the vast square rises a low half-muted hymn or the intoning of a prayer. But the real prayer and hymn is the tremendous silence that for long periods envelops all those present, so that even the sound of the loudspeakers giving news or making some announcement cannot break or profane it.

Ever since, more than a week before, the seriousness of John XXIII's illness had become known, thousands of people had begun to take their stand in the square, as if to mount a guard of honour never previously envisaged by any tradition or convention. But when he grew worse and there was no more room for hope, the whole of Bernini's enormous bowl was invaded and filled by the silence and tension that only the announcement of his death – first given mutely when the lights in his room went on at 7.49 p.m. – was to dissolve.

20 July 1903 – 3 June 1963: two dates – the dates that open and close the chronological compass of this book – that correspond to two symbols, for they mark the extremes of the parabola of the Papacy in our century: from an apex of temporal and, so to speak, domestic, exclusively Roman-Catholic, glory, to an apex of spiritual and ecumenical glory, the patrimony of all without distinction of race or confession or even religion. And it is symptomatic that

while the first event aroused only a moderate stir and curiosity, the echo of the second was without precedent not only in Rome but in the whole world.

We have, of course, to remember the kind of atmosphere prevailing in Rome at the dawn of the century: the still watchful, suspicious rivalry between the Vatican and the Quirinal, seat of the monarchy; the Masonic influence pervading the Italian Government and its home and foreign policy; the enfeeblement and humiliation of religious feeling. Many people, especially among the leading classes, believed that the Church was a lost cause and that only Leo XIII's exceptional personality had delayed its end. In addition to this Pope Leo, now over ninety, had for years been living on the threshold between life and death, displaying a sort of lively and provocative flirtatiousness. It was as if it vastly entertained him to keep on a string those who, after a twenty-five-year pontificate, longed for a change of men and methods. 'We elected a Holy Father, not a Father Eternal,' Cardinal Oreglia di Santo Stefano, Dean of the Sacred College, used to go about saying – in feigned annoyance but really delighted at his own *bon mot*.

Be that as it may, the pontificate that came to an end on that torrid summer day of 20 July 1903 was undoubtedly one of the greatest in history. And the frail old man with the extreme pallor and keen, malicious eye who had just abandoned his throne was one of the giants among the Popes. To find a pontificate that bore comparison with his it was necessary to go back beyond Benedict XIV, in the middle of the eighteenth century, to the heart of the seventeenth century at least. Why then this near-indifference at his death?

Because – the answer can be given now – Leo XIII nevertheless did not seem the ideal Pope; just as later his most impressive successors, Pius XI and Pius XII, were not ideal Popes. No Pope, for example, had ever so occupied the public gaze as did Pius XII; yet no pontiff of modern times had so lonely an end as he, or one so surrounded by unfitting drama. Pius X and Benedict XV, the first two Popes of the century, seemed for a moment to approach the ideal cherished, if largely from confused intuitions, by the Christian world. Both destroyed these illusions, if for different reasons – the first from excess of manichean masochism, the second from the misfortune of a too brief reign.

It is, moreover, certainly no mere chance that the death of the last great traditional Popes should continually have prompted Catholic writers from their various standpoints to sketch the portraits of ideal Popes. Barely a year after Pope Leo's death there appeared in England *Hadrian VII* by Frederick Rolfe (Baron Corvo), with its sparks of prophetic intuition, many of which were destined to wait half a century before being realized; and the year after, in Italy, came Antonio Fogazzaro's *Il Santo*. And it was still in Pius xii's lifetime that Giovanni Papini brought out his controversial *Celestino VI*.

The truth is that only the advent of John xxiii was to give the true answer to that question, revealing that the object of Catholicism's most authentic aspirations was not merely the end of old-style temporalism, still less its replacement by another more equivocal and insidious form of temporalism. What it awaited was neither more nor less than a new conception of the Papacy and hence of the Church. Up to the time of Pope John's election, the prevailing conception of the Church in the Catholic world had been of a structure descending from top to bottom, from the head, the seat and fountainhead of authority and all other power, to the members. This was essentially a juridical conception, concerned almost exclusively with establishing the rights of authority and uniting them in the supreme pontiff, while the 'subjects' were merely a subordinate consideration. The new ecclesiology under Pope John, which was to be ratified by the Ecumenical Council, Vatican ii, provided instead for an ascending structure: it still culminated in the head, but its starting-point was the members, regarded as 'the people of God' and hence as constituting the fundamental reality of the Church. Essentially theological, based on the Scriptures and tradition, this new ecclesiology strives above all to know God's designs for His people and to activate the whole body towards their realization through the help of the various directive organs. Consequently, while according to the first conception the Pope is a sovereign who can never be given enough honour and praise and power, according to the second conception he is truly 'the servant of the servants of God', as he was defined in earliest tradition.

This is the fundamental fact that makes the advent of John xxiii the most revolutionary date in the history of Catholicism. With him, in fact, the over-long chapter of the Constantinian or temporalist Popes, the absolute theocrats, is closed, and a new chapter opens in the history of the Papacy – a chapter that will also have its complications and setbacks, but whose path is inexorably traced and defined. Temporal power came to an irrevocable end under Pius IX: the new direction initiated under John XXIII will be equally irrevocable. It took sixty years (from 1870 to 1929, the date of the Lateran Pacts) to bury the Roman Question completely. Whether it will take more time or less to bury the old idea of the Papacy is unimportant: what matters is that it has been condemned in principle alike by a Pope and a Council.

This latest evolution of the Roman Papacy – a Papacy whose claims in the past proved a stumbling-block first to Orthodoxy and then to Protestantism – could no doubt be analysed more thoroughly by the complex and difficult method of examining all the component factors that produced it. But a more concise and all-embracing way is to study its development through the lives of the twentieth-century Popes, its protagonists.

True, Leo XIII put an end to the negative and bankrupt period of Pius IX and his predecessors, and restored the prestige of the Church after the Papacy had sunk almost to the level of the darkest ages of Christianity. He established and exercised a new influence for the Church in the world, but he does not go beyond his own century. He does indeed form a bridge between his predecessors and his successors, at least up to Pius XII, but as theoretician of the juridical conception of the Church inherited from the nineteenth century and earlier he belongs to the end of the period of certainties that reached its highest point under him. Immediately after him, under Pius X, the modern crisis of the Papacy opens, a crisis of recognition. The Papacy was not yet aware that its problems arose from putting into practice the Leonine ideology, then believed to be definitive and immutable – so much so, indeed, that it was taken as the basis for the Code of Canon Law brought into effect by Pius X and Benedict XV. In vain was Pius XI to strive to adduce in support of the juridical neotemporalism of the Church the ideological thesis of the Kingship of Christ; in vain was Pius XII to re-evoke the dogma of the Mystical Body and attempt a spiritual interpretation of the Church as the Kingdom of Christ: the crisis both within Catholicism and outside it became increasingly apparent.

The biographies in this book will show whether and to what
extent the five Popes who are its subjects were aware of this
crisis. But in any case, and quite apart from their various degrees
of awareness, the important point is the objective reality of the
crisis that led to the reversal of the whole conception of the
Church and the Papacy under John xxiii. The first four Popes of
the twentieth century may have cherished the illusion that their
worries and struggles arose merely from anxiety about their
failure to establish permanent and close relations with the non-
Catholic world, whether civil or religious: in fact they were
struggling against a conception of their function which made all
their efforts sterile.

Up till now all the histories of the modern Church, and hence
of the Papacy, especially when written by Catholics, have steered
clear of this fundamental drama, not only in relation to its main
protagonists but also to the more enlightened of its members.
Lives of the Popes have been written mainly to satisfy the
curiosity of those who want to know the exceptional story of
that handful of men who in each century have come to occupy
one of the most isolated and exalted positions in the world. This
is of course a perfectly legitimate curiosity. It is natural that
people should want the answers to questions such as, where did
these men come from? how were they chosen? what spiritual and
natural gifts are sought in them? what are their feelings as they
see the papal tiara gradually approaching them and what kind of
shock they experience when suddenly confronted with it? what
is their real attitude towards their own almost unlimited power
in religious and diplomatic affairs? how do they conceive of the
nature of their tasks and how do they gird themselves to fulfil
them? how do they react towards the men who do indeed serve
them, but for the most part, whether courtiers or ministers, with
the intention of proving their masters? . . . All these are natural
questions, but their importance and interest wane in the face of
a fact of such exceptional historical significance as we have suggested – the revolution of the whole situation and conception of
the Papacy. True, that revolution will more especially affect the
history of future pontificates, but it will also have repercussions
on those of the past as they are increasingly seen to have been
troubled about their own inadequacy, and as they come nearer
to the culminating moment of catharsis reached by John xxiii.

This book is the first attempt to view the modern Papacy in such a perspective, even though up to the last pages the reader may be hardly aware of it. Indeed what might be called its thesis had little or no influence on its drafting. It was only when the book was finished that the author discovered that a thesis had imposed itself on him, and after long reflection he found himself compelled to recognize its truth and testify to it in these opening pages.

In an earlier preface, drafted before writing the individual biographies, the author's main object was to try to explain the reasons for the tremendous interest of the past twenty years in the affairs of the Catholic Church and especially in its Popes. (Among such reasons, apart from the new role of broadcasting and television which is undoubtedly the most immediate practical cause of the phenomenon, are the increasingly central and dominating part played by the Papacy during the last century within the Church itself; the re-entry of the Church, if largely in the moral sphere, into international politics, as a result of the de-temporalization of its central organs following on the loss of the Papal States; and, lastly, the inclusion of the Roman Church into the ecumenical movement of the Christian Churches, in which it has come to play a vital role through the proposals it has advanced.) That is an important and interesting subject in itself but one which I came to feel must yield place to my other central theme.

As for the lives of the Popes themselves as given in this book, they are here based only to a small extent on the more or less official published biographies. These, being largely of a hagiographical nature, have been used merely for the essential facts, especially the facts directly relating to each pontiff's government, which are also recounted in the official publications of the Holy See. Otherwise the works consulted have included the best of the ecclesiastical histories, from whatever source, and all the other available literature on the subject such as memoirs and letters of churchmen or diplomats, as well as articles in periodicals and the press.

In addition to this, in the absence of the Vatican secret archives (still closed as regards the period of the Popes dealt with in this book) the author has been able to make use of various unpublished and generally inaccessible sources such as the records of the various stages of hearings leading up to the

beatification or canonization of Pius x, his Secretary of State
Cardinal Merry del Val, Cardinal Andrea Ferrari, Archbishop of
Milan under the pontificates of Leo xiii, Pius x and Benedict xv,
etc. These hearings took place during the past fifteen years, but
they also made use of testimonies collected earlier during the
preliminary stages of the inquiries, and so bring before the
reader practically all the personalities of the Curia, great and small,
from the heads of the Secretariat of State to those of the minor
Congregations, as well as many representatives of the Italian and
foreign episcopate.

The biographies of the five Popes related in this book are thus
certainly not 'conformist' biographies. But their unorthodox
treatment is confined to avoiding the methods of ritual hagio-
graphy while at the same time steering clear of the partisanship
or sectarianism of the professional anticlericals. The sole criterion
has been respect for historical truth, so that the author, besides
dissipating some misplaced haloes, has sometimes found himself
according recognitions unusual among lay historians. Thus while
devotional readers may deplore it or even feel shocked when
here and there some thing or person seems belittled, some
revelation too crude, those of an opposite view may be astonished
at certain recognitions of agreement or approval. But just because
of these opposite reactions, the book will, it is hoped, emerge in
the end as a serious attempt at investigation untrammelled by
preconceived standards or unjustifiable inhibitions, carried out
purely in the spirit of historical veracity.

Rome, 31 March 1966

Note. Some passages in the chapter on Pius xii have been taken from
the author's essay, 'Note sul Pontificato di Pio XII', published in *Nuovi
Argomenti*, no. 6, January–February 1954, pp. 61–117, and from his
profile of Pius xii in *I Protagonisti* (Milan, C.E.I., vol. xii, 1965,
pp. 29–56; 'Giano' edition, 1966). Some passages about Leo xiii
occurring in the early pages of the chapter on Pius x have been taken
from the author's profile of Leo xiii, published in *I Protagonisti*,
vol. xi, 1966, pp. 225–52 ('Giano' edition, 1967). Some pages in the
chapter on John xxiii have been taken from the introduction to the
author's *Documents secrets du Conseil* (Monaco P., 1965).

The Popes in the Twentieth Century

Pius X : Giuseppe Sarto

4 August 1903 – 20 August 1914

'Sede Vacante'

The plenary congregation of cardinals had decided on the evening of Saturday, 25 July, for the burial. The embalming had been done on the 21st (after the removal of the heart, lungs, and entrails which, enclosed in an urn, had been escorted and deposited by night, in accordance with tradition, in the church of Saints Vincent and Anastasius), and from late on the 22nd the body had been lying on the catafalque in St Peter's. For three days, from six in the morning to three in the afternoon, people had been able to pass in procession before it within the gates of the Chapel of the Sacrament, though they could not kiss the feet, as another tradition demanded, because of the unusual heat – or so the official explanation ran: malicious rumour said it was because the embalming had not been successful.

The ceremony began at seven in the evening with a funeral rite beside the body, now transferred to the Chapel of the Choir on the other side of the basilica. After the service the frail little corpse of Pope Leo XIII had been placed in the ritual triple coffin with a primitive and exhausting ceremonial that lasted until 9.30 pm, by which time the authorities' and the cardinals' seats had begun to empty. First the official seals had to be affixed by the Cardinal Chamberlain, the Majordomo, and the Cardinal Archpriest, then the technicians had to seal the second coffin with lead. When it came to the third coffin, this was fastened down not with screws but with nails, and the hammer-blows added a further sinister note to the sombre ceremony.

Finally, at 9.30 pm, the laborious business of winching up and raising the coffin began. When it had been transported to the crypt it only remained to place it in its appointed tomb. In the

words of *Civiltà Cattolica*, 'the *sanpietrini* carried out the operation
with the greatest skill and care'. But one of the cardinals who
had stayed on, perhaps the most modest among them but also
the most observant, the Patriarch of Venice, Giuseppe Sarto,
noticed a detail that chilled his blood. Next day he remarked to the prefect of pontifical ceremonies, Mgr Carlo Respighi, 'Did you notice how the *sanpietrini* gave Leo XIII's coffin
a final kick to shove it into the tomb? That's how the Popes
finish.'

Twenty-odd years before, on 13 July 1881, something much
worse had happened to the body of Pius IX: while it was being
transported by night from the Vatican to St Lawrence Without
the Walls where its tomb had been prepared, a street crowd
shouting insults against the dead Pope halted the cortège and
even tried to throw the bier into the Tiber. But if those days were
now forgotten it was largely due to Leo XIII himself, who had
aroused admiration even among many of his opponents. Kings and
heads of State and politicians of renown from all over the world
had been on cordial terms with him or had shown their respect for
him – men such as Umberto Rattazzi, Ruggero Bonghi, and
Francesco Crispi in Italy, Gambetta in France, Bismarck in Germany, the Tsars of Russia Alexander II and III and Nicolas II, the
Sultan of Turkey, the Shah of Persia, the Mikado of Japan, the
Emperor Menelik II of Abyssinia. Only two or three months
before his death he had been visited in the Vatican by King
Edward VII of England, and, a few days later, by Kaiser Wilhelm
of Germany: when the latter heard of his death while on holiday
on his yacht he pronounced a funeral oration before the crew. As
someone said with a touch of kindly malice, the most ferocious
enemies of the Church could hardly refuse their sympathy to a Pope
who, with his great eyes and wide sardonic mouth, remarkably
resembled Voltaire.

Literary men, too, vied with the statesmen in their praise of
him. D'Annunzio lauded his graceful Latin and boasted of his
favour, Bourget described him in the last pages of his novel
Cosmopolis, Pascoli hymned him in 'La Porta Santa' . . . Mommsen
alone did not rise from his table on the day he saw him come into
the Vatican Library. He was the only Pope in history to re-
capitulate (at the twenty-fifth anniversary of his accession, in 1902)
the story of his own pontificate in a strong encyclical which

included a realistic appraisal of the inheritance he was soon to leave to his successor.

When, in 1878, Giovanni Pecci was elected Pope Leo XIII at the age of sixty-eight a good many people had thought he was in poor health because of a strange trembling of his right hand, the result, it would seem, of inexpert bloodletting. 'If they unfortunately elect me,' he had given people to understand, 'they'll have to have another Conclave soon.' As if to bear out this prophecy, he refused to have a whole private apartment in the Vatican, contenting himself with a single room at the entrance to the official apartment, divided in two by a partition. He used half of it as a bedroom, the other half as a study and had his meals served on a little table on which was placed the sealed box brought from the papal kitchens. But, while it may be true that he never expected to receive the tiara (he had left behind all his papers open and unsealed at Palazzo Falconieri in Rome), it is no less true that, once he took possession of the Vatican, he made no secret of his intention of leaving an indelible mark.

During his predecessor's pontificate he had been openly in opposition, although in a noble and dignified way, rather as befitted an exile. In point of fact, his chief adversary was Pius IX's Secretary of State, Giacomo Antonelli, who is said to have been largely responsible for delaying for some years his receiving the cardinal's hat. In any case, as Archbishop of Perugia he had established there a sort of little 'anti-Vatican' with a court of faithful followers, bringing into being literary and philosophical academies and writing pastorals which were the complete antithesis of Pius IX's encyclicals and in which he significantly anticipated the themes he was later to pursue to a very different public as Pope. It was after reading these writings of his and reflecting on the situation in the Sacred College that Ruggero Bonghi, in his *Pio IX e il Papa futuro* (Pius IX and the Next Pope), of 1877, with remarkable foresight deduced Pecci's election to the pontificate a year later.

When he left his pseudo-Vatican in Perugia for the authentic one, Pecci changed in one thing only, the consciousness of his supernatural investiture. Outwardly, he continued to be rather careless and untidy in his dress (he took snuff and, though he nearly always had a handkerchief in his hand, its traces could be seen on the upper part of his white robe), but when a visitor was announced or he had to appear at some ceremony or at a public audience he at once became transformed, assuming the hieratic pose of a sovereign and creating around him an impressive atmosphere of inaccessibility.

If he wished to be in every way the opposite of Pius IX, he succeeded most effectively in the sphere of policy. Only a few hours after his election he was heard to say, 'I want to carry out a great policy,' and that 'I' on the lips of one who never once forgot to use the royal 'We', left no doubt that he and he alone would hold the reins of Vatican policy, whoever his collaborators might be. An infallible judge of men (among the 146 Cardinals he created, nearly all of whom predeceased him, were Newman, Gibbons, Lavigérie, and Capecelatro), he chose collaborators of exceptional stature, especially as Secretaries of State. Concerned about the position of the Holy See *vis-à-vis* Italy, then governed by the demagogic and anti-clerical Left, he strove constantly to ward off the danger that he might end up as merely the head of the national Church in Italy. He thus did for the Church what Cavour did for the little state of Piedmont, successfully bringing it back into the orbit of the great Powers until it occupied a position of prestige in international affairs. He was openminded, first in accepting the bait offered him by Bismarck and then in furthering, at all costs, good relations with the French Republic, but his diplomatic activity was equally tireless towards all the Chancelleries both within and outside Europe. Perhaps one of his greatest moments of pride was when he was called upon to arbitrate in the question of the Caroline Islands and Cuba; and certainly one of the greatest disappointments of his life was the exclusion of the Holy See, through the instrumentality of Italy, from the international conference at The Hague in 1899.

All this high-level diplomatic activity did not, however, prevent Leo XIII from perceiving, despite his advanced age and lack of direct experience, the importance of the newly arising problems in the social and economic spheres. Not that he was particularly attracted to such problems in themselves, for he always remained substantially a conservative even if much more progressive than his collaborators (his *Rerum Novarum*, or 'Encyclical on the Condition of the Workers', is very limited in scope and takes good care not to mention, let alone condemn, capitalism); but he had grasped the fact that power was now moving down from the top to the lower levels of society and that the popular masses, especially the peasants, would constitute the future basis of the Church's power.

As a genuine humanist, moreover, he was proud to be able to react against his predecessor's obscurantism by pursuing a courageous cultural policy. True, it is open to question whether the revival of Thomism – the theology and philosophy of St Thomas Aquinas – was an enlightened decision on his part, especially in the forms in which he at first seemed to accept it on the suggestion of the experts around him. But it must not be forgotten that during the eighteenth century Catholic culture had lost not only its own philosophical tradition but even its faith in philosophy, particularly in metaphysics. Thus the Thomist revival was really an essential stage towards the acceptance of a philosophical and theological pluralism which even now the Catholic Church has not yet in fact achieved. In any case, that he had more long-sighted aims can be seen from his faith in it and from the encouragement given to the neo-Thomism of the future Cardinal Mercier.

In the field of biblical studies, too, his encyclical *Providentissimus Deus* may, indeed, have had restricted horizons, but it had at least the merit of establishing biblical criticism in its own right among the other ecclesiastical disciplines, and the blessing he gave to the Biblical School in Jerusalem founded by Père Lagrange testifies to his desire to see it prosper and develop. The fact remains that where it was possible to act without restrictions, he did so, as for instance in the sphere of historical studies. The opening, by his wish, of the Vatican archives makes him truly the father of ecclesiastical history in modern times.

The great ambition of Leo XIII was to bring the Catholic Church to the same level of progress as the secular world in every sphere. Many of the acts of his pontificate repeat in new terms, or with more authoritative decisions, the declarations of sympathy and belief in science and progress to be found in his last pastorals from Perugia, under such symptomatic titles as 'The Catholic Church and the Nineteenth Century' or 'The Church and Civilization'. In one of these he declared:

How grand and majestic man appears when he summons the electric spark and sends it, messenger of his will, across the ocean deeps, the mountain heights, and the limitless plains! How glorious he is when he harnesses steam to give him wings and take him with the speed of a whale by sea and through the land! How powerful, when his genius develops this force, imprisons it, and leads it through prepared paths to give movement and almost intelligence to crude matter which takes the place of man and relieves him of his hardest labours!

In the same pastorals the then Archbishop of Perugia had even dared to play down Pope Pius IX's *Syllabus*, declaring that it should not be 'set up as a scarecrow to frighten the world', but understood according to the truth of each of its propositions in the light of the relevant documents, which, when carefully examined, would be found to obviate any suggestion that it might condemn the modern State or true civilization. As Pope (and it is significant that his sole opponent in the Conclave was the author of the *Syllabus*, Cardinal Bilio himself) he no longer permitted himself to use such strong terms: his opposition to Pius IX was concrete and positive rather than verbal and negative. He even went so far as to maintain the desirability of a dialogue with the world at large and himself initiated such a dialogue, though, in accordance with his way of seeing things, as teacher rather than as between equals – indeed his role as teacher is undoubtedly the most lasting side of his whole pontificate. A good many of his sixty encyclicals are of relatively minor importance (and reveal, incidentally, the most unexpected aspect of Leo XIII as a man if not as Pope, his devotional piety – ten of them are on the rosary alone!) but at least a third 'make history'.

His one real mistake was that, in concentrating on the teaching role and on political, social, and cultural activities, he neglected the need to modernize the Church's central and peripheral organization. The departments of the Curia should, of course, have seen to this, at any rate with some prompting from him, but the Curia continued to live in a chaotic state of muddled and over-lapping organizations, and virtually nothing was done to reform it during his pontificate. His gaze was fixed too high and too far off to take in realities nearer home.

Quite apart from his lack of interest and belief in technical organization, Leo XIII was really deeply concerned only in matters that he dealt with personally. The government of the Church and the prestige of the Papacy were for him strictly personal questions in which he would countenance no assistants or collaborators who might impinge too closely. This was one reason for his isolation, and for certain forms of the 'personality cult' about which he was highly sensitive (the use of the gestatorial chair, the large escort of guards and prelates that accompanied him even in the Vatican gardens, his strange withdrawals into the Chinese pavilion or the Swiss chalet in the gardens, and so on).

The Conclave of 1903

The greatness of Leo XIII's pontificate can only be really appreciated today, when, at this distance in time, we find ourselves constantly having to refer back to him over all kinds of questions relating to the Church in modern times. But it is understandable that at the time of his death, and especially after the last weary years of his rule, contemporaries thought of him only as a colossal and wellnigh fraudulent publicity machine. At a time of growing political crisis the diplomatic activity of his reign appeared particularly ephemeral and delusory. A truer impression was of a certain spiritual aridity. The biggest gap in Leo XIII's pontificate was, as has already been suggested, on the pastoral side, but since there was no such term in those days (although Pius X used a somewhat similar expression – '*pastoratico*'), doubts about the extent of his failure in that sphere tended to become disproportionately exaggerated.

As early as 1894, Contardo Ferrini, a devout layman who was on familiar terms with Mgr Ratti, the future Pius XI, when he was librarian at the Ambrosian Library in Milan, wrote:

At present we have a Pope who with profound knowledge, sure insight and subtle skill has prodigiously improved the Church's position in the world beyond all expectation. But at the death of Leo XIII, the Church may have need of a supreme head who will more conspicuously lead it back to the evangelical virtues of the days of the apostles, to goodness, charity, poverty in spirit, meekness; and in this sense a most fitting choice might be Sarto, who has in the highest degree the reputation of such virtue.

The mention of Sarto nearly ten years ahead of time is undoubtedly an impressive point, but even more impressive is the writer's analysis of a hope and expectation that was to become increasingly widespread – especially as coming from a university lecturer, and thus from a cultivated scholar likely to be dazzled by Leo xiii's achievements.

In October 1903 an Italian politician of strong religious feelings, Senator Tancredi Canonico, who shortly after was to become President of the Senate, made the following diagnosis of the state of the Church on the morrow of Leo xiii's death:

> The life of the Church has come to a standstill: it does not respond as it might and should to the needs of adult humanity – needs that for the most part are not even understood. Even in the transmission of the truth and of revealed precepts it is rare to hear the vibrant and vivifying note of the spirit. The secret has been lost of the word that moves the soul to its very roots and creates the Christian conscience therein without which there can be no true conversions ... and humanity finds itself deprived of the spiritual support that is its destined right.

Weariness of Leo xiii's over-long reign, and above all the conviction that its underlying weakness had been his policy of temporal aggrandizement, were decisive factors in the outcome of the Conclave. Too much importance has generally been attached to the episode of the Austrian veto against the election of Leo's Secretary of State, Cardinal Rampolla, exercised at the Emperor Franz Josef's behest by Cardinal Kniez de Kozielsko Puzyna of Cracow. The old Pope's followers who sought Rampolla's election had in fact small chance of imposing their view against the opposing group's desire for a new man who would resolutely further modernization. Moreover there was also an anti-Leonine party which, in Cardinal Mathieu's words, reproached Leo xiii and his Ministers with having 'steered the ship of Peter too exclusively within French waters'. There was, too, the long-standing tradition, based on a profound knowledge of psychology, that a pontificate with a very definite character should be followed by another of a quite different kind.

Pius xii introduced the rule that every cardinal at a Conclave must hand over all his notes about the outcome of each ballot, to be burnt together with the voting papers; but before his day it was always possible to find out how the voting had gone. In 1903 there were even two published reports about the Conclave, one by a German cardinal, Kopp, and the other by the French Cardinal Mathieu. Recently yet another such report has come to light, even more interesting and rich in details than the others since it was not intended for publication, comprising twelve pages of the secret diary of Cardinal Domenico Svampa, then Archbishop of Bologna.[1] From all these reports two facts emerge clearly: first, that there was never any mention of the possibility of a foreign – non-Italian – Pope, and secondly, that the candidature of Cardinal Gotti, supported by the third group including a strong contingent of Austrian and German cardinals, was never more than a provisional stage towards the eventual nomination of the candidate of the 'young and brilliant cardinal of Northern Italy', Giuseppe Sarto.

The first fact can cause no surprise; as long as the 'Roman Question', the dispute between the Holy See and Italy about the former Papal States, remained unsettled, a foreign Pope was inconceivable. On the other hand the fact that the Patriarch of Venice, Sarto, should have been from the outset the chosen candidate of the group that was to win the day completely contradicts the long-standing belief that his choice came only after a laborious compromise in the course of which all the more important names were eliminated. There seemed to be sound reason for this view, for Sarto was regarded as one of the most modest and obscure members of the Sacred College. This was undoubtedly true of the public in general, even in Italy. The press there, especially the lay papers, only rarely mentioned his name; its favourite was old Cardinal Capecelatro, famous both for his culture and writings and also for his liberalism. After him, but a good way after, the names most frequently mentioned were those of the cardinals of the great sees, Ferrari of Milan, Svampa of Bologna, and Richelmy of Turin. It is not surprising, therefore, that the practice of telegraphing by gestures from the windows of the Sacred Palaces the name of the elected Pope before its official announcement by the Cardinal Dean should in this instance have broken down completely. Nobody thought of Sarto when someone appeared at a window of the Majordomo's apartment and made the gestures of sewing and cutting.[2] Indeed the only thing that emerged from his diligent gesticulations was the movement of the index and the middle fingers, meant to represent scissors, but interpreted as the initial 'V' of the two

[1] The original is in the Archives of the Bologna Curia. See V. L. Bedeschi, 'Il Conclave del 1903 nel diario segreto del cardinal Svampa', *L'Avvenire d'Italia,* 16 June 1963.

[2] The name 'Sarto' means 'tailor'.

Vannutelli brothers – in itself an ambiguous message – so that
when, an hour later, Cardinal Mocchi announced Sarto's name as
the elected Pope, the crowd, taken aback, paused for a moment
before bursting into the customary applause.

For the foreign cardinals, too, the Patriarch of Venice was a
completely unknown quantity. Not only had Cardinal Sarto
never travelled outside Italy: no action of his had ever even been
mentioned abroad. Cardinal Mathieu himself, though a member
of the Roman Curia and thus resident in Rome, had never seen
him, and when he happened to find himself next to him at a
general congregation before the Conclave he asked him in
French what diocese he came from. Receiving the ritual answer
that he could only speak Latin, Cardinal Mathieu concluded, and
took a malicious pleasure in telling him so, that he was not
'*papabile*' (likely to become Pope).

Sarto may have been unknown to the twenty-four foreign
cardinals at the Conclave (the only one absent was Morvan,
from distant Australia; but Gibbons came from Baltimore, land-
ing at Le Havre in an ordinary unclerical dark suit with a white
straw hat showing his scarlet skull-cap beneath, and arriving in
Rome in this costume to the shocked astonishment of the Curia).
But he was at least a more familiar figure to the Italian members
of the Sacred College, whether of the Curia or from the various
dioceses. For them, even though he could not be said to have
put himself forward in any way, Sarto was no newcomer.

A bishop since eighteen years earlier and a cardinal for the
past ten, he had begun to make an impression between 1885 and
1894 as Bishop of Mantua, a diocese of Lombardy situated between the Veneto and Emilia and certainly not among the more
prosperous ones, religiously speaking, in those three regions.
In his first year there he ordained only one priest and one deacon,
for the local seminary had been closed for ten years. The clergy
themselves were far from docile. Among the more notorious to
leave the Church was Canon Roberto Ardigò, a gentle and disciplined man who lost his faith and became the greatest exponent
of positivist philosophy in the country. But that had happened
fifteen years before, in 1871. Among the secessions under Mgr
Sarto was that of Don Giovanni Grisanti, Archpriest of Rovere,
one of the main towns in the diocese, who became a Protestant.
To counteract that scandal Sarto himself preached a special

sermon given, to emphasize the solemnity of the occasion, in the presence of the Host. But even then the scandal was not over, for the monstrance disappeared, abstracted, so it was said, by the chaplain, who himself later quitted the Church.

The new bishop lost no time in reopening the seminary and three years later held the first diocesan synod for two hundred years there. He also made two tours of pastoral visitations and to galvanize the apathy of this difficult diocese organized the celebration of two centenaries, that of the patron saint, St Anselmo of Lucca, in 1886, and of St Luigi Gonzaga in 1891. When transferred to Venice he was no less active there, undertaking a pastoral visitation and organizing a synod and a successful eucharistic congress.

Both as bishop and as cardinal, Sarto had also come to notice outside his diocese and in manifestations of a national character. In 1889 he took part in the first National Catechistic Congress, held in Piacenza, where his proposal to adopt a single text was approved and forwarded to Rome. In the next two years he appeared at the Catholic congresses at Lodi and Vicenza. In 1896, by then a cardinal, he made a speech on the distribution of wealth and the duties of the rich at the first congress of the Catholic Union of Social Studies in Padua. He was already a familiar figure to his colleagues in that Union, for it was under his auspices that it came into being in 1889 through the work of Mgr Callegari, Bishop of Padua, Professor Toniolo, and Count Medolago Albani.

Lastly, the stand adopted on two occasions by Sarto as Patriarch of Venice had had nationwide repercussions, the first time because it caused a good deal of talk, the second for the astonishment and admiration it aroused. These two episodes in a sense characterized the beginning of his pastoral reign in Venice. In April 1895 he forbade priests and Catholics to visit the first Art Exhibition in Venice because it included a picture which he considered offensive to religion; and in the following July he gave his support to the Catholic-moderate coalition which turned out the Radical Democrats from the city council, thus maintaining the promise he had given on the day of his arrival in Venice when, seeing the Town Hall windows shut, he said: 'Never fear! We shall get them opened!'

Some of those present at the Conclave must certainly have

reminded their colleagues, especially the Leonines among them,
of how Leo xiii once described Sarto as 'the jewel of the Sacred
College'. Leo had moreover given public proof of his esteem for
Sarto in first making him a Cardinal before appointing him to
Venice, thus making it plain that the honour of the cardinalate
was being conferred on him personally rather than on the see. In
addition, when, a few months earlier, Leo xiii's Vicar in the
diocese of Rome, Cardinal Parocchi, had died he had wanted to
make Sarto his successor.

Be all that as it may, Cardinals Ferrari, Svampa, and Richelmy,
supported by others in the Curia, such as Satolli, were from the
outset of the Conclave extremely active in putting forward Sarto's
name. Svampa wrote in his secret diary: 'I have the consolation
of being able to say that at the first ballot and in all the others I
gave my vote to Cardinal Sarto.' Even before the Conclave his
name was being put about. On its eve a curious leaflet circulated
both in the Vatican and outside in which the various Cardinals
were described by scriptural quotations. Among the Italian cardinals, the quotation for Gotti was *'Cogitationes eius peribunt'* ('His
thoughts will perish'), for Svampa *'Ignis evanescens'* ('A warning
fire'), for Mocenni *'Ecclesiae diabolus'* ('Devil of the Church'), for
Agliardi *'Cor eius vanum est'* ('His heart is empty'). Rampolla even
got two: *'Flagellum Dei'* ('The scourge of God') and *'Incidit in
foveam quam fecit* ('He falls into his own pit'). The descriptions
were clumsy and often in poor taste. But the remarkable thing
was that only Sarto came well out of it, getting a quotation that
was both apposite and witty: *'Tutis Sartis redimet Israel'*.

The malicious leaflet at least had the courage to speak plainly.
It did not get things muddled, as, for instance, in the famous
pseudo-prophecy of St Malachy, according to which the new
Pope was indicated as *'Ignis ardens'*. Rampolla, in fact, given his
Sicilian origins, recalled the flames of Etna; Vannutelli, who had
the Christian name of an angel, Serafino, had 'wings of fire'; and
Gotti, Prefect of the Propaganda Fide, was not only the 'red
Pope' but as such had under his jurisdiction the line of the
Equator.

The Conclave was not without incident: besides the famous
veto against Rampolla, the law of secrecy was indubitably violated
at least at the beginning; one cardinal persisted in registering a
blank vote, indeed in the first round he wrote on his voting slip

'*neminem eligo*' (I choose nobody); and there was a rumoured attempt at intimidation by poisoning[1] after the penultimate ballot when the outcome was already clear – several cardinals were taken so ill on the last night that fifty orders for remedies were placed with the chemist next morning. To sum up briefly what happened in the seven ballots between 1 August and the morning of the 4th, for the first two days Rampolla was always in the lead, though without appreciably increasing his number of votes; starting with twenty-four at the first ballot, he got twenty-nine at the second, and reached only thirty at the third. Even reaction to the veto secured him only one more vote: he had plainly reached his limit. At the same time Gotti's vote fell steadily (seventeen, sixteen, nine and three) while Sarto's rose (five, ten, twenty-one and twenty-four) even though at the beginning of the fourth ballot he urged his supporters to concentrate their votes on a less inadequate candidate than himself.

At the beginning of the third day, the fifth ballot for the first time put Sarto in the lead, with twenty-seven votes, but while Gotti pulled up slightly (to six), Rampolla still stayed where he was. But the vote was decisive enough to cause Sarto to withdraw his opposition to election, and in the next round that afternoon he came a good deal nearer to the necessary quota of two-thirds of the total (or forty-two votes), while the Rampolla front began to collapse (sixteen votes, against Sarto's thirty-five). As was expected, the battle came to an end at the seventh ballot: the Patriarch of Venice got fifty votes, Rampolla ten, and Gotti two.

'I shall renounce the cardinalate and become a Capuchin friar,' Cardinal Sarto had said to Ferrari on the second day of the Conclave. But although he gave in later, when finally elected he showed signs of being deeply perturbed. When all his ex-colleagues hastened to leave their stalls to hear what name he would take, and the Dean, Oreglia, stood before him with his usual surly demeanour and asked him '*Acceptasne?*' – 'Do you accept?', his only answer was a sigh. He was being called on to accept the cup of Christ at Gethsemane, and Oreglia insisted almost roughly: 'Well, do you accept or not?' Sarto then hurriedly assented. 'By what name do you wish to be called?' asked Oreglia. This time there was no hesitation about the slow, calm

[1] Mentioned in Cardinal Svampa's diary, op. cit.

answer: 'Pius, trusting in the help of the holy Popes who have honoured this name by their virtues and defended the Church with strength and gentleness.'

The New Pope

If those present had been able to detach themselves at that tense moment from the atmosphere of curiosity that dominated the Sistine Chapel, they would have realized in what unusual terms the new Pope had justified his choice – for his was obviously more than a simple answer: it was a programme for his pontificate. 'Defence' meant reaction not merely to a threat or danger but to a siege, an attempt at suffocation. This signified neither more nor less than a return to the latter days of Pius ix, when, after fulminating anathemas against progress and civilization, he had immured himself in the Vatican as in a fortress to ensure the Church's survival. It was as if the whole pontificate of Leo xiii, who had brought the Church back into the world and a large part of the world back to the Church, had never existed. The new Pope, in other words, was presenting himself to his ex-colleagues as a general who, after the sensational experiment of a war of movement carried on under his predecessor, was returning for reasons of sentiment to the old tactics of a war of position.

Ever since the days of Sergius iv in the eleventh century when the custom of taking a new name began, a Pope's name has always been symbolic, almost like a *nom de guerre*. When Giovanni Pecci took the name of Leo, though he did so partly out of gratitude to Leo xii, he did not conceal his hopes of measuring himself against the greatest of his predecessors, Leo the Great, Leo ix, Leo x: Popes who had overcome the barbarians, rebuilt the power of Rome, or patronized the arts in the Renaissance. Sarto, on the other hand, can hardly have had in mind Pius ii and perhaps did not even remotely envisage St Pius v; the Piuses he chiefly remembered were those of the calvary under Napoleon, and most of all Pius ix, the martyr Pope *par excellence* in spirit even though he shed no blood. In contrast to his predecessor's optimism he resolutely if modestly opposed his own pessimistic, not to say masochistic, conception of the Church in the world: a Church not inured to triumphs but, as in the Bible, rejected, misunderstood, isolated and humiliated.

Even physically, and in his whole bearing, the new Pope strikingly recalled Pius IX. Both of them impressive though of only medium height, it was above all the faces of the two Popes, open, luminous, and of a harmonious regularity, that drew people to them and evoked their sympathy. Their regular features were enhanced by the gentle, rather mournful liveliness of their great eyes, which were deep and intense, while a rebellious lock of hair in the middle of the forehead gave to each a touch of almost youthful boldness. Pius IX, especially before he became Pope but also in the early days of his astonishing election at the age of only forty-eight, was quick, lively and almost ostentatious in his movements and walk. But from the very beginning Pius X in this respect resembled him only in the composed and solemn majesty of the last bitter years of his reign.

From the very beginning, however, what inevitably struck people most was the antithesis between him and the dead Pope. This antithesis emerged as soon as he set foot in the Vatican. The famous Bishop of Cremona, Mgr Bonomelli, in a letter of 6 October 1903 quoted the impressions of his own secretary: 'The Vatican is no longer what it was under Leo XIII: there is a simplicity about it that it does one good to see.' The apartments reserved for Leo and his close colleagues had always been inaccessible to everyone else and so seemed immensely remote; but when Pius X inherited and extended them (he himself had his private apartment on the third floor) they soon became, especially in the early days, the most frequented quarter of the Sacred Palaces. The Venetians in particular invaded them, bringing their friends and filling them with their lively chatter in the dialect of the Lagoons to the scandalized astonishment of the Roman courtiers. But the most incredible thing was that the new Pope seemed to adapt himself to all this bustle and did not even bother to turn away the many *arrivistes* and adventurers in priest's clothing who thronged Rome at that time. He could not say no to the many sculptors and painters who vied to portray him, and sacrificed hours of his day to them. It seemed that the Vatican had been invaded not so much by the Patriarchate of Venice as by a whole lively, noisy parish which it was hard to imagine adapting itself to the traditional atmosphere of Court and Curia.

Those closest within the circle were quick to notice other significant details of difference between the two Popes, the one more regally aristocratic, the other more intrinsically proletarian. For example, Leo XIII, out of respect for the customary etiquette, never wore a watch; Pius X made no mystery of the fact that he used a simple nickel watch worth a few shillings which he valued because it had been at his mother's deathbed. Leo XIII used a quill pen, not only to sign important documents or to inscribe elegant Latin hexameters in his leisure moments, but also for letters or jotting down notes; Pius X used a perfectly ordinary pen and himself cleaned its nib or changed it, sometimes so hurriedly that he would rub it on the sleeve of his pontifical white robe. Leo XIII always received Catholics on their knees, the only exception being for cardinals, kings and princes, and when presiding over congregations of cardinals he always made the prelates and advisors stand; Pius X made them all sit down, sometimes even in private audiences offering his own seat.

Everyone, however, was immediately impressed by Pius's cordial friendliness and simplicity. Unlike his predecessor, a sovereign of the old stamp who in twenty-five years had never exchanged a word with his coachman, he talked to everybody and often joked with them. These jokes, like his acts of kindness to humble people, were repeated and enlarged upon until it became impossible to distinguish fact from fiction. This simple familiarity made an even greater impression because Pope Sarto openly confessed to anyone who came near him in the early days his dismay at finding himself buried in this magnificent and labyrinthine palace, at every turn under the eye of a prelate or a gendarme. His admitted nostalgia for Venice aroused particular sympathy. Most of all he missed the contact with people and with nature. In those days general audiences were rare events, and he had to content himself with seeing the faithful only on the occasion of some religious ceremony, on the other side of a grille or from the height of his detested gestatorial chair. True, he could walk in the Vatican gardens whenever he wanted; but with all those neat flower-beds and pebbled paths he seemed, as he used to say, to be moving in a cemetery. Accustomed to the wide plains and flat countryside around Venice, the hilly landscape he saw from his apartment in the Vatican gave him a feeling of insecurity and unrest. He liked Rome only because of its climate, warm enough even in winter to allow him to go without a heavy cloak or overcoat.

Thus, little by little, the legend emerged of the country Pope a prisoner in the Vatican: a legend nourished by all the most minute episodes of his life, becoming more precious day by day like a golden legend of medieval days. There is nothing surprising about this. The story of the gentle melancholy Pope, caught up in Rome – where he had been only a few times in his life because its complicated immensity always embarrassed him – by the surprising decision of the cardinals of the whole world, and compelled to live there till his dying day, was like an incredible fairy-tale. He, no less than his relatives, would have been the first to laugh incredulously if anyone had foretold it. Between the modest one-storey cottage on the outskirts of Riese in the Treviso plain, dwarfed by comparison with the nearby inn of the Two Swords whose sign can still be seen today on the fading plaster walls, and the Vatican palaces, there was no visible link. Yet God had woven that link from the virtues of the bailiff's little son destined to wear the tiara.

The first of these legendary virtues was the simple, serene poverty that remained with him from his earliest childhood. At that time the necessary means to send him into the priesthood had had to be found by the parish priest and a generous benefactress, Countess Marina Loredan-Gradenigo, a former lady-in-waiting at the court of Napoleon I, whose estate was near Riese. But for his lesser expenses such as books and clothes the boy Giuseppe had to go round and collect from door to door in the village before going back to the seminary each year. What he collected was not always enough, especially after his father died when he was seventeen and the family found itself in debt. When his first cassock had to be bought his mother, Margherita, had to take an old mattress to the pawnshop in Castelfranco. Yet at his first Mass she and Giuseppe's three sisters were, so said one of them, Maria, 'so happy to have a priest in the family that they felt as if they had become fine ladies'. Giuseppe himself, however, whether as the young chaplain of Tombolo, parish priest of Salzano, canon and monsignore of the Chapter of Treviso, as bishop, or finally as Patriarch, was never allowed to cherish any such illusion – as can be seen from his letters, where a recurrent topic is his personal budget and his need to ask for loans or for time to repay them. Writing from Venice, from one of his two little ground-floor rooms amid the vast magnificence of the

Doges' Palace, he said: 'At Mantua I was always poor, but here I have become positively a beggar.'

But this was not meant as a lament but rather as a cry of joy. For this was the way he wanted to live, having no idea how to save nor any interest in doing so. When he was an impoverished chaplain at Tombolo with the debts for his studies still to be paid, his success as a preacher used to bring him hitherto un-dreamed-of sums – a golden napoleon, a *genova*, a *fiorella* (coins worth, respectively, twenty, eighty and thirty-six Venetian lire); but by the end of the day they had usually ended up in the pockets of people poorer than himself. When such unexpected sources failed, his watch or his priest's ring would find their way to the pawnshop, and the furthest possible pawnshop so that no one should suspect what he was doing. At Salzano, though it was quite a prosperous benefice, his barn was alway empty, and for dinner he had 'a heap of lean, consumptive-looking beans'.

Another virtue to adorn the legend of the new Pope was his humility. The obscure chaplain of Tombolo had certainly no grounds for self-indulgence, but once a parish priest he might at least have allowed himself some small satisfaction, if only the pomp of a ceremonial induction such as was customary in the dioceses of the Veneto. Instead, both his arrival at Salzano and his departure from it were as quiet as possible. He genuinely disliked ceremonies in his honour, and hated to be thanked. He had little ambition to rise in his career. When, after four years in the Chapter at Treviso, it was rumoured that he was to be made an auxiliary bishop, he wrote to a cousin: 'The experience of four years in the Chapter has made me realize what thorns and dangers and responsibilities there are in such a post; the seeming fame of becoming a bishop is no compensation for them, for everything vanishes away when one reflects, with St Philip Neri, "And then? – and then? – and then? . . . death!" '

The public legend about the new Pope was not aware of the final stage of the episode at the burial of Leo XIII which we mentioned earlier. It was revealed only later by Mgr Respighi. When his friend the prefect of the pontifical ceremonies came to kiss his foot after his election, Pius X just said: 'Do you remember that kick?' The legend, however, expanded, nourished on ever more vivid and appealing details illustrative of his simplicity and goodness. At Venice, it was said, his nickname was the Patriarch

of the Gondoliers; at Mantua, when he found time to take a
walk he would go beyond Porta San Giovanni to the banks of
the Mincio to gossip with the fishermen. There was never any
mention of connections with the great or wealthy or of meetings
and conversations in the more elegant quarters of the city.

Such was the man, or rather the saint, so the legend ran, whom
the dove that Cardinal Rampolla turned away from his window-
sill on the first day of the Conclave, and that then alighted at
Sarto's window, made prisoner of the Vatican.

The Parish-Priest Pope

The image of the new Pope that the legend tended to form was,
in fact, that of a Pope who, in spite of everything, remained
simply and solely a parish priest. This was undoubtedly true, and
not only in relation to the past but also, at any rate in part, to the
present as well. Sarto had remained a parish priest not only for
practically the whole of his life in the diocesan priesthood but
also as bishop and Patriarch. Mantua to him was really just a
much bigger parish than his earlier cures. Mgr Ratti, librarian at
the Ambrosiana, arriving by chance at the bishop's palace one
morning found no one there but Sarto, who hastened to serve
Mass himself and afterwards prepared him some coffee. He often
acted as his own secretary and clerk, and also regularly gave
lessons in the seminary.

In Venice the situation changed only outwardly. Venice, moreover, is not really a diocese but just a town that is also diocese,
enclosed within its group of islands and only near enough to the
mainland not to feel quite cut off from the other dioceses on its
borders. Thus despite the magnificence of the purple, which
incidentally he donned as seldom as possible, Sarto came to look
on himself as simply a super-parish priest among his subordinates,
and to behave as such.

In Rome he maintained a number of parochial customs, at the
same time imposing the ideas that had matured in him throughout forty years of pastoral ministry. One of the new Pope's
greatest surprises for his court was his resolve to hold an explanation of the catechism for the public every Sunday afternoon in
the courtyard of San Damaso. No Pope had ever dared so to
humble himself. But to Pius x these catechism afternoons were

among the most delightful hours of his pontificate. Only six months after his election he decided to make closer contact with his new diocese and on 11 February 1904 announced an apostolic visitation throughout Rome. He had already, on St Cecilia's day, 22 November, issued the *motu proprio 'Tra le sollecitudini'*, later to become famous, announcing the reform of sacred music throughout the Church. Later, in 1905 and 1910, he promulgated two decrees, *'Sacra Tridentina Synodus'* and *'Quam Singulari'*, concerning, respectively, frequent and daily Communion and the admission of children of tender years to their first Communion.

Instruction in the catechism – liturgical piety – devotion centred on the Eucharist: these were the three distinguishing features of his pastoral ministry from the first moment he assumed the responsibilities of a priest. All three were plainly inspired by the needs of the deepest and most fundamental religious feeling. A proof of this was the absence of the cult of the Virgin Mary. Indeed Sarto always held aloof from all marginal aspects of religious practice prompted largely by reasons of sentiment or folklore; this can be seen from the fact that before taking steps against the aberrations and excesses of city life his first care was to bring about a return to the pure spirit of the gospels in the villages of the Venetian countryside.

The rural religious life of the Veneto in those days, and indeed still today, was characterized by 'the fear of God' – a fear of God curiously similar to the Lutheran idea in its pervading sense of sin but also, and perhaps even more, in its complacent attitude towards sin and especially towards the sweetest of sins, the sin of the flesh. This in no wise contradicted the fact that, especially in the countryside, conformity (of the legalistic Austrian stamp) allowed of no deviation. Catholicism was the overruling tradition, absorbing and sublimating all others: and this very complacency towards sin, the object at once of attraction and repulsion, of fascination and fear, induced a compensatory urge towards faith and towards the outward practice of it – a faith and a practice whose public manifestations merely intensified in proportion to any secret yielding to forbidden pleasures. In the words of an imaginary priest in a contemporary Venetian novel, 'In our countryside men are born Catholics and never become Christians'. In any case, especially in the Veneto of those days, in that magically smooth land softened by the sirocco breeze that lends a feminine pliancy even to the most virile character, permeating the habits and even the dialect of the inhabitants and tempering them to a resigned and almost innocent gentleness, the only manifestation of austerity was in religion. And since in the life of man the years of the temptations of the flesh are only a parenthesis, austerity easily won the day, supported by the authority of the elders strong in their uncompromising guardianship of tradition.

Conformity, the outward acceptance of religion, was the great enemy against which Sarto began to fight as soon as he became a priest. In his view, people could only arrive at a consistent belief in their own faith through a wider knowledge about it, and above all through its inculcation from their earliest years. Religious practice should be reduced to its essential elements, untrammelled by purely decorative features. These conclusions of his are not particularly surprising in themselves, but it was remarkable that he should have arrived at them in a region such as the Veneto where there was still no sign whatever of any weakening of faith. The need, for instance, to give children a feeling of religion from their earliest days had not yet become urgent there, where the new social and economic factors at work in other regions did not apply. The Treviso plain knew nothing of the phenomenon of industrialization that elsewhere was beginning to cause children to leave school early, to quit their homes and go into new and often undesirable surroundings. There was, in fact, as yet no need there to evolve a means of protecting children from the unhappy experiences to which they might be exposed as they grew up. That Sarto should nevertheless have made such a point of establishing an early age for the first Communion, instead of the then customary age of fourteen, is highly significant.

His own conviction on the subject cannot, of course, suffice to eliminate doubts about a child's receiving the sacrament when too young to understand its meaning and importance. But if once infant baptism, and indeed the obligation of parents to see that babies are baptised as soon as they are born, is admitted, then the criterion adopted by Sarto as a parish priest, and the rule enunciated by Pius x in *Quam singulari*, follow as a logical conclusion. It is also true that in putting back confirmation and the first Communion to a very early age – both in order to impress the

solemn event on children's minds and to afford their parents a
new stimulus towards religious observance – Pope Sarto was in
no wise going against conformist opinion, as can be seen from
the costly and elaborate customs that grew up around the new
practice. But in any case there can be no doubt about the Pope's
good faith, especially after his views had been confirmed by
experience both in Mantua and in Venice. It is also significant
that the *motu proprio* on frequent Communion preceded by five
years that on early Communion for children. His basic care was
clearly to make the sacramental relationship between the believer
and God as constant and continuous as possible; and seen in this
perspective early Communion for children was only a detail.

The scandalous secularization of Church music which Sarto
tackled in *Tra le sollecitudini* was not a very pertinent question in
the villages of the Veneto; but in the larger towns it took on
increasingly elaborate forms. This was no doubt partly due to the
drying up of religious inspiration; but another reason was that
composers of church music, impressed by the contemporary
vogue for opera, decided that the best way to preserve the
renown of the cathedral choirs was to provide them with music
that drew its inspiration from opera. Thus the *Gloria*, the *Credo*,
and the motets in the variable parts of the Mass were soon
burgeoning with themes in the style of Verdi, Rossini, Puccini,
or even Wagner, accompanied not by the harmonium or organ
alone but by whole orchestras or bands. Trumpets vied with
flutes, violin solos with the harp, and cymbals and the bass drum
accompanied the choir. Cathedrals and the more ambitious parish
churches were invaded not only by dozens of instrumentalists
and choristers but also by solo tenors or sopranos who sang in
operatic style for the edification of a congregation packed as for
a theatre. Naturally the worshippers paid more attention to the
choir than to the altar, waiting for the moment when their idol
would appear in a cavatina or duet, for all the world as if they
were on the stage. When it was not possible to raise a full choir or
orchestra, or at less solemn festivals, the accompanist at the organ
or harmonium was nearly always a virtuoso who drew on
operatic overtures for his voluntaries, elaborating their themes
or reproducing them whole even during the most solemn
moments of the Mass such as the consecration and elevation.

In the eighteenth century and for much of the nineteenth,

churches used to draw their biggest congregations during Lent, but by the early 1900s they were filled to capacity only for such performances as these, which in vying with the theatre amounted to a profanation of the church. The liturgy lost all its sacred atmosphere and became a mere excuse for a concert. The sacraments ceased to be understood and valued, and prayer itself was reduced to an emotion whose only religious element lay in its surroundings. Pius x's reform, urging the restoration of Gregorian chant and polyphonic music, put an end to this scandal and made the churches once more places for prayer and meditation centred around the most solemn liturgical celebrations. Moreover Sarto when he came to Rome already had behind him an example of successful reform in church music. His own interest in the subject dated back to the days when he was choirmaster in the seminary at Padua and in his own early parishes. Just before he went to Venice he had got to know the musician Lorenzo Perosi, from the lagoon village of Tortona, and he made him conductor of the choir of St Mark's, imbuing him with his own ideal of music as a spiritual and elevating factor.

The Forgotten Curial Clerk

As with all legends, the legend that grew up around Pius x from the earliest days of his pontificate tended to neglect certain things in his life which did not quite fit in with the story.

What significance could it have, for instance, that the young student in theology had been for three years 'prefect-in-charge' of some classes at the seminary in Padua (where he went thanks to a grant for students from the Treviso neighbourhood)? And was it really important for the legend of the parish-priest Pope that he had been a curial clerk?

As to the first of these facts, the authors of the legend were really not to blame for neglecting it. For it was only a few years ago that the registers were found in the seminary library in which Sarto as prefect used to make six-monthly reports on those in his charge.[1] The discovery proved both fascinating and unexpected. For these notes provide a key both to the young Sarto's gifts of psychological insight and to his idea of the priesthood. Unfortunately, in accordance with the traditions of the institution

[1] See note in Bibliography, p. 372.

the notes were written in Latin, which plainly somewhat inhibited the writer. At first he evaded the difficulty by relying
almost entirely on biblical terms (of one seminarist he said '*Deum
precatur corde non ficto*' (He prays to God with an open heart), of
another '*ambulat iustus in simplicitate cordis*' (He walks uprightly in
simplicity of heart)), which led to somewhat unrevealing and
generic descriptions, as when of a third he said '*Dominus haereditas
eius*' (The Lord is his inheritance). Later on, however, he evolved
a more personal kind of formula which conveyed his meaning
better, such as, when speaking of a subordinate given to gossip,
'*Durum illi linguam in officio continere . . .*' (It is hard for him to keep
a watch over his tongue), and if he found it really difficult to
express his thoughts he even had recourse to Italian. '*Ipse curam
habere demonstrat, at nihilominus, ut vulgo dicitur: Un poco freddo*' (he
strives to be considerate but is, in vulgar parlance, a cold fish).
But the main importance of these notes is that they constitute
the background for his pontifical action on seminaries (the reform
of 16 January 1906), on the training of young clergy (the encyclical *Pieni l'animo* of 28 July 1906), and in the exhortation to
the clergy of the world on the occasion of his Jubilee in the
priesthood (4 August 1908).

Documents such as these, and far-reaching decisions such as
those on seminary reform and on the establishment of regional
seminaries in Italy (in regions split up into several dioceses the
small diocesan seminaries were in no position to provide adequate
training in philosophy and theology), were of course also the
fruit of Sarto's much wider experience as teacher and spiritual
director in the seminary at Treviso and later as bishop. But the
germ of it all lies in those early notes.

The other neglected aspect of Sarto's life, his activities as a
curial clerk, also had an important influence on his decisions as
Pope. It would indeed be strange were this not so. For this work
occupied him on an average six hours a day, for eighteen years
of his life, and under three different bishops. True, it was an arid
task, concerned chiefly with the technical and material side of
spiritual activities; but since it had to do mainly with the rights
and duties of the bishop and the priests and with their relations
with the Congregations of the Roman Curia, it afforded him an
exceptional insight both into the needs of his fellow-priests and
the functioning of church management. From this experience

Sarto became profoundly convinced of two needs: the codification of canon law, and reform of the Roman Curia.

How urgent he felt these needs to be, can be seen from the speed with which he tackled them on becoming Pope. The decision at last to give the Church a code of canon law came only eight months after his election, with the *motu proprio Arduum sane munus* of 19 March 1904. It was a fulfilment of his earlier aspirations both as curial clerk and as student. For with his instinctive bent towards clear and concrete ideas Sarto must have felt even in his seminary days that law was the answer. Philosophy and theology could not provide precise enough guidance; moral theology with its casuistry did not differentiate sufficiently. Law alone went to the heart of the matter. The only difficulty, and it was a serious one, lay in the chaotic state and number of the laws.

As a chaplain at Tombolo, Sarto used to divide his leisure hours between reading the *Somma teologica* of St Thomas Aquinas – itself a text of exemplary clarity – and the *Decretali* of Graziano. But it was of course his experience as a curial clerk that chiefly made him aware of the problem of codification. He became convinced that the average clerk was profoundly ignorant about canon law, and as bishop he constantly urged its study. Indeed, in Venice he got permission from Leo XIII to establish a chair of canon law in the seminary, with the right to award academic degrees.

Fate played into his hands when he became Pope in providing him in the Secretariat of State with the very man for the job: Mgr Gasparri, Under-Secretary of the Congregation of Extraordinary Ecclesiastical Affairs, had in fact been Professor of Canon Law for over twenty years at the Catholic Institute in Paris. He was, moreover, both a tremendous worker and an inspiring colleague. When the Pope told him what he wanted, he guaranteed to codify the canon law within twenty years and at a minimum cost. Pius x had no difficulty in believing him: Mgr Gasparri wore big shoes like himself and, much more than Sarto, had kept the measured, steady pace of a mountaineer. He had nothing of the honeyed mildness of the Venetians – on the contrary, he was rough and rugged almost to hardness. But he was a man of extremely clear and penetrating thought, decisive in action and wellnigh infallible. Pius x had nothing in common with Gasparri who, despite his humble origins, had all the characteristics of an intellectual and a consummate diplomat; but he recognized his abilities and gave him *carte blanche*. He had, besides, observed some differences of opinion between Gasparri and the Secretary of State, Merry del Val, and this offered a means of separating them. Thirteen years later – seven years before the proposed date – and at a cost to the pontifical Treasury of only fifty thousand lire of those days (although at times as many as fifty thousand collaborators were at work on it in Rome and other parts of the world in addition, of course, to the fifty members of the special commission), the Code of Canon Law was completed according to promise with all its 2,414 articles, and at Whitsun 1917 Benedict xv promulgated it to the whole world.

Pius x missed by just three years being present at that solemn event, which set the seal on one of the most lasting undertakings of his pontificate. Whether as well as promoting this great work he should also be thought of as constantly inspiring and directing it, is difficult to say today. The new Code naturally included all the measures initiated by Pius x concerning the Curia and the reforms of the clergy, seminaries, and the liturgy, but that in itself would not suffice to establish his personal imprint upon it. The Code was first and foremost a synthesis of the canon laws accumulated throughout the centuries, chief among them being the deliberations of the great ecumenical councils and of lesser synods. The contribution of certain legally-minded pontiffs, in particular Benedict xiv, is also clearly apparent in some sections (such as the reasons for beatification and canonization, in the case of Benedict xiv). Lastly, the influence of Benedict xv, himself an experienced jurist, must not be forgotten, coming as it did in the vital latter stages. Nevertheless the marks of Pius x are plain enough to be seen, especially in the parts suggested by his experience in the offices of the Curia. And his spirit, at times that of a simple priestly piety, at others more nearly resembling inquisitorial zeal, emerges beyond question here and there. But Pius x's chief responsibility in relation to the Code of Canon Law undoubtedly lies in its pervading conception of the Church and of its rigid hierarchical structure, constituting the most solemn ratification of the ecclesiology that culminated in the nineteenth century with the first Vatican Council and the encyclicals of Leo xiii: thus demonstrating incidentally, his unawareness of the strident contradiction between his own work of evangelical reform and the suffocating effects of legal curbs and checks not sufficiently attuned to purely spiritual needs.

Pius x also devoted himself in the early years of his pontificate to reform of the Curia, and on 28 June 1908 promulgated the apostolic constitution *Sapienti consilio*. But this reform was by no means so radical and far-reaching as the title sometimes accorded him, of 'second founder of the Roman Curia', would suggest. This is not merely because only a few years later his successor had to introduce substantial modifications to it. Pius x's plan for reform of the Curia was in fact simply a technical reorganization of the Vatican departments, with no attempt at reform of personnel, recruitment, or training. Such a reorganization was the very least he could do – especially in drastically reducing the number of departments and sub-departments which had multiplied under Pius ix, largely to provide posts for former officials of the civil pontifical administration dismissed after the suppression of the Papal States Pius x inherited thirty-seven from Leo xiii, and reduced them to nineteen). His main aim was certainly to distinguish administrative from judicial authority (the two had hitherto existed side by side in each department) but this, though doubtless necessary, did not touch the heart of the problem. So *clientelismo* – the seeking of favours from the higher prelates, especially the cardinals – continued to characterize the Curia, and pursuit of their career persisted in most of its members at the expense of the true priestly spirit and zeal for the Church's progress which should have been its hallmark.

A peripheral reform of the clergy without reform of the Roman prelacy was a decapitated reform, and this Pius x failed to realize. He merely succeeded, and this was at least something, in putting an end to or at any rate greatly reducing the scandal of those 'wandering priests' who, prompted by ambition or disputes with their bishops or just by loneliness and poverty, came to seek their fortunes in Rome from the poorest parts of Italy. They came in their hundreds and of all ages in search of a benefice, some without degrees, some staying on in Rome after graduating, often miserably poor and living only on alms from collections taken in the churches where they said Mass and from the charity of some religious institution, ready to do anything if only they could get into some department or secure the protection of some high prelate. The Romans called them '*scagnozzi*' (beggar-

priests) and they were easily recognizable by their ragged clothes
and hungry look. Their existence was a disgrace to the dignity of
the priesthood even if they did not actually compromise it, as not
infrequently happened, by stealing or some other offence. Pius x
established severe laws against priests staying in Rome when not
directly under its diocese, and this scandalous situation gradually
died down though it never completely ceased to exist.

The Unknown Aspect

Not all the gaps in legends are due, like those mentioned above,
to an understandable need for simplification. Sometimes, unfortunately, details that do not fit in with an idealized picture are
eliminated without regard for completeness or historical truth.
This is what happened with the legend of Sarto: the exaltation
of the parish-priest Pope had the sole aim of showing Pius x as by
definition the 'good Pope' – good both idyllically, all sweetness,
gentleness, and kindliness, and in an appealing way, as the silent
and forgiving victim of cruel enemies.

But in Sarto there was not only the simplicity that charmed
and the kindliness that conquered all hearts: there was also a
strength that stiffened and a toughness that reacted firmly. This
dual aspect of his personality must have been apparent from the
earliest days of his training in the seminary, for it is the consequence of the ascetic ideal which he then embraced never to
abandon it. His cordial expansiveness to others was counterbalanced by his severity towards himself. But when he became a
priest it was at once evident that in him gentleness was not
synonymous with weakness, nor compassion with compromise.
And in this he was merely conforming to the accepted ideal of a
priest in his part of the world.

It should be borne in mind that the most typical characteristic
of the Veneto from the religious standpoint is its place as, so to
speak, the Vendée of Italy. There is no need to go back to the
Middle Ages to realize the truth of this. The historical events that
most deeply affected it are of more recent date: the Council of
Trent in the second half of the sixteenth century, and the annexation to Austria in 1797. The first event made it a sort of experi-
mental ground of the Counter-Reformation; the second subjected
it to the no less decisive experiment of Habsburg jurisdiction.

Both events caused it to remain apart from those contacts with the enlightenment of the eighteenth century and the secularism of the nineteenth which so profoundly influenced, for example, Piedmont through its relations with France and Switzerland (even the Napoleonic occupation of the Veneto was short and superficial, lasting only ten years). Consequently when, after its reunion with Italy in 1866, it was invaded by the new secular bureaucracy and ideas, the reaction of the local aristocracy, and even more the clergy, except for a few open-minded spirits like the poet Giacomo Zanella, took the form of an extreme integralism.[1]

Even a superficial knowledge of the Catholic movement in Italy from 1870 to the First World War will show that many of its leaders came from the Veneto – such men as Toniolo and Paganuzzi, Saccardo and Sacchetti, the Scottons and Cerutti or Giuseppe della Torre. Romolo Murri, trying to explain in one of his essays why among all the regions of Italy only the Veneto remained obstinately impervious to the Christian Democrat movement which he founded, wrote:

The Catholic Veneto, except for Rosmini whose powerful intellect and mind outstripped all narrow local confines, never entered into the spirit of the Catholics in the Risorgimento; and in the period under review it stood chiefly for the anti-Risorgimento. Its idea of authority was Austrian, developed in an atmosphere of complete agreement between ecclesiastical and civil authority and a supine acceptance of authority by the subjects; and Austrian, too, was its unreadiness to adapt itself to freedom.

He might also have added that because in the Veneto respect for authority and for seniority were linked together, it had little understanding for his own movement, which aimed at rejuvenation and bringing in the young.

As for the clergy of the Veneto, fundamentally conservative and docile in relation to civil as well as ecclesiastical authority, the two being linked in their minds by respect for the maxim 'throne

---

[1] Used here (and throughout) in the sense of total acceptance of the laws of the Catholic Church. In particular, 'Catholic integralists' was the name given by themselves, during the Modernist controversy (see below, pp. 34 ff.) to those who unreservedly adhere to Catholicism excluding everything that diminishes the Church's rights. Some French theologians distinguish between *intégrisme* and integralism, the former involving a closed approach to the world and the latter an open approach. *Translator.*

and altar', they were in general exemplary for their strict behaviour
and often for their austere ascetic practices, and at the same time
active in charitable and social works as well as in works of piety.
Accustomed to enjoying high consideration under the Austrian
régime, they continued to regard themselves as the supreme
authority in their own districts, excluding any idea of equality
between the municipality and the parish or between civil and
religious authorities.

Now Sarto was perhaps the most perfect specimen of a priest
according to the traditional Veneto concept – the more so inasmuch as he accepted the priesthood in complete faith and with
no self-interest. As we have seen, no ordinary human desire to
improve his own or his family's position ever entered his head.
His novitiate in the seminary was a true novitiate for the sanctity
of the priesthood, and he became a priest simply for the love and
glory of God. Because his sacrifice of himself to this ideal was
complete, the priesthood was in his eyes something beyond
question, the obvious corollary to which was the miniature theocracy represented by the power of the parish priest: a peaceable
and non-violent theocracy, no doubt, but also if need be a rigid
and inflexible one, whose demands gradually expanded with the
added responsibilities of episcopal office. But in the more favourable local situation of Venice moderation prevailed over his theo-
cratic-autocratic tendencies, thus attracting the sympathy and
trust of such men as Cardinal Ferrari of Milan and Cardinal
Svampa of Bologna.

Nevertheless in the depths of his heart he never wavered from
his early idea of authority. When, as Bishop of Mantua, somebody
was one day praising his colleagues, he said bluntly: 'I myself
prefer that they should say to me, as they do in the Veneto,
"Paron, comandi!" ("Master, yours to command!")'. And once
as Pope he let slip: 'It's enough if the Pope has a head on his
shoulders.' But even before that, and indeed right from the
earliest days when he seemed most confused and embarrassed in
his new world, he showed his authority. It was customary in the
Vatican after the Conclave for the new Pope to distribute
gratuities to the pontifical guards in place of the permission to
sack which from the Middle Ages onwards had been granted to
the soldiery of the Sacred Palaces during the Conclave, who
generally ended by looting the palace of the cardinal appointed

Pope. However, in view of the situation of pontifical finances after the occupation of Rome Leo XIII had abolished this privilege. In vain the guards threatened to mutiny: there was no joking with Leo XIII, and order was at once restored. But with Sarto, a provincial with no quarterings of nobility (he was the first Pope since Sergius IV not to come from the aristocracy, except for Gregory XVI, who was of middle-class, not peasant, origin) and so obviously stunned by his incredible promotion, the Swiss guards thought it would be easy game. They threatened to rebel, but they got an unexpected answer – the Pope declared the corps dissolved. They could hardly believe their ears; and it was only after heartfelt petitions, particularly from Switzerland, that the ban was withdrawn.

This episode was naturally unknown outside the Sacred Palaces. Had it been otherwise, people would have realized much earlier the most unlooked-for aspect of the new pontificate, namely its rigidity. A few months later, however, saw the first public confirmation of the 'good Pope's' resolute methods. The *motu proprio* on the reform of church music had aroused pretty strong reactions and opposition in Rome itself. And on 8 December 1903 we find Pius X addressing a letter to his Cardinal Vicar in the following terms: 'My lord Cardinal, show no indulgence; allow no delays. Difficulties increase rather than diminish with postponement. The cut has to be made: make it at once, and resolutely.' People could hardly believe that these words could have come from the gentle, smiling Pope whose image had aroused enthusiasm throughout the world. But it was true, for this was indeed his other face, the face of a man burnt up with zeal for God and wellnigh transported by a sacred fury to defend His cause. This was his first sortie to cast out the profaners from the temple.

Other episodes of the same kind were soon to confirm the later definition of Pope Pius X as a mixture of the *curé de campagne* and the angel with the fiery sword. They concerned, moreover, the Vatican's foreign relations and in particular its relations with France, then veering towards radicalism under Combes. The first such episode, and one which received resounding publicity, was the Pope's refusal to grant an audience to the French President, Loubet, who arrived in Rome on 24 April 1904 to return King Victor Emmanuel III's visit to Paris of the previous October. This refusal was embarrassing enough in itself, even when represented as being in accordance with the rule established under Leo XIII for the visits of Catholic rulers to Rome (in accepting the hospitality of the Quirinal, they were, according to the Pope, implicitly giving *de facto* recognition to the King of Italy's possession of Rome, which could not but cause offence to the Pope). Worse still, however, on 28 April the Secretary of State, Cardinal Merry del Val, addressed an indignant protest to the various Chancelleries about the affair. This document was published in a French newspaper, and a few days later the French Ambassador called at the Vatican to ask Merry del Val if he acknowledged the text as authentic. The Cardinal's hesitant replies were regarded in Paris as obvious proof that he wished to evade the question, and the decision was taken, and approved by a large majority in the Chamber on 27 May, to recall the French Ambassador, leaving only a chargé d'affaires at the Vatican. A few weeks later the French Parliament was called upon to approve the law excluding members of the religious fraternities from the teaching profession. Early in 1905 the Combes Cabinet fell, but that did not prevent the progress of the law on the separation of Church and State, which was approved on 3 July and came into effect on 9 December. Pius x's reaction came swiftly: on 11 February 1906 he solemnly condemned the French Government's decision in an encyclical severe and stern from its opening words: *Vehementer nos.* This was only the beginning of a change in his attitude which, hitherto on the whole cautious and moderate except for the Loubet episode, from then onwards became increasingly stern and intolerant not only towards the French Government but also towards the episcopate despite the latter's generally moderate trend. As we shall see, the crux of the matter was the so-called *associations cultuelles*[1] envisaged in the law, whereby the Church in France was to continue in control of its own property and of State allowances for the clergy, a measure which Pius x decided to reject.

An Unexpected Crusade

All this, however, was to pale by comparison with the drama secretly preparing in the Vatican and which burst upon the public in the second half of 1907. The first premonition of it came a year

[1] See p. 75.

earlier when, in April 1906, Antonio Fogazzaro's novel *Il Santo* (The Saint) was put on the Index.

Fogazzaro had reached the apex of his literary career and success ten years before with the publication in 1895 of his *Piccolo Mondo Antico* (The Little World of the Past), a novel of Risorgimento patriotism which also had as its subsidiary theme the superiority of religion over rationalism, demonstrated in a passionate conflict between the two main characters. Ten years before he had written an even more combative novel from the liberal Catholic standpoint, *Daniele Cortis,* but the tortured irresolution of his hero failed to satisfy even the author, who thereafter abandoned the narrow theme of political dispute for the revival of religion. After *Piccolo Mondo Antico*, Fogazzaro became drawn to the idea of promoting a partnership between science and religion, as advanced in the new moderate evolutionary theory launched in Europe by certain Catholic scholars; and to propagate this idea he gave a number of lectures, still famous today, in various Italian towns. He was temporarily distracted from this purpose by a moral crisis which inspired the somewhat obscure *Piccolo Mondo Moderno* (The Little World of the Present, 1901), but then reverted even more resolutely than before to his mission of arousing the Church by proclaiming a new reform. It was thus that *Il Santo* was born.

The novel had one fault from the outset in that it harked back to the equivocal atmosphere of the *Piccolo Mondo Moderno*, whose hero appeared again in *Il Santo*. True, Pietro Maironi, the son of Franco and Luisa, the chief characters in *Piccolo Mondo Antico*, was now quite a different person, not only in habits and way of life (the idle nobleman had repented and become a gardener in a convent in Subiaco) but also in name, having been rechristened Benedetto; but he still trailed behind him the drama of his passion for Jeanne Dessalle. The central idea of the book, however, lay in Benedetto's mysterious and complicated meeting with the Pope, whom he admonished to embark without delay on a reform of the Church, and in Benedetto's speech, near the end, to his followers in Rome shortly before his death.

At his meeting with the Pope, Benedetto denounced the four spirits (of falsehood, domination, greed, and sloth) which in his view held the Church prisoner; and he also found time to tackle the question of relations between the Vatican and the Quirinal.

In his speech, on the other hand, his main theme was the re-habilitation of the laity within the new ecclesiastical community. The real aim of Fogazzaro's reform was, in fact, the Church's return to evangelical simplicity and its purification of all traces of legalism and authoritarianism, in short a new fervour which would reaffirm the validity of religion and raise its prestige in the eyes of non-believers.

As a work of art, *Il Santo* added nothing to its author's reputa-tion; but it had the great merit of bringing to the notice of Italy and all Europe the religious crisis that the Church was under-going and the need for a revival among believers, both clergy and laity. It was only from *Il Santo*, in fact, that the public learnt, and in a most sensational way, of the existence of that reforming trend which Pius x was soon to name 'Modernism'. Indeed Fogazzaro had this aim in mind. The novel was given a spectacular launching. Several weeks before the publication date it was an-nounced in huge advertisements (the review *Civiltà Cattolica* wrote caustically of 'big multicoloured posters such as comedians use for their plays or Roman innkeepers to advertise new wine'). The first editions were over-subscribed. But if publicity helped, the demand for the book was even greater because of the polemics it at once aroused, which reached a fresh pitch when the book was put on the Index and the author had to submit to authority. The scandal led to student demonstrations when Fogazzaro was banned from the Higher Education Council, and there were questions in Parliament; while abroad, where it was translated into several languages, *Il Santo* became the most discussed book of the year.

By this time the press had become alarmed: for the crisis, hitherto concerned chiefly with politics and outside matters such as relations with France, had now moved into the bosom of the Church itself and was becoming increasingly an ideological affair. Throughout 1906 the newspapers closely followed every develop-ment in the Catholic world. In the early part of 1907 the reformers could still have their say: on 18 January Fogazzaro at the invita-tion of the Ecole des Hautes Etudes gave a lecture in Paris, which he later repeated in Geneva and various towns of Italy, on 'The ideas of Giovanni Selva', a character in *Il Santo*. But soon came a whole series of interventions by the Roman Curia: on 14 June Pius x signed a letter on the errors of Hermann Schell;

on 3 July he promulgated the decree *Lamentabili*, containing sixty-five erroneous propositions to be banned; on 28 August the Holy Office directed an instruction to the superiors of the religious orders indicating means for the protection of clerics from such errors; on 26 July the Index included among works to be condemned the international review *Coenobium* and books by Dimet, Le Roy, Houtin, and others; on 16 September the *Osservatore Romano* published the encyclical *Pascendi* on Modernism; on 29 October Cardinal Respighi, Vicar of Rome, excommunicated the anonymous authors of the volume *Il Programma dei Modernisti* ('The Modernists' Programme); lastly, on Christmas Eve the year closed with the major excommunication pronounced by Cardinal Ferrari against 'all the publishers, editors, authors, and collaborators' of *Il Rinnovamento*.

It was the beginning of a storm that was to die down only with the outbreak of the First World War, and which grew in intensity throughout the years from 1907 to 1912. The Church was showing a quite new aspect of itself, devouring its own children; nothing short of such a spectacle could have attracted to it the inquisitive attention of a society accustomed virtually to ignore its existence.

In the concluding section of the encyclical *Pascendi* Pius x had outlined a method for suppressing Modernism; all teachers infected with the heresy were to be excluded from the seminaries and Catholic universities, reliable censors were to be elected in all episcopal Curias to revise texts intended for publication, and a vigilance council was to be established in every diocese. Finding even these means inadequate, he further, on 1 September 1910, imposed on all aspirants to the priesthood, and on clergy fulfilling duties as ministers, teachers, or in ecclesiastical jurisdiction, that 'oath of faith' which was soon to become known as the 'anti-Modernist oath'.

To all appearances there was nothing special about these provisions. But in fact they, and in particular the measure about vigilance councils (though perhaps the last one was even more paralysing for honest consciences), signified neither more nor less than the reconstitution of the Inquisition adapted to modern form. Except for occasional rare oases, the Church, especially in Italy and France, but elsewhere too, as in Germany and England, was oppressed by an atmosphere of suspicion and insecurity that spared none, not even the bishops and the members of the Sacred College. The higher clergy and those most in the public view from the intellectual standpoint were naturally the most closely scrutinized; but even simple parish priests and chaplains were liable to be suspected, if not of 'scientific Modernism', at least of social or vaguely reformist leanings in that direction. No one was safe; people informed against each other, often simply from personal vendetta. As in time of war or special tribunals, judgements were both swift and secret, being concerned above all to protect the accusers' anonymity and allow no likely fomenter of rebellion to escape. The accused, whose mere semblance of guilt facilitated their condemnation, were suspended from office, stowed away in monasteries and isolated to prevent their doing harm. Seminaries were shorn of teachers of the more delicate theological subjects, as well as of rectors and spiritual directors. And lest silence should give a false impression of the gravity of the situation, public informers appeared too, holding forth even in the most worthless newspapers. Secure in their protection from above (which, of course, meant Rome), they launched their accusations against the most irreproachable personalities: the higher their objectives, the greater their merit and hope of reward.

In case these should be regarded as merely unsupported statements, it may be worth while to quote some contemporary testimonies. Those from victims who in a sense acknowledged their own guilt by later leaving the Church are naturally the most suspect; but they are by no means the most numerous. In any case, we will cite only two examples from Loisy's memoirs, and those merely to show how they do not differ substantially from the statements of innocent victims, especially when expressed privately, even to the highest Church authorities. According to Loisy, the main exponent of so-called Modernism in France, 'under the pontificate of Pius x no bishop had the right to be absolutely moderate', and the reign of Pope Sarto was 'a veritable orgy of fanaticism and senselessness'.

As is understandable, testimonies from those accused of Modernism who remained faithful to the Church are either much more cautious about making personal references to Pius x or omit them altogether. In general they refer to the abuses of the integralists in flinging themselves into a virtual 'man-hunt'. Thus Padre Semeria, bearing posthumous witness:

Fervid, impassioned, and over-zealous Catholics everywhere discovered the relics or seeds, the old traces or new marks [of Modernism]. Where they could no longer speak of modernists they spoke of modernizers, invoking and provoking stern measures against persons who were either innocent or less guilty and dangerous than they believed and proclaimed. The better to attack the so-called modernizers, they called them by new names, thus inadvertently incurring the very fault of seeking after new words and things which they violently attacked in others: *integral* Catholics, as if the word Catholic did not convey everything; or *papal* Catholics, for their habit of appealing direct to Rome over the head of the local authority, their legitimate pastors the bishops. And when some bishops protested in the name of church discipline, these zealous souls, who were usually priests even if they had the title of monsignor, described as episcopalian (using it as a term of reproach) what was merely a proper conception of the ecclesiastical hierarchy.

Their intentions [Father Semeria continued elsewhere] were naturally beyond question . . . But there still remained the interference with discipline, the injustice of accusations launched in public without letting the accused defend himself in the calumniating newspapers, the systematic denial of fraternal charity. They no longer knew what or how to write. Someone I know quite well [probably himself – *author's note*] found himself reproved for having in a speech applied to the Heart of Jesus the line from Dante: '*Se il mondo sapesse il cuor ch'egli ebbe*' ('If the world knew the heart he had'). What did the carping critic find to reproach in that? The word 'had', because it would imply that He *no longer has it*! Worse still, this friend of mine found himself violently criticized for having denied the existence of God in a book in which he had made every effort to demonstrate it in the way most effective for our contemporaries. The calumniator cited in quotes improbable passages which my friend had never written.

These passages constitute silent if indirect accusations of Pius x. Henri Brémond made much more open use of the method of silent accusation in his installation speech at the French Academy, when he succeeded Mgr Duchesne. He said of himself: '*J'ai vécu sous quatres pontifes: Pie IX, Léon XIII, Benoit XV et Pie XI.*' Evidently under Pius x his existence was not a 'life' at all.

Speaking of anti-Modernist fanaticism in his Lenten letter of 1915, Cardinal Mercier, who had been among those accused of philo-Modernism, wrote:

In some Catholic countries, and especially in Italy and France, anti-

Modernism had drawn some impetuous spirits, more courageous in words than deeds, into violent and insidious personal controversy. It seemed almost as if the profession of Catholic faith did not suffice to satisfy these extempore defenders of orthodoxy, according to whom humble obedience to the Pope involved ignoring the work of the bishops. Petty scribes or worthless journalists, they excommunicated all those unwilling to pass beneath the Caudine forks of their integralism. Sincere hearts were troubled by unrest: the more honest consciences suffered in silence.

More outspoken and impressive were the complaints reaching Rome in private letters from church leaders deeply concerned about the situation. Cardinal Pietro Maffi, the Archbishop of Pisa, for example, on 10 February 1911 wrote at length to his colleague De Lai, Prefect of the Consistorial Congregation and Pius x's right hand in the repression of Modernism:[1]

Bishops are becoming increasingly divided against each other, suspicion is growing everywhere, and instead of the bond of faith, a single newspaper becomes arbiter of the fate of a diocese! Who are the informers? I don't want to paint things too black; but there is no concealing the grief and shame a bishop sometimes feels when he finds himself put on the same level with, or even below, some wretched person more worthy to be denounced to the Holy Office than himself to denounce others! ... A flush rises to my cheeks when I think that I, a Cardinal and Archbishop, who have given incontrovertible proof of my faith and devotion to the Holy See, am accused, attacked, publicly insulted and denounced by two or three priests of no authority and of equivocal mode of life! And the accusation found a warmer welcome than the defence, and there was no repair, and it all happened just because I showed obedience – and only in the Pope's greatness of heart did I find any consolation! And how many others have suffered the same as I! For ourselves, in secret, the word of the Holy Father sufficed: but in public? ...

... What afflicts one is having to submit to persecution ... It causes a general feeling of mistrust, paralysis, inability to act. Of course, anyone who acts may make a mistake; but since mistakes are pounced upon while good deeds go unnoticed, most people decide to play safe and do nothing! Look at the literary corruption there is – quantities of pamphlets all advertising anti-Modernism; and the bishops live from hand to mouth, putting ten lire-worth of professions of faith in

---

[1] The letters exchanged between Maffi and De Lai are in the *Disquisitio,* cited in the Bibliography (p. 370).

common newspapers and then keeping quiet! And no publication of
any value appears! . . . Are there any societies, clubs, or libraries in the
quarters that so loudly proclaim orthodoxy? Nothing of the kind. Do
they bother to hold any meetings? Of course not. Who are the first
to evade their obligations? . . . It has come to this. The intimidated
bishops hourly await orders about some individual concrete affair in
their dioceses – orders that they often think are not in the best interests
of the Church – and they don't know what to do . . . To bring the
Holy Father into particular cases *so often* (I repeat, *so often*), and cases
that *in the general way* the local bishop knows more about than a far-off
Congregation, is to create confusion, discredit the bishop, and produce chaos. The effects can already be seen. And I would dare to point
to instances of it even in the most solemn documents. Imperative and
detailed directives of this kind cannot be carried out, and in practice
it is better to leave it to the bishops.

In another letter of 31 July 1912, more especially concerned with
the question of Catholic newspapers, Cardinal Maffi wrote to the
same correspondent:

Here we are in the midst of controversies that amount to a veritable
man-hunt. They are doing their best to make an apostate of Semeria,
and treat Meda as a rebel. If Meda were to transcribe the *Pater Noster*
they'd accuse him of heresy . . . With all these insinuations [of Modern-
ism] they have alienated the best men, from Grosoli to Pini: they have
even thrown suspicion (whether more absurdly or more wickedly I
can't decide) on Toniolo. There is danger in everything – and then
who is there left? People lament that the Pope is not loved or obeyed;
that enthusiasm is waning, pilgrimages dwindle, and so on. But the
people to be blamed for this are those who try to enforce love with a
cudgel, who treat genuine enthusiasm with mistrust and suspicion,
who claim a monopoly of orthodoxy. One could weep when one sees
how the good has been obstructed by the very people who claimed
to further it!

We have said that the Inquisition had come again, and this is no
exaggeration, though happily, given the absence of the secular
arm, there were no burnings at the stake. In the historical times
of the Inquisition there was only the Holy Office: during the
years of repression of so-called Modernism, the period of what
has been described as the anti-Modernist 'purges', there was in
Rome not only the Supreme Congregation of the Holy Office,
working in conjunction with the Congregation of the Index, but
also the Consistorial Congregation and, later on, in 1909, the

secret police of Mgr Benigni,[1] under the control of the Cardinal Secretary of State and soon, as will be seen, to receive the blessing of Pius x himself.

The Holy Office and the Index acted solely on the basis of the denunciations they received, with which, indeed, they were virtually inundated. The Consistorial Congregation, on the other hand, initiated investigations and inquiries all over the place, mainly by means of 'apostolic visitations'. There was usually no fixed time for these; they took place from time to time according to the decisions of the Secretary of the Congregation, Cardinal De Lai. On 7 March 1904, however, Pius x himself by his decree *Constat apud omnes* decided on a visitation to every diocese of Italy. This was still three years before the encyclical *Pascendi*, and it was to prove the most tolerant of the visitations during his pontificate. But there were, all the same, exceptions. On the situation in Milan, and especially in its seminary, Mgr Nicola Canali, personal secretary of Merry del Val and himself a high dignitary in the Secretariat of State, gave a quite unwarrantably severe verdict which elicited indignant protests from Archbishop Ferrari and the Congregation of Ecclesiastical Discipline of his Curia. But the sternest apostolic visitors won the highest appreciation, and this spurred on the more moderate to increase their zeal. After *Pascendi* their powers also increased, and soon the effrontery of these *missi dominici* knew no limit. There was no counting the number of apostolic visitations (Milan had three in the eleven years of Pope Pius x's reign) and many resulted in the closing down of seminaries, the removal of eminent ecclesiastics, and uncompromising reports on the bishops. The visitors vied with each other in reproducing the manner and actions of the early Inquisitors. Among the most notorious and awe-inspiring were Mgr Beda Cardinali and Mgr Pio Tommaso Boggiani, bishop of Adria and Rovigo, a rigid Dominican. Mgr Cardinali, who had already been in Milan in this capacity in 1908, was responsible for closing, in September 1910, the seminary in Perugia whose Rector was the celebrated Umberto Fracassini. Mgr Boggiani, sent to Milan in 1911, announced his coming in a letter dated only the day before, arrived in Cardinal Ferrari's absence, and at once established himself in the theological seminary to begin his

[1] The inquisitorial organization known as *Sodalitium Pianum* ('Fellowship of St Pius v') – see pp. 51, 54–5. *Translator.*

visitation. When the Archbishop returned in haste, instead of receiving the visitor's homage in his palace he had himself to render homage to the visitor as the representative of the Holy See.

As for Benigni's secret police, its methods were infinitely more arbitrary. The brother of a priest who collaborated with him even became a Freemason in order to ascertain whether the lodges had any links with the Modernists. Another priest, or possibly the same one, a friend of the future historian Antonino De Stefano, who was later to leave the Church, was sent to Geneva when it leaked out that De Stefano was preparing to launch a review of international scope, the *Revue Moderniste Internationale*. Received as a friend and guest, when left alone for a few hours he proceeded to photograph all the correspondence connected with the review which he then passed on to the Holy Office. In this way the Office secured a list of the promised collaborators, among them Ernesto Buonaiuti, the future leader of Modernism in Italy.[1]

Amid all the voluntary or paid spies of Benigni or the Holy Office, there was no escape in those years even for the most casual encounters. Giorgio La Piana, who later on went to the United States and became a professor at Harvard, as a young priest was once travelling from his native Sicily to Rome when he met an unknown colleague in the train. They got into conversation, and when his companion confided his sympathies with Modernism, with true Sicilian verve he replied in kind. On arrival in Rome the two separated great friends. A few days later La Piana was called *ad audiendum verbum* and at once sent back to his diocese. His unknown travelling companion was a Curia official who knew how to make good use of his time.[2]

As we have said, the Roman Congregation acted mainly on secret denunciations, but certain Catholic newspapers operated in the full light of day. Of these the most audacious and provocative in Italy was the Florence *Unità Cattolica*, but the most virulent was *La Riscossa,* from an unknown village of the Veneto, Breganze, in the diocese of Vicenza, where it was supported by the trading activities of three brothers, all priests, the notorious Scotton brothers. Its crude attacks were an epoch-making event of the times, among their chief targets being the diocese of Milan and

[1] See E. Buonaiuti, *Il pellegrino di Roma*, 2nd ed., Bari, 1964, pp. 104–6.
[2] See note in Bibliography, p. 372.

its Archbishop. After one such strident attack on Cardinal Ferrari, Mgr Bonomelli wrote in a private letter on 23 February 1911: 'You will have seen the tepid protest of the Lombard bishops. Never mind. It's all the same thing, with the triumph of the Scottons who still go unscathed and the Cardinal and bishops at a loss what to do. It's an immense moral defeat for the Pope . . .'

Canonization in Danger

But what was Pius x's personal role in all this? When the question of his beatification arose, the debate on the heroic nature of his virtues, begun on 28 October 1949, brought to light some serious and unexpected doubts. Quite a number of the *consultori* (consultors) advanced objections and reserves to which they sought a reassuring answer. As the 'Promoter of the Faith', Father Ferdinando Antonelli, wrote in the *Disquisitio* addressed to Pius xii on 29 June 1950, 'in addition to various objections concerning one or other particular virtue . . . there is a whole series of objections and reserves of a positive kind which, on due consideration, appear to have one single common denominator: namely, the method of action of the Servant of God (that is, Pius x) in the struggle against Modernism. . . . The general objection is substantiated and supported by various positive facts. The main ones are: having allowed the so-called integralists to lay down the law in the Church even to bishops and cardinals; having fought the partly-secularized press;[1] having made use of a secret-police instrument like the *Sodalitium Pianum*; and having struck at innocent and worthy men and induced a deep division among Catholics'.

As it was the intention of Pius xii to proceed as quickly as possible with the beatification and canonization of Sarto, Father Antonelli at once prepared to answer these and other objections. But the objections cited required documented answers, and from documents which were not to be found in the various published histories of Modernism but only in the archives of the Roman Congregations. The Consistory was asked on 3 May 1950 to provide the necessary information, and on 6 May its secretary, Cardinal Piazza, handed over to the *rapporteur* of the Historical

[1] i.e. papers which included the type of secular news generally excluded from Catholic newspapers. See also p. 72. *Translator.*

Section of the Congregation of Rites (the body dealing with causes for beatification and canonization) 'a voluminous folder of original papers, the subject of which was indicated by a slip on which the late Cardinal Rossi had written "Pius x and Modernism" '. This folder when examined proved to contain material on the accusations in question. With astonishing speed Antonelli, aided by a single collaborator, Father Giuseppe Loew, managed in the record time of fifty-four days to study all the material and present it in relation to the pre-ordained thesis of the sanctity of Pius x, producing a volume of some 350 pages in large format which was published by the Poliglotta Vaticana that same year.

Whatever may be said of the optimism of the 'Promoter of the Faith', Pope Pius x's personal responsibility in the anti-Modernist struggle is beyond dispute. The first anti-Modernist action (taken before the term was current) – the condemnation of five of Loisy's works, among them *L'Evangile et l'Eglise* and *Autour d'un petit livre* – was taken only five months after his election, and was followed in the succeeding years by a constant infiltration of other measures up to the promulgation of the key document, the encyclical *Pascendi*. The Pope was obviously seeking a suitable way in which to intervene decisively and had not yet found it; but that does nothing to controvert, indeed it rather confirms, the fact that he intended from the outset to take repressive measures against the trends he feared. It would almost seem as if this urge, neither concealed nor held in check, corresponded to a long-felt wish.

It is, however, far from easy to find presages of his anti-Modernism in the future Pope's actions while still a bishop. True, there is a striking passage in a pastoral letter of 7 February 1887:

Not a few persons, although they have hardly even a superficial knowledge of the science of religion and still less put it into practice, claim to set themselves up as teachers and go about declaring that the Church must adapt itself to the needs of the times; that it is impossible to maintain the pristine integrity of its laws; that the holiest men will from now onwards be the most pliant, prepared to sacrifice something of the old forms in order to preserve the rest. In this modern Christianity, forgetful of the ancient folly of the Cross, the dogmas of the faith must adapt themselves to the demands of the new philosophy; the public law of the Christian era must go warily before the great principles of the modern era and confess at least the legitimacy of its defeat. Over-severe evangelical morality must lend itself to compliance and accommodations, and discipline must withdraw all its sanctions as being contrary to nature, and itself further the joyous advance of the law of liberty.

In his first pastoral letter to the Venetians, too, there are explicit references to that evolution of dogma which was to be one of the hallmarks of Modernism; and he also speaks there of the negation of the 'most established prophecies and most manifest miracles of Christ', an obvious allusion to certain affirmations of biblical criticism. But such generic expressions could easily be attributed to quite different motives; moreover, especially at the time of the first pastoral quoted, to refer to Modernism would be a chronological heresy. And both the evolution of dogma and the negation of the prophecies referred to in the second passage are among the errors condemned in the *Syllabus* (1864).

As far as can be proved, in fact, the future Pope Pius x had only a general and superficial knowledge of Modernism up to the last period of his patriarchate in Venice. Then, it seems, when about to make his last journey to Rome, anticipating that Leo xiii might question him about Loisy's new standpoint on biblical matters, he sought information from the professor of Holy Writ in his seminary. He also seems to have had in his hands, possibly on that same occasion from Father Genocchi, Loisy's celebrated little book *L'Evangile et l'Eglise*; but, unexpectedly enough, in speaking of it to Don Minocchi he is said to have remarked: 'Here is a theological book that at least is not boring.' The 'at least' suggests that Sarto had not been taken in by it but not, apparently, shocked either.

Certainly there is room for correction in the legend, prompted by his humble peasant origins, that Pius x had only a superficial knowledge of ecclesiastical disciplines. A perusal of his correspondence while a seminarist shows that he must have learnt quite a lot at Castelfranco. His sentences are perhaps too latinized in construction but they are strong and surely-worded, and neither artificial nor empty of content; indeed these early writings show a striking clarity of thought and spontaneity, even wittiness, of expression.[1] It must also not be forgotten that Sarto later

[1] His style from youth onwards emerges from his letters – see *Lettere di San Pio X*, edited by Nello Vian, Padua, 2nd ed., 1958.

went, with a scholarship for the most promising seminarists of Treviso diocese, to the seminary of Padua. Now Padua was undoubtedly one of the best seminaries in Italy, well known for its stiff courses and enlightened discipline; and the marks he got there for philosophy and theology suggest that he was among the top students.

There is a significant episode dating back to the start of his theological studies. From a letter of the Rector's dated 10 November 1854, preserved in the seminary library, we learn that young Sarto really wanted to follow the theology courses at Padua University rather than at the seminary, because at the University he could also have studied oriental languages. The rules of the seminary, formulated in 1671 by Bishop Gregorio Barbàrigo, recommended the study of Hebrew, Syrian, and Chaldean for a right interpretation of Holy Writ; but this practice must have lapsed by Sarto's time. His bishop must have objected for some reason, so that he could not fulfil his desire or even crown his studies with a degree in theology or canon law (when Leo XIII made him Bishop of Mantua he had to dispense him from the title of doctor). Had the young theological student's aspirations been granted the history of the Church in the early 1900s might have been very different.

As we have seen, the activities of the pastoral ministry diverted the future Pope's cultural inclinations first towards more concrete disciplines, and he then became increasingly detached from a culture which, even when religious, bore no direct relation to the service of souls. As Sarto advanced in pastoral activity he came to have less and less understanding for the leisure aspects of culture. For example, he probably thought it unseemly for a Pope, even so efficient a Pope as Leo XIII, to indulge in Latin verse composition (unless, of course, on some sacred subject intended for the breviary). The catechism and the gospel should, in his view, suffice for a parish priest and a bishop, with the possible addition of some serious theological manual; all the rest was profanity or temptation. In case of need a bishop could always have recourse to experts for information on more topical points.

He may have received some stimulus to take an interest in the great philosophical, theological, and biblical problems under discussion at the turn of the century from his protector and friend

Cardinal Parocchi, Leo XIII's vicar for the diocese of Rome. Parocchi, who was from Mantua and had known Sarto a long time, was probably influential in bringing about his promotion to the see of Mantua: in any case he made a point of personally consecrating him bishop in Rome. After that they were frequently in contact, especially after Sarto's promotion to be Patriarch of Venice. Parocchi, who was a highly cultivated man with wide interests, followed closely the new ideas then maturing in various spheres of the Catholic world in Italy and abroad. An eminent member of the Curia and of several Congregations, he kept himself up to date both out of personal enthusiasm and from a sense of duty. In 1901 Leo XIII had given fresh proof of his esteem and confidence by appointing him one of the three Cardinals to preside over the Pontifical Biblical Commission. But, despite all this, it seems likely that Sarto's friendship with Parocchi (who died in January 1903) did relatively little to arouse his interest in those new ideas. How, then, are we to explain his impulsive condemnation of Loisy in December 1903 and the even earlier allusion, in his first encyclical of 4 October 1903, to 'a certain new science'?

The answer seems clear: it was mainly the result of pressure from the Archbishop of Paris, Cardinal Richard, and the group of prelates supporting him in the Roman Curia. At that time the greater part of the French episcopate was deeply concerned about the question of the '*abbés démocratiques*'. Richard, in particular, seconded by Cardinal Perraud, Archbishop of Rouen, and some of the bishops, believed that the first step must be to secure the surrender of the intellectual abbés such as Loisy. At his last meeting with Leo XIII, in February 1903, he used every possible argument to achieve this end, but without succes. In his own diocese and among his clergy Richard went by the half-affectionate half-ironical nickname of 'the holy mule'. He refused to give up, and when after Leo XIII's death he encountered Pope Pius X he thought he saw his chance. This time, however, he felt the need of support and took Perraud with him. His success was immediate, as was confirmed by the reference in the encyclical two months later.

In the meantime Loisy had followed up *L'Evangile et l'Eglise* by a short explanatory work, *Autour d'un petit livre*, which, far from placating the dispute, added fresh fuel to it. A commission of three theologians was set up by the Archbishop of Paris to prepare a memorandum for the Holy Office, and armed with this Richard returned to Rome in October for the third time that year determined to settle the matter.

Loisy, though he owed to Richard the sharpest rebuffs of his whole career, nevertheless presents an attractive and sympathetic picture of him in his *Memoirs*:

He was a man of another age. The language he spoke was almost foreign to me, and he, in his turn, did not understand the way in which I was used to express myself. He was not particularly cultivated, though by no means so limited as his clergy used to suggest; like so many men, he had become fossilized in his original form. He brought with him from his native Brittany a granite-like faith that had probably never been touched by the slightest doubt. Moreover throughout his career in the Church he had been almost entirely absorbed in administrative duties or liturgical offices. Reading his biography, one learns that he was involved in the religious events and Church politics of the day, but the major impression is of a life filled with pastoral visitations, presiding over spiritual and ecclesiastical exercises and Synods, and consecrating churches; in short, he lived by ritual. He wanted to be fair; and he was good, but within the limits permitted by orthodoxy and the Church's rules. But he lacked the background to enable him to understand the biblical question, or, indeed, any contemporary question.

The picture could equally be applied without the change of a comma to Sarto. Thus the two were made not only to understand but also to influence each other and become allies.

Richard stayed twenty days in Rome devoting his time entirely to his single objective. He saw the Pope again and once again impressed him; and he had long talks with Merry del Val and the heads of the Holy Office. In the meantime he had written to the French cardinals asking them to join with him and Perraud in requesting the proscription of Loisy's books, but only two of the other five agreed. Nevertheless he boasted of this success in a long letter to Pius x after his return to Paris. The Pope did not disappoint him. On 16 December the Holy Office ordered five books by Loisy to be put on the Index, and the Pope next day approved the decree.

Pius x, in deciding to adopt so severe a measure, may have meant it to serve mainly as a warning. But the spark had touched powder, and the first to be burnt was himself. At the time of the notorious Modernist repressions, many maintained that responsibility for Pius x's sternest measures against the Modernists lay with his highest collaborators, in particular with the Secretary of State, Merry del Val, Cardinal Gaetano De Lai, and Cardinal Giuseppe Calasanzio Vives y Tuto. While this may be true of the later and most active period of anti-Modernism, it cannot apply to the beginning of the dispute as described above. For Merry del Val became cardinal only on 9 November 1903, and De Lai on the morrow of *Pascendi*, 16 December 1907; while Vives y Tuto was still wrapped up in nostalgia for Leo xiii during the first months of the new pontificate. But were they really chiefly responsible later on, even to the point of acting independently of Sarto and without his knowledge?

It is admittedly almost impossible to approach without prejudice these three key figures of Pius x's reign, so deeply have they become involved in the sinister legend representing them as insidious *éminences grises*. The most enigmatic among them is certainly Merry del Val and, more surprisingly, he remains so even after reading all the depositions collected by the Roman tribunal for the cause of his beatification. That this elegant and severe young aristocrat, the Secretary of the Conclave, should from the first have made such an impression on the new Pope that he at once appointed him pro-Secretary of State, is not surprising. He had had the same effect on Leo xiii from the moment that Leo first knew him as a seminarist. In the eyes of Pius x, Merry del Val combined all the brilliant qualities that he himself lacked – noble birth, culture, *savoir-faire* – qualities attuned and subordinated, moreover, to the demands of an ecclesiastical discipline embraced and practised with conviction. But what even more impressed the 'country Cardinal' that Pius x knew himself to be, was the maturity of judgement and the calm self-assurance that distinguished this Spanish-Irish descendant of two noble families. But the very strength of this fascination was enough to arouse the peasant mistrust still watchful within Giuseppe Sarto. After three months of close observation and reflection he ended by choosing him as head of his Secretariat of State, passing over men of real worth with a brilliant past like Ferrata (who, aged only fifty-six in 1903, had behind him a well-nigh unequalled curial and diplomatic career, as under-secretary and then secretary of the Congregation for Extraordinary Eccle-

siastical Affairs, President of the Academy of Ecclesiastical Nobles
in Rome, and, outside the Vatican, as apostolic delegate in
Switzerland and nuncio in Belgium and France). He reached this
decision because he knew he would find in Merry del Val both a
trusty collaborator and one who would carry out his wishes: the
difference in age (Merry del Val was only thirty-eight), his
limited experience, his ascetic austerity would all combine to keep
this man of his choice in a suitably modest position, a state of
affairs that Pius x rightly foresaw would have been impossible,
given his own inexperience in affairs of high policy, had he placed
at his side an old hand with an impressive past.

The relations between Cardinal Merry del Val and Sarto were,
moreover, completely different from those of his distant predecessor Antonelli and Pope Pius ix. Antonelli kept Pius ix
literally under his hand, to such a point that he was sometimes
positively paralysed with fear. On only one occasion at the beginning of their relationship did Pius ix manage briefly to elude his
grip. Antonelli was a real despot more especially in the sphere of
Vatican policy; but through the links between that policy and
the internal affairs of the Church, in which the Pope was nearly
always the unquestioned arbiter, he also succeeded in imposing
his views in other spheres (it was he, in fact, who delayed the
publication of the *Syllabus* and secured the postponement of the
Vatican Council). More than once the link between the two
men was strained to near breaking point, but Pius ix never quite
dared to dismiss his 'Satan'. (This was apparently because of
Antonelli's extraordinary ability in financial matters. Coming
from a modest family of pig-dealers in Latium, together with his
brother he made one of the most notorious fortunes of the day,
and he later proved himself a wizard in Vatican finance, especially
during the crisis of the Papal State and its progressive absorption
by Italy.)

There was nothing remotely resembling all this in the relations
between Pius x and Merry del Val, still less between the Pope and
his two other collaborators. The Spanish Capuchin Vives y Tuto,
nicknamed '*Vives fa tutto*' (Vives does everything), was certainly
a fanatic to excess, but always within the limits of his own sphere,
the Congregation of the 'Index'. He too had become a cardinal
at an early age under Leo xiii, and at the Conclave of 1903 was
so ardent a supporter of Rampolla that when his candidate was

defeated he fell ill and nearly died. But he recovered and flung himself with equal enthusiasm into the anti-Modernist struggle, which ended by driving him literally off his head. This was almost certainly an after-effect of excessive study and penitences (he was regarded as a walking encyclopaedia, for he was immensely learned and had a prodigious memory: people in Rome used to peer at the ghostly little figure crouched over a book in a corner of his black carriage as it passed by with its black horses and black-liveried servants on its way to the Vatican from the house of his Order in Via Boncompagni). The scandal was hushed up by sending him to a convent of Spanish nuns outside Rome, at Monte Porzio Catone, where he was kept under constant surveillance by the nuns and eventually died.

An end less dramatic and not without some feelings of remorse befell Cardinal De Lai, a Venetian (from Vicenza) and therefore closely linked with Pius x, who made him head of the Consistorial Congregation. This Congregation is the Roman department in charge of bishops all over the world, and given its importance it comes immediately after the Supreme Congregation of the Holy Office. But the powers accorded him as its head did not suffice for De Lai's anti-Modernist zeal. As Father Antonelli recognized in the *Disquisitio* quoted earlier, he extended his influence to cover not only the state of the dioceses but also the press, preaching, and education; he even 'concerned himself with the life of the seminaries, their discipline and teaching and details about individuals'. Among other things, he took upon himself the question of Mgr Benigni's secret inquisitorial organization, the *Sodalitium Pianum,* although it really fell within the sphere of the Congregation of the Council.

De Lai's tendency to invade the sphere of others, and his colleagues' fear of protesting against it in view of his influential intimacy with the Pope, find confirmation in an outspoken testimony by Cardinal Schuster, Archbishop of Milan, who died in the odour of sanctity in 1954 and whose beatification is under consideration. Describing the relations between Cardinal Ferrari and Pius x during the cause for Ferrari's beatification, he said: 'An atmosphere of suspicion and disapproval had developed, such that it was forbidden to read even respectable newspapers in the seminary in Rome. This was why Cardinal De Lai took it upon himself to build the new Roman Seminary at the Lateran, relieving the Cardinal Vicar of the task, and himself gave the inaugural speech there while the Cardinal Vicar had to sit in silence.'

In the anti-Modernist dispute itself De Lai made no mystery about his convictions. For example, in a letter to Cardinal Ferrari on 9 Feburary 1911 (a letter which, incidentally, won Pius x's warm approval), he wrote:

> Have the methods used gone too far? But one must understand the situation, and it's no bad thing if in uttering warnings the situation is somewhat exaggerated. It is always better to exceed in warning of evil rather than to keep silence and let it grow . . . It is unwise to tie too closely the hands of the defenders [the integralists and, in this case, the Scotton brothers[1]] or to reprove and discourage them for every little mistake.

As we have said, he did entertain latterly some scruples and feelings of remorse; and he also took pains to conceal, if not destroy, certain documents. When the notorious Scotton brothers died, he sent orders by telegram for all the correspondence and papers of the three Monsignori of the *Riscossa* to be sent to Rome. But it would be untrue to suggest that his prudence was dictated only by the desire to disguise from posterity his own responsibility. Though his behaviour towards the *Sodalitium Pianum* might be thought equivocal, inasmuch as he allowed it to continue even after Pius x's death, he never wholly approved it even when Pius x was showering blessings on the organization. On the back of the programme and statute of the *Sodalitium Pianum* presented to him by Mgr Benigni on 1 March 1913 he wrote in his own hand, 'Pamphlets sent in by Mgr Benigni and Padre Saubat for approval. But I have told them that the S.C. (= the Sacred Congregation) cannot approve either of a secret society or of a secret inquisitorial body over the bishops etc. They have agreed; but . . .' (the dots are the Cardinal's).

All this confirms that, to use another expression of Cardinal Schuster's, the collaborators of Pius x 'put too much of their own stern spirit into serving him'; and, as Schuster cautiously added, 'perhaps they made some victims'. Nevertheless it does not suffice to warrant the much more serious accusation levelled against them, namely that they held the Pope in thraldom, abusing his goodness and gentleness and above all his ingenuousness

[1] See p. 41.

even more than did the Venetians of his entourage. Pius x
was being anything but timid or ingenuous when, for instance, he
appointed a trusted friend like the Venetian Mgr Sanfermo as
Canon of Santa Maria Maggiore in Rome, with the express task
of reporting to him what was being said in curial circles about
his rule. And, in any case, no proofs of that accusation have
hitherto come to light. On the contrary, to judge by the existing
but still reserved documents one cannot but accept Cardinal
Schuster's definition of the 'right and left arms' of Pius x –
Merry del Val and De Lai – as 'men of most upright intentions'.
Had they not been so Pius x would not have placed them so
close to himself and put such confidence in them. If they abused
their power this happened only rarely. It is, moreover, unlikely
that later evidence will contradict this estimate. It is inevitably
almost impossible to find documentary proof of the extent of a
close adviser's influence on a sovereign. Such influence lies rather
in cautious suggestions, calculated silences, subtle ways of presenting a situation, avoiding any open suggestion of the steps
desired, and so on. Then at a certain point the degree of trust and
intimacy reached by the adviser establishes a circuit in which he
no longer needs to take the initiative and solicitations come mainly
from the sovereign; so that, if imprisonment there be, it is
voluntary and sought, not submitted to or struggled against.

Malicious tongues said that the Pope got the collaborators he
deserved. But as a good Venetian he could only have chosen such
subjects as these. Convinced by his congenital pessimism that the
situation of the Church was not only dramatic but tragic, he had
decided to take drastic measures against the Modernist peril.
Anyone inclined to temporize, to let action wait on conviction,
to go slowly in taking repressive measures, shocked and exas-
perated him so much that he would have nothing more to do
with them. He would tolerate around him only men determined
to use fire and sword to save the Church. He was therefore
prepared to grant them a certain autonomy: but he never allowed
them to precede him in action. From the first moment he put
himself in the forefront and right to the end he was the undisputed head of his implacable crusade.

His private letters to the episcopate or official communications
to heads of departments of the Curia or to his Secretary of State
all reflect *ad nauseam* that the responsibility for the anti-Modernist

struggle was his and his alone, his the strategic directives in the fight against the Church's enemies, his the measures chosen to destroy them. He is frequently ironical about those who try to create friction between him and his collaborators: 'We are back at the same old tune,' he says, commenting on a letter from Cardinal Maffi to De Lai of 25 February 1911, 'with the Pope and for the Pope; but not with those (imaginary) beings who surround him.' 'The others,' he boasted one day, 'read what is written [by the Modernists], but I read what is hidden between the lines and find mistakes there.'

In the depositions for the process for beatification, all Pius x's collaborators, whether direct or indirect, confirmed that the decision about the anti-Modernist struggle was the Pope's alone. His personal secretary, Mgr Pescini, said on oath: 'The great struggle undertaken and conducted with such energy and efficiency against Modernism was personally directed and sustained by Pius x despite considerable opposition and protests'; similarly Mgr Canali, at that time Vice-Secretary of State: 'The line to be taken and the measures to check the Modernist movement were all the work of the Pope ... I remember how closely and knowledgeably he followed that harmful movement in the press, in education, in propaganda of all kinds, and through the daily reports made to him by the Cardinal Secretary of State, giving his personal encouragement.'

It was, in fact, the fight against Modernism that revealed, even more clearly than did his uncompromising attitude in foreign relations, that other aspect of Pius x – the angel with the fiery sword. But for that, no one could have believed him so inexorable. Convinced that the Modernist movement, as he himself named it, represented a serious threat to the very cause of God, he showed no pity towards the erring. The epithets used of Modernists, and the references to them in *Pascendi* (where in paragraph VIII the causes of Modernism are given as curiosity, pride, and ignorance), astonished the whole world. But in private he was even more inexorable. 'These miserable wretches,' he called them writing to Cardinal Ferrari on 17 February 1910, 'whom, by command of the apostle St John, we should refuse even to greet'; and to Mgr Bonomelli, as early as 31 December 1905: '... there are too many who have turned aside from the truth and, in demanding a reform of discipline, dare also to aspire to a reform of dogma and harass the Church with the sophisms used by its most violent opponents.'

After that, stern repression comes as no surprise. 'I am astonished,' he wrote to the Archbishop of Cremona, 'that you should find excessive the measures taken to confine the flood that threatens to swamp us, when the error they are striving to spread is much more deadly than that of Luther, because it aims directly at the destruction not only of the Church but of Christianity.' 'Kindness is for fools,' he said to someone who begged him to show pity towards a Modernist. And on another such occasion: 'They want them to be treated with oil, soap, and caresses. But they should be beaten with fists. In a duel, you don't count or measure the blows, you strike as you can. War is not made with charity: it is a struggle, a duel. If Our Lord were not terrible, He would not have given an example in this too. See how he treated the Philistines, the sowers of error, the wolves in sheep's clothing, the traders: He scourged them with whips!'

To seek out the Modernists he would use any allies and sanction the most repugnant methods. All his aids and watch-dogs (and they existed even in the Sacred College, such as, for example, Cardinal Andrieu, Archbishop of Bordeaux, who was later to help in opening the way to the condemnation of the *Action Française* under Pius XI) were not only protected and defended by him (like the Scotton brothers, with whom he had been friendly long before becoming Pope) but had their careers assured (like Mgr Gamberoni who, sent away from his seminary by Cardinal Ferrari, was then appointed Bishop of Chiavari, or the Jesuit Mattiussi – about whom, incidentally, the young Giuseppe Roncalli made a shrewd and critical report to his bishop – who was also turned out by Ferrari, only to be promoted by Sarto to succeed Billot at the Gregorian University in Rome). But the protection accorded to Mgr Benigni and his activities goes beyond any possible justification. Cardinal Gasparri, when called on to give his deposition about the heroic virtues of Pius X, did not hesitate to mention this as the most important of the 'obscure points':

Pope Pius X approved, blessed, and encouraged a secret espionage association outside and above the hierarchy, which spied on the members of the hierarchy itself, even on their Eminences the Cardinals; in short, he approved, blessed, and encouraged a sort of Freemasonry in the Church, something unheard-of in ecclesiastical history. Now this seems to me serious, and not to me alone, for it also seemed so to Cardinal Mercier (who was on the list of suspects to be watched) . . . And not only did Pius x approve, bless, and encourage the *Sodalitium Pianum*, but the denunciations emanating from it also afford the explanation for some serious attitudes adopted by Pius x in the government of the Church, although in this the Holy Father was, I do not doubt, in perfect good faith.

Cardinal Gasparri cited in particular his behaviour towards Cardinals Ferrari and Maffi and his mistrust of the Jesuits.

According to one of the theologians acting as censors *de scriptis* of Cardinal Ferrari in the cause for his beatification, there is no doubt that 'Pius x believed he saw in Cardinal Ferrari a truly rebellious spirit'. The letters exchanged between the Pope and De Lai prove this beyond all doubt. Moreover Ferrari is known to have been more than once on the point of resigning from the posts of Archbishop and Cardinal. The lack of understanding between the two was not merely temporary but lasted throughout practically the whole of Sarto's pontificate. The strangest thing about it is that Sarto had known Ferrari ever since he was Bishop of Como, which should have made it easy for him to realize how 'biologically improbable' it was that he should be a Modernist, and how blindly devoted and dedicated he was to the Pope. But in fact there had always been a certain incompatibility of character between the two, and indeed, according to Cardinal Schuster, 'a long-standing antipathy'. Schuster's deposition in the Ferrari cause goes on, 'Cardinal Sarto's jocular, friendly manner towards the clerics of the Lombard seminary may have been displeasing to the dignified, aloof Archbishop; but Pius x also found something to object to in Cardinal Ferrari's perpetual preaching. "He preaches," the Pope would say, "and he doesn't grasp that he's boring everyone." ' But such differences of character should obviously have been easy for a saint to overcome, if for no other reason than the gratitude he owed his opponent for having been one of the firmest supporters of his election as Pope.

But Loisy was right: 'Pius x was not at daggers drawn with anyone; but he was not master of his decisions, and once he felt himself to be the Pope he ceased to know anyone and reached the point of "unconscious brutality".' Few documents show this so eloquently as Pius x's letter to Cardinal De Lai of 26 February 1911 after seeing the latter's reply to Cardinal Maffi's letter:[1]

Your Eminence, May God reward you for your sacrifice in devoting so many hours of work to giving a triumphant answer to the senseless letter you received. If the author has kept a copy of it he will certainly blush to read this refutation ... How small certain men become who think themselves great! And how they show what they are without meaning to! Modernism, indeed! ...

Others besides Ferrari and Maffi fared no better – among them Cardinal Amette, Archbishop of Paris, Cardinal Fischer, Archbishop of Cologne, Cardinal Mercier, Archbishop of Malines, Mgr Bonomelli, Bishop of Cremona, Mgr Radini Tedeschi, Bishop of Bergamo, to cite only a few. Pius x did indeed show understanding in some cases, especially if the persons under suspicion were well known to him, as with Padre Genocchi ('that sort of wizard', as he used to call him) or Don Orione. Tommaso Gallarati Scotti has described the extraordinary audience given to Don Orione. 'Kneel, my son,' Pope Pius suddenly told the priest, his face clouding, though up to that point he had been talking to him with his accustomed familiarity. Don Orione fell at his feet in a posture of such humility that all Pius x's doubts vanished. He merely made him recite the *Credo*, which Don Orione did with such fervour that at the end Pius x brusquely raised him to his feet in anger not against him but against his traducers. 'Go, my son, go, I'll see to your enemies.'

But for the few who were not struck down by his 'paternal and implacable goodness', there were many others who fell victim to it, and unfortunately in some cases not without a suspicion of personal animosity. It is almost impossible, for example, to reject the doubt that Murri and Fogazzaro, in particular, experienced Pius x's vendetta. Had Pope Pius followed Cardinal Svampa's advice and summoned Don Murri to Rome to meet him personally, Murri would probably never have left the Church and his movement might have received papal approval – with far-reaching consequences, religious, political, and social, for Catholicism in Italy. But instead, as is now known, the whole process of ques-

[1] See pp. 38-9.

tioning and persecution to which Don Murri was subjected by his
bishop, Mgr Castelli of Fermo, was carried out step by step in
accordance with precise directions from the Pope, down to the
famous pastoral on the Murri case which was written on the basis
of pontifical letters. Pope Pius's conception of political action
certainly differed profoundly from that of Don Murri – the Pope,
in particular, would not countenance 'priests in politics'. But the
whole Murri affair, which tormented Pius x for years, has quite
different origins, going back to the days shortly before he became
Pope, when Murri lodged a complaint against the then Patriarch
of Venice for defamatory references to himself occurring in the
Patriarch's defence of Paganuzzi.

Resentment and susceptibility also undoubtedly played a part
in Pius x's relations with Fogazzaro. While Sarto was Patriarch in
Venice, Fogazzaro had dared to defend openly a picture by
Giacomo Grosso which Sarto considered offensive to religion.[1]
For the time being nothing happened, but the incident came home
to roost when *Il Santo* appeared. Anyone familiar with the book
will know that it neither expounds nor insinuates any theological
or moral errors. Even the highly cautious *Civiltà Cattolica*, review-
ing it on publication, found nothing to object to of a reformist
nature. Nevertheless the book was at once put on the Index. This
was a result of the Pope's personal decision. Pius x himself said
as much to Filippo Crispolti, admitting that he could not bear
Fogazzaro's having in his novel given a lesson on how to be
Pope and reform the Church, as if what the Pope himself was
doing was all wrong and useless; moreover he had drawn so
unattractive a picture of the Pope that he was bound to consider
it an offence. That *Il Santo* was condemned by Pius x's personal
wish was also confirmed during the cause for the beatification of
Cardinal Merry del Val by Canon Alberto Serafini, who had heard
it in confidence from Padre Pasqualino of the Holy Office.

An even greater puzzle is presented by Pius x's equivocal
treatment of eminent personalities in the Church hierarchy who
became the subject of a denunciation. He hardly ever dared to
speak to them himself, preferring instead that criticisms and
admonitions should be conveyed to them by subordinates. It quite
frequently happened that a cardinal or bishop would come away

[1] See above, p. 11.

deeply moved from an audience, only to be brusquely addressed
by the Secretary of State or Cardinal De Lai (who, incidentally,
did not even accompany his colleagues to the door after giving
them one of his terrible reprimands). Other methods of Pius x's
appear inexplicable, such as writing personal letters to parish
priests which they could then make use of *vis-à-vis* their bishops
(for example, letters to two priests, both in Milan diocese, of
19 March 1911 and 20 October 1912); or dividing bishops against
each other. An example of the latter occurred when all the
bishops of Lombardy wished to express their collective sympathy with Cardinal Ferrari for the calumnies published in
La Riscossa. The only non-signatory of this document was Mgr
Archi, Bishop of Como: he had asked the Pope's opinion and
Pius x telegraphed in reply: 'Best advice silence'.

The Paper Tiger

Nevertheless Pius x's most serious fault was not that he let himself be so far drawn into the anti-Modernist struggle that he was
unable to remain superior to the atmosphere of doubt and mistrust
created by all the accusations and suspicions. Paradoxical as it may
seem – especially since in the end he became the victim of his own
policy – his greatest real responsibility lies quite simply in having
'invented' Modernism.

No one would deny that so-called 'Modernism' (which incidentally is a constant feature of all ages, tending to become
accentuated in periods of crisis) corresponded to a reality which
was certainly complex, and for that reason difficult to grasp, but
which also included other quite different features. Modernism, in
fact, was never an ideological system but only a climate: a
climate made up of aspirations, plans and hopes for a universal
and profound modernization of the Church, of the kind put forward by those most in tune with the times and the advances made
by society. This climate was no sudden or recent phenomenon;
it was the continuation and development of aspirations and trends
at work throughout the nineteenth century which had been
largely frustrated during the pontificates of Gregory xvi and
Pius ix and only partially satisfied under Leo xiii.

In Italy, the idea of a reform of the Church took its inspiration
from such nineteenth-century figures as Antonio Rosmini,

Vincenzo Gioberti, and Raffaello Lambruschini, but especially Rosmini, whose philosophy had become in the last quarter of the century the watchword of Catholic liberalism, just as Thomism was for the integralists. His *Cinque Piaghe della Chiesa* (Five Wounds of the Church), however, was condemned during his lifetime, in 1849. In that year Rosmini had prepared himself by order of Pius IX to receive the Cardinal's hat; instead, there came the condemnation of the *Costituzione* and the *Cinque Piaghe*. In that courageous work, written with the humility of a saint, the philosopher of Rovereto attributed the crisis of the contemporary Church to five evils: social remoteness of the clergy from the people, the low standard of education of the priests, disunion among the bishops, the dependence of lay appointments on secular authorities, and church ownership of property. Rosmini, incidentally, was the spiritual father of Alessandro Manzoni; and another of his followers was Fogazzaro.

Gioberti and Lambruschini revealed themselves in their posthumous works as much more radical than Rosmini, seeking a reform that would even affect some essential points of the Church's constitution and creed. Though they never remotely envisaged the results of applying scientific methods to theological disciplines, they were ahead of their times in anticipating the answer to problems raised by later Catholic biblical critics such as Giovanni Semeria, Giovanni Genocchi, and Salvatore Minocchi.

These critics too had an independent scientific approach of their own, though chronologically speaking they came slightly after their French counterparts. Minocchi, in particular, drew his tools for biblical criticism mainly from the liberal Protestant or rationalist German scholars. Their earliest writing or teaching activities (Genocchi was a celebrated lecturer in Rome) went back to the 1890s, and Minocchi's periodical *Studi Cattolici* was first published in Florence in January 1901. Theirs was no vaguely reformist trend, nor was the parallel movement, concerned mainly with ecclesiastical historiography, of Umberto Fracassini, Padre Bonaccorsi, and others. By subjecting ecclesiastical disciplines to modern scientific methods, they showed what important changes could be achieved to the advantage of religion and the Church through cautious advance along the lines suggested.

Romolo Murri, in his turn, while agreeing with the ideas of both the more generic and the critical reformist groups, was himself above all the leader of a new social movement. Leo XIII's approval of this movement cast into confusion the Catholic Congress and its awe-inspiring Venetian leaders; but Murri, as we have seen, thereby earned himself the mistrust and hostility of Pope Pius X.

Thus the Italian reformist movement developed out of three groups: the 'generic' reformists, who aimed at a simplification and purification of Church organization and religious expression; the scientific critics; and the social movement. A similar development took place in France, where the earliest movement in this direction is usually forgotten, though it produced some significant manifestations. The Church congresses of Rheims (1896) and Bourges (1900) brought together from six hundred to eight hundred clergy, mainly parish priests, determined to examine on a basis not of principles but of facts the problems raised for the Church by modern developments in French society. The dominant note of the two congresses, corresponding to their aim of rendering pastoral action effective, was 'We must belong to our own era' – speak its language, respond to its aspirations, be adaptable to its methods. It was significant that reform of theological studies, though neglected at the first congress, played a large part at the second.

This was not surprising, for recent advances in religious studies had been much greater in France than in Italy, and had aroused wide interest among the French clergy, notoriously more intellectually inclined than the clergy in Italy. In the course of a few years the French scientific reformist movement acquired such notable leaders as the biblical scholar and historian of religion Loisy, the philosophers Hébert and Le Roy, specialists such as Tournel, the historiographer Houtin, and Mgr Mignot, Archbishop of Albi – not to mention isolated figures such as the great ecclesiastical historian Mgr Duchesne, precursor of the movement itself, Père Lagrange, founder of the Biblical School in Jerusalem, Mgr Batiffol, Rector of the Catholic Institute in Toulouse, Père Laberthonnière with his *Annales de philosophie chrétienne*, and Blondel with his *Philosophie de l'Action* and *Méthode de l'Immanence*. And the French progressive movement also had its social wing in the '*abbés démocratiques*' and Marc Sangnier's Christian Social movement, *Le Sillon*.

These various groups, nourished spontaneously by the prevailing climate of expectation, were not, either in Italy or in France, rigidly separated from each other: their members met and knew each other both because of their common interests and because many of them were versatile and often in demand. But there was no overall organization uniting them, no combined planning, and certainly no single secret leadership. What we earlier called the 'generic' group included reformists of all kinds of views and trends, whose most distinctive characteristic was their individualism and isolation. Members of the intellectual groups, too, worked in physical and, even more, in ideological isolation. They may have collaborated on certain periodicals, but for the most part they were solitaries who barely communicated with each other. Only the social group could really be said to be organized, for it could only act in combination, and was therefore the more readily destroyed and scattered.

Still less was there any international organization between these groups, unco-ordinated as they were even within the individual countries. Modernism was really a purely Latin phenomenon, affecting only Italy and France, and having only small-scale repercussions beyond, in England and Germany (in England its main representatives were the ex-Jesuit George Tyrrell and Baron Friedrich von Hügel, Austrian by birth but who spent most of his life in England). Germany, it is true, acted to some extent as a link between the various representatives in the different countries, but largely on a basis of personal contacts; and there was never any plan for co-ordination of the national movements. In its whole history Modernism held only one congress, at Molvena in Italy in 1907, where the sole foreign representative was von Hügel. Even the various reviews describing themselves as international were the products of personal initiative, not of any organization. A volume entitled *Il Programma dei Modernisti*, published in Rome just after the encyclical *Pascendi*, was indeed translated in several countries; but, besides expressing the views of a small group of Roman Modernists for which the other Italian groups disowned responsibility, it also differed from the encyclical in stating emphatically that the so-called Modernism denounced there was not a clearly defined system but a method of work aimed at verifying certain hypotheses.

Even more important was the fact that Modernism was a movement from within the Church itself, initiated by believers determined to work and sacrifice themselves for the Church's development and progress. Its most typical characteristic, by comparison with the heresies of the past, was the absence of any idea of schism or separation from the Church. The cause for this is obvious: the whole *raison d'être* of the movement, in its members' eyes, was the reform, not the replacement, of the Church. All the historical heresies of the past had confronted the hierarchy of the day with an ultimatum: either accept the proposed changes or a new Church will be set up. No Modernist ever thought along these lines: those who bowed to Pius x's edicts had the courage to renounce the spreading of ideas evolved through years of study and meditation (ideas which, incidentally, the Church often later came to accept) and frequently to sacrifice all their research activities; while those who decided against submission continued their studies as isolated scholars or adopted other professions, but never with any idea of establishing a Modernist Church. Lastly, the smallest group, those who were forcibly ejected, showed their loyalty to the Church even more openly, continuing, like Ernesto Buonaiuti, upon its threshold and protesting that they were still its devoted sons.

Among the many autobiographies by Modernists, none perhaps more eloquently describes the intentions of the best of them than this extract from a letter of Padre Semeria's to Mgr Bonomelli:

I know that I – we – might have kept apart from these crises [of those who strove to find a point of contact and harmony between faith and science] and pretended to ignore them; we should have led peaceful and honoured lives . . . But we had not the courage to turn aside certain souls that came to us . . . we thought it our duty as priests to diagnose and understand their doubts. They were fine souls: souls that wished to remain faithful to Christ, that felt the mysterious powers of the Church, but did not want to renounce the scientific methods that had served to illuminate their work and that of others in the lay field – they wanted to live in Christ a joyous life, a life of thought, affection, art, democracy. Like our fathers, those whom you, Your Excellency, have understood so well wanted to remain good Catholics but also to live to the full the life of their country. We tried to preserve these souls for the Church: we told them to be patient and hope. The Church is slow to move, but it moves. We tried to resolve some of their difficulties and problems. Our sincere attempts at a solution – and they were only attempts – may have been inaccurate or wrong in part and were certainly only provisional. But our intentions were, in God's name, upright, [word missing in text] an uprightness for which the dignity of our lives and our intellectual work would answer. But we who desire the unity of the Church but who also believe that unity is compatible with honest freedom, we suffer because of this, and if we have done something for these young people, it was and is in order to keep them *malgré tout* faithful to the Church ... The problems remain even when unfortunate attempts to solve them are discarded, and unhappily for anxious hearts they are not solved by decrees and condemnations. Just as the grievous problem of relations between Church and State in Italy is not solved by reaffirming every six months the indispensable need for temporal power ...

Some instances of ideological degeneration, and hence of heresy, did occur, but this merely meant that while so-called Modernism undoubtedly constituted a crisis in the life of the Church, it was a crisis of involution in only a few insignificant cases, whereas in general the crisis was one of growth and as such should have been met and dealt with accordingly. Now there can be no doubt whatever that in reversing Leo XIII's diagnosis his successor committed the most tragic blunder that he (and the Church with him) could possibly have made. This does not mean that Pope Leo can be absolved from all responsibility. In the last years of his reign he should have suspended the repressive measures proposed in the case of the more suspect scholars and taken practical steps to utilize the positive aspects of what they had to contribute, while eliminating what might prove harmful; and he should have urged them particularly to exercise caution in making public critical opinions or plans for reform which might otherwise come as a dangerous shock to the public. But it is easy to see why Leo XIII did not act in this way: it was partly due to his own limited background – for he was no great theologian, let alone a biblical scholar – and partly to the illusion that the spell of his authority, before which the best minds had always bowed submissively, would continue to function; and in any case he was a tired man at the end of a long reign.

A much greater responsibility than that of Leo XIII rests upon the Sacred College in their choice of his successor. The cardinals' estimate of what the situation called for, whether reached individually or in groups (for there was no attempt to do so as a body), was clearly very superficial; the supporters of Rampolla probably took too much account of the political aspect, and those who supported his opponents too little. In view of the recognized crisis through which the Church was passing, the need was to analyse its component parts. If, as we have seen, the aspiration for renewal was represented by three main groups – generic and spiritual, critical and scientific, and social – the election of a 'religious' pope would certainly go some way towards meeting the needs of the first and third groups but not of the second, unless the pope in question had sufficient personal authority to deal with its members. Now this central group was, in the second half of 1903, not only the most delicate but also the most important, because of the influence that the progressive intellectual leaders were acquiring within the Church.

To choose a candidate for the tiara who lacked the necessary cultural background and expert knowledge in at least some branch of theology could well prove disastrous. It was by their failure to realize this that Pius x's electors brought the catastrophe of Modernism upon the Church. And the crowning misfortune, as we have seen, was that the new Pope was at once assailed and besieged by the most reactionary elements, with as their representative a fanatical saint like Richard the Archbishop of Paris, who literally transmitted all his own fears to the Pope; and the first incautious step decided the whole future. Had the danger come from some other quarter in the progressive field, Pope Pius would have been sufficiently cool-headed and detached to see it in its true perspective. But arising as it did in the sphere of criticism, the threat seemed the more dramatic because he found it nebulous and hard to understand. The Loisy episode took on nightmare proportions. The spectre of heresy loomed large in his imagination and, like Richard, he saw in the exercise of authority and discipline the only possible means of checking the advancing danger. If Richard was a Breton, Sarto was from the Veneto, and if Richard was, as Mgr Mignot jestingly put it, 'the old legitimist of the Vendée', the same could be said of Sarto. To both of them, not only was the Church everything but it had thought of and provided for everything. It had envisaged in detail every possible form of future. To speak of new needs, unfold new ideas, invoke new and untried alliances with profane knowledge, was for them the equivalent of being steeped in devilish poison and predestined to betrayal and schism. The only course for them, therefore, was to pluck out the error as quickly as possible. To delay condemnation was to let the canker spread. To yield to discussion was to favour its advance. 'He could not have done so,' Loisy wrote of Richard, 'but in any case, on principle, he allowed of no discussion.' Exactly the same was true of Sarto. An authority given from above, from God Himself, and on matters directly concerning God, could in their eyes only lose prestige by self-justification – and so the axe of the Index was made to fall.

Even if some of Pius x's excesses in repressing Modernism can be forgiven, it is hard to forgive the haste with which, only a few months after his election, he instituted a reign of ideological terror. His own inadequacy to deal with the complex cultural problems involved should have made him especially cautious in a sphere where his great predecessor had shown such prudence. In any case, before taking drastic action against errors and the erring – many of whom were in good faith – it would have been wise to examine the situation carefully and work out the best means of dealing with it in collaboration with the relevant experts and departments. The mere fact that danger came not from ill-disposed sources outside, but from within the Church, and for the most part from clergy sincerely zealous for its effective modernization, might have suggested other methods less harsh than condemnation and outright humiliation.

True, the first sudden condemnation was followed by a pause in which only minor interventions occurred. But this was not due to any lack of suitable objectives or to Pope Pius's preoccupation with the French crisis, still less to any search for a different method on his part. The delay in bringing out the series of bombshell anti-Modernist announcements of 1907 was because the Pope was seeking for a really decisive weapon to destroy all the various forms of heretical unrest at work within the Church. Draft condemnations of the new errors piled up on his desk, but they were all formulated on the outdated lines of the old *Syllabus* of Pius IX or of Leo XIII's attacks on Rosmini's views. Now the *Syllabus* of 1864 had failed precisely because its vast list of errors revealed no common element or weak point for attack. Perusing the lists before him, Pius x found the errors seemed lifeless and fossilized, whereas he knew them to be active and exerting an irresistible attraction for the young clergy and laity. Hence his resolute refusal to act on such feeble documents, and hence his

repeated exhortations to trusted theologians to give body to
these scanty limbs and find some unity among this collection of
scattered faults in which his sons continued to indulge. The
celebrated Padre Billot, '*Thomas redivivus*', Professor of Dogmatic
Theology at the Gregorian University, burst into tears one day
before his students when confessing the failure so far of all the
efforts to obey the Pope's wishes and combine all the lists of
errors into a single document to be refuted at a blow.[1]

The wrong course had in fact been adopted in seeking to find
the lowest common denominator among the widely differing
standpoints of the reformers. No such common denominator
existed even among the various doctrinal or scientific standpoints
of the biblical scholars, philosophers, or ecclesiastical historians
denounced or suspected by the Roman tribunals; what hope
then was there of finding one that would also be valid for the
many-sided group of the religious reformists or the social
movement?

The way was found at last in deciding to abandon the search
for a common ideology and adopt instead the method of grouping
by headings, each under a generic name, all the heretical or near-
heretical phenomena to be eradicated. Once find an original and
striking name and the myth of the new heresy would be created,
to which all the most diverse and contradictory imputations
could be attributed without the need to justify their strange coexistence. A name presupposes a reality, and a reality does not need
to be explained: it imposes itself by the mere fact of its existence.
Indeed the more intricate, unfathomable, and complex it appears,
the more fascinating and impressive it is. In short the thing was
to find an '-ism' which would be the quintessence of all '-isms',
combining within it all the '-isms' then fashionable, from agnosticism to criticism, immanentism to evolutionism, and the rest.

The name chosen was 'Modernism', till then a word seldom
employed, and it was used here as a catalogue-heading rather
than a term to express a philosophical principle. The method did
not attempt to explain why or by what criteria such diverse
elements had been brought together, but confined itself to insinuating that it had come about by the law of affinity. At most
it was vaguely suggested that the catalyst of the various errors
making up the 'heresy of heresies' was the desire for new things,

[1] See note in Bibliography, p. 372.

in keeping with current fashion, which had arisen among certain sections of the clergy and laity who had let themselves be tempted by worldly ideas and who, instead of striving to bring the world to the Church, wanted to bring the Church to the world, reducing sacred things to a natural level and depriving the supernatural of its revolutionary content.

In short, the process was one of an extreme simplicity and incredible audacity. Instead of trying to reconstruct the presumed face of the unknown heresy from the fragmentary features known, as by a sort of Identikit process, a name was invented and a face and body were attributed to it irrespective of whether they really existed. The invention of Modernism consisted simply in this: in an audacious mystification, carried out in the encyclical *Pascendi*, thanks to which not only the Catholic but the non-Catholic world, and not only contemporaries but posterity, came to believe in the existence of the Modernist Devil. *Pascendi*, in fact, did not define something that existed, but something in whose existence it was convenient that people should believe.

The operation was, of course, highly risky, but its success was never in doubt since it had the backing, in a solemn document such as an encyclical, of the authority of the Pope himself. According to Catholic doctrine, in guarding against dogmatic or moral errors the Pope, even when not speaking *ex cathedra*, is supported by divine aid which protects him from erring. Consecrated, even if not formally and explicitly, by the chrism of infallibility, the announcement made in *Pascendi* was sure to be received by all Catholics with the necessary docility. Prudence, however, suggested that the papal document should include additional causes for credence. So the encyclical after a theoretical analysis of error provided a list of types of persons in error, which lent itself much more easily to concrete verification and acceptance than the earlier general theory of Modernism as a synthesis of all errors. Hence the detailed description of the Modernist theologian, philosopher, biblical scholar, reformer, politician, and sociologist.

The authors of the encyclical even had the temerity to explain to readers that in Modernism:

It is not a question of isolated and disconnected errors but a genuine organized system of error, whose different parts are so closely associated that it is impossible to admit one without admitting all the others. Therefore, viewing the system as a whole, can anyone be surprised if we call Modernism 'the complex and synthesis of all heresies'? Certainly, if anyone had taken the trouble to assemble together all the errors which arose to combat faith throughout the centuries, and had concentrated them in one alone, he would not have done better than the Modernists, who, as has been said, demolish not only the Catholic religion but all religion.

Needless to say, widespread protests came at once from the 'Modernists', beginning with the *Programma* published in Rome.[1] But that could have been a mere question of tactics. The fact remains that no one, whether opponent or defender or historian of the Modernist movement, who was not just pedantically repeating the words of the encyclical was ever able to discern in the ideology or works of the individual Modernists the existence of a system even remotely resembling that set forth with such wealth of imagination in the pontifical document. Regardless of this, however, Pius x's faithful followers organized themselves for the great struggle. The encyclical had provided against all possible accusations of a discrepancy between its own full and lucid exposition and the fragmentary, cautious, and allusive statements of the Modernists, by accusing them of adopting a gradual method in revealing their errors, so as not to be found out and checked at once. There was a grain of truth in this, for to avoid reprisals the 'Modernists' had indeed put forward their aims singly, advancing cautiously from one to the next. But this method, while it furthered the manoeuvres of the real heretics, ended by compromising even the most upright and orthodox persons because of the suspicions their allusions aroused.

Thus, since Modernism was in reality simply a desire for modernization on the part of people sincerely attached to the Church who deplored its reactionary ways, the battle launched against it ended by involving indiscriminately everyone who expressed such a desire or who followed, however cautiously, the various advocates of reform. *Pascendi*, in trying to cover every possibility, had included under the label of Modernism every form of dissent, however legitimate, from tradition or authority; but the effect of this was to present the Church as a target to itself, or rather to the most retrograde elements whom the encyclical

[1] See pp. 35, 61.

had so ingenuously entrusted with the fate of the future of Catholicism. The most serious responsibility of its authors and its supreme promoter lies in this – in having brought Catholics to the point where they could no longer distinguish between each other but dealt each other mortal blows in the dark, and all in the name of a non-existent spectre.

Beneath the Ruins of Victory

Modernism, in short, was the spectre which Pope Pius employed to give consistency to all the shadows nourishing his fears when faced with a progressive movement that had attained a certain position, whose aims he could not understand, and whose novelty frightened him.

Naturally, like every movement still uncertain about its ultimate aims and strength, the progressive movement of the 1890s–1900s brought together doubtful and dangerous elements as well as conscientious and God-fearing ones. And, as so often happens, the extremists came to be regarded as typical of it, especially in the eyes of those responsible for the established order. Only calm reflection and far-sighted intuition could have helped such critics to view less pessimistically a phenomenon which was in fact inevitable, being part and parcel of the transition from one cultural era to the next.

The Catholic Church was undoubtedly, as the official historians aver, purified by the recourse to 'sword and fire': but it emerged from it sterilized. To cite only the instance of theological studies, a great many scholars who as clergy wanted to remain faithful to their priesthood, or as laymen to their baptism, and give dutiful submission to the pontifical measures, ended by abandoning completely the fields of study most subject to reactionary attack and withdrew to more peaceful spheres or gave up intellectual work altogether, concentrating exclusively on pastoral or charitable duties. In Italy alone, for example, men of such standing as Fracassini, Mari, Bonaccorsi, and Semeria gave up any attempt to pursue scientific research.

Pope Pius naturally had no wish to appear a cultural iconoclast, and he sought some counter-initiative to demonstrate the Church's permanent interest in advancing theological studies. He had inherited from his predecessor the Pontifical Biblical Commission, conceived of by Leo XIII as a guide for Catholic biblical scholars in the more complex aspects of their studies. Pius X somewhat precipitately, on 23 February 1904, altered its structure and scope, making it also an examining body with the power to confer degrees in biblical studies. A more opportune step would have been to moderate his inquisitorial zeal for producing all those ill-fated decrees which for decades afterwards had to be continually modified or tacitly disregarded. But instead, on 18 November 1907, by the *motu proprio, Praestantia Sacrae Scripturae,* he declared his judgements obligatory *in foro conscientiae,* giving them the same value as the doctrinal decrees of the Sacred Roman Congregations.

Pius X decided to entrust to the Benedictine Order the critical edition of the Latin version of the Bible produced fifteen centuries earlier by St Jerome: this might have been a useful undertaking but for the fact that what was really needed at that time was a critical edition of the Bible in the original text (Hebrew for the Old Testament, Greek for the New). An excellent idea, on the other hand, was his decision to establish a college for biblical studies in Rome (the Pontifical Biblical Institute), entrusting it to the Jesuits (7 May 1909), although it naturally had to conform to all the cautionary regulations for biblical teaching in seminaries which the Pope had laid down three years earlier. The plan, in any case, dated back to Leo XIII, who would certainly not have wished to see the *Biblicum* in Rome wasting itself in sterile dispute with Lagrange's Institute in Jerusalem.

Pius X's anxiety to avoid the slur of obscurantism is, indeed, clear from *Pascendi* itself, where in the concluding section the proposal was announced to establish an Academy of Sciences which, with the collaboration of world-renowned Catholic scholars, would give practical proof of the Catholic Church's interest in cultural and scientific questions. This Academy too got as far as the planning stage, and Cardinals Rampolla, Maffi, and Mercier, with Ludwig von Pastor as Secretary, were charged with drawing up its statutes. But for some reason their work was never finished, perhaps fortunately, for however imposing the new Academy might have been it would have ended up as just another of the numerous pontifical academies in Rome, bearing within itself the original fault of an impossible attempt to confessionalize scholarship.

These limited proposals were, in fact, typical of Pius x, and afford the clearest demonstration of the antithesis between him and Leo xiii: Pope Leo with his eyes always fixed on the non-Catholic world, whether secular or Christian, eager to establish relations and increase contacts with it; and Pope Pius concerned only with the defence of the Church and its religious restoration to the exclusion of any attempt to keep up with the times. As he once said in reproof to Padre Semeria who was explaining that in his books he aimed at a wide public: 'You are opening the doors to bring in those outside and meanwhile you chase out those within.'[1]

A temporary check in the field of ecclesiastical studies, as a prelude to further advance, might have done no harm. But the check ordained by Pius x was meant to be, and was, absolute, and it hit not only the scholars of his own time but future generations virtually right up to the pontificate of John xxiii. His anti-cultural measures produced a half-century of sterility that, taken in addition to the earlier slowing-down (it was not for nothing that Benedetto Croce described the Modernists themselves as 'delaying factors'), was to weigh as a tragic inheritance upon the future of Catholicism.

Inasmuch as the Modernist dispute played so large a part in the pontificate of Pius x, his reign inevitably ended by being partly submerged beneath its accumulated ruins. One thing about it is certain: the impression it gives of something unfinished, in suspension, of an unexpected arrest that suddenly paralysed it, leaving undone nearly all the enterprises planned. One needs only to recall the chronology of the various reforms undertaken by Sarto: all of them without exception go back to the first five years of his pontificate, and only a few were partially completed later. Now this certainly did not come about through some sudden physical weakening on the part of the Pope, for of this there is no trace. And it was only partly because the good country priest's modest handful of ideas became exhausted. Modest though they may have been, Pius x had barely begun to put them into effect: how was it, then, that they were carried out only up to a certain point, and then left in suspense? The answer is clear: the cause was the massive reaction against Modernism, which

[1] See Mgr Girolamo Bortignon, *Pio X e il Modernismo*, Rovigo, 1951.

was given absolute and immediate precedence over everything else.

Certainly, Pius x's could hardly have been a great pontificate. Great history in the making calls for great ideas, and Pius x's ideas were modest and limited in number. His narrow mentality is obvious even in that sphere, the pastoral, in which he was most at home. The fact that as parish priest of Salzano he undertook such extra tasks as ordering the village's supply of gravel or supervising teaching in the elementary schools may testify to his zeal to pay off his debts, but not to his breadth of view as a pastor. He did not think, like Don Bosco, of oratories for young people or, like other colleagues of his, of agricultural credits for the peasants. It is the fate of the conservative-minded not to open up new forward-looking ways, and therefore not to become really great. Richard, in Paris, for example, refused, despite all his zeal, to build new churches in the suburbs even though he admitted their falling away from Christianity. But an even worse defect of conservatives is their unwillingness to recognize the good side in new things.

When, on becoming Pope, Sarto found himself faced with the question of the Catholic press in Italy, and in particular with the choice between a partly-secularized press,[1] upheld by such men as Cardinal Maffi of Pisa and Cardinal Ferrari of Milan, and a purely confessional press, he did not hesitate to support the latter with every weapon available. A confessional press was the formula of the intransigents and the ultra-papalists, but journalistically speaking it was a mistaken formula, for such papers had a purely symbolical circulation and were read only by people already devoted to the cause of reactionary Catholicism. The partly-secularized Catholic press on the other hand, was in competition with the whole lay press, which was nearly always anti-clerical and agnostic; it was still in its early stages, but despite mistakes the results were on the whole promising. Pius x was probably also worried that the power of the partly-secularized Catholic press in Italy might increase after it came under Count Grosoli's press Trust, and that he might not be able to control it. But that does not alter the fact that he supported, once again, a thesis contrary to the Catholic cause.

Despite its limitations, however, the pontificate of Pius x

[1] See footnote, p. 42.

might have left a permanent mark or even proved a turning-point in the history of the Church, because for the first time in modern history it put into practice an anti-temporalist ideal which had been lost sight of since the early centuries of the Church. It is, indeed, in the political sphere that admirers and opponents find the greatest contrast between his pontificate and that of Leo XIII. But it is perhaps just here that the greatest misunderstanding has arisen through a confusion between diplomatic and political activity. It was with diplomacy, not politics, that Pius X refused to concern himself – at one point he even wanted to suppress the entire diplomatic corps of the Holy See and replace the nuncios by a bishop or the Superior General of an Order as the Church's representative in each country. An irrefutable text on this subject exists in the allocution at his first consistory, of 9 November 1903:

To restore everything in Christ! That is our programme, as we have already announced. And since Christ is the Truth, our first duty will be, first and foremost, to teach, proclaim, and defend the truth and law of Christ. Hence the duty to illustrate and confirm those principles of truth, both natural and supernatural, which in our day we often unfortunately see obscured or forgotten; to consolidate the principles of dependence and authority, of injustice and equity, which today are trampled upon; to direct all people according to the laws of morality, and in social and political matters as well: all people – we say – both those who obey and those who command.

We know well that we shall shock many in saying that we shall necessarily concern ourselves with politics. But anyone who takes a just view of things must see that the Supreme Pontiff, invested by God with Supreme Authority, is absolutely unable to separate the things belonging to faith from the conduct of politics. Since he is also the Head and First Magistrate of the society of the Church – a society composed of men and living among men – it is necessary that he should have mutual relations with the heads of nations and with the civil authorities if he desires that wherever there are Catholics provision should be made for their security and liberty, not forgetting that, in defence of the faith, our apostolic duty is to confute and reject such principles of modern philosophy and civil law as may urge the course of human affairs in a direction not permitted by the restrictions of eternal law.

Thus from the beginning of his pontificate Pius X was fully prepared to concern himself with politics, taken in the sense of a religious policy, or the defence of the rights of the Holy See regarded, in accordance with the Catholic tradition, as of similar force to the rights of God. If he avoided entering into international politics, and cared no more for the Triple Alliance than for the Triple Entente – and that, of course, is to his credit – he undoubtedly did so in conformity with this principle, in which he firmly believed; though it must also be borne in mind that, unlike Leo XIII, he no longer had to concern himself about alliances with the Great Powers. As has been mentioned earlier, Pope Leo's efforts to put the Holy See back into the orbit of the Great Powers were inspired by the need both to recover his predecessor's lost prestige and also to safeguard his own survival as a dethroned sovereign, keeping a constant threat hanging over Italy lest an extremist government should try to deprive him of even the protection assured him by the Law of Guarantees, and so reduce him to the status of an ordinary Italian citizen at the head of a private religious society. Any danger of this had virtually ceased to exist by the early years of the twentieth century, despite the persistence and even increase of anti-clericalism under Nathan's régime as Mayor of Rome. The survival of the Papacy for over thirty years in the Italian capital was by then an accomplished fact of history. With the disappearance of resistance, even the Roman Question might soon lose its force.

Pius X, in short, could embark on a religious policy free from temporalist preoccupations. Recent history had shown that the strength of the Church lay in the spiritual, not the temporal sphere. Pius X's aim was to conduct a policy in accordance with the Church's interests in every country having Catholics among its population. And, contrary to what is often claimed, he did so quite irrespective of the type of régime in each State, prepared to accept flexibly the various different situations he found. In the countries where Catholics were in the majority, he naturally favoured their pre-eminence in the political sphere, but where this was not so, he accepted their participation in mixed associations, as for instance in the German trade unions; where they were not even independent, as in Poland or Ireland, he supported their irredentist cause and protected and supported them against possible persecution.

In Vatican relations it is never the countries with a Catholic minority that present the greatest problems: in such cases prudence and tactics alike counsel a policy of wait-and-see. Pius x's greatest difficulties came from the Latin countries, and in particular from France; and his conduct in relation to that country, especially in the question of the *associations cultuelles*,[1] was typical of his policy as a whole. While he never dreamt of acting like Baron Corvo's Hadrian vii in deposing all the French cardinals from their sees and making them apostolic missionaries in a de-Christianized France, he could nevertheless quote Ruskin and say with him of the bishops and priests left without funds or office: 'They will starve and go to heaven'; which caused everyone to admire the heroic aspect of his decision. It was also equally successful politically, and he refused to barter the Church's freedom, won by its separation from the State, for the dish of lentils offered by the episcopal incomes and parish allowances. Through the *associations cultuelles* the French Government aimed at imposing on the Catholic Church in France the jurisdictional control that it could no longer maintain after the separation of Church from State, thus making void much of the advantages the Church derived from its autonomy. All these schemes were brought to naught by Pius x's refusal.

But even a policy that gives absolute primacy to the spiritual is not without its temptations, and Pope Pius might have echoed the words of his imaginary counterpart Hadrian vii: 'We, having no personal sovereignty, exercise Our prerogative as Father of princes and kings.' That, at least, was the key to his conduct in relation to Portugal and even more to Spain. No one would wish to suggest that the revolt of 1909 in Catalonia was not an extremely serious matter for the Church, with its dozens of priests and monks killed and churches and monasteries destroyed; but a tragic equilibrium was restored with the shooting of Francisco Ferrer and his companions. The notorious law against the religious Orders approved in the Cortes during the subsequent phase of the disturbances was certainly a grievous matter for Rome; but did it really justify the withdrawal *ex abrupto* of the Nuncio from Madrid? And this, moreover, just when the Pope was lauding the splendour of the Eucharistic Congress in the

---

[1] Recognized religious associations to which, under the separation of Church and State, Church endowments and revenue were to be handed over – see p. 32. *Translator.*

capital with the words: 'Spain, invincibly Catholic, will never accept separation from the Church'?

It is therefore not surprising that by the end of Pope Pius x's pontificate diplomatic representation to the Holy See had been severely cut down by Merry del Val's needlessly gladiatorial methods, carried out with the unreserved support of his master.

Though not without its contradictions and compromises, Pius x's behaviour towards the Catholic parties is even more significant than his anti-temporalist aspirations. His real wish would have been that they should not exist. He once said of the German *Zentrum*, even with all its background of resistance to Bismarck's *Kulturkampf*, 'I do not like it, because it is a Catholic party'. Naturally he never thought of dissolving the parties already in existence so long as they docilely let themselves be controlled. But his ideal was that they should not exist, and this for various reasons. First, because he believed the mixture of politics and religion to be the most hybrid and dangerous possible for the Church; secondly, because in general, and especially at that time, they fostered the participation of priests in politics; and lastly, because he thought them useless, for Catholics could always seek support for their religious claims from the lay parties favourable to the Church or at least not hostile to it.

The danger of socialism in Italy, associated at that time with an anti-clericalism that certainly did nothing to encourage the Pope in dreams of Christian Socialism, convinced him of the need for Catholics to unite and form, together with the Liberals, a bulwark against it. He therefore agreed to a modification of the *non expedit*, the prohibition declared by Leo XIII in 1895 against voting by Catholics; but at the same time he forbade Catholics elected to the Chamber to call themselves Catholic deputies, thus preventing them from uniting in an autonomous party. Don Murri's Democratic League should have been such a party, but the Pope disavowed and banned it, as he also did with Marc Sangnier's movement in France *Le Sillon* – though there perhaps mainly because it seemed to him a particularly scandalous example of an invasion by politics of purely religious territory. He also found other justifications such as the movement's excessive cult of democracy, its philo-socialism, and its non-confessionalism; but the only real reason was its mixture of religious and political activity.

The condemnation of *Le Sillon* was chiefly surprising because of the different treatment accorded to the *Action Française*. Marc Sangnier's movement had never adopted an attitude that struck at the heart of any dogma or precept of Catholic morality, or that might constitute an invitation to rebellion or secession from the Church. And Marc Sangnier himself, despite his mystical totalitarianism, had always been a loyal son of the Church, as was shown clearly and most movingly by his submission after the condemnation. The situation in relation to Charles Maurras and the *Action Française*, on the other hand, was quite different. Though Maurras took good care not to repeat the blasphemies of his youthful works against Christ (the 'Jew' who from the Cross had cast darkness over all humanity) and the Church (which for eighteen hundred years had 'monstrously soiled the world'), his essentially pagan and positivist view of life had not altered. And though it did not openly inspire his paper, it nevertheless made itself felt in its comments on current political events, in supporting the primacy of the individual against society (hence its anti-democratic and royalist tone), the immorality of means of defence for the established order, and so on. But Catholic integralism, given its anti-republican, anti-democratic, and anti-liberal character, had ended by sympathizing with Maurras' paper, which, in turn, found it useful to attach the Catholic conservatives to its cause; and this it did by openly aligning itself with them in the anti-Modernist dispute, in combination even with Mgr Benigni's *Sapinière*, as the *Sodalitium Pianum* was ironically called in France.

These were more than sufficient reasons for Pius x to look kindly on the *Action Française* and its movement. In fact, he not only privately encouraged its leaders' activities but also, when the Holy Office took action against Maurras' works and his newspaper and prepared the decrees for their prohibition, Pius x decided not to sign them but merely kept them by him. It fell to Pius xi, in 1926, to bring them to light again and promulgate them; but just as Pius xi then bowed to the dictates of politics in order to clear the ground of Maurras' movement as an obstacle to a second *Ralliement* of Catholics to the French Republic, so too Pius x, in refusing to sign those decrees, recognized the wisdom of utilizing what was then perhaps the only lay voice openly to defend the cause of the Church in France, even if it meant perpetuating the equivocal union between the Catholic integralists and a largely anti-Catholic ideology. Which shows yet again that the parish-priest-Pope was not so innocent and ingenuous as to shun a 'pact with the Devil' if he found it advisable.

Moreover Pius x sometimes showed quite remarkable indulgence in relation to the Catholic parties, even to the point of supporting an anti-semitic campaign which, while it might have had some practical justification, was none the less blameworthy both morally and on principle. The episode is worth mentioning because it also shows the conservative and anti-ecumenical mentality of Pius x. Sarto was most certainly no typical anti-semite. While Bishop of Mantua, when passing the Jewish cemetery one day he jokingly asked his secretary if he could recite a *De Profundis* for those buried there and, sensing his companion's embarrassment, said: 'Look, you've just taken your degree in theology at Rome. That is the sovereign science and the one most necessary to us. But, you know, Our Lord has his own theology, and it is a quite special system. Therefore I want us to pray for those poor people.' But there is also another story of him in Mantua. It was the custom there on 14 May, King Humbert's birthday, for the civil and military authorities to attend a service first in the cathedral and then in the synagogue. Now in 1889, although he had made no objection to this custom during his previous five years there, Sarto refused to go on with this 'indecorous comedy', as his official biography describes it, telling the Prefect that he must choose between the cathedral and the synagogue, otherwise the cathedral doors would be closed – which is in fact what happened by decision of Crispi, the Prime Minister, who when asked his view just said: 'Neither cathedral nor synagogue.'

Many years later, in order to win votes during the local elections in Vienna, the Austrian Christian-Social (i.e. Catholic) party stirred up a violent anti-semitic campaign (so violent that Hitler recalled it as one of the most significant memories of his youth), thereby provoking protests that even reached Rome. Pius x came down on the side of the Nuncio, Agliardi, who had represented the protests made to the Holy See as being a manoeuvre of the Christian-Social party's opponents. In other words, he refused to criticize publicly the Christian-Socialists' behaviour, although in private, being obviously worried about the affair, he advised the party's leaders to moderate their attitude.

The explanation for these and other contradictions in Pius x's attitude to Catholic parties lies not only in the different situations *vis-à-vis* the Church in the various countries but also in his own social conservatism. Notwithstanding his proletarian origins, and, indeed, precisely as a result of the acceptance and ascetic glorification of poverty that he had assimilated from his family and social surroundings in the Veneto, Pius x was always a convinced supporter of a public order based on the recognition of social and class distinctions as something immutable. In his *motu proprio* of 18 December 1903 he reiterated his predecessor's most conservative tenets with regard to property and class differences; and in 1909, addressing pilgrims from the Abruzzi, he said: 'Let the rich be generous in alms-giving. Let the poor be proud to have been chosen as the images of Christ! Let them remove envy from their hearts and have patience and resignation.' And early in 1913 Cardinal Merry del Val, acting in his name, criticized in a letter those who put too much emphasis on the idea of justice rather than of charity and regarded the right of property as a function of justice no longer involving charity.

Whatever limitations and contradictions there may have been in Pius x's political and social outlook, there can be no doubt about his anti-temporal ideal. This was something quite new and even disconcerting for Vatican practice, but it was also one of the most important, and indeed revolutionary, innovations of his pontificate. This anti-temporal ideal had obviously to be worked out in terms of all the consequences it involved, avoiding, in particular, the temptation of allowing the spiritual side to reclaim for the Church, in the name of the rights of God, benefits which it had been ready to renounce out of respect for the rights of civil society. The sternness of Pius x's religious policy was a direct result of this possibly unconscious dilemma.

Withdrawal from a world in flames

After all that has been said about the anti-Modernist crusade and its effects on Pope Pius x's pontificate, the question unavoidably arises whether it did not in part involve also the moral figure of the man himself. The fact that the Church did not hesitate to canonize him, and in record time (only forty years after his death), constitutes no proof even for Catholics; if anything it gives them an additional reason to exercise their faith.

A saint, in any case, in certain respects at least, Giuseppe Sarto undoubtedly was: if for no other reasons, for the dour, reserved, tenacious consistency with which throughout his life he followed the hard ascetic road he had laid down for himself; for his numerous virtues; for the wellnigh supernatural disinterestedness of which he gave constant proof. His ascetic austerity is to be measured not so much by his renunciation of material things (though that too counted) as by his total dedication of himself in the fulfilment of his duties, his complete forgetfulness of self and unawareness of self-sacrifice (this unostentatious self-sacrifice had in it something of the taciturnity and tenacity of the peasant that he was at heart – his father was a humble local official, his mother a dressmaker, but his whole background was of peasant origin). Nevertheless the character of his saintliness was typically medieval, being the fruit of suppression and annihilation rather than of renunciation and contemplation, of negative rather than of positive virtues.

Medieval, too, was much of the incidental ballast that went along with his saintliness: the occasional coarseness of speech in his jokes and witticisms (much less so after he became Pope, but sometimes, as was recognized during the cause for his beatification, bordering on the scurrilous, though free from any sexual tinge – the typical rather heavy facetiousness, in fact, of many parish priests even today in the Veneto and elsewhere); the tendency to slightly malicious gossip or banter; the instinctive antipathies; the lack of restraint in speech and action (for example, speaking to a layman of the French bishops, whose collective views he had three times ignored, he burst out: 'Oh, I know just what your bishops are like!'). And then, too, the occasional recourse, if not to double-dealing, at least to ambiguity and that kind of tortuous scheming already described in relation to his conduct during the anti-Modernist struggle; to say nothing of certain rather obscure aspects of his administration of Church property, such as, for instance compelling the owners of property around the sanctuary of Pompeii to give it up. . . . Certainly, all these negative aspects are much more than counterbalanced on the positive side; yet the mere fact that both sides existed suggests a certain rather disconcerting volatility, a lack of balance, moderation, serenity and unquestioning superiority, surprising in a canonized saint.

Yet the aura of pathos that surrounded him – partly because of the pessimism that caused him to attract misfortunes and reverses, to see situations as blacker than they really were, and to create a void around him when others did not share his intransigence and bitterness – always won in the end and reconquered lost sympathies. Towards the end of his pontificate, moreover, the Modernist battle was dying down and the transfiguring legend of the Pope came uppermost again. The majority of the faithful and clergy had indeed never fully realized the grievous events going on under their eyes within the Church, and had never believed that the Pope was directly involved in them, tending rather to think of him as the victim of the heretical folly of the Modernists who, so they believed, had profited by his ingenuous goodness to do violence to the Church and impose their subversive views. And the Pope, though it wrung his heart, had been forced to take extreme decisions alien to his whole being. As the years passed by, the increasing sadness of his demeanour and speeches and reprimands convinced them beyond all doubt that this was the right interpretation.

Between 1912 and 1914 another constant anxiety added to the Pope's sorrow: the state of a world which, moving ever farther from God, was travelling towards an abyss of unbelievable ruin. Truth to tell, these vague prognostications of doom – a constant theme of papal discourses throughout the ages – were not immediately given the significance later attributed to them. It was only after the outbreak of war between Austria and Serbia and the swift sequence of the First World War that they came to be regarded as prophetic.

The old Pope's unostentatious exit from the world at such a time made a lasting impression on people's imaginations. During the afternoon of the feast of the Assumption, 15 August, he felt unwell and spent much of the next two days in bed. But on the afternoon of the 18th he talked cheerfully with relatives who had come to visit him and but for the mid-August heat seemed to have got over his earlier exhaustion. That night, however, the fever rose and he became breathless and by the morning of the 19th he was plainly much worse. With his consent he received the viaticum and was given extreme unction. He turned his palms upwards to receive the unction of the hands, but by the time the *Sacrista Maggiore* anointed his feet he had lost consciousness. He never regained it except once or twice for a few seconds. He was in this state when, in accordance with custom, all the cardinals then in Rome filed past his bed. Later that evening his breathing became easier and he was left almost alone. His approaching end was announced at 1 am by one of the Vatican staff watching over him. He died at 1.16 am on 20 August.

Three weeks before, the Archduke Franz Ferdinand had been shot at Sarajevo. The war, they said, had killed the Pope. His tender heart had given way before the rising tide of mobilizations, declarations of war, and the first casualties after the Austrian ultimatum. Like the prophet Elijah, a chariot of fire had borne the gentle Pope away. It was the last flicker of the legend, a legend that was never to fade. It was nourished by a host of confidential rumours and exclusive statements from his close colleagues. The Pope had lived under the shadow of the coming conflict since at least 1911 – other sources put it even as far back as 1906, when he was said to have prophesied war to Mgr Luçon when appointing him Archbishop of Rheims. 'I see a great war, something truly colossal,' he told his sisters on one occasion. Another time he told his Secretary of State: 'Your Eminence, things are going badly – A great war is on the way – I do not mean this war [the Libyan war] – all this is nothing by comparison with the great war to come.' And in the last months of his life he said: 'We shall not get through 1914 without war.'

While it would be pointless to question the truth of these statements, they obviously cannot be regarded as genuinely prophetic. It is an axiom of Catholic theology that except for weighty reasons supernatural explanations must not be attributed to phenomena that can be explained naturally. The prophecies of coming catastrophe attributed to Pius x have a simple explanation in his own pessimism: a pessimism that was partly congenital, absorbed into his nature together with the need for resignation learnt through his family circumstances and background, and partly the result of his manicheistic conception of life and of human history as destined for progressive dissolution but for the regenerating power of God.

How purely subjective this pessimism was, can be seen by comparing Pius x's estimate of his times with the completely different view held by most of his contemporaries, who quite justifiably regarded the years between 1900 and 1914 as a period of exceptional peace and prosperity. That more optimistic view is shared also by present-day historians. One of them[1] gives the following objective picture of a period which to many who were alive then seemed like a golden age now irrevocably lost:

As the twentieth century opened, Europe, still sovereign throughout the world, enjoyed conditions of solid stability. Frontiers had for long remained unchanged, and there was no thought, at any rate on the part of governments and the leading classes, of calling them in question. A concert of Europe formed of the six major Powers peacefully settled such international questions as arose from time to time in areas of unrest such as the Balkans and over recurrent colonial problems. This international stability had its counterpart in domestic affairs: governments, most of them constitutional, parliamentary, and democratic, were under no threat of uprising: the events of 1898 and King Humbert's assassination in Italy had closed the anarchist era. Political parties contended within a framework of freedom which itself stood for order – an order allowing for a peaceful and regular contest and exchange of power between majority and minority.

There was the social question; but even in the Socialist camp legal parliamentary methods had been universally adopted, and governments respected the freedom and activities of the trade unions; thus a reformist trend was developing in the Socialist parties and even moving towards collaboration. Economic and cultural relations and associations created a vast network of internal and international solidarity which powerfully contributed to the general atmosphere of peace and law-abidingness.

All this existed in combination with a widespread increase of general culture and spiritual life, a broadening of horizons, and a reduction in social inequalities. Education became at once more specialized and more generally available, with greater opportunities within the grasp of those of modest means, and even in certain sectors free. These advances in the cultural field were associated with complete freedom of thought, finding expression in all kinds of different ways and quarters; different opinions, faiths, and confessions existed peacefully side by side as never before, or indeed after. There was a feeling in the air of added wellbeing, joy of life, and general happiness . . .

True, during those first fourteen years of the century there was also a series of crises (the Russo-Japanese and Moroccan wars, the Bosnian crisis, and the Libyan war), but 'each of these crises was overcome without ever really touching the abyss of war'. In

[1] Luigi Salvatorelli, in an article in *La Stampa* (Turin).

short, it was 'the classic era of diplomacy, whose success reached its apex in the London conference, after the first Balkan War, when Germany and Britain were seen working shoulder to shoulder for peace. Between October 1913 and June 1914 two important colonial agreements were concluded between the two Powers . . .'

The optimistic colours of this general picture were somewhat dimmed when it came to the particular problem of relations between Church and State, a problem that inevitably loomed large to Pius x. But, even taking into account the disputes it aroused in Latin countries where the Church was still strong enough to defend its outworn privileges, the fact remains that Pius x was in a very different situation from Pius ix as far as secular claims were concerned. In Pius ix's time such claims were closely associated with extreme anticlericalism, and this made him suspect that their true aim was not merely greater autonomy for the civil authority but the eviction and suppression of the Church itself. But misconceptions about the real nature and aims of secularism had gradually disappeared during the pontificate of Leo xiii, who had accepted a large part of the lay revolution's claims and secured in return an understanding of the Church's rights, including even such spectacular successes as the end of the *Kulturkampf* in Germany and the *Ralliement* to the Republic in France. Although secularism pressed for separation of Church from State, the century-long experience of the United States and of Belgium, for example, showed that the aim of separation was not to create perpetual opposition, let alone war, between them, but simply to guarantee a more peaceable distinction between their spheres of competence such as might eventually provide the basis for fruitful collaboration. By the early 1900s it was, in fact, absurd to suppose that the States' autonomist claims might conceal any idea of war on religion. Unfortunately, however, that absurd idea with all its terrors and anxieties dominated Pope Pius x and his Secretary of State, urging them to adopt a policy of vengeful reaction which inevitably weighed upon the Church itself and exacerbated the conflict. A typical example was their lack of understanding, during the dispute with France, for anyone who, like Briand, toiled to smooth away difficulties and achieve a satisfactory *modus vivendi* with the Church. The truth is that Pius x's attitude towards civil society

was governed by a subconscious and irrational (or preter-
rational, in view of its mystical components) manichean pessimism which prevented him from viewing the world and its
potentates, whether political, cultural, or economic, as other than
basically antithetic to the Church, something that the Church
was called upon to exorcise and purify as best it could. Adopting
the oversimplified interpretation of some of the more extreme
mystics he believed, not without pain and grief, that the world
was in truth fatally *positus in maligno* – sunk in evil. Hence his
pessimism as to its inevitable deterioration and its predestined
course towards the abyss of self-destruction.

Any discussion of the true significance of his vague premoni-
tions of war must also take into account the concrete and unequivocal fact of his public actions and utterances. The text
generally regarded as the most outspoken and striking in this
connection is the following, read on the occasion of his last
consistory (25 May 1914): 'Today more than ever this peace
must be sought, while we observe the widespread spectacle of
class hostile to class, people to people, nation to nation, discords
growing daily more bitter, we see fearful struggles suddenly break
out.' Within a month of the outrage of Sarajevo the allusion could
well have been a good deal more perspicacious.

Pope Pius's anguished bewilderment in the last weeks of his
life ('*Poveri figli miei, poveri figli miei*') is certainly characteristic of
the man: had he still been the parish priest of Salzano his attitude
on seeing the first soldiers leaving for the front would have been
just the same. But when on 2 August he set about writing his
Exhortation to the Catholics of the World the vein of inspiration had
run thin and all he produced was a few lines in which he did
not even call directly upon the Heads of State to revert to peace,
merely confining himself to a weary exhortation to prayer. The
most resonant part of this short document is the beginning, but
it bears no comparison with the later texts in similar circumstances of Benedict xv and Pius xii:

While almost the whole of Europe is dragged into the vortex of a
most terrible war, the dangers, slaughter, and consequences of which
none can contemplate without an oppressive feeling of grief and
horror, We too cannot fail to be concerned and to feel Our heart torn
by the bitterest grief for the safety and life of so many Christians and
so many people who are very near to Our heart.

The published documents from the archives of the various States (excluding the Vatican, which has not yet made them public) and the testimony of statesmen in touch with the Holy See during the last two months of Pius x's pontificate give the impression that the Vatican Secretariat of State was dumbfounded at the sudden and precipitate course of events and reacted only feebly and inadequately. Some discussion has arisen about the reports sent by the Austrian Ambassador to the Holy See, Prince Schönberg, to his Minister, Count Berchtold, according to which the Secretary of State, Merry del Val, invited Austria to react vigorously in relation to Serbia. The terms used by the Cardinal, though susceptible of an extreme interpretation, have the diplomatic virtue of avoiding explicitness. But it would certainly seem that Merry del Val was not alluding to war and, had he been asked for his opinion, would have firmly advised against it, for he would not have thought so extreme a step necessary to effect the humiliation of presumptuous little Serbia.

That does not, however, obviate the undeniable predilection cherished by the Pope personally and his principal colleagues for Austria and in general for the Central Powers. The fact that only a few days before the outrage at Sarajevo Serbia and the Holy See signed a concordat is quite irrelevant. The Vatican had naturally seized the opportune moment to secure support for its own minority in a State of mixed religious composition like Serbia. But the agreement over religion carried no political implications, least of all any suggestion of Vatican support for Serbia in her dispute with the former Holy Roman Empire.

Even without all the reasons of the past, more recent developments would have led the Vatican to sympathize with Austria-Hungary. Of recent years many considerations had contributed to direct the preference of most of the Curia towards Austria and Germany: the long-drawn-out struggle with France, the collapse of any prospect of agreement with the Church of England, where Protestant resistance to Catholicism in Britain was stiffening, the complete failure of agreements with the Orthodox Church in the Russian sphere, coupled with resentment of Russian provocation in Poland. In addition to which the Central Powers were the only countries to have normal and indeed very cordial diplomatic relations with the Holy See.

Pius x felt no particular sympathy for the Kaiser (when on the occasion of the Constantinian centenary ceremonies Kaiser Wilhelm sent him a banner showing the well-known scene of the appearance of the Cross to the Emperor Constantine, he at once decided – probably in annoyance at the implicit allusion – to put it in an attic); but he had a genuine regard for Franz Josef. Many things about this eighty-year-old Emperor, from his asceticism to his inexhaustible activity, appealed to Pius x. He had always been impressed by the idea of his living in bare rooms, sleeping on an iron bed and sticking to a régime worthy of a hermit in the desert, getting up at four in the morning and starting work at once without a secretary, giving orders by telegram (never by telephone) and writing all his letters in his own hand, as well as giving an incredible number of audiences and appearing at all kinds of functions. He also knew that the Emperor, though extremely courteous even with his own servants, never gave his hand to bishops so as not to have to kiss their ring; but he over-looked that detail, remembering instead the lavish homage he paid to religion through his official participation in all the great festivals of the Church. At the close of the Eucharistic Congress in Vienna in 1912, the Emperor had himself taken part in the procession behind the monstrance at the head of all the Arch-dukes, the members of the imperial family, and the entire court. Pope Pius, who never quite lost his peasant ingenuousness, had been so struck by this gesture (which was subsequently portrayed in one of the frescoes in the chapel beside the throne room in the Vatican) that he even spoke of it – unfortunately not prophetic-ally – as a 'sign from Heaven'.

The Holy See under Pius x exercised less of an active policy towards the Central Powers themselves than a passive and acquies-cent policy in relation to the behaviour of the Catholic parties in Austria and Germany. In Germany, after the death of Ernst Lieber in 1902 the *Zentrum* came increasingly close to the govern-ment, even eventually endorsing the Kaiser's *Weltpolitik* and voting the military credits he demanded. Pius x, alarmed at the party's growing nationalism, asked its leaders, Spahn and Hert-ring, to show more moderation, but he did not impose his will on them, as had been done in the case of other Catholic political movements. This weakness towards the leaders of the German *Zentrum* and the Austrian Christian-Socialists was to bear bitter fruit in 1914.

No support for, still less incitement to, war, but a yielding in face of its inevitability: such were the limits of the Vatican State Secretariat's responsibility towards the conflict of 1914. Pius X himself never, of course, remotely desired the war; but, sentiment apart, an active religious and political horror at its onset was not in him. Perhaps at those last moments of his life physical exhaustion weakened his proper moral reaction. As has been recognized by the best and most objective among his Catholic biographers, 'he raised no strong prophetic voice in a world already convulsed by storms, but almost extended himself as a victim upon the altar'[1] – a renunciation and an offering which in their ultimate contrast symbolize the contradictions that characterized and tormented his whole pontificate.

[1] Nello Vian, 'Cinquant' anni dal transito di San Pio X nell' alba di sangue dell'-Europa', *L'Osservatore Romano,* 20 August 1964.

Benedict XV : Giacomo Della Chiesa

3 September 1914 – 22 January 1922

A Wartime Conclave

A few days after the announcement of the death of Pius x – who, incidentally, had given instructions that he should not be embalmed – many members of the Sacred College were already on their way to Rome. The latest batch of seven new cardinals, appointed only three months before, had brought their numbers to sixty-six. However Cardinal Lugari had died on 31 July, and of the sixty-five others five (Vaszary, Bauer, Prisco, Martinelli, and Dubillard) were prevented by illness from attending the Conclave, while three others only arrived after the election was over (Gibbons of Baltimore and O'Connell of Boston on 4 September, and Bégin of Quebec on the 6th). Cardinal Serafino Vannutelli had a narrow escape on 20 August when he took the morning express to Rome from Naples as soon as he heard of Pope Pius's death, for a bomb exploded on the train wrecking a first-class carriage and injuring nine people. But all the cardinals from countries already involved in war arrived safely, convinced that they would be performing a patriotic as well as a religious duty in giving the Church a pope who was at least no adversary to the cause of their own particular country.

By a curious coincidence, Pius x at his last consistory, on 25 May, had called to the purple five prelates from the major countries now at war: the English Benedictine Aidan Gasquet, the only British cardinal; the Germans Bettinger and von Hartmann, Archbishops respectively of Munich and Cologne; and the two Primates of Austria and Hungary, Gustav Piffl, Archbishop of Vienna, and Johan Czernok, Archbishop of Esztergom. Towering above them all, both for his personal prestige and heroism and as representative of a people so lately victim of aggression, was Cardinal Mercier, Archbishop of Malines and Primate of Belgium.

The climate of war already weighed upon these men, and they were anxious at having to be away even for a short time from their duties at home. Moreover the tide of events had mounted during the short period of *sede vacante* since Pius x's death. On 23 August the Russians had attacked East Prussia and Poland, on the 28th Britain had won the Battle of Heligoland, and by the end of the month the Germans in the east had annihilated Samsonov's Russian army at Tannenberg, while their advances on the western front had compelled the transfer of the French Government from Paris to Bordeaux.

Passing through the streets of Rome, normally a rather distant host towards its guests, they were gazed at and scrutinized more as representatives of the belligerent countries than as members of an international community superior to the conflict's vicissitudes; and there was something tense and almost military about the bearing of these high church dignitaries that attracted attention. People's curiosity was aroused, and they wondered how these men from both sides of the struggle would get on when they met in the Vatican. But if any awkward episodes occurred they were never made public. Instead, various stories went the rounds, like the one about the German cardinal who kept on repeating solemnly: '*Cito vincemus in bello*' (We shall win the war in no time) until his colleagues from the other side nicknamed him 'Cardinal Cito'. But if an occasional joke lightened the tense atmosphere, the war soon thrust itself afresh upon their consciousness, as when Cardinal Billot got the news, when the voting had just begun, that two of his nephews had been killed. And since even the most hardened senators of the Church are also human and occasionally swayed by sentiment, such news doubtless played some part in the choice of the future Pope.

The international situation also inevitably made itself felt in the pressure of the various governments, especially of European countries, on the individual cardinals. The ecclesiastical sanctions threatened by Pius x soon after his election, against any intervention such as might cause a repetition of the Rampolla episode at the 1903 Conclave, made it unlikely that any political power would try to exercise a veto; but that did not prevent other kinds of pressure. Two days after the death of Pius x, for example, the

Austrian Foreign Minister, Count Berchtold, sent his ambassador at the Vatican the following instructions:

Cardinal Ferrata is regarded as francophile, Cardinal Maffi as a convinced nationalist, while the Benedictine Serafini is described as a pious and learned man devoid of political prejudices. I make known to the Cardinals representing Austria at the Conclave that we have no wish to influence the papal election in any way, but at the same time we are bound to take into consideration the fact that it would be in the common interest both of the Church and of the Hapsburg monarchy that the coming Conclave should not produce a Pope of marked political or nationalistic leanings.

In any case, the war, though it formed the ever-present background, was not the only factor to influence the labours of the Conclave. After all, it involved barely a quarter of the members of the Sacred College and, inexorable though it might seem, it had broken out so recently that there might still be some justifiable hope of a diplomatic solution or a speedy end to it. In the view of a good many of the Cardinals present in Rome, an extraneous factor such as war ought not to influence the Conclave one way or the other.

On the other hand, the outbreak of war prompted reflection as to the responsibilities which, even if only indirectly, the policy of the pontificate just ended might bear in relation to it. Pius x's policy was, if not wholly negative, at least marked by detachment from the real political situation: now it was bound to be asked whether the Church's exclusive concentration on its own interests had not been carried to dangerous excess – not so much because it had overstressed the Church's claims, but rather because it had led to an almost complete neglect of the mediating function which a moral guide such as the Church should exercise in the world. Except for a single act of arbitration by Pope Pius between certain Latin-American Powers, the Holy See had not only remained uninvolved in international affairs but appeared not even to take a detached interest in them. Hence the question arose whether the discreet type of intervention desired by and carried out under Leo xiii might not be more beneficial for the world and the Church itself than the ascetic absenteeism practised by Pius x. In other words, the cardinals assembling for the Conclave were faced with an acute comparison between Leo xiii's policy, of intervention, and Pius x's, of withdrawal; and naturally this most closely concerned those who had lost the day in the 1903 Conclave.

Only fifteen of the cardinals who had been present in the Sistine Chapel eleven years before were there now, and only half of those now remained pro-Leonine to the last, while others had yielded unwillingly to the majority when convinced that it would not alter. All of them were now determined to fight for a return to Leo XIII's line of policy. They were, inevitably, joined by the victims, whether direct or indirect, of Pius X and his collaborators: the cardinals who under his pontificate had been suspected or persecuted as philo-Modernists, and those who, like the French cardinals, had never approved of his religious policy towards their countries.

From a consideration of the present situation of the Church and the world yet another critical aspect of Pius X's pontificate emerged. Not only had the Pope made no attempt to intervene as Europe and the world advanced towards the abyss of war, but seven years earlier, far from preventing internal strife within the Church, he had positively encouraged and provoked it. His anguish at the last was certainly genuine in the face of his own impotence to avert the onset of a world war; but he had not even thought to invoke peace within the Catholic world.

By comparison with such criticisms of Pius X's pontificate, the pontificate of Leo XIII took on an added stature – a Pope who, though over ninety, had up to the last kept within bounds the Church's internal disputes and those of the Holy See with foreign Powers, never ceasing to strive for international equilibrium. Yet quite a number among even the sternest critics of Pius X's pontificate were nevertheless convinced that precisely because of the wartime situation it would be inadvisable to concentrate on electing a political Pope. Had Rampolla been alive an exception would doubtless have been made for him, given his personality and prestige; but it was difficult to do as much for a Ferrata or a Gasparri. Certainly it was important that the new Pope should not be at sea in diplomatic waters, but the really vital thing was that he should have a true pastoral spirit and experience.

Both in the General Congregations and in private groups it was soon agreed that the new Pope should be elected as quickly as possible. This was necessary both to enable the cardinals of countries at war to return home as soon as possible and in order to show the world that the Church remained outside the political interests and passions of the belligerents and superior to their grounds of conflict. Everything suggests that even before the Conclave opened the Leonine majority had decided on the new Pope and on the provisional candidate who should try out the ground. In any case, on 30 August, the day before the opening, the Austrian Ambassador to the Holy See reported to Vienna that 'luckily' Ferrata, Maffi, and Ferrari had not much chance of being elected, adding 'Della Chiesa (Archbishop of Bologna) is at present the most frequently mentioned; our own Eminences, in particular, seem determined to support his candidature, since they regard him as fully worthy'. By the first ballot of the second day (and thus at the fifth ballot, since, contrary to the irregular practice of 1903, four votes were taken each day) Cardinal Della Chiesa was already well ahead of the provisional candidate, Cardinal Maffi.

Maffi, the Archbishop of Pisa, was in fact not likely to be elected. The fact that his previous experience had been exclusivey pastoral was to some extent counterbalanced by his great reputation as a mathematician, astronomer and man of letters; and though he had no direct experience in diplomacy, many diplomats might envy his ability in establishing relations with the secular world. But his Achilles' heel lay in his too close association with the House of Savoy. True, the King's shooting-lodge of San Rossore was quite near to Pisa and in its diocese; but it was certainly not just religious sentiment that caused Victor Emmanuel to go and greet the Archbishop in person at the villa gate when he called to pay his respects. When an attempt was made on their Majesties' lives in March 1912, Cardinal Maffi not only took part in the service of thanksgiving for their escape, held in the historic church of Santo Stefano ai Cavalieri in Pisa, but he also personally addressed the congregation, an audacious act in those days when the Roman Question was still alive.

While in a manner of speaking chaplain of the excommunicated dynasty, Maffi could also be described as bishop of the Italian army. At the time of the Libyan war in 1911 he made a far from pacifist speech to the troops leaving from Pisa:

Go! with the blessing of Moriconi, the bishop who from these shores set forth with his Pisans to conquer the Balearics:[1] at Messina

---

[1] In 1114. *Translator.*

our Daiberto will renew the blessing, who there transformed the fading laurels of the east into eternal palms. And see how from the historic walls of this church a hundred banners dip to do you honour and godspeed, the envied and glorious trophies of your ancestors united in their wishes for you; and you will soon bring other banners back to redeem the new glories of Italy, our country . . .

Not all the difficult times under Pius x and Merry del Val and Cardinal De Lai could weigh in the balance against this inflamed nationalism, which might burst out afresh if Italy were to be drawn into the war (as indeed it did, on the morrow, of Italy's declaration of war, in Maffi's appeal containing the famous sentence repeated by Salandra to an applauding Parliament: 'Yesterday you could still discuss, tomorrow you can do so again, but not today!').

When it became plain who the Leonines' real candidate was, the group led by Merry del Val also disclosed their choice: the Benedictine Cardinal Domenico Serafini, Assessor of the Holy Office, who, like Della Chiesa, had worn the purple for only three months. Though belonging to a monastic Order (in which, incidentally, he had reached the highest office, having been for four years Abbot General of the Benedictine Congregation) he had had a brilliant career as member of the Curia – where he was adviser to the Holy Office, the Propaganda Fide, and the Congregation of Bishops – Bishop of Spoleto for eleven years, and in the Vatican's diplomatic service, where as Apostolic Delegate in Mexico he had fulfilled a delicate mission in 1904. But this dynamic though ascetic Roman had the great defect of being too young – he was only fifty-one.

At the ninth ballot the two rivals each got twenty-two votes. But the die was already cast: the votes given earlier to Cardinal Maffi and others converged at the tenth ballot on the Leonines' candidate, and Della Chiesa was elected.

An Intransigent Aristocrat

If votes converged sooner than had been expected upon the Archbishop of Bologna, this was not the result of any capitulation by the Merry del Val group. All in all, Della Chiesa combined in himself qualities sufficiently reassuring even to the strenuous minority that had earlier opposed him. His Italian colleagues were all more or less familiar with his origins and career; and if the caution he had imposed on himself during his seven years as Archbishop of Bologna testified to his moderation, his consistent ideological integralism and social conservatism made of him a candidate generally acceptable even to the opposition.

Lay historians have popularized a picture of Benedict xv which, through its stress on his liberalism, corresponds in some sense to the widespread legend of Pius x as the 'good Pope'. Yet such a picture was contradicted from the outset by the known facts of his childhood and youth. There was a tradition of rigid clericalism among his ancestors, and his father, Marchese Giuseppe Della Chiesa, was a rigid practising Catholic, enrolled as an active member of numerous confraternities. Perhaps not much significance need be given to his regular appearance in the streets of Genoa with the banner of the Misericordia at the funeral of every prisoner who died in the Sant' Andrea gaol; but his work as prime mover in organizing, in 1864, an association for the care of released prisoners, and in 1867 a home for delinquent children, was of real importance. All the same, when the question arose of what school Giacomo should go to, his father's first choice was for a secular school; and when, towards the end of the *liceo*, the boy asked to be allowed to enter a seminary for theological studies, he refused, saying that before embarking on an ecclesiastical career he must first take his degree in law at the State university.

This sense of responsibility, this belief that faith, and even more a vocation for the priesthood, should be qualified by a knowledge of the world and its difficulties, is perhaps to be explained by the fact that Giacomo had been over-sensitive to religious influences from his earliest childhood, when his favourite pastime was to play with the elaborately-furnished toy altar given him by his maternal grandmother, Marchesa Ersilia Migliorati Raggi. His inclinations in this direction, far from diminishing at school, were strengthened when, following a disagreement between his father and the school authorities, he was sent to finish his *liceo* studies as a day pupil at the archbishopric's seminary. Those last two years at school fell between 1869 and 1871, thus including both the Bersaglieris' entry into Rome in 1870 and the first Vatican Council at which papal infallibility was declared. These two events made an indelible impression on the sixteen-to-seventeen-year-old boy not only in themselves but also because of the atmosphere of impassioned dispute that surrounded them.

In the years leading up to 1870, Genoa had contributed two outstanding figures of national stature to the ranks of the Church's adversaries: Mazzini, herald of a new religion of humanity, and Ausonio Franchi, the most acute and critical mind of nineteenth-century Italian rationalism. The romantic fascination of Mazzini, the thought-provoking intellectualism of Franchi, represented the two different aspects of a secular revolt that threatened to strangle the Genoese tradition of Catholicism, still widespread among the masses but wearing thin among the aristocracy and even more among the bourgeoisie.

In the seminary and elsewhere Giacomo Della Chiesa must have heard sinister references to that Satan of unbelief, Ausonio Franchi, whom many people in Genoa had known, before he embraced his new doctrines, as the upright priest Cristoforo Bonavino (Ausonio Franchi was a later pseudonym and *nom de guerre*). Against these great figures of heresy and rebellion, the only protagonist that the Genoese clergy could produce was the city's archpriest, Canon Gaetano Alimonda, later Archbishop of Turin and a Curia Cardinal, a prolific orator who distinguished himself from most of his local and national colleagues by his remarkable erudition even in scientific matters, and by the sound logical structure of his Lenten sermons. These sermons when published proved to be among the most original and important volumes of apologetics of the day either in Italy or abroad. One of them, on 'Man under the law of the supernatural', had a great influence on Giacomo Della Chiesa; and he also knew Alimonda personally as a friend of his father.

Priests and monks hardly ever attended Italian universities in those days, especially after 1872 when the theology faculties were suppressed; and even practising Catholics were only a small minority, tending to keep apart and form little groups among themselves which, while not seeking provocation, defended their faith when need arose; it was only much later that they became organized on a national basis. Giacomo Della Chiesa seems to have been the head of one of these 'clerical' groups – a group so small that it had only three members besides himself, all of them like him students in the faculty of law; but the bond between them was strong enough to withstand the passage of time.

A number of letters exchanged between Della Chiesa and his closest friend Pietro Ansaldo, which have fortunately survived,[1] provide valuable witness to the fervent faith and apostolic zeal that inspired the future Pope at that time. From one of them we learn the significant fact that the four friends called themselves 'sons of Pius IX'. In another he confesses that if God had not called him to the priesthood he would have 'devoted his spare time to the Catholic press'. In another letter written from Rome, where he went after taking his degree in 1875 to pursue his theological studies, he exhorts his friends in astonishingly vigorous accents for the small, frail, emaciated youth he then was: 'Never be dismayed by difficulties. Where would the Church be if the Apostles had counted heads after the Last Supper? Let your faith rest on the justice of the cause, and I,' he added, with a symptomatic certainty and authority, 'stand surety for the result!' In another place he said: 'Certainly one of the main needs of our times is to bring into being a true lay apostolate: I don't need to write to you at length about this, for you will remember all we used to say about it at the university . . .'

Such effusions as this testify, even more convincingly than do his enthusiastic letters about entering the priesthood, to the profound conviction and courage with which he was preparing to confront a world then largely hostile to the Church. Clearly his choice of a career was no longer based merely on the sentiments and yearnings of his childhood but on the reason and conviction of maturity. After getting his degree he had every opportunity for a successful worldly career: though his father's means were modest he could have given him a good start: one of his brothers ended up as an admiral. When Giacomo left the port of Genoa for the unknown mirage of Rome he could not know that the life of renunciation he had chosen would call him too to command a ship, the invisible and mysterious barque of Peter.

The Church and its defence were, in short, during those years of study the aspiration of his whole being for this 'son of Pius IX'. This can already be seen from his notes for some talks to young people even before his ordination. But the final proof is provided

[1] See Francesco Vistalli, *Benedetto XV*, Rome, 1928.

by the first of two Latin inscriptions printed on the picture commemorating his first Mass. It is addressed to St Peter – another strange instance of unconscious presentiment – and says:

O Peter, prince of the apostles, whom we venerate in Rome as illuminating the nations with the light of truth, sustain me, Giacomo Della Chiesa, pupil of the Divine Capranica College, who upon thy altar and thy sainted body today, 21 December 1878, celebrated the first Mass. Give me strength to maintain thy rights sacred and inviolate and to repel with unconquered heart the wrongful assaults of the enemies of the pontificate! (*Tu mihi adde ardorem quo tuae potestatis iura tuear intemerata et integra et forti pectore male ominatos hostium impetus in Pontifices maximus contundam.*)

When, later on, Leo XIII succeeded the Pope of the *Syllabus,* the new Pope undoubtedly helped to moderate the young Della Chiesa's intransigence, especially since it fell to his lot to live in close contact with him in the Vatican Secretariat of State. But he never admitted any discussion about the Supreme Pontiff's temporal rights. Some of the Curia Cardinals must certainly have been aware of how, for instance, under Pius X he had opposed the trend headed by Padre Lepidi, Master of the Sacred Palaces, which favoured the suppression of the *non expedit*, the veto on Catholics presenting themselves as candidates for the Italian Parliament. The recent discovery of some hundred letters which he wrote as Pope to his former vicar-general in Bologna, Mgr Menzani, and which are now in the archives of the seminary at Piacenza,[1] has confirmed the remarkable way in which these convictions of his persisted right up to and beyond the war. In one of these letters, dated 20 May 1915 but written on the morrow of the outbreak of hostilities between Italy and Austria, referring to the precarious situation of the Holy See and the Catholic press's apparent unconcern he wrote:

It is làmentable that there seems to be no awareness of what may happen! We certainly do not wish to provide any occasion or pretext for disputes, but if tomorrow we were denied free communication with a part of the Catholic world – for example if a cypher telegram to the Nuncio in Vienna were rejected – we should at once raise our voice in protest, not against the war, but against the state of affairs

[1] See Lorenzo Bedeschi, '*La questione romana in alcune lettere di Benedetto XV*', in *Rassegna di Politica e di Storia*, no. 119 (1964).

introduced on 20 September 1870 . . . which may have seemed tolerable in peacetime but which would prove intolerable in wartime. In that case it would be seen how in Italy the duty of Catholics can be superior to that of citizens . . . and in view of that is it prudent to insist so much on the observance of the *whole* duty of citizens? But we commit ourselves to the hands of God *ex quo omnia, in quo omnia, per quem omnia!*

Stranger still, coming as it did in 1920, was his reaction to the fiftieth anniversary celebrations of the entry into Rome at Porta Pia. The Italian railways had granted a fifty per cent reduction to enable people to come to Rome for the occasion. Three priests from Bologna took advantage of this to celebrate their own anniversary of twenty-five years in the priesthood and come to Rome to see their former Archbishop as Pope. Benedict xv refused to receive them and in justifying his action to Mgr Menzani added a reproof to the Bolognese Curia for their failure to supervise priests leaving the diocese without the regular *discessit*: '. . . I had made it clear that I would not receive any priest who had taken advantage of the reduction of fares granted for the fiftieth anniversary of Porta Pia. The celebration of this date is an offence to the Holy See, and it is deplorable that among those condoning this offence (if only in a material way) there should be priests – and priests of my Bologna!'

Similar episodes, going back to his time in the Curia and as bishop, must have been recalled and discussed by the Fathers in Conclave in their efforts to form a precise idea of what manner of man he was. But his intransigence was not the only characteristic to effect a breach in the ranks of the cardinals attached to Pius x's pontificate. Another factor was undoubtedly Della Chiesa's noble origins, origins which, without ever obtruding them, he himself had shown no tendency to underestimate. Now a descendant of one of the most ancient and famous families of Genoa was bound to be conservative in trend, unwilling to indulge in innovations of a social kind, a defender of the established order, and so on.

Cardinal Della Chiesa had in fact never been a lover of cultural novelties, let alone what might be called a militant intellectual. His three years of theological studies had given him an adequate but not exceptional grounding in basic ecclesiastical subjects, without apparently arousing his interest in any particular aspect. At the Gregorian University, his most famous teachers were

Padre Antonio Ballerini for moral theology and apologetics and Padre Camillo Mazzella – whom Leo XIII was soon to make a cardinal, according him the same influence and near-monopoly in the sphere of ecclesiastical studies that Cardinal Rampolla enjoyed in the political sphere – for dogmatic theology. But the main thing he got from the former was a distaste for Protestantism, of which more later; while he does not seem to have thought much of the latter, for when asked to draw up the papal brief honouring a collection of his works he showed Leo XIII a review of the book by Padre Genocchi which effectively liquidated Mazzella's whole system of theology, with the result that the brief was withdrawn.[1]

Della Chiesa got his degree in theology, as everyone expected, but his favourite subject, as was natural given his earlier training, was canon law ('It's a good course,' he wrote to Ansaldo; 'the professor is a follower and successor of Cardinal Tarquini.'). During the anti-Modernist campaign he was the object of some denunciations (he is said to have come upon one of them, from the Bishop of Piacenza, Mgr Pellizzari, when going through Pius X's last papers), but we may be sure that they concerned his conduct of affairs rather than his theological standpoint. As far as is known, the accusations, which were quite unfounded, referred to his alleged approval of partly-secularized Catholic journalism.[2]

All this gave reason to hope that the anti-Modernist struggle would be continued. But what was likely to happen about the pastoral aspects of Church reform under a man trained in the most arid of bureaucracies, that of papal diplomacy, and, moreover, under Leo XIII? This objection was the most difficult to get over, and it was only partially satisfied. One of the most striking characteristics about Della Chiesa to those who met him was, in fact, his complete lack of 'unction', of the priestly aura. The man they saw before them wore the garb of a prelate and obviously had the manner and behaviour that went with it, but nevertheless his general bearing and speech did not suggest the priest or bishop. Even in his cardinal's robes he was first and foremost the born aristocrat. How could they choose as Pope a man who had

[1] See Alfred Loisy, *Mémoires pour servir à l'histoire religieuse de notre temps,* Paris 1931, vol. II, p. 103.
[2] See footnote, p. 42, also Bibliography, p. 373.

no hieratic quality, who did not emanate an atmosphere of holiness, who simplified all his words and gestures instead of lending them an aura of the supernatural and eternal?

On the other hand, could such outward appearances be a substantial objection? Certainly not: the more so since to anyone who knew him well Della Chiesa was a truly pious man, conscious of contact with God and eager for the ideals of his own vocation, who performed his duties punctiliously and sincerely loved the Church, even if his manner had, so to speak, something of the profane. The best proof of the authenticity of his faith and his religious feeling, apart from the letters already quoted, is afforded by the facts of his own life, from his decision to prepare for the priesthood not as an external seminarist living on his own but as an internal student at the Capranica College in Rome, to his intensive pastoral activity as bishop. No doubt he brought to the Archbishopric of Bologna a good deal of the meticulousness of the bureaucrat after his over-long sojourn in Rome, but if Della Chiesa was a most careful administrator with an eye for everything on the technical side in the running of his diocese and the conduct of his subordinates, he was also a bishop of action, who in four years carried out a pastoral visitation of his whole diocese as well as organizing eucharistic and catechistic congresses. He also succeeded in overcoming his natural aversion to speaking in public, and if his oratory owed nothing to artifice, it was the more attractive and compelling by its lucid and logical simplicity. This aristocrat with his irreproachable but chilly manner, slow to abandon his reserve except with close friends, had never become popular, but he had shown frankness and sincerity in mingling among humble people, and above all he had appealed to people's hearts and imaginations by the tremendous generosity of his donations, even though it was difficult to tell whether it was the nobleman or the bishop who found the greater satisfaction in giving.

Setback to a Promising Career

The strongest reason for the opposition of Merry del Val's group to Della Chiesa's candidature was the line of policy of which he had been the main exponent as close friend, follower, and protégé of the great Rampolla.

Their relationship had begun when Della Chiesa was still a mere student – if with three degrees to his credit – at the Academy for Church Noblemen, whither he had gone with the help of his parents and of its president, Mgr Placido Maria Schiaffino, an Olivetan from Genoa soon to become a cardinal. Like his fellow-students at the Academy, Della Chiesa went to gain experience at the Secretariat of State, and it was there that the decisive meeting of his life took place with Leo XIII's future Secretary of State who had them, in 1881, just been appointed Secretary of the Congregation for Extraordinary Ecclesiastical Affairs. The friendship that dramatically linked the imposing Sicilian prelate and the shy little Genoese student was the result of one of those reciprocal intuitions that have no rhyme or reason. It developed as they came to know each other better, and the two realized that their destinies were bound together. Physically so different, they both had the gifts of intelligence and character calculated to command each other's unreserved admiration. Rampolla del Tindaro could have found no trusted collaborator of more exceptional qualities than Della Chiesa, and Giacomo Della Chiesa could have wished for no more gifted protector and master than Rampolla who, though not yet at the apex of his career, already showed the capacity for the heights to which he would rise.

Only a year later Leo XIII made Rampolla Nuncio in Madrid and five years afterwards Cardinal, soon appointing him Secretary of State. Della Chiesa went with him to Spain as his personal secretary and afterwards to the Secretariat of State, but the friendship of his superior never degenerated into favouritism. First taken on as a clerk (*minutante*), he remained in that office for fourteen years. Anyone might have thought Rampolla had forgotten him, and his mother was seriously worried about it and even one day diplomatically took the Cardinal to task. His reply was: 'Be patient for a little while; your son will take few steps but great ones.' Rampolla could not guess how prophetic that remark was to prove. But the first of these steps was Della Chiesa's appointment, in 1901, as Under-Secretary of State and Secretary of Cypher. When, two years later, the death of Leo XIII brought with it the fall of Rampolla and his isolation by his successor Merry del Val, that step seemed likely to be the last.

If he could have chosen his own colleagues, Merry del Val

would certainly have replaced at once the two section heads in
the Secretariat, Mgr Gasparri, Secretary for Extraordinary Affairs,
and the Under-Secretary, Della Chiesa. This would have eased the
situation in the office, since both prelates disagreed with his
policy. The chief point of dispute emerged at once over relations
with France, which had already become difficult before Leo xiii's
death with the advent to power of Emile Combes. The depositions made at the hearing on Merry del Val's beatification leave
no room for doubt on this subject, though they naturally differ
in detail and approach. Canon Francesco Rossi Stockalper, for
example, affirmed that:

Mgr Della Chiesa saw in Cardinal Rampolla a pope *manqué* and
therefore did not see with pleasure the servant of God (Merry del Val)
in the post of Secretary of State. Mgr Della Chiesa often came out
with such remarks as 'But Cardinal Rampolla would not have done
that!' But the servant of God, though aware of this, never complained
but continued to treat Mgr Della Chiesa kindly . . .

Canon Alberto Serafini, in turn, testified:

The very English strictness of the servant of God in fulfilling his
office, and the fact that Della Chiesa was, if not turned out, at least put
in a subordinate position, were undoubtedly the reason why subsequent relations between the two men . . . were always tinged with a
reserve which the diplomatic experience of both prevented from becoming open hostility. This I infer from allusions made to me by
Della Chiesa himself after he became Archbishop of Bologna . . .

Probably not all the manifestations of these disagreements were
quite so restrained, and there may have been occasional explo-
sions outside the offices of the Secretariat of State. Possibly Della
Chiesa's remark at a reception of his mother's in her house in
Rome, that 'Church affairs march haltingly, like me', may have
referred to this situation. But, given the frank and forthright
character of both Gasparri and his colleague, that doubtless
happened only rarely. The Church's whole policy under the new
pontificate depended to some extent on relations with France; in
addition to which it was only natural to feel some resentment at
seeing the work of years of diplomatic effort gratuitously compromised.

A change was finally brought about in 1907 when both Gasparri
and Della Chiesa were transferred, Gasparri becoming a Cardinal

on 10 December in recognition of his work as Secretary of the Commission for the codification of Canon Law, and Della Chiesa being appointed on 8 October to the archbishopric of Bologna. The suitability of Gasparri's promotion was widely recognized, but Della Chiesa's appointment was viewed in a very different light.

The normal promotion for an Under-Secretary of State is to a nunciature of the first class, after which, having done well in that office, it is customary for him to receive the Cardinal's hat. Advancement in the diplomatic career signifies recognition of his professional qualities, and such recognition is considered to be withheld, or at least in doubt, if instead he is given some other post such as the government of a diocese. For this reason Della Chiesa's appointment to the archbishopric of Bologna was generally regarded, despite the importance of the see, as a step down – more especially since at the time when that see became vacant the post of nuncio in Madrid also had to be filled, and rumour had it that he was sure to be given it. The Spanish Government, or the King himself, had almost certainly had their eye on Della Chiesa and put forward a formal request to Pius x; also, Spanish interest in him may well have been skilfully fostered by Cardinal Rampolla in order to extricate his protégé from an increasingly awkward situation in the Vatican; or perhaps these two schemes just happened to coincide. In any case, the Spanish Ambassador to the Holy See got the impression that the whole thing was settled and said as much to Della Chiesa, and also let the news leak into the press. But just at that point the unexpected happened.

Cardinal Nicola Canali, in his extensive deposition during the beatification hearing on the heroic virtues of his former superior Merry del Val, has given a highly edifying version of the affair:

When Cardinal Svampa, Archbishop of Bologna, died, Pius x was much concerned as to who should succeed him in that important See, where unhappily there had been some infiltration by Modernism and the press of the so-called 'Trust' . . . He mentioned his anxiety about the choice of the new archbishop to his closest colleagues, particularly the Cardinal Secretary of State, Cardinal De Lai, and others, asking them to pray for light from the Lord. One day in the second half of 1907, at the beginning of his usual morning audience with the Secretary of State, the Holy Father said: 'Your Eminence, I have found the

new Archbishop of Bologna, and I am glad for I feel it is the true will
of God.' The Cardinal expressed his pleasure even before learning the
name, and Pius x went on: 'I think Your Eminence will never guess
who my candidate is so I will tell you at once: it is Mgr Giacomo
Della Chiesa' . . . The Cardinal was astonished but quickly said he
thought it a real inspiration of God. The Pope then asked the Cardinal
how he thought the news should be given to Mgr Della Chiesa: 'What
do you think, Your Eminence? Would it be best, so as to leave him
free to answer, if the first news of my intention were given him by
Your Eminence, or do you think I should tell him myself?' The
Cardinal at once replied that in his view it would be preferable for
the Pope to tell him personally of his own inspiration, both because it
would give Mgr Della Chiesa greater satisfaction and comfort, and to
avoid giving the impression that the Cardinal might himself have made
the proposal in order to remove him from his office, which was certainly not the case. Pius x fully agreed with this view, and at the next
audience with the Under-Secretary, on 4 October 1907, the Feast of
St Petronius, Bishop of Bologna, he gave him the news, adding that
the Cardinal Secretary of State had been informed and considered it
inspired by God. The official announcement was published in the
Osservatore Romano of 8 October 1907.

This is almost certainly what actually happened, and in that case
one may suppose that Pius x, knowing of the strained situation
in the Secretariat of State, was glad of the opportunity to end it
decisively and in such a way that there would no longer be any
direct connection between the Secretary of State and Della
Chiesa, such as would have arisen had the latter become Nuncio.
But this aspect of the truth does not exclude the possibility of
others, as, for instance, that friends of Merry del Val may have
exercised pressure on Pius x to take the step which he believed
to have been his own idea and which, indeed, he took for an
inspiration from on high.

Be that as it may, Della Chiesa presents yet another facet of the
truth in his letter of 5 October to his brother Giovanni Antonio:[1]

So I am not to go to Madrid as Nuncio because, so it has pleased
God, I am to be Bishop of Bologna. The will of God has been made
manifest in so clear a way that I cannot be in any doubt about it.
Yesterday morning the Holy Father asked me if I had read the *Messaggero* and I said no. His Holiness took it and read me the 'Vatican
decree' according to which the day before Mgr Della Chiesa had been

[1] Quoted in Vistalli, op. cit.

appointed Nuncio to Madrid. I told the Holy Father that I was sorry about this intrusion of the press. His Holiness interrupted me: 'I am sorry too because I would have liked to ask a favour of Mgr Della Chiesa.' 'Command me, Holy Father, there is no question of favours on my part.' 'Yes,' the Pope answered, 'I wanted a charity from you. I know that Mgr Della Chiesa does well wherever he is put; the Cardinal Secretary of State has told me that he would be an excellent Nuncio in Madrid, but I have to think of the dioceses too. I want to have good bishops, and I would like Mgr Della Chiesa to go for me as Archbishop to Bologna.' 'Holy Father, I am embarrassed at Your Holiness's kindness and also because of the difficulty of the situation . . . Bologna is a difficult place . . . but I am ready to do what your Holiness commands.' 'No,' the Pope replied, 'I am not in the least demanding your obedience. I am merely expressing a desire and asking whether you might not like the way of the Sacred Ministry which offers so many consolations.' 'Oh, I have always felt inclinations towards the ministry; Bologna frightens me because of the difficult situation there, but I have not sought it – indeed I never thought of it – I will not conceal from Your Holiness that I had heard from the Spanish Ambassador of the probability that I might be sent to Madrid, and I never thought of Bologna . . . It just occurs to me that today is festival of St Petronius in Bologna, and I take it as a good omen!' The Holy Father had the kindness to say that he thanked me, and then added: 'Cardinal Rampolla would certainly do it gladly, and so would the Cardinal Secretary of State for his Under-Secretary, but the Pope reserves for himself the consecration of Mgr Della Chiesa.' This announcement greatly moved me . . .

This letter clearly does not say everything – for instance, it omits a great deal about Cardinal Merry del Val's part in the business – but it says much more than it seems, and in particular it gives an eloquent speaking likeness of the two protagonists and their different attitudes. Pius x is drawn to the life merely by the tone of his words, with all his clumsy, heavy countryman's diplomacy and its tortuous, unctuous circumlocutions and ingenuous attempts to gild a pill probably prepared for him by others, showing himself really sorry for the part he had agreed to play, even to the point of apologizing to his companion for having to use his overwhelming sovereignty to thwart his legitimate hopes. Mgr Della Chiesa, on the other hand, despite all his submissive correctness shows no servility and is clearly impatient at all this ceremony, wanting to cut it short and come to the point without futile manoeuvring between men who know only too well the distance of their respective positions and, above all, the complete inadmissibility of play-acting in face of what a man of faith cannot but believe to be the will of God, however and by whomever it may be communicated to him.

The real importance of the document, however, lies elsewhere. It is obvious that the letter is dictated by anxiety to forestall the recipient's wrath about the failure of the Madrid appointment. This explains its silences about both Merry del Val and Rampolla. Once again, in fact, the real struggle had gone on over Della Chiesa's head, and once again, despite appearances, the true victim was not he but his friend and protector. Merry del Val was certainly aware that it was Rampolla who, in 1902, had dissuaded Leo XIII from appointing Della Chiesa as Archbishop of Genoa (an appointment of great prestige, for it would have made him spiritual head of his native city when only forty-eight) in order to keep his protégé in the diplomatic career. Similarly, he must also have known of Pius X's decision (Cardinal Canali's silence about the date of Merry del Val's audience is highly significant) and doubtless took a sardonic delight in appearing up to the last to support and agree to the Spanish Government's request.

Of the conversations between Rampolla and Della Chiesa after the audience only one sentence has come down to us, but a sentence fraught with implications: 'Go to Bologna,' said the Cardinal, 'to be archbishop, and let everyone know that you are the archbishop.' In other words, Rampolla advised Della Chiesa to submit to the wrong done to him and let himself become completely absorbed in his new pastoral task, for the hour of his rehabilitation would come when he least expected it: an hour he would jeopardize by either refusing to accept the appointment or by coupling acceptance with an attempt to fabricate an opposition that could harm and diminish him in the esteem of those who knew he was the victim of an injustice.

Mgr Della Chiesa's removal from Rome recalls forcibly the similar experience in 1954 of Giovanni Battista Montini, then pro-Secretary of State under Pius XII. In that case too no manifestation of esteem and honour was omitted to give the impression of a genuine promotion; and but for Pius XII's illness he would certainly himself have consecrated his former Under-Secretary as bishop (as it was, he let his voice sound over the loud-speakers in St Peter's as he read from his room a short address overflowing with praise for his 'most faithful' collaborator). And as with Montini removal from Rome to the diocese of Milan was not an end in itself but was followed by a long delay in awarding the cardinal's hat, so too with Mgr Della Chiesa just the same thing had happened.

Bologna, the second city of the Papal States, was by long tradition regarded as a cardinal's see. There might be a delay of some months or a year, but the people of Bologna could never remember having an archbishop without the purple, and to them such a thing seemed unthinkable. But six long years and no less than six consistories passed by before Mgr Della Chiesa was made a member of the Sacred College. And, significantly, the cardinal's hat was at last granted him at the first consistory after Cardinal Rampolla's death, thus confirming yet again that the real target of the humiliations inflicted on Della Chiesa was not himself but Rampolla. Della Chiesa himself undoubtedly believed this, for the one implacable step he took on being elected Pope was to vindicate his great protector, making Merry del Val cede the Secretary of State's apartments to Cardinal Ferrata within the space of forty-eight hours.

Cardinal Canali, in his baffling deposition before the Ordinary Roman Tribunal assembled to pronounce on the heroic virtues of Merry del Val, attempted to justify the long humiliation inflicted on Della Chiesa. It makes painful reading:

In the interval between his assumption of the Archbishopric of Bologna in 1908 and his elevation to the sacred purple in 1914, only one consistory was held near the time of his appointment as Archbishop of Bologna. I think it worth mentioning that the usual promotion for an Under-Secretary in the Secretariat of State was to an apostolic nunciature of the first class, with an indefinite period before his eventual promotion to the Sacred Purple. In general such an interval corresponds to the duration in office of an apostolic Nuncio of the first class.

The Cardinal further dared to add:

Benedict xv, when raised to the Pontifical Throne, always showed the most delicate consideration and regard towards the Servant of God, being concerned from the outset to demonstrate such sentiments publicly by some official act. At first he thought of specially reviving for Cardinal Merry del Val the office of Abbot-in-command of Subiaco with ecclesiastical jurisdiction, an office always reserved for Cardinals and regarded as a particular distinction from the Pope. The Servant of God, while deeply appreciating this kind thought of the new Pope's on his behalf, asked to be excused, especially since such an appointment would have involved the responsibility of pastoral care. The Holy Father did not insist but at the first suitable opportunity appointed him Secretary of the Sacred Congregation of the Holy Office and established for him a regular periodical audience, which did not exist previously, for hitherto the Secretary had to ask for an audience each time.

The feigned candour of these words must have astounded the judges of the Roman Tribunal, men much too shrewd and experienced in Vatican intrigues to suppose that the appointment to Subiaco had been rejected by Merry del Val for the reasons given and not because he saw it for what it was, as an attempt to remove him from Rome to a prestige-bearing but baleful sinecure. As for the regular audience established by Benedict xv, it is easy to see that it signified for his secretary not only a weekly rendering of accounts about his important department but also the discomfort of having to present himself before his one-time ill-tolerated subordinate and pay him all the honours of which he had failed to deprive him.

In short, the cardinals associated with Merry del Val clearly bore a heavy responsibility in relation to Della Chiesa, even though he himself was not, or at least only indirectly, the real object of their aversion. On the other hand, in supporting his election they seized an extraordinary, indeed unique, opportunity to repair the wrongs done and transform the victim's resentment into gratitude, to their own advantage. As for the Leonine cardinals, the impositions inflicted on their candidate added lustre both to himself and to their own proofs of loyalty to him. But the real test of the man's measure lay not in those impositions themselves but in the way he bore them. Far from displaying Cardinal Ferrari's almost feminine sensibility under attack, or reacting angrily like the impulsive and bellicose Mgr Bonomelli, he always showed a supreme indifference even to calumny. (When a reporter from the Catholic daily *L'Avvenire* caught him in the midst of a pastoral visitation in the Apennines with a request for a reply to a violent attack in a secular paper reported with malicious glee by an integralist news-sheet, Della Chiesa sent him back with an order to the editor to steer clear of polemics and keep silent.)[1]

He showed particular dignity and restraint in his conduct towards Rome, never failing to make clear his own differing views when need arose or even to impart shrewd lessons to the curial strategists. For example on 1 July 1911 Pius X disavowed the five Catholic papers belonging to the Grosoli Trust: Della Chiesa at once seized the opportunity to remind Cardinal De Lai that, as everyone in Bologna knew, he had never held any brief for *L'Avvenire*, indeed it was rumoured that he had set up the *Diocesan Bulletin* as a rival to it; and his letter went on:[2]

And here let me add that it makes a bad impression among the bishops and the better priests that the Holy See's condemnations should come *after* the criticisms and censures of *L'Unità Cattolica*. I confess that I would make the editor of *L'Unità*, and perhaps the editor of *La Riscossa* too, general advisers of the Sacred Congregation of the Index, authorizing them to communicate *privately* to the Holy See any observations they might think fit about books and pamphlets in question, so that the Sacred Congregation of the Index might base its examination, and even its decrees, on those observations; but the *prior publication* by *L'Unità* of criticisms and censures of such works is harmful to the Holy See, because people say 'If *L'Unità* did not speak, the Holy See would keep silence!' I would like the Holy See to speak first, acting on the *secret opinions* given by the 'general advisers', and afterwards *L'Unità* and *La Riscossa* would illustrate and *justify* the Holy See's condemnation.

In his retreat in Bologna, Della Chiesa had in fact shown not only that he could be a good pastor of souls as well as a skilful diplomat, but also that he possessed strength of character and self-control, a sense of balance that restrained him from extremes, and a no less admirable ability to overcome adversity; all this, in addition to the lucidity and farsightedness that had won appreciation during his long sojourn in the Secretariat of State.

The Natural Pope

Thus majority and minority – the first determined to win but not to abuse its victory, the second relieved not to have to make greater concessions – agreed on the choice of the Archbishop of

---

[1] See Maria Torresin (*v.* Bibliography, p. 370), p. 267.
[2] ibid., pp. 280–1

Bologna, and he accorded his electors the rare surprise of seeing him accept perfectly naturally and serenely his designation to the highest responsibility. Every Conclave in fact expects that the cardinal called to the pontificate on realizing his fate should try, or pretend to try, to evade the task and seem downcast and overwhelmed at his colleagues' insistence, feigning to give in only in order to comply with the divine will. Pius x, though in complete sincerity and dismay at the prospect, lent himself, so to speak, to this comedy. Benedict xv, on the other hand, appeared calm and at ease, as if nothing unusual had happened: he naturally admitted that the task entrusted to him was considerable, but added at once that he felt 'serene and confident', since the help of God would surely not fail him. The Master of the Ceremonies told Della Chiesa's secretary, Mgr Migone, to go and join his cardinal, and Migone, on entering the Sistine Chapel and grasping what had happened, staggered and almost fainted. 'What a child he is!' commented Della Chiesa in gentle amusement. 'You'd almost think it was he who had been made Pope!'

Some people might find this naturalness an irritating pose or in bad taste. But Giacomo Della Chiesa was a very honest person, and he had no patience with false modesty or concealing one's genuine natural feelings by pious lies. Once when a prelate whom he had appointed bishop made an embarrassing scene, dramatizing his unworthiness and begging to be excused from that high office, he waited a few minutes and then answered curtly, noting almost with satisfaction his companion's shocked dismay, 'Very well, we will content you – you are free. We want to make a bishop and confessor, not a bishop and martyr.'

How, moreover, should he have been other than satisfied and serene at his election? As an ingenuous but sincere youth he had embraced the way of the priesthood with the purest intentions, and since then he had always let himself be guided by Providence whether for good – as in his meeting with Rampolla – or ill – as in the fiasco of the nunciature in Madrid; every step he had taken was because he was guided, not because he had let himself be influenced by personal considerations. If now God had chosen him, with perhaps lesser gifts of nature and grace than some of his colleagues, and with his insignificant physique – indeed probably the most insignificant and awkward of the whole Sacred College – it was because He wished to mock, as the Scriptures say, at the proud and presumptuous thoughts of men, deciding to entrust the fulfilment of His designs to one who was seemingly the least fitted for the task.

When Pius x appointed him to the diocese of Bologna he wrote with significant frankness to his diocesans: 'So I will say, surprised at myself and perhaps causing surprise to others, that my feeling after my designation was one of spiritual joy. This feeling was from God, and I cannot conceal its strength, because I must and wish to give glory to God.' He might have included such expressions in his first encyclical as Pope; but instead he confined himself to avoiding the references usual in such documents to his feelings of dismay on hearing of his election. On the day of his coronation Mgr Arborio Mella, his personal chamberlain, noted that when he was raised for the first time on the gestatorial chair in the Sistine Chapel and according to rite a chaplain approached him with a burning bundle of straw on a silver platter, saying: '*Pater Sancte, sic transit gloria mundi*' (Holy Father, thus vanishes the glory of this world), he made an expressive face, as if to say that his glory was at the service of God and he had nothing against staying in that service as long as possible. He was never, in fact, throughout his whole pontificate, found weary or downcast. His optimism recalled that of Leo xiii, and was in sharp contrast with the melancholy and jeremiads of Pius x.

But the first twenty-four hours of his pontificate provided a mixture of disappointments and surprises. His presentation to the faithful in the basilica of St Peter was disappointing, and so too were the first photographs bringing the picture of the new Pope before the world. The crowd assembled in St Peter's for the benediction from the inner loggia could get only a vague idea of what he looked like: perhaps they did not guess, given the distance, how very small he was, but they could not help realizing his frailness: it was as if a child pope sat in the gestatorial chair, with a head out of proportion to his stature, set on shoulders one higher than the other, which gave an uneven motion to his arms as he raised them. And this child pope, too, though he made gestures of blessing, was quite extraordinarily immobile; most immobile of all were his eyes, with their strange fixity and depth, the black pupils standing out enigmatically from the emaciated pallor of his face. But it was not only a child pope but a sickly pope that the crowd gazed at curiously as they turned their backs to the Altar of the Confession dedicated to the memory and tomb of the first pontiff. And when the newly elected Pope opened his mouth to intone the liturgical verses before the benediction, an even more unpleasing impression seeped through the crowd, evoked by the tuneless, hollow quality of his voice.

But Giacomo Della Chiesa was used to arousing this kind of disappointment, and knew how such judgements could later swing the other way. His badly-built body had been a handicap even in his games as a child; at school, as he grew older he found some consolation in the fact that the poet Leopardi had had the same kind of affliction. In the Secretariat of State, and perhaps even earlier at the Capranica College, his nickname was '*piccoletto*', 'a little scrap of a thing'; first conferred in a half-pitying half-sarcastic spirit, it later came to denote a mixture of envy and admiration, for the '*piccoletto*' soon proved himself an invaluable support for anyone seeking explanations, advice, or a way out of difficulties. His installation in Bologna also caused disappointment. Its townspeople, notoriously accustomed to good living and appreciative of fine physical stature, looked askance at this scrawny little archbishop who looked more like one of his own choirboys. The contrast with his late predecessor, the massive and majestic Cardinal Svampa, merely accentuated his deficiencies. Yet as time went on and they discovered his many good qualities, the Bolognesi came to feel in sympathy with their small, frail archbishop, and they resented Rome's unreasoning persecution in refusing to make him a cardinal. So the new Pope was not unduly perturbed about the initial disappointment he now aroused.

Moreover he had already begun to astonish people by his decisiveness in assuming command. The white smoke, announcing his election to the waiting crowd beneath their straw hats and sunshades in St Peter's Square on that blazing September day, was seen rising at 11.30 am, and only an hour later he appeared on the balcony of St Peter's (the tailor had had to work at top speed in the meantime to fit as best he could the shortest of the white cassocks kept ready in three sizes for whoever should be chosen Pope). So he had no chance to have something to eat until about 2.30 or 3 pm after the cardinals and heads of the Secretariat and the Court had taken their leave; nevertheless that same afternoon the whole Vatican was set in turmoil by a series of immediate orders from the new Pope.

It was, of course, only natural that he should find no difficulty in going into action, for every stone and denizen of St Peter's was familiar to him; but this speed and assurance were, all the same, amazing. 'Goodness!' exclaimed a prelate, 'we've got a professional Pope', and the description seemed to fit. A good many of his orders were naturally of a technical kind, but some were both authoritative and daring. One of the first, destined to arouse widespread comment, concerned his coronation – not its pomp and ceremony, however, but its restriction to the most modest possible affair: it was to take place not, as usual, in St Peter's but in the Sistine Chapel, as a mark of the new Pope's respect for the general sorrow caused by the war. Another order concerned the letters communicating the news of his election to the various Heads of State: he would send a letter in his own hand to the President of the French Republic, despite the ten-year-long separation between State and Church in France. The choice of the person to act as unofficial channel between the Italian Government and the Holy See was also made in those first hours. Lastly, the new Pope wished to learn at once about the state of Vatican finances, and set aside a huge sum for charitable donations to be made without delay.

These four main decisions of his first day as Pope displayed the characteristics that were to distinguish him in future as a Pope of peace between nations, conciliation within the Catholic world, apostolic zeal, and charity.

The name he had chosen, Benedetto or Benedict, itself provided a happy augury for his reign. He explained that he had assumed it out of homage to his last great predecessor from Bologna, Lambertini (Benedict xiv), but perhaps he was also unconsciously influenced by the recollection of Fogazzaro's hero Benedetto in *Il Santo*. Be that as it may, no name among all those chosen by the successors of Peter could have been more auspicious for this frail but resolute son of the Della Chiesas embarking on office amid a world at war and a Church in mourning.

Peace Above All

Yet this name was fated soon to become involved in the passions and partisan hatreds of war and be cruelly transformed into a term of abuse and offence. For this Pope, who had himself decided to celebrate his coronation in minor key lest the father's splendour should intrude on the grief of his sons caught up in the tragedy of war, at the height of an unreasoning and unjust campaign was even called Maledetto xv.

On the morrow of those passion-fraught years, and still in his lifetime, that insult was found to be completely unfounded, if largely for political reasons. Any discussion of Benedict xv's attitude to the war has, indeed, always been based primarily on political rather than on ideological or religious grounds, whereas the psychological aspect ought really to be considered first. Benedict xv had in fact no need to think out a line of policy in relation to the war, for that policy imposed itself on him of its own accord, as a natural need: it was inspired by his heart and feelings even more than by his intellect. His biographers tell the story of how one day during his pontificate when receiving in private audience a former priest of his from the Apennines above Bologna a strange sight met his eyes. For the priest came in accompanied by a bird of remarkable size with a proud and angry eye, though it was still quite young. He had captured this young eagle up in the mountains after a stiff battle with its mother and, as he said, 'at the risk of my own life'. 'And that was a bad thing to do,' rejoined the Pope, visibly angered; 'I accept your intention, but this cruel capture of yours displeases me greatly.' And he kept and fed the young eagle and then had it set free.

Such was Giacomo Della Chiesa, with his instinctive repulsion for any violent or cruel action: for him war was something terrible that should never be allowed to happen, that should be resisted at all costs, and for which one could only feel horror and the desire to suffocate and prevent it. It was as if the fact of war was in some way directly connected with his own physical weakness, the instinctive defence of a disabled being against a situation of exceptional ferocity that rendered him even more defenceless. His public and doctrinal attitude and his diplomatic action in relation to the war are all to be explained primarily by this paralysing and almost physiological horror of it.

Certain of the recently-discovered letters to which we have already referred leave us in no doubt on this point. A few days before leaving for the Conclave he wrote to his Vicar General: 'I do not want any priest to take sides openly for one or other of the belligerent countries; I have caused it to be suggested that they should ask God for the cessation of the war without indicating to the Lord the "way" in which this terrible scourge should be brought to an end.' And on the morrow of Italy's declaration of war on Austria in 1915: '... I thank you for your expressions of sorrow at the present time: they have pleased me much, especially since *L'Avvenire d'Italia* seems to me to be excessively hysterical about the war. On Thursday I read the announcement of a service "for the *public* blessing of the banners" and I feared that the so-called Catholic Associations of Bologna had extorted an act of too great condescension from Monsignor the Archbishop. Now it seems the affair has reduced itself to more Christian terms.' A man who can write thus – and who in June 1916 refused to approve the entry of a Catholic, Filippo Meda, into the Boselli Government, and would never allow chaplains to appear in the Vatican in military uniform – has not a single fibre in his body that responds to war and is bound to be an unqualified pacifist; but he is also a man who, in addition to his natural intolerance of war, feels the shocked and grief-stricken horror of a Christian.

To realize this, we need only reread the moving prayer for peace beginning 'Shocked by the horrors of a war . . .', which he composed at the beginning of 1915 and caused it to be recited therafter throughout the world, thus arousing the first adverse reactions to his 'policy'. But as Pope, his attitude to the war is naturally to be sought chiefly in the public actions of his government. In his first message to the world, of 8 September 1914, he calls it 'the scourge of the wrath of God'. In his first encyclical, *Ad Beatissimi*, on All Saints' Day (1 November) 1914, he traces the following dark picture, in words completely free from the false rhetoric and sentimental style that were to mar so many similar passages in the wartime messages of Pius XII.

Truly those days seem to have come upon us of which Our Lord foretold: *Audituri estis proelia et opiniones proeliorum . . . Consurget enim gens in gentem et regnum in regnum* (Ye shall hear of wars and rumours of wars . . . For nation shall rise against nation and kingdom against kingdom). The terrible spectre of war dominates everywhere and there is hardly any other thought in men's minds. Great and flourishing nations are there on the fields of battle. What wonder is it, then, if, being well furnished as they are with those horrible weapons that the progress of military science has invented, they inflict tremendous carnage on each other. There is no limit to the ruin and slaughter: every day the earth is steeped in fresh blood and covered anew with dead and wounded. And who would believe that such peoples, armed against each other, are all descended from the same progenitor, have the same nature and belong to the same human society? Who would think they could be brothers, sons of a single Father in Heaven? And in the meantime, while huge armies fight on both sides, nations, families, and individuals groan under the sorrows and miseries attendant on war; day by day the ranks of the widows and orphans swell; trade languishes because of destroyed communications, the fields are abandoned, the arts suspended, the rich are in difficulties, the poor in abject misery, and all in distress.

On the first anniversary of the conflict, 28 July 1915, in the famous appeal in which he reminded statesmen and peoples that 'nations do not die', he described the war as 'a horrible carnage that dishonours Europe'; in his Christmas message of that year, the world was said to have become 'a hospital and a charnelhouse'; on 4 March 1916 he spoke of the 'suicide of civilized Europe'; and four months later, on 31 July, he described the recourse to arms as 'the darkest tragedy of human hatred and human madness'. Significant too were the passages in which he referred to himself as prisoner of such exceptional circumstances:

Oh! how often in the months of Our Pontificate, made long by the fatal delay of any settlement of these human conflicts, have we taken refuge in prayer!... We felt the anguish of a father who sees his house devastated and abandoned through a violent hurricane... throwing ourselves, so to speak, into the midst of the belligerent peoples, like a father amid his warring sons, We have exhorted them, in the name of that God Who is justice and infinite charity, to renounce their designs of mutual destruction... It is not permissible for the Father whose sons are engaged in violent strife to cease from admonishing them merely because they resist his prayers and tears...

No wonder, then, that he chose 'neutrality' or rather 'impartiality' between the two sides at war. The only wonder is that he should have contented himself with a mute and negative role of indirect protest, never officially condemning the war but merely expounding the main lines of a theology that showed it to be useless and inadmissible. Apart from the hard terms used in opposing war – which, though indubitably sincere, were liable

to be confounded with the commonplaces of pontifical oratory in
any era – the doctrine advanced by Benedict xv consisted almost
exclusively of rejections and silences. He never once, for example,
recalled the classic distinction made in Catholic theology between
a just and an unjust war (usually taken to mean a war of defence
or a war of aggression); and, unlike most of the bishops in the
belligerent countries, he refused to indicate in the war an opportunity for moral revival, expiation, or the rediscovery of forgotten
virtues, and hence for conversion and return to God as well as
for heroism and courage. His silence did not, certainly, signify the
repudiation or condemnation of all this traditional teaching, but
by implication he declared it inadequate, a childish morality in an
adult age, and inadequate above all because it helped to nourish
rather than extinguish war.

But what was the reason for this attitude of reserve, this refusal
to adopt an unequivocal position in relation to the belligerent
Powers or to give clear directives to the episcopates and clergy
or the faithful? These questions are not difficult to answer,
especially as far as concerns the failure to condemn the aggressor,
a request repeatedly made by both sides. Even admitting that
Benedict xv might be constrained by the obligations of his office
to adjudge responsibility for aggression (which is simply not the
case), insuperable practical difficulties prevented his doing so.
A Curia cardinal acutely observed to Charles Loiseau:

> This century seems to demand of the Papacy of today precisely what
> it reproved in the Papacy in the past. It would like the present pontiff
> to hurl himself into the midst of the warring peoples thunderbolt in
> hand, sparing no one. Such advice may be generous, but we today are
> more modern and know what would happen to us if we followed it.
> The result would be that we should no longer be at peace with any
> nation once they became reconciled. Because, quite frankly, to follow
> this idea to the end we should have to condemn one after the other,
> and with great publicity, all nations, all social classes, and every
> category of sinner.

This was not just a display of diplomatic wit on the part of the
anonymous cardinal: it was sound realism. True, the Papacy is a
seat of moral teaching, but it is a tribunal for sins, not for sinners:
to put it more precisely, explicit condemnations are reserved for
offences, while for those responsible for them the general rule of

secrecy remains valid. The pontifical practice of medieval times, when the Church itself was also a political power, ceased to have any force after the Papal States came to an end. Any declaratory intervention by the Church must now be confined to conflicts arising out of religious causes. And that was certainly not the case in the war of 1914–18.

At most, pontifical injunction might be invoked in instances of a serious violation of natural ethics, but even then only if it could be proved beyond doubt. But the propaganda efforts of both sides, each determined to attribute, whether rightly or wrongly, the most sinister responsibilities to its adversary, made it extremely difficult to ascertain the truth of such accusations. Individual bishops or episcopates could easily make mistakes, and even the nuncios, where such existed, sometimes sent in reports which later proved unfounded, thus casting doubts on any other information of the kind. Obviously certain points were beyond dispute, such as the violation of Belgian neutrality by the Germans, and it is true that Benedict xv chose to condemn them only generically, but this was certainly not out of calculation or timidity; he did so, rather, in order to retain the possibility of influencing all parties to the conflict when the time should come to call them to a reciprocal understanding. Moreover, as in the case just mentioned, he spoke extremely openly through the medium of his Secretary of State, Gasparri (in the Note sent by the latter on 6 July 1915 to the Belgian Minister to the Holy See), who significantly recalled the fact that the German Chancellor Bethmann-Hollweg had 'publicly confessed in the Reichstag on 4 August and 13 September 1914' that Germany had violated Belgian neutrality. In short, Benedict xv confined himself to adopting a definite standpoint only on the basis of incontestable and officially recognized facts.

On the other hand, as regards his influence on the Catholic world, to issue an encyclical radically condemning the war presented serious problems: it would need to justify the rejection of theories approved by the Church for centuries (some of which, such as that of a war of defence, it would be hard to prove unfounded); and it must also avoid creating confusion or rebellion among the episcopates, clergy, and faithful, who were involved in the defence of their own countries and convinced of the justice both of their own cause and of the crusade to defend the values of civilization and progress. (For instance, a pastoral letter from the German bishops in December 1914 declared: 'We are innocent of the outbreak of war; it was imposed on us; this we can testify before God and men.') In the first case, there would have had to be a preliminary theological examination of the thesis of the absolute inacceptability of war, which would have taken time to organize, and it would have been difficult for the theologians conducting it to remain uninfluenced by the existing conflict. And in the second case any intervention would have come too late and defeated its own ends: the war had not only aroused resentments and prejudices in men's minds but had also caused the leaders of the countries involved to adopt standpoints which it would now be hard to alter. Efforts confined to deploring the war, describing it as futile, and attempting conciliation on the basis of the *status quo* had several times caused reactions approaching open rebellion (as when, in the Madeleine in Paris, in the presence of Cardinal Archbishop Amette and the highest State authorities, the Dominican Père Sertillanges cried amid the applause of the whole congregation: 'Holy Father, we cannot accept Your peace'); it is easy therefore to imagine what would have been the effect of taking up a doctrinal stand, which would have required the inner assent of all believers.

For all these reasons, Benedict xv confined himself to expounding his evangelical conception of the war as occasion offered, at the same time supporting or promoting diplomatic efforts to prevent its further extension or help to bring it to a speedy end. In pursuing the first of these aims, to avoid arousing cases of conscience that could have no outlet without the wholehearted collaboration of the episcopate and the clergy, he restricted himself to expounding the purely rational arguments which in his view condemned the conflict. A celebrated instance among many such was his exhortation to leaders on the first anniversary of the war:

The copious riches with which God the Creator has furnished the lands under your control permit you to continue the war; but at what cost? . . . Nor let it be said that this vast conflict cannot be settled without the violence of arms . . . Recollect that nations do not die: humiliated and oppressed, they chafe against the yoke imposed on them, preparing revolt and transmitting from generation to generation a tragic heritage of hatred and revenge . . .

As for his diplomatic efforts to stem the conflict, we know, for example, that in January 1915 he counselled the Emperor Franz Josef through his Nuncio in Vienna to cede the Trentino to Italy, with the aim of depriving interventionist movements in Italy of one of their most forcible arguments, that of irredentism. Among all the steps he planned or took towards suspending the war, the most notorious and the most unfortunate, especially for the reactions it produced against himself, is the celebrated Note to Heads of States at War, of 1 August 1917. But a careful consideration of the timing and contents of this Note reveals that its true intention went far beyond the immediate aim. It was a logical extension of the lessons constantly preached in his allocutions and messages – which themselves unfortunately failed to get the response they should have done, largely because owing to press restrictions they were not sufficiently widely known; and in it Benedict xv strove to diffuse a knowledge of the ideal conditions calculated to prevent any future reversion to armed violence. These conditions, he said, could be summed up as the re-establishment of the rule of law, to be achieved in three phases: suspension of fighting; 'simultaneous and reciprocal reduction of armaments, according to rules and guarantees to be established to the extent necessary and sufficient for the maintenance of public order in each State'; and lastly, 'in the place of armies, the establishment of arbitration with its exalted pacifying function, on lines to be concerted and with sanctions to be settled against any State that should refuse either to submit international questions to arbitration or to accept its awards'.

How far from utopian this programme was could be seen only a few months later when President Wilson's Fourteen Points were published. But a letter from Cardinal Gasparri to the Archbishop of Sens a week or two after afforded concrete illustration of the most delicate of these aims, that of disarmament:

The practical method of realizing it exists. The Holy See in its appeal of 1 August did not see fit to indicate it, out of deference to the leaders of the belligerent countries, preferring to leave it to them to decide about it. But the only practical method, and the easiest of application, given the good will of the parties concerned, would be the following: compulsory military service should be abolished by mutual agreement among all civilized nations; an arbitration tribunal should be established; ... lastly, to prevent infractions, the sanction of a universal boycott should be instituted against any country attempting to reintroduce compulsory military service, etc. Britain and the United States normally had voluntary service and in order to play an effective part in the present war were forced to introduce conscription. This proves that voluntary service can provide the contingent needed to maintain public order ... but does not produce the enormous armies demanded by modern war ... For more than a century conscription has been the real cause of a number of ills that have afflicted society: the true remedy lies in its simultaneous and reciprocal abolition ...

In making this attempt, Benedict xv must almost certainly have been aware of what its fate would be. There were the discouraging precedents of the failure, in December 1916, of the Central Powers' Note to the Entente and President Wilson's appeal; and some months later pressure from the German deputies Naumann and Erzberger, and Cardinal Bisleti's letter to the Empress Zita, had failed to disperse the doubts prevalent about German and Austrian offers for the suspension of hostilities. Moreover the general political and military situation had developed in the meantime, producing different conditions from those in which the Note had been envisaged and prepared. The Nuncio in Berne was urging the Holy See to abandon its immobility and take some initiative before the Socialists did so at their Stockholm congress. But it was the promptings of his own ideals and intentions, and not such arguments as those, that decided Benedict xv to intervene all the same (and with what haste, can be judged from following the movements of the Nuncio in Munich, Pacelli, between June and August). He hoped against hope as he anxiously awaited some reaction from the Powers concerned. When weeks passed by without a sign, he was perhaps the first to abandon any illusion.

But this same quality of single-mindedness helps us to understand the moral greatness of Giacomo Della Chiesa. Between the diplomatic victory he might perhaps have achieved without so total and drastic a denigration of war, and his own deeply-felt need to maintain his unbiased stand against it, he never hesitated. Instead, he insisted that his unqualified repudiation of war should clearly dominate the document, the secret ambition of which was to secure not only the end of the current 'useless carnage' (an expression that he insisted on including though his collaborators thought otherwise) but also the definite suspension of all wars. True, he made this attempt for its own sake, both for the immense benefit Europe would gain by abandoning hostilities and for the prestige that would accrue to the Holy See from acceptance of his proposals; but diplomatic success should not, in his view, be sought independently of its deeper evangelical motivation. The greatness of Benedict xv, in other words, lies in the fact that he subordinated the diplomatic argument to the moral and evangelical, and forfeited a considerable if ephemeral prestige for the announcement of a startling and revolutionary principle understood by only a tiny minority; and this he did, and remained irremovably fixed in his decision, in spite of the most ferocious campaign conducted against him by contemporary politicians and the press.

It is remarkable to find how, right from the beginning of his pontificate, his peace policy was not understood, even by men whose intelligence and idealism put them beyond suspicion. To take only such sources as diaries and little-known correspondence published much later, Léon Bloy, for example, writing between December 1914 and February 1915, said in his journal (*Au seuil de l'Apocalypse*): 'Stupefying mediocrity. The Pope, in his first encyclical, naturally deplores the horrors of war, but accuses no one . . .'; 'the Vicar of Jesus Christ declares himself neutral . . . Monstrous declaration'; '. . . I wonder what kind of Pope we have been sent'; 'he deceives *infallibly* . . . I think we shall have to pray for Benedict xv . . .'. And von Hügel, writing to Loisy after the war was over, on 17 November 1918, went so far as to say that 'not only in the interests of humanity but also of the Church, it would be advisable to insist on the abdication both of Wilhelm II and of Benedict xv';[1] he had always agreed with Loisy, who wrote to him on 17 December 1914: 'What is very strange about the present situation, and what I confess I never foresaw, is that a political Pope like Benedict xv should be even more inadequate than a fanatical Pope like Pius x to fulfil the (moral) function which a Pope could still be permitted to assume, if he could and would assume it.'[2]

But after the Note of 1 August 1917 the scorn and derision

---

[1] Loisy, op. cit., vol. III, p. 373.
[2] ibid., vol. III, p. 297.

for the 'Boche Pope' reached fantastic heights. His proposal was called a 'white peace', and accusations that he was pro-German multiplied, despite the fact that while Benedict xv certainly could not welcome the idea that the balance of Europe might be shattered by the collapse of the two German-speaking empires, what he feared most of all was a crushing military collapse, whereas in his view any desirable readjustment should have been decided at an international conference. But, far from clinging to an untenable situation, he was ready to accept without useless regrets even the most unexpected innovations, as can be seen from his wish for the Holy See to enter speedily into diplomatic relations with Poland and the new Successor States. He may have had some sentimental feeling for the Catholic Hapsburg Empire, whose importance for the Church in a predominantly non-Catholic Europe he was bound to recognize, and for Germany, which since the days of Leo xiii had shown increasing sensitivity towards the Roman Church; but he would not allow such considerations to influence him in making political decisions of immense importance for the Church, still less to cause him to sacrifice his profound desire for peace. Quite apart from which, it was a very odd way of showing pro-German feeling to make it a first duty, on becoming Pope, to notify the French President of his election, and to choose as his Secretary of State first Cardinal Ferrata, ex-Nuncio in Paris and universally regarded as francophile, and then, on Ferrata's death within a month, Cardinal Gasparri, for twenty years Professor of Canon Law at the Catholic Institute in Paris.

But, far from weakening in the face of opposition, Benedict xv pursued his appointed path undeterred. From the documents at present available it is difficult to say how far he strove in private as well as in public to advocate peace at all costs; but certain actions speak for themselves, as, for instance, his exhortation to Marc Sangnier, immediately after the war, to concentrate on articles about a referendum of the nations and the abolition of military conscription. To Sangnier's reply that he thought public opinion was not ready for that kind of propaganda, he countered: 'Then you must work to educate public opinion.' During the war his verbal exhortations to members of the clergy or laity had to adapt themselves to the circumstances and could happen only rarely, given the difficulty of travel to Rome at that time; and correspondence was hampered in view of the censorship. In any case, anyone following his advice would, if he acted cautiously, either not have been understood or would have aroused useless suspicion, while if he spoke openly he ran the risk of being called defeatist.

It was only after the war that Benedict xv's pacifist idealism became more widely understood, as can be seen from such episodes as the establishment, in July 1921, of the 'Pax Romana' association, promoted by Catholic students from three neutral countries – Holland, Switzerland, and Spain – and including both victors and vanquished; or the collective letter from German bishops, published on 30 September 1923 while the Ruhr was still under French occupation. In that letter the bishops firmly repudiated nationalism and declared: 'We renounce all diets, all plans of hatred or revenge; we do not strive after any such reprisals. We content ourselves with that vengeance which St Paul calls the vengeance of heaven, and which consists in loving our enemies and praying for them.' Another example of such better understanding of his teaching was the ethical-ideological study of war promoted by such writers as Vanderpol, Sturzo, Yves de la Brière, Regout, Mausbach, Batiffol, the authors of the Fribourg manifesto of 1932, and others.

Post-war disillusionment naturally contributed to some extent to the sucess of Benedict xv's teaching, but so too did his own work for peace during the second part of his pontificate, beginning with his defence of peace in face of the semblance of peace imposed by the Versailles conference. In pursuance of Leo xiii's policy, Benedict xv aspired to give his support to the new international order which should come into being after the war. Positive proof of this can be seen in the attempt made by his Secretary of State in the last days of July 1918 to secure, through the Belgian Government's mediation, a modification of Article 15 of the Pact of London, made known some time earlier by the new Russian Government, according to which the Holy See was explicitly excluded from participation in the peace negotiations. True, the Holy See also aimed to bring forward the Roman Question, but that was certainly not the sole aim of so risky a step – which in fact failed partly as a result of a rumour from the Sacred Palaces which came to the ears of the Italian Ministry of Foreign Affairs.

Foiled in this hope, Benedict xv in his allocution on Christmas Eve 1918 announced his firm intention of ensuring for the 'equitable deliberations of the Peace Congress' the support of his influence with the faithful. Some saw in this a suggestion that he still wished to take part in the Peace Conference. The *Osservatore Romano* waited until 19 March 1919 before publishing an official denial of this interpretation, but its aim was obviously not so much to deny the Pope's desire to participate but rather to make it clear the he would only have wished to do so if there were a prospect of a truly conciliatory peace, at which the victors did not appear to be aiming.

He therefore abandoned such illusions and concentrated his efforts on the defence of the vanquished, on whom he rightly believed the future fate of peace depended. In the spring of 1919 he addressed apostolic letters to the German episcopate and to Cardinal Amette, Archbishop of Paris, inviting Catholics in both countries to cease from hostility towards each other; on 16 December 1919 he deplored hatred between nations and the excessive nationalism of some ecclesiastical hierarchies; he conveyed to Washington the German proposals on the settlement of reparations; and on 24 January 1921 he wrote to his Secretary of State of the intolerable situation to which Austria had been reduced. Most important of all these steps was his stern condemnation of the Versailles peace treaties, expressed in his encyclical *Pacem Dei munus* of 23 May 1920, and of that 'peace of a sort (*pax aliqua*)' which would not eradicate the seeds of ancient rivalries. Lastly, he refused to recognize the League of Nations, which, in his view, lacked the necessary foundations for ensuring a lasting peace.

Conciliation in Civil Affairs

Once again, this was not a policy likely to make him popular; but once again it was an attitude of high moral significance and completely consistent with the standpoint he had maintained throughout the conflict. Equally consistent were Benedict xv's efforts for civil pacification within the individual countries, where he strove in particular to eliminate as best he could causes of dispute between Church and State.

The most important case was clearly that of France, though

after the war conditions had greatly changed in that country of extreme secularism. The wartime union of all the national forces, the Church included, had dealt a blow to the old anticlericalism. But for the presence of Clemenceau at the head of the Government, the *'Chambre horizon bleu'* would quickly have voted for the resumption of diplomatic relations with the Holy See. The question was raised immediately after that Government's fall. But Benedict xv had not stood passively by in the meantime. Mgr Cerretti, his envoy attending the Versailles Congress to arrange the question of Catholic missions in the ex-German colonies, had had frequent contacts with Briand, and at the same time in Rome the Congregation of Rites speeded up the preliminaries for the canonization of Joan of Arc, which took place on 16 May 1920. The French Government was officially represented at the ceremony in Rome by an ambassador extraordinary accompanied not only by all the French upper clergy but by eighty Members of Parliament. Soon after, for the feast-day of the new St Joan, Cardinal Granito Pignatelli di Belmonte arrived in France as pontifical legate and between ceremonies raised the question of resumption of diplomatic relations. The Government welcomed the proposal, and it was approved by the Chamber on 30 November 1920 by 391 votes to 179.

This was a sensational event of far-reaching significance; but for Benedict xv it was not yet enough. His conciliation with the Third Republic aimed to dissipate the last shades of Pius x. And in this he once again found an ally in Gasparri, as he had done fifteen years earlier in their resistance to Merry del Val. The Congregation for Extraordinary Ecclesiastical Affairs even declared itself in favour of recognizing the *associations cultuelles*. This was a clamorous refutation of Pius x's decision, but not even the danger that it might be controversially interpreted could divert Benedict xv from his aim; and though he himself did not live to achieve it, it came to pass under his successor.

In Italy itself, Benedict xv went so far as to approve and encourage the first official approaches to the Italian Government for a settlement of the Roman Question. The first indication of his new and promising attitude on this question had been given as early as 1915 through his Secretary of State, following an audience-interview granted to the French journalist Latapie, correspondent of *Libertè*. In the counter-interview with the

Corriere d'Italia 128 June 1915), Gasparri said that the position of
the Holy See at that time could not be accepted as normal, 'although,' he added, 'the Holy See, as befits its neutrality, has no
intention whatever of embarrassing the [Italian] Government; it
puts its trust in God and awaits a proper readjustment of its situation, not through foreign arms, but through the triumph of those
sentiments of justice which, it hopes, are steadily gaining ground
among the Italian people in conformity with its true interests'.

The approaches to the Italian Government came about four
years later as a result of meetings between an American Bishop,
Mgr Kelley, first with Marchese Brambilla of the Italian delegation to the Peace Conference and then with the Italian Prime
Minister, Orlando. Convinced that something definite might be
achieved, Kelley then came to Rome and met Cardinal Gasparri.
Benedict xv at once gave precise directions to Mgr Cerretti, who
on 1 June 1919 saw Orlando in Paris, and at that meeting the
Holy See's conditions were accepted concerning the cession to it
of a territory under its own ownership and sovereignty and the
revision and harmonization of the Italian ecclesiastical laws – the
two points, in fact, which contain the seeds of the future treaty
and concordat. Unfortunately the Orlando Government's resignation on 17 June put a stop to the project, which was not revived
by any of the succeeding Governments for fear of arousing opposition in Parliament and among anticlerical circles. Later, in May
1920, Benedict xv permitted Catholic Heads of State to visit the
Quirinal[1] and also allowed contacts between the diplomatists
accredited to the Holy See and those accredited to the Quirinal.

Bearing in mind that during the war Benedict xv not only
refused King Alfonso xiii's offer of hospitality in the Escurial
but also rejected all the proposals made to him by the Central
Powers for the re-establishment of a miniature Papal State (the
'Erzberger project', drafted by the leader of the *Zentrum*), the
judgement of his policy on Church and State, given by Senator
Morello (well known as a political writer under the pen-name of
Rastignac) after his death, will seem in no way exaggerated:

Benedict xv . . . never pursued a policy of strife against Italy and
never adopted towards the Italian State those forms and formulas
which even the gentle Pius x employed, if regretfully, or was forced

[1] See note in Bibliography p. 373.

to employ. Benedict xv was the first Pope since 1870 to show an acceptable inclination towards pacification and not to belie it by such words and deeds as to make it impossible. He was the first Pope who, either from natural sensitivity or from natural correctness of behaviour, did not contribute to making neighbourly relations with the Italian State an impossibliity.

This attitude is the more remarkable since in private he never renounced the intransigent views on the Church's temporal rights which (as was shown in the letters quoted earlier) he had assimilated in youth. But Benedict xv's desire for pacification within the individual States was not confined to improving relations between them and the Holy See (though no concordats were signed during his pontificate, several were set in motion, for instance those with Latvia, Poland, and Bavaria); it extended also to avoiding such indirect interference in their affairs as might arise through the establishment of Catholic parties. In Italy itself, though he did not forbid the formation in 1919 of Don Luigi Sturzo's Partito Popolare, he never encouraged it. This became clear in 1922 with the publication of Cardinal Pio Boggiani's memoirs, *Due Anni di episcopato genovese* (Two Years as Bishop of Genoa), and was further confirmed in a letter to the *Giornale d'Italia* of 29 October 1922 from the Italian deputy Monti-Guarnieri:

I remember how one afternoon in the summer of 1920 while talking about politics . . . Benedict xv mentioned certain attitudes of a well-known member of Parliament which did not seem to him consistent with Christian doctrine. I interrupted him to ask: 'Why does Your Holiness not ask him to mend his ways?' The Pope answered: 'First of all, because I don't know him; and then too it is a good thing that you should know once for all, and tell your friends among the moderates, that the Pope has nothing to do with the Partito Popolare. I have never recognized it as a party, and I do not wish to recognize it, so that I may be free to disown it when it seems advisable and when I want to.'

These statements of Cardinal Pio Boggiani and Monti-Guarnieri, further authenticated by the *Osservatore Romano*, received recent confirmation from the publication of a letter from Gasparri to Count Santucci, dated 1 April 1928, in which the Cardinal explicitly denies that the Partito Popolare was formed by Benedict xv and himself:

The Partito Popolare was created by all of you without any intervention from the Holy See; you showed me the statutes already drawn up and I objected to the article which said that the Partito Popolare was non-religious (an obvious slip for *non-confessional*) and also to one or two other articles which I don't remember. I often deplored the fact that the President or Director of the Partito Popolare was a priest, but I never either got Don Sturzo to resign or the party to give up. My view of the Partito Popolare by comparison with the other parties striving for power in Italy before Fascism was that it was the *least bad* of the lot, in other words not so bad as the Communists, Socialists, Radicals and Liberals.

These remarks of Cardinal Gasparri's might seem to suggest that Benedict xv was unable to get rid of Don Sturzo as head of the Partito Popolare. This was of course not the case: obviously it was only a wish on the Cardinal's part that the Catholic party in Italy should not be headed by a priest; had the Pope expressed the same wish, Gasparri would certainly not have put up with disobedience from the party. Not that Benedict xv approved of priests in politics, but he knew where to draw the line. Thus he raised no objection to a man of Mgr Seipel's high spiritual qualities becoming Chancellor of Austria. As for Don Sturzo, he had given substantial proof of his prudence in the past, and was known to the Pope, who had appointed him to a position of trust in the central office of Catholic Action: so why not allow him his experiment? The important thing is that the Partito Popolare did not come into being with investiture from on high or at the Holy See's instigation, as a Trojan horse to undermine Italian political life from within. It could develop at its own risk without hindrance but also without any special approval from the Vatican, and the only condition imposed on it, once it was formed, was that it should not define itself as Catholic, so as not to involve the Holy See in any way in its internal affairs and decisions.

The End of Anti-Modernism

A Pope of peace in a world at war, and of conciliation between Church and States, Benedict xv was also from first to last throughout his pontificate a peacemaker among his own spiritual sons. They, as we have seen, had become involved in a violent dispute among themselves over the anti-Modernist measures of Pius x. This strife, which had exacted many victims, had now been going on for seven years. Such a situation could not continue, and the electing cardinals, several of whom had suffered from it themselves, had openly asked the new Pope to put an end to it. Benedict xv was himself anxious to do so, and he took prompt action with the issue of his first encyclical, *Ad Beatissimi Apostolorun Principis*.

It was naturally not to be expected that he should repudiate his own predecessor's standpoint about the alleged errors of Modernism: to do so would have created even worse ideological chaos than Pius x's denunciations had produced. He therefore recapitulated the condemnation of Modernism and the measures taken to make it effective, even adopting some of the hard terms used of Modernism in *Pascendi* ('daring innovations', 'monstrous errors', and so on). After saying that Pius x had rightly defined it as 'the synthesis of all the heresies', he went on:

We hereby renew that condemnation in all its fulness, Venerable Brethren. And as the plague is not yet entirely stamped out, but lurks here and there in hidden places, We exhort all to be carefully on their guard against any danger of contagion. We desire that Catholics should shrink not only from the errors of the Modernists but also from their tendencies and from what is called the spirit of Modernism. Those who are infected by that spirit develop a keen dislike of all that savours of antiquity, and become eager searchers after novelties in everything, in the manner of speaking of divine matters, in the celebration of the sacred rite, in Catholic institutions, and even in private exercises of piety.

Benedict xv followed up this condemnation of Modernism (regarded, however, as a 'trend' rather than a 'system') by another stronger and more detailed condemnation of the anti-Modernist crusaders:

Let no private person, by the publication of books or newspapers or in public speeches, comport himself as a teacher in the Church. Let all know to whom God has entrusted the office of the Church's teacher, and leave the field free for him so that he may speak as and when he thinks fit . . . With regard to those things about which – where the Holy See has not pronounced its own judgement – it is possible in due faith and discipline to discuss the pros and cons, it is certainly permitted to everyone to give and maintain his own opinion. But in such discussions let everyone refrain from excess in speech, which may cause grave offence against charity; let everyone freely defend his own opinion, but with courtesy, and let him not accuse others of suspect faith or lack of discipline for the simple reason that they hold different views from his own.

We also wish our sons to refrain from those appellations which have recently begun to be used to distinguish Catholics from Catholics; and let them avoid them not only as *profane innovations of speech*, which correspond neither to truth nor to justice, but also because neither the more nor the less is admissible . . .; faith is either professed wholly or not at all. There is therefore no need to add epithets to the profession of Catholicism; it is enough for each one to say 'Christian is my name and Catholic my family name'; but let all who call themselves so, be so in very truth.

These last remarks obviously referred to the term 'integral' employed by Mgr Benigni, the Scotton brothers, and others who took part in their incredible crusades. It therefore seems strange that Benedict xv should not at once have decided to suppress the *Sodalitium Pianum* but waited to do so until 1921, when certain documents of the organization were published which had been found in the house of one of its secret agents and sequestrated by the German army in Ghent in 1914. But the extraordinary fact is that neither Benedict xv nor his Secretary of State Gasparri was aware of the survival of the *Sodalitium,* which they believed to have been dissolved, as in fact it was, provisionally, by a shrewd decision of Benigni's, on 22 August 1914, immediately after the death of Pius x. Cardinal Sbarretti, Prefect of the Sacred Congregation of the Council, under whose control the organization was supposed to be, was at once charged by Gasparri to take the necessary measures. Asked by him to explain his actions, Mgr Benigni drew up a memorandum on the origins and activities of the *Sodalitium,* concluding by saying that he was ready to dissolve it anew (it had been reconstituted with Cardinal De Lai's approval in the summer of 1915) if that was the wish of the Holy See. This gratuitous offer was evidently designed to enlist the Cardinal's sympathies, but Sbarretti took it at the foot of the letter, thus putting an end to the recognized activity of the *Sodalitium,* which thereafter reorganized itself on a completely clandestine basis to continue its own battles regardless of the Pope's objections.

But if Benigni's *Sodalitium* managed to survive, the encyclical *Ad Beatissimi* dealt a mortal blow to all the anti-Modernist activities of the other groups and exponents of integralism, including their press organs. In this it was helped by the war, which caused Italy, like other countries, to sink its internal disputes in resistance to the common enemy. Letters exchanged between some of the Modernists mention a number of instances of the Pope's moderation and wish to introduce a 'thaw' in the Modernist dispute, the most important being the fusion of the Congregation of the Index with that of the Holy Office. Clearly, Benedict xv found two inquisitorial Congregations too many for the twentieth century.

That did not mean that the Holy Office's activities were completely suspended during the seven and a half years of his pontificate, especially since at its head was Cardinal Merry del Val; but the Supreme Inquisition only rarely exercised censorship and in all those years put only ten works on the Index. Apart from Vigouroux's Biblical Manual, Funk's *Von der Kirche des Geistens,* and another work on the Church by Macaire, all the rest were by Italian authors, among them Salvatorelli, Gallarati Scotti (his *Life of Fogazzaro*), and Ernesto Buonaiuti. Buonaiuti, the most prominent representative of Modernism among the Italian clergy, was also excommunicated in January 1921 and suspended from ecclesiastical office 'with the approval of the Holy Father', but this was because he had published an article in which he went so far as to deny the dogma of the real presence of Christ in the Eucharist.

Buonaiuti had already been suspended once, in the spring of 1916, together with three other priests who collaborated with him on the *Rivista bimestrale di scienze delle religioni,* as usual 'with no previous warning and no contesting of presumed errors'. But times had changed, as was shown by the fact that when Buonaiuti queried the matter with the Cardinal Vicar of Rome, Pompilj, the latter, aware of the strained relations between the Secretary of State and the Holy Office, sent Buonaiuti straight to Cardinal Gasparri. Gasparri, with his famous legal flair, suggested an interpretation of the anti-Modernist oath that completely satisfied the four priests, and he and Buonaiuti became firm friends. Gasparri had been a colleague of that other Modernist, Loisy, when he was teaching at the Catholic Institute in Paris, but in their frequent weekly meetings it was certainly politics rather than theology or historical criticism that he and Buonaiuti dis-

cussed. Surprising as this friendship between the Secretary of
State and the Modernist priest may seem, even more astonishing
is the fact that it never faltered despite the periodical condemnations of Buonaiuti's works. The explanation probably lies in the
Cardinal's scheme for making Buonaiuti head of the Vatican
Press Office, possibly with the idea of distracting him from his
researches on the history of Christianity. Be that as it may, no
surer proof than this friendship, based on mutual esteem, could
be found of the atmosphere of clemency carried to the extremes
of tolerance that was typical of Benedict xv's pontificate.

Fabulous Charity

Benedict xv's clemency arose not from agnosticism or scepticism,
still less from weakness, but from a genuine magnanimity. His
horror of ideological coercion was equalled only by his horror of
physical violence. The Italian diplomatist and future Foreign
Minister, Carlo Sforza, described him as 'ironical, reserved,
distant, not . . . made for easy friendships', adding that the particularly striking thing about him was the 'complete absence of
unction': which is perfectly true with regard to his conduct as an
official in diplomatic and political affairs, but anything but true
of his personality as pontiff. His frankness and simplicity certainly deprived his gestures and words of any of that redundance
or unctuous insistence typical of so many ecclesiastics, but that
in no way detracted from his innate piety or his manner of
bearing as pontiff. The witty irony and calculated reserve of the
diplomat vanished at once when he left such spheres to be once
more the sovereign living in human relationship among his subordinates, from the lowest to the highest.

One of his most frequent and sympathetic exclamations was
'*Che bambino!*' – 'What a child!' – and he would use it as readily
of his Secretary of State as of a simple priest or a coachman. He
showed the same cordiality to his servants every day, not merely
on the special anniversaries when he would invite them all to
lunch and each one would find beside his cup of chocolate an
envelope containing a generous gift. When he became Pope, his
two men-servants, cook, scullion, and chauffeur from Bologna
at once set off in their archbishop's car and arrived in the Vatican;
and that same day they were all given the purple livery of the

'*scopatori segreti*', the Pope's personal servants, or the red livery of the '*sediari*', the sedan-bearers. The only one not quite so easy to place was the scullion, who was hunch-backed, but not even he was sent back to Bologna; every effort was made to find him a suitable job, and finally he was installed as porter at the hospice of St Martha. Benedict showed the same consideration towards his servants' families. One day after he had received in audience a servant's mother, whose name was Regina, he went with her to the door of his apartment, saying: 'When the Pope receives queens (*regine*) he always accompanies them as far as this.'

His friendly conversation often included jokes, occasionally against himself. One day, for instance, when receiving the teachers and pupils of the pontifical 'Schola Cantorum', he said: 'Nobody can appreciate your courses better than I; if there'd been something of the sort when I was a novice, I shouldn't sing out of tune as I do now.' Leo XIII would never have permitted himself to say anything like that. Benedict XV differed from him not only in this but also, and much more, in his generosity. Leo, great and magnanimous though he was in all else, was not so where money was concerned. The critical state of the pontifical treasury in his day forbade it – a situation due at least in part to unfortunate speculations by financiers he had trusted. Benedict XV was certainly, by comparison, not much better off, for especially in the early days of his pontificate the war seriously affected the channels through which that vital international source of income, 'Peter's Pence', flowed to Rome. But it made little difference to him whether he had more or less, for he would distribute it in any case with the greatest ease.

A psychologist might say that Benedict XV's generosity was at least in part a reaction against his family's not particularly prosperous financial situation. That may be so. In Genoa the Della Chiesas lived in a rented apartment in the Palazzo Magliavacchi, an ostentatious bourgeois five-storeyed building with a massive tympanum over the entrance-door which later contained an inscription commemorating the birthplace of the future Pope. The family house was in the nearby village of Pegli, and it too was modest despite its severely majestic interior; outwardly with its stunted turrets and painted façade it differed little from its neighbours. And the family income cannot have been large if the future

Pope's expenses at the Academy for Ecclesiastical Nobles had to be covered by a cousin, Giacomo Durazzo Pallavicino.

His biographers speak of Della Chiesa's fantastic, indeed almost eccentric, generosity right from the time when he was Rampolla's secretary in Madrid. There they called him '*el cura de las dos pesetas*' (the two-pesetas priest) for that was what he used to give poor beggars instead of the usual few centimes. It was just the same during his seven years as Archbishop in Bologna, and this generosity seems to have been a constant characteristic throughout his life.

It corresponded to his conception of the aristocracy and nobility. Far from having a progressive social conscience, Pope Benedict, within the framework of gospel teaching, believed the upper classes should fulfil two basic functions: to give the lower orders a consistent example of Christian practice, and to assist them with the most generous charity. In his New Year speech of 1921 to the Roman nobility he laid stress on their duties of leadership in Catholic Action – a surprising attitude to take then, for by that time the majority of the organization's leaders were of the middle class, and Catholic Action itself was ceasing to be an affair of the élite and becoming increasingly an organization for the masses.

But Benedict xv was an aristocrat by choice as well as by blood. One had only to look at him to know this: his manner and bearing made people forget his physical defects even before they came under the spell of his intellectual qualities. But nothing showed the aristocrat in him more than his generosity. He enjoyed lavish giving like a *grand seigneur* or even a king; and as Pope his generosity took on fabulous forms. It would however be a mistake to think that natural explanations accounted wholly for his munificence, for its real reasons were supernatural and religious. A rich man or a sovereign is normally generous out of vanity or desire for popularity and fame, and so his gifts are apt to be ostentatious and receive much publicity. Benedict xv, instead, was generous both in public and in private, and private giving was what he preferred.

True, people used to be puzzled by some of his ways, as for instance when, standing among his servants, he would take a gold piece from his pocket and show it to them, amusing himself by watching their reactions, and then throw it in the air to see who rushed first to pick it up. But it was done with affability rather than malice. He enjoyed combining a gift with a joke, as when one day he went up to a group of workmen attached to the Sacred Palaces and asked one of them where he lived. When the man answered timidly, 'A long way off,' pretending not to know the answer he asked him if he went home on foot or on horseback. 'On foot, Your Holiness,' the man replied in amazement, 'I can't afford a horse!' 'Well, tonight you shall have a horse,' countered the Pope smiling, slipping into his hand a bright gold piece with the mounted figure of St George.

Private acts of charity gave him the greatest pleasure, and thus the most remarkable revelations about it came from his chamberlain, later Master of the Chamber, Mgr Arborio Mella di Sant'Elia, whose duty it was to administer his personal beneficences. 'One morning,' Mella recounts in his memoirs, 'I found him sitting at his desk taking out some thousand-lire notes and murmuring the while, "Poor thing, poor thing!"' Benedict xv had just had a letter from a poor servant who could not keep her child with her in the house where she worked and so asked the Pope for help to send it to a relative. The Pope was so touched that he at once decided to send her the money himself without passing on the request to his secretaries; he put the notes in an envelope and wrote the address and stamped it with his own hand. The poor woman's amazement when she opened this pontifical communication can easily be imagined. Fifteen or twenty thousand lire was a fortune in those days, and the servant's astonishment was equalled only by that of her master, a marquis, who was sure there must be some mistake and himself went to the Vatican to give the money back. He could not believe his ears when the Pope told him there was no mistake at all – he had sent the gift himself.

Donations out of all proportion to what was asked were the normal thing with Benedict xv. He once interested himself, for example, in three children afflicted with a skin disease; he not only sent them to a hospital until they were cured but also gave two hundred thousand lire for a clinic to be built to enlarge the existing institution. The legend of the Pope's fabulous charities soon spread, and naturally some tried to profit by it. A Roman seamstress once made a bet with her friends that she would manage to get as much as fifty or a hundred lire from the Pope by writing him a letter describing in excessively moving terms her family's terrible state of poverty. She won her bet easily, but what she had not foreseen was the huge sum that arrived – not fifty or one hundred, but twenty thousand lire. She was covered with shame and remorse: by her lies, she felt, she had not only deceived the Pope, but positively robbed him. She wrote to him again and confessed. The answer was that the Pope's charity could not be given back: she should herself distribute the money to others in the best way she could think of.

In addition to these private acts of charity there were all the donations that Benedict xv made no less generously to religious organizations. It can easily be imagined what alarm and criticism this fabulous munificence caused in the Vatican. 'They say,' the Pope confided one day to Filippo Crispolti, 'that I am ruining the Holy See's property. Except for the part of the patrimony I found there, I believe that what comes into my coffer should punctually go out again. The Lord will provide: that is His task.' But the story of ruining the Holy See's property was not just a rumour: it was sober truth. On the last day before the Pope took to his bed to die, Mgr Mella presented him with a petition from a forty-year-old priest who was blind, poor, and paralytic. Mella expected a large donation for him, but for the first time in his life he was disappointed. Raising his hands helplessly, Benedict xv confessed, 'We have not the money.' In fact, when he died there was not even enough in the Vatican coffers to cover the expenses of the Conclave, and Gasparri, the Treasurer, had to provide a loan.[1]

In considering objectively Benedict xv's conduct in this connection, it must be borne in mind that the years of his pontificate coincided with the war and its troubled aftermath. The calls on him went far beyond the mere distribution of charity, impressive though this was. The various forms of aid he devised or approved and encouraged were so complex as to defy description: the list of them in Vistalli's biography occupies fifty pages. Suffice it to say that all that Pius xii did later, during and after the Second World War, was only a pale replica of it. And certainly the charitable activity of Benedict xv was one of the reasons that drew the gratitude of nations to him, despite the campaign of

[1] See note in Bibliography, p. 373.

denigration representing such acts as prompted by political rather than religious motives. Perhaps the most convincing testimony to popular admiration for his charity was Turkey's decision, made in his lifetime, in 1919, to erect a monument to him on the Bosphorus in the name of the whole Orient. In particular, mention must be made of his actions on behalf of Russia, then in the throes of a terrible famine: not only did he send generous aid but he also, on 5 August 1921, issued an appeal to the whole world and sent an official mission which remained there two years distributing aid and supplies.

The Fascination of the East

The horizons of Benedict xv's apostolic zeal extended even further than those of his material charity. Benedict undoubtedly possessed all the characteristics of a meticulous and painstaking administrator. He had an extraordinarily detailed knowledge of every question as well as a remarkable memory. He would astonish people long afterwards by his accurate recollection of situations and people. Many who were impressed by these administrative qualities, however, misjudged his true capabilities, believing that they went no further than a minute and clear-headed attention to detail. In point of fact, his pontificate marked a return to the wide horizons, both political and religious, but more especially religious, of the days of Leo xiii; and, in particular, to concern for the Eastern Orthodox Church and for missionary activity.

Under Pius x these subjects had vanished behind a misty curtain. Relations with Russia had deteriorated because of the Tsar's anti-Catholic policy in Poland; while missionary activity had become confined to a bureaucratic routine. The war created great difficulties for missionary work, especially for German missions and because of the near-impossibility of sending missionaries and funds to the various continents; but at the same time it opened up unhoped-for possibilities with regard to Russia and the countries hitherto within its sphere of influence. The provisional Government, set up in Russia after the overthrow of the Tsarist régime, during its brief period of rule from February to October 1917 seemed to justify great hopes for a relaunching of Catholicism in those peripheral regions. Under the Tsars, the five Catholic ecclesiastical districts surviving in Russia between the Balkans and the Ukraine – which together had seven bishops, some nine hundred priests, and over six hundred parishes, with a total of six million believers – were the object of a suspicious tolerance: they were allowed to survive but they were forbidden to proselytize and could not communicate with each other or with the Holy See except through State-controlled organs. The Catholic episcopate explained its desiderata in a memorandum to the new Government, but while it awaited an answer Benedict xv in Rome was preparing the Church for the long-hoped-for reconquest of the East.

The year 1917 was important not only for the Pope's famous Note of 1 August to Heads of States at war but, even more, for the establishment in autonomous form of the Sacred Congregation for the Eastern Church (founded by Pius ix in 1862 but since then always a subordinate part of the Congregation for the Propagation of the Faith) and the foundation of the Pontifical Institute for Oriental Studies which, as a daring innovation, was also open to Orthodox students. These two events took place at Benedict xv's instigation on, respectively, 1 May and 15 October 1917, and thus with remarkable sense of timing. But in October the provisional Government in Russia was replaced by a Communist Government which made no attempt to conceal its atheist ideology and anti-religious programme. So explicit was it, indeed, that the first act of the Patriarch Tychon on election by the Orthodox Church Council was to pronounce an anathema upon the new rulers. This gesture was courageous but it was also unwise; for four days later, on 26 January 1918, they answered with the notorious decree 'on the separation of Church from State and of education from the Church' in accordance with which the various Churches were deprived of all educational or social influence and reduced to the status of mere cultural communities bereft even of those rights which the law conceded to professional and cultural organizations. They thus lost the right to possess property of any kind, landed or otherwise, including even the objects necessary for their church services.

For the Russian Catholics this meant the collapse of all their hopes, but for the Holy See it meant only a delay. As to the Catholics in the Baltic States, Poland, and the Ukraine, everything depended on the outcome of the war and its local after-effects. In

1918 Benedict xv sent Mgr Achille Ratti, destined to be his successor as Pope, to Warsaw as Apostolic Delegate for Poland, Lithuania, and Russia itself; and in 1920 he appointed Padre Genocchi in a similar capacity to the Ukraine. Ratti managed to reach the Baltic States, but neither he nor Genocchi ever managed to get into Russia or the Ukraine. But as long as Bolshevik Russia maintained its isolation from the rest of Western Europe the Holy See could continue to hope. For the Soviet Union, anxious to obtain some sort of recognition from the Powers it banned, strove to secure it even from the Vatican; it therefore left the door open for possible meetings and negotiations, and Benedict xv profited by this to organize the charitable mission already mentioned (the Pizzardo-Vorovsky conversations), and later to set on foot the diplomatic *démarches* which eventually took place soon after his death, at the Genoa conference of 1922.

The most remarkable thing in the relations between Benedict xv and the Eastern Orthodox Church is the fact that he predicted a year ahead the possibility that war might bring about a *rapprochement* between Catholicism and Orthodoxy. His apostolic constitution concerning the Eastern rite is in fact dated 22 March 1916 and it was followed on 15 April by the apostolic letter *Cum Catholica* in favour of union of the Christian peoples of the East with the Roman Church. This far-sightedness and sense of timing are certainly not the virtues of a hidebound bureaucrat; and these qualities are also discernible at different points all over the vast religious-cum-political chequer-board under his control, the various lines never crossing or interfering with each other in any way.

This has already been seen earlier in relation to the establishment of diplomatic relations and concordats with the new States emerging after the dismemberment of the Russian and Austro-Hungarian Empires, but it comes up too over that highly delicate region, the Middle East, where British influence was replacing that of France, as witness the new directives issued on 15 November 1918 concerning the Apostolic Delegations in Constantinople, Egypt, Mesopotamia, Persia, and Syria.

On the other hand, Benedict xv was traditionalist in his approach to the establishment of the Jews in Palestine. In his consistorial allocution of 13 June 1921 he said:

142 The Popes in the Twentieth Century

When the Christians by means of the Allied troops regained possession of the Holy Places, We joined with all Our heart in the general
exultation of men of good will; but Our joy was tempered by the fear
that as a result of so splendid and joyous an event the Israelites might
find themselves in a position of preponderance and privilege in
Palestine. To judge by the present situation, unhappily what We
feared has come about. It is in fact known that the position of Christians in Palestine is not only no better, but has actually worsened by
the new civil arrangements established there, which aim . . . at evicting
Christianity from the positions it hitherto occupied to replace it by
the Jews.

It would be crude to interpret this attitude, which has remained
unchanged down to the present Pontificate, as a manifestation
of anti-semitism, for its real if not sole concern is the 'defence of
the Holy Places'. In the same way, we should avoid exaggerating the,
undoubtedly negative, significance of certain unfortunate expressions used by Benedict xv in connection with Protestants in Italy,
and particularly in Rome. 'Whoever robs the faith,' he said in December 1915 to the President of the Association for the Preservation
of the Faith in Rome, 'deserves the name of thief.' In the same
speech the Protestants operating in Rome were actually defined
as 'emissaries of Satan who in the midst of the Holy City raise
temples where the true worship of God is denied, who set up
pestilential pulpits to diffuse errors among the people, who dis-
seminate with both hands lies and calumnies against the Catholic
religion and its ministers'. He also spoke of 'diabolical arts' and
an 'iniquitous assault' because 'undertaken against the centre of
the Catholic religion'. Benedict xv's views on this subject had
not altered in August 1920 when, receiving a pilgrimage of the
Knights of Columbus, he spoke of 'odious and harmful propaganda' and 'aims worthy of execration'.

As far as Protestants were concerned, Benedict xv was undoubtedly still living in the atmosphere of the Counter-Reformation and the Council of Trent; but for that very reason his
openmindedness towards the nascent ecumenical movement is
the more remarkable. That movement had emerged in response
to a common demand of many evangelical Churches at the World
Missionary Conference in Edinburgh in 1910, but by 1914 it had
only reached the point of appointing a committee under a layman, Robert Gardiner, to organize an ecumenical conference.

When, in that year, Gardiner approached, among others, Cardinal Gasparri, he received a courteous reply in which the Cardinal assured him that the Pope was praying for the success of the undertaking. The war naturally postponed further plans for the conference, but when they were revived the Protestants, not content with dispatching a written invitation to the Head of the Roman Church, sent a deputation to Rome in 1919 to invite Benedict xv personally. The Pope received the delegates cordially, though he declined the invitation on the ground of 'the teaching and practice of the Roman Catholic Church' in relation to unity. 'But His Holiness,' said the official communiqué on the visit, 'does not mean in any way to disapprove of the conference in question for those who are not united to the See of Peter; on the contrary, he seriously desires, and asks with prayer, that if the conference takes place those who participate in it may, by the Grace of God, see the light and become reunited to the visible Body of the Church, by which they will be received with open arms.' Two years later, moreover, Benedict xv approved the Malines Conversations on inter-faith problems between Lord Halifax and Cardinal Mercier.

Anti-colonial Missionary Work

The few dark patches fade when we move on to consider Benedict xv's work in the missionary sphere, where he brought about one of the greatest revolutions ever attempted by a Pope. Here, too, nothing was left to chance even when circumstances were favourable; and here too, the daring and timeliness of certain steps he took were no less striking than his long-range decisions.

The maintenance of the missions involved both defence and initiative in attack. Success in defending them was largely due to the invaluable efforts of Mgr Cerretti, the pontifical representative who put the case of the Catholic missions in the former German colonies at the Versailles conference. Benedict xv had the gift of choosing men well: foremost among his collaborators was Cardinal Gasparri, but there were also such men as Pacelli, Ratti, Genocchi, Cerretti, Pizzardo, Roncalli, and others. Some of them had not even graduated in the *carriera* of diplomacy, for Ratti was originally a librarian, and Genocchi a missionary and inspired promoter of religious and cultural works. Cerretti, whom we have already met in his discussion with Orlando for the basis of the future Conciliation between the Holy See and Italy, was in contact with the Allied plenipotentiaries, and especially with Balfour, and secured the recognition, under Article 448 of the Peace Treaty, of the Church's rights in relation to the missions.

More unexpected, and much more daring, was Benedict xv's attempt to withdraw the missions in China from French protectorate. As far back as 1846 France had secured an edict of tolerance for Catholic missions from the Chinese Empire, thus initiating a form of protectorate which Rome had never asked for, but which the majority of the missionaries, especially the institutes and bishops, had all too readily come to appreciate – not realizing that in this way they became, in the eyes of their converts, privileged clients of a Western foreign Power. In 1858 another treaty concluded between Britain and France and the Chinese Emperor not only gave the missionaries the protection of extra-territoriality and secured for their churches a considerable part of the indemnities exacted from China but also established that 'the members of all Christian communities' should 'enjoy complete security of person and property and in the free profession of their worship'. This, in the words of the historian Latourette,[1] 'tended to remove Chinese Christians from the jurisdiction of their government and to make of Christian communities *imperia in imperio*, widely scattered enclaves under the defence of aliens'. As K. M. Pannikar commented,[2] 'To have believed that a religion which grew up under the protection of foreign Powers, especially under humiliating conditions following defeat, would be tolerated when the nation recovered its authority shows extreme shortsightedness.'

Leo xiii was far from short-sighted. In 1886 he made approaches to the Chinese Government with a view to establishing direct official relations with China; but violent opposition from France caused him to desist for the time being. During the First World War Benedict xv judged the moment opportune to revive these efforts. In July 1918 the Peking press suddenly announced that following negotiations China and the Vatican were about to exchange representatives: a Nuncio had in fact already been

---

[1] Kenneth Scott Latourette, *A History of Christian Missions in China* (1929), p. 279.
[2] K. M. Pannikar, *Asia and Western Dominance* (1953), p. 425.

appointed to Peking and a Chinese Minister Plenipotentiary to the Vatican. But France again reacted strongly, accusing the Holy See of playing into the hands of the Central Powers. Unable to exert direct pressure on Rome, with whom she had broken off diplomatic relations, she intervened instead with the Chinese Government, sending Peking a threatening Note signed also by the other Allies, and this time Peking capitulated.

But Benedict xv did not give in. On 22 July 1919 he appointed the Bishop of Canton to be Apostolic Visitor to China, with the task of carrying out an inquiry into the state of the Church there; and without waiting for its results he published, on 30 November, his great missionary encyclical *Maximum illud*, still today the charter of the Catholic missionary movement of modern times. The significance of this pontifical document was so obvious that a veritable insurrection took place against it in China, and every effort was made to prevent its being put into effect. But Benedict xv was by now resolved to carry the matter through, and although the appointment of the first pontifical representative to Peking came only under his successor (in September 1922), Pius xi was merely reaping the fruits of Benedict's initiative.

Missionary organization under Benedict xv was largely carried out from the centre, through the new powers given to the three great organizations, those of the Propagation of the Faith, the Holy Child, and St Peter the Apostle for Native Clergy; and a new body, the Missionary Union of Clergy, was also created. These great international organizations both spread the missionary ideal at all levels and provided financial support for the missions.

In the mission lands themselves, the revolution was carried out in accordance with the three fundamental principles put forward in *Maximum illud*: promotion of native clergy, renunciation by missionaries of all spirit of nationalism, and recognition of the objective importance of the mission lands' own civilization (this last idea, being still in its infancy, was less strongly emphasized than the others). Today, twenty years after the onset of the end of colonialism, these principles do not strike us as sensational. But to realize their revolutionary character, we have only to read the life of one of the greatest missionaries of the 1900s, Père Vincent Lebbe,[1] a Belgian, one of those pioneers of anti-colonial-

[1] Jacques Leclercq, *Vie de père Lebbe*, Tournai-Paris, 1955.

ism who by his work and contacts helped to provide the impetus for Benedict xv's great encyclical.

When he came to China in the spring of 1901, just after the Boxer rebellion, Lebbe was not even a priest. The superior who came to meet him in Tientsin was scandalized to find him carrying his own bag: 'A missionary,' he told him, 'does not carry his bags.' In the refectory he found European and Chinese priests sitting at separate tables, and only white clergy at the high table. He very soon realized that the missionaries nearly always spoke French: few of them knew Chinese well, and some could not even read it. The native seminarists' courses were of a superficial nature, 'to keep them in humility' – they were destined for purely subordinate duties. Servants were often beaten, 'the only language they understand'. In missionary work, a European missionary was never sent, even in cases of need, to help a Chinese priest. The faithful were never allowed to sit in a missionary's presence, and had to greet him kneeling on both knees. Persons under instruction were rewarded for attendance at courses on religion either by a gift of maize or with money, which meant that, whether intentionally or not, conversions were virtually paid for. Quite a number of Chinese would travel from one mission to another getting themselves baptized so as to enjoy these benefits; many others gave way before their neighbours' criticism and reverted to paganism after being baptized.

These first impressions multiplied in the succeeding years, and Père Lebbe became convinced of the need for radical change if the missions were not to collapse at the first touch of persecution. He said then:

Chinese Christians have the right, indeed the duty, to be patriots just as much as Christians in Europe and America . . . what is a virtue for European Christians should be a virtue for Christians in China too; and why should a source of pride for European clergy be a blemish for the clergy here . . . ? The impression left on me by my seventeen years' apostolate . . . is that the fundamental obstacle – I do not say the only one – to the coming of the Kingdom of God among these people is the *national question*, and that, humanly speaking, barring a miracle the barrier that separates them from the Church is insuperable for them and can only be broken down by us . . . The protectorate is an obstacle to the entry of the élite into the bosom of the Church . . . If the Church in China were to have to suffer persecutions like those in

France or Mexico or England under Elizabeth, it would be taking a poor view of our Christians to expect them to prefer the protection of a foreign flag to keep them safe. All the élite would prefer persecution, and they would easily carry the masses with them.

Maximum illud gave an authoritative interpretation to this and other similar appeals, thus marking a new turning-point in the history of missions. The following passage of the encyclical obviously has China in mind:

It is to be deplored that there are regions in which the Catholic faith has been introduced for centuries, without any indigenous clergy being as yet to be found there, except of a lower class; and that there are certain nations which have attained a degree of civilization, such as to possess men excelling in all the varieties of the civil arts, which yet, after many centuries of the influence of the gospel and the Church, can show no bishops to govern or priests to teach their own countrymen. This shows that there is something wanting and defective in the method up to now employed for the education of clergy for the missions.

Later the encyclical touched on the subject of a nationalistic spirit among missionaries:

It would be deplorable if any missionaries should be so forgetful of their own dignity that they should think rather of their earthly country than of the heavenly, being unduly desirous to widen its influence and to extend its name and fame. This would be one of the saddest calamities for the Apostolate, which would paralyse the missionary's zeal for souls and weaken his authority among the indigenous people ... His work will become suspect to the population, who may easily be led to conclude that the Christian religion is the religion peculiar to some particular nation, and that anyone who embraces it makes himself dependent on a foreign State, thus renouncing his own nationality. We have been greatly grieved by certain missionary periodicals which have appeared in the last few years, in which, coupled with the desire for the increase of God's Kingdom, there is also apparent the desire to enlarge the influence of the writer's own country ...

It was on the basis of Benedict xv's three revolutionary principles that Pius xi guided the missions towards greater autonomy within the various countries, speeding up the process by promoting some indigenous priests to the episcopate. On 28 October

1926 the first six Chinese bishops were consecrated by him in St Peter's; but as early as 1920 Cardinal Van Rossum, Prefect of the Propaganda Fide, had asked Père Lebbe, whom Cardinal Mercier had introduced to him, for a list of possible candidates. The little Belgian missionary wrote the names down there and then with a pencil which he always kept afterwards as a memento. In the summer of 1922 the first priest on his list became secretary of the first Apostolic Delegate in China, Mgr Celso Costantini; and four years later he headed the list of the six new Chinese bishops.

An Unfinished Destiny

Those who knew Benedict xv well at the time of his sudden death said that he was full of great ideas and plans. The prospects opening up for the apostolate in the Orthodox world, in the Islamic world of the Middle East, and in the wider missionary field afford convincing proof of this. But his tremendous activity was of course not confined to these spheres. It has already been said that he was not an intellectual either by nature or by vocation. His natural bent was for practical, concrete work to a definite end; abstract, universal ideas, metaphysical problems, or abstruse ideological debates held little interest for him. Yet even his initiatives in the cultural field show an astonishing modernity and breadth of view. It was through a decision of his, for example, of as early as 4 November 1915, that the department of the Consistorial Congregation concerned with seminaries was united with the Congregation of Studies in charge of the Catholic universities, with a view to establishing the new Congregation of Seminaries and Universities that became, and still is, the Ministry of Education of the Catholic Church. How important he considered this new unified department is shown by the fact that he made Cardinal Mercier its first Prefect – a prestige appointment that was inevitably largely symbolical at that time, for the Primate of Belgium could clearly not leave his country in the middle of the war. It was also under the pontificate of Benedict xv and with his encouragement or approval that the Academy of St Thomas Aquinas, for the study of Thomist philosophy, was modernized, the Catholic University of the Sacred Heart in Milan was founded, and the Higher Institutes of Religious Study for Laymen were established at the Gregorian and Catholic Universities.

So it is not to be wondered at that, absorbed as he was in plans for the future, possessing an iron constitution and only sixty-seven years old, he never remotely foresaw his approaching end. He, who had found his election the most natural thing, welcoming it without the slightest qualm, and who had always loved his job of being Pope, gazed with alarm and incredulity at this death which came to cast confusion into the midst of his work, so full of promise and but half done. The way of its happening was almost unbelievably banal. He had promised to go, on 21 November 1921, to celebrate Mass in the chapel of the Sisters of St Martha, on the far side of St Peter's from his apartment. An early hour had been fixed – five o'clock in the morning; but the Pope arrived a few minutes too soon and waited outside the door of the Chapel of the Holy Sacrament leading into the Basilica. The verger with the keys arrived only at the last moment, but those few minutes of waiting in a draughty passage were to prove fatal. He had only once in his whole life gone into a chemist's to buy a box of cough lozenges. But by an irony of fate the cold he caught that morning, and needless to say neglected, turned into a bronchitic infection which two months later suddenly worsened and brought the end.

It all happened with a rush in the few days between 18 and 22 January. Pope Benedict submitted to the ritual ceremonies, but with no conviction. He kept on insistently asking his closest friends and relatives if it was really true that people were praying for him in the churches of Rome. Right up to the last evening they had to prevent him from getting up and going to work at his desk. Perhaps only in the last moments he became resigned, understanding that God had wished to mock even him, confounding his ingenuous hopes and too facile calculations.

His end, wrote the Paris *Temps*, was suffused with that shadow of melancholy associated with unfinished destinies. But the saddest part is that the shadow of melancholy soon dissolved before the resounding pontificates of Pius XI and Pius XII, whereas the quiet, unspectacular reign of Benedict XV was relegated to the archives. Taking it all in all, one might be tempted to conclude that Della Chiesa was born too late (in Pius X's place, he would have avoided the Church's isolation from the lay world and the absurd anti-

Modernist crusade) and died too soon (without being able to spare Catholicism and the world the degrading compromises with totalitarianism that came about under his successor). But hypotheses after the event do not make history. And, in any case, even unfinished destinies can be fruitful – quite apart from the fact that they often avoid ending in anti-climax. If today men's minds are beginning to turn once again towards what till recently was the most disregarded pontificate of the century, that is because only now, after the revolution under Pope John, can they form a true estimate of its originality and importance, and in particular of its courageous advance in the diplomatic and temporal spheres and its disinterested and deeply evangelical preaching of peace. With regard to the temporal or 'Roman' question, it is, indeed, difficult to say whether the idea of a 'concordatory separation', which revived under Benedict xv, would have later on protected his pontificate from the excesses into which those of his immediate successors fell; whereas it is beyond doubt that Pope Benedict xv's message of pacifism suffered only a temporary eclipse from totalitarian warmongering. It took the horrors of the Second World War, and the inadequate conduct of Pius xii in relation to them, to cause that message to be revalued at its true worth. If, in fact, any pontificate foreshadowed and prepared the way for the miracle of John xxiii, the robust and genial Bergamasque peasant, it is that of the frail, reserved Genoese aristocrat, Giacomo Della Chiesa.

Pius XI: Achille Ratti

6 February 1922 – 10 February 1939

The 1922 Conclave: Excommunication and a Surprise Candidate

Benedict XV's pontificate was cut short less than four years after the end of the First World War and only two years after the signature of the peace treaties. Those treaties themselves raised a whole series of new problems; the victors in the war were restless and half-disillusioned, the vanquished in the throes of serious economic difficulties; in Eastern Europe, the new States, from Finland to the Balkans, were still uncertain about their future; while the Bolshevik revolution spread a question mark over the whole vast territory of the ex-Tsarist empire. Thus the sudden ending of Benedict XV's pontificate brought not only grief for the death of such a Pope but also serious anxieties within the Holy See as to the future. But it was not till years later, after the experience of the involution brought about by his successor, that the extent of the catastrophe now beginning was fully realized. And if theologizing about history were anything but a form of pointless apologetics, at once ingenuous and presumptuous, one might be tempted to say that rarely in modern times has history been confronted by a more difficult and insuperable obstacle than the pontificate of Pius XI. Yet the new Pope was undoubtedly more richly endowed with gifts, of a personality more complex and impressive, than either his two predecessors or his successor.

History itself, indeed, inured though it is to threading its way among the mysteries of individual and collective psychologies, stands in doubt before the third pontificate of our present century. To begin with, there is the primary enigma of the choice of the man himself. Once a Pope is elected, dozens of prophets who had foretold it invariably emerge, even though only an hour before the odds may have been quite uncertain. Sometimes, for one reason or another, it is fairly easy to make a safe guess. But this was certainly not the case in 1922. Even the cardinals who shut themselves up in conclave on 2 February had far from clear ideas on the subject; the more so since they were anything but clear as to their general estimate of the pontificate just abruptly ended, paralysed as it had been by the war for half its duration, and only just preparing to embark on plans for the future. Pope Benedict's actions had certainly shown remarkable wisdom and sense of timing, and he had preserved a careful balance between political and religious activities; under him the Church had gone far towards regaining international prestige. Nevertheless a good many people felt doubtful about his so-called liberalism, and about particular points such as the newly-resumed relations with France. Consequently, while some cardinals inclined towards a continuation of his gentle but firm policy, a nucleus of pertinacious supporters of Pius x's more clear-cut conservatism wished to put an end to it.

The four ballots of the first day were little more than a preliminary testing of the ground for both sides, in the course of which the two most unlikely candidates, Merry del Val and Maffi, were eliminated. To find these names turning up again is almost as if the clock had been put back seven years to the Conclave after Pius x's death. It was not till the following day that the real candidates, La Fontaine and Gasparri, came on the scene and the battle around them began.

It was, as a matter of fact, clear that neither of these two original candidates had a serious possibility of success. Under Pius x, Gasparri had won merit through his codification of the Canon Law, but he had never become reconciled to Merry del Val's policy and had, indeed, reversed it under Benedict xv. Moreover he had no real first-hand pastoral experience. La Fontaine, on the other hand, had the opposite disadvantage, lack of experience in diplomacy – a serious matter given the delicate post-war international situation. Against him, too, was his past as an inquisitor and *éminence grise* of the Curia under Pius x; while certain resemblances in their careers – La Fontaine too was Patriarch of Venice, and their pastoral activity was somewhat similar – almost suggested a reappearance of Sarto. Despite his aristocratic manner, with his intransigence in matters of doctrine and discipline, his rigidity as a canon lawyer, might he not end by reawakening the now almost quiescent anti-Modernist struggle? Lastly, the fact that he was only sixty-two weighed against him by comparison with his more mature rival Gasparri, who was seventy.

Nevertheless both sides made every effort to prevail; but to no purpose. Gasparri got as far as twenty-four votes and then stuck. La Fontaine, though a close runner-up, only once reached twenty-three. The few floating votes first given to other candidates were not enough to solve the deadlock. Both sides therefore had to abandon the field and seek a new candidate likely to command the necessary majority. It was at this point that the figure of the Archbishop of Milan, Achille Ratti, began to emerge.

Like Cardinal Della Chiesa in similar circumstances, the new candidate had worn the purple for less than a year; but unlike him, he was almost completely unknown to his foreign colleagues, having spent his whole life as a librarian up to 1918, when he went to Poland first as Apostolic Visitor and then as Nuncio. Though his present See of Milan was an important one, he had been there too short a time – only five months – to make his mark. The only point in his favour was that he had won the confidence both of Pius x, who made him Vice-Prefect and later Prefect of the Vatican Library, and of Benedict xv, to whom he owed his later rapid promotion. Thus in him the two sides could find a possible point of convergence and reconciliation, supported by the esteem he had aroused in both pontiffs.

But if Ratti's personality and suitability were an unknown quantity for his colleagues in the Sacred College, how was it that their eye fell on him rather than on, for instance, Lualdi, Archbishop of Palermo, or Mistrangelo, Archbishop of Florence? The answer is simple: it was thanks to the skilful manoeuvring of Cardinal Gasparri, who was perhaps the only one of them (except for his friend of student days and later, Lualdi) who had had a good deal to do with Ratti when he was Prefect in the Vatican Library and later during his mission in Poland, when Gasparri was his immediate superior. The two men's characters had a good deal in common in such things as their fondness for hard work and their political outlook. Gasparri had had fresh confirmation of this during the interim after Benedict xv's death, and had probably decided then to support Ratti if his own candidature should fail.

He conducted his manoeuvres to swing his supporters' votes over to Ratti so skilfully that it was only belatedly that De Lai, leader of the 'reactionary' group of nostalgics for Pius x, realized that Gasparri was the great protector of the Archbishop of Milan. Foreseeing what in fact happened, namely that if Ratti became Pope he would retain Gasparri as Secretary of State, De Lai approached Ratti with a promise of his group's votes if Ratti would agree to appoint someone else to that post. So blatant an attempt to influence a papal election automatically signified its author's excommunication. But it would seem that De Lai was not the only one to incur the extreme penalty, for Gasparri often afterwards told his friends, and even mentioned in his *Memoirs* (in the unpublished text preserved in the first section of the Secretariat of State's archives), that both Merry del Val and De Lai incurred excommunication during the Conclave of 1922.[1] In any case, the threat of scandal sufficed to overcome the obstacle of De Lai, and Ratti, who at the eighth ballot had only five votes, secured forty-two out of fifty-three at the fourteenth. Thus the Church found itself with a surprise candidate as successor to Benedict xv – a man who only three-and-a-half years earlier had been living buried among the manuscripts and *incunabula* of the Vatican Library, and had had no diplomatic or even ministerial experience.

Unclouded Childhood on Lake Como

Surprising though the outcome of the Conclave may seem, the real mystery about Ratti lies in his own personality: a personality so complex that even the man who had imagined he knew him and could dominate him, Cardinal Gasparri, was forced seven years later to admit his mistake, when he found himself summarily dismissed by his former protégé whom he had helped not only to become Pope but also to secure the most resounding success of his pontificate, the Lateran Agreements with Italy.

What manner of man was Ratti? The official biographies contain a quantity of information about him, going right back to his childhood. Indeed of the first five Popes in this century he is certainly the one, after John xxiii, about whom most is known.

[1] See note in Bibliography, p. 374.

Cardinal Tisserant even revealed not long ago[1] that his father and uncles, who were all textile workers (the father worked in the Conti mills at Desio and a number of other factories), used to remove the knots from defective pieces of fabric from the Lebanon and exchange them for selected silkworm cocoons from the local breeders.

Such marginal scraps of information, however, do not get us far towards penetrating the secret of his personality. The story of his childhood and youth is, in any case, fairly clear. It so happens that the present writer passed a good deal of his own young days in the same district where Achille Ratti used to spend his holidays as a boy – in the Upper Brianza, a picturesque triangular peninsula separating the two lower branches of Lake Como. There, at Pieve di Asso, an uncle of his, Don Damiano Ratti, was rector – one of those clergymen who, being regarded as a good deal superior to their particular job, have the habit of winning the confidence both of people in the lay world and of their own superiors. His church, celebrated for its magnificent altar of carved wood painted in black and gold, still stands there today, as it always did, with the quiet little piazza beyond and the avenue of great plane-trees leading to the cemetery. And at the nearby rectory a frequent visitor, coming from Count de Herra's house at Visino, was no less a person than the Archbishop of Milan, Mgr Nazzari dei Conti di Calabiana. Significantly, this venerable prelate used to call the boy Achille his 'little old man': even in childhood, evidently, he must have shown something of that pensiveness and reserve characteristic of him throughout his life.

That hilly triangle of country, the scene of Manzoni's *I Promessi Sposi*, with at its base the magical Lake of Pusiano immortalized in Segantini's pictures, and to the east, towards Lecco, the jagged mass of Monte Resegone and the peak of Monte Grigna, soon became both the training-ground for Ratti the future mountaineer and the ideal refuge for his studies and meditations. At the *liceo*, his lessons with Luigi Mercalli (for whose book *Geologia d'Italia* only a few years later he wrote a long chapter on historic earthquakes in Italy) aroused his enthusiasm for natural sciences. Thus the sights he saw around him during his holidays not only afforded him aesthetic and romantic delight but were also an invitation to investigation and discovery. Natural sciences

[1] In a speech in Rome, 17 June 1964, reported in *L'Osservatore Romano*, 19 June 1964.

were not his only interest, for he was good all round, both in mathematics and in literary subjects. And, as sometimes happens, though not often, this variety of intellectual interests in his case co-existed perfectly naturally side by side with a vocation for the priesthood. For right from the very beginning, both at the elementary school under Don Giuseppe Volonteri and in the seminary, and above all with his uncle the priest, he breathed a liberal atmosphere of spontaneous harmony between knowledge and belief.

This atmosphere, however, surviving relic of a homogeneous society destined soon to be superseded by a more composite, contradictory, and restless, if more vital, social set-up, was already invaded by hostile forces, a fact which the young Ratti began to realize even at the *liceo* and later on in the seminary. Things were not all peaceful in the ecclesiastical world around him: for the diocese and particularly its cultural centres, the seminaries, were divided into two camps at loggerheads with each other, the one seemingly more democratic and violent, the other more aristocratic and reserved.

The first camp was that of the intransigents or anti-liberals, whose programme combined defence of the temporal rights of the Holy See against oppression by the Italian State with the ideological intolerance of the *Syllabus*. They regarded as betrayal and apostasy any sign of leniency towards the State or the secular ideals of the contemporary world. The higher the station and repute of such 'traitors' the more drastic was the reaction against them. Thus these intransigents openly opposed the Archbishop, who, as a Senator of the Kingdom, had voted in Turin in 1861 for Rome as the capital of Italy and during the first Vatican Council had sided with the minority against papal infallibility, thereby forfeiting for good the cardinal's hat, a traditional appanage of his see for the past four centuries. They even attacked, during his lifetime and after, Alessandro Manzoni, the greatest glory of Milanese Catholicism.

Their head was a priest from Pavia, Don Davide Albertario, who had come to Milan to edit the *Osservatore Cattolico* and had quickly become one of the most despotic leading churchmen of the Lombard capital. A fiery and vehement orator, he was even more vivid and effective as a journalist. His immense physique gave the impression of a tremendous and uncontrollable natural force. His passion for action led him to embark on innumerable enterprises which he carried through with truly remarkable skill and ability for intrigue. Strife and dispute were his natural milieu, into which he threw himself so violently and indiscriminately that it was difficult to say which was the stronger, the ideals he fought for or his own love of a fight. It was rumoured at one time that before celebrating Mass he used ostentatiously to drink a cup of coffee in public (he started a lawsuit against his opponents about this). Worse still, his freedom in sexual matters was certainly not in keeping with the priesthood (once, as guest of a priest in Cremona where he had gone to preach, he seduced his colleague's niece, and made no attempt to deny the subsequent slanders put about concerning this unfortunate man, who ended by committing suicide). But his charm was such that everything was forgiven him – by his followers, at least; and though he nearly always lost his countless lawsuits, in the columns of his newspaper he seemed invincible. Even such personalities as Bonomelli of Cremona or Scalabrini of Piacenza, the greatest Italian bishops of the day and justly renowned for their liberal views, were attacked by him like obscure priests. Such rare admonitions as he received from Rome had no effect whatever on him: more papist than the Pope, he knew he was too necessary to Leo XIII to be dispensed with.

The other party, that of the liberals, was largely the heir of a group of priests centred, at the time of Italy's unification, around the periodical *Carroccio* and in a Milanese cultural association such as also existed at that time in various other Italian towns. This original nucleus had gradually widened but it still remained representative of the cultural élite among the Milanese clergy, reinforced by teachers from the seminaries and diocesan colleges and by occasional isolated but important individuals from the larger provincial centres. They had no actual leader but hardly felt the need of one, for among them were persons of such national and international repute as the well-known scholar and writer Abbot Antonio Stoppani, the Prefect of the Ambrosian Library Mgr Antonio Ceriani, Abbot Giulio Tarra, known for his work among the deaf and dumb, and Don Luigi Vitali. Moreover the Archbishop, Di Calabiana, though maintaining the impartiality due to his office was generally regarded as their protector. They derived their inspiration from Antonio Rosmini

(1797–1855), the saintly founder of a religious order whose personal philosophy succeeded in reconciling faith with learning and religion with patriotism.

Ratti's equable temperament and tendency towards moderation, his passion for scientific and philosophical inquiry, and the example of others around him all inclined him as a seminarist towards the second party, the liberals, though he appreciated the justice of their opponents' ideals. He seems already to have had an instinctive tendency against taking sides which kept him aloof from the excesses of party rivalry in either camp. Moreover he was so deeply absorbed in his studies that he took little interest in anything that might distract him. Two important factors preserved him from being dragged into the disputes that aroused many of his fellow-students: first, he was able to do his theological studies privately, and secondly, when deacon, he was chosen out by Mgr Calabiana to complete those studies in the Lombard seminary in Rome, rather than going to Turin to take a degree in mathematics.

In thus choosing Ratti for what was intended as a reward and privilege, Calabiana certainly had no idea of the danger to which he was exposing him and his fellow-student Lualdi. Besides taking their degrees in theology and canon law, the two friends also wanted to study for a degree in philosophy at Leo XIII's recently opened Academy of St Thomas Aquinas. Now the Prefect and organizer of that Academy was the Jesuit Padre Matteo Liberatore, regarded as not only the greatest Thomist revivalist in Rome but also one of the most violent opponents of Rosminianism. And of course to him it seemed too good to be true to have the opportunity of training, among his first students in Thomist philosophy, two Milanese priests whom he could then send back as apostles into the den of heresy itself. He got their mission confirmed by a special pontifical blessing given to them both in a private audience; and only a few months later he had them appointed members of the Pontifical Academy which had just given them their degrees.

Political and Social Distractions of a Librarian

Padre Liberatore's dreams were destined, however, to remain unfulfilled, at any rate as far as Ratti was concerned, for Ratti was anything but eager to go back to Milan as an inquisitor among his Rosminian friends, and derived no fresh enthusiasm from the jobs he was given. After a short vacation period as chaplain at Barni, a small village under the rectorate of Asso, he was appointed teacher of oratory in the theological seminary in Milan, later going on to teach apologetic theology and eventually Hebrew. These sinecures were not particularly calculated to stimulate any zeal he might have felt for the spread of Thomism. He might, of course, have dedicated his free time to that cause, and indeed three years later a long chapter by him, entitled '*De hominis origine quoad corpus*', appeared in the second volume of Mgr Federico Sala's *Institutiones Scholasticae*. Sala was a follower of Don Albertario and an active contributor to the anti-Rosminian *Scuola Cattolica,* a highly polemic review founded by the editor of the *Osservatore Cattolico*. Had Ratti, then, gone over bag and baggage to the intransigents? And was this really his only contribution to the great struggle?

No one who knew him could entertain any such doubts. That first contribution was also the last, and thereafter he became increasingly absorbed in those learned researches into Milanese church history which were to occupy him almost exclusively for the next thirty years. Had he decided, then, to bury himself in the dusty world of the past and make his sole objective a doctor's chair at the famous Ambrosian Library? For a time it really seemed that this was so. True, he was chaplain at Our Lady of the Cenacle, an aristocratic institution where ladies from Milan's best families joined with humbler people in organizing welfare work; but every priest without a cure is expected to take on some such post.

It was only later, when people realized that through acquaintances met at the Cenacle he had made friends among the Milanese upper bourgeoisie and aristocracy, that they began to suspect he might have other quite different secret ambitions. During the next few years, and especially after 1888 when he got a doctorate at the Ambrosiana, he came to be on visiting terms with all the most influential Milanese families. Some of these doors had already been opened to him by the Gallarati Scotti family, where he went as catechism teacher and tutor to their little son, Duke Tommaso, with whom he afterwards remained on friendly terms. He used to go to dinner every Friday evening with Tommaso's paternal grandparents, where there were interminable conversations on religious and political topics of the day; and he also frequently visited the Melzi D'Eril in their villas at Vaprio d'Adda (where the 'Madonnone' by Leonardo da Vinci even inspired him to write a sonnet in reply to one by Count Guido, his friend and companion in mountaineering excursions) and at Oreno near Bellagio. Soon, too, through the Gallarati Scottis he got to know Marchese Lodovico Trotti, whose house was a meeting point for the best of the eclectic Cavourian tradition in society, and where, among others, he met the Minister, Emilio Visconti Venosta, by whose decision Rome was occupied in 1870. Another house he often frequented was that of General Genova Thaon di Revel, where the city's civil and military leaders used to congregate, among them the writer Gaetano Negri, mayor from 1884 to 1889 and a senator in 1890, and General Bava Beccaris, who later sternly suppressed the disorders of 1898. He was also on friendly terms with a number of other aristocratic families such as the Borromeo, the Caccia-Dominioni, the Jacini, and the Greppi.

What was the attraction of all these contacts for the Desio cotton-spinner's son? A desire for worldly society? A natural inclination for politics and the hope of exercising a secret influence there? Or the zeal of a priest anxious to make contact with a world at least partly remote from and hostile to the Church? These questions, frequently asked at the time among his acquaintances and ecclesiastical colleagues, still remain unanswered today. For none of those hypotheses, whether alone or in combination, gives a really satisfactory answer. To solve that enigma is tantamount to solving the enigma of Ratti's own personality before he became Pope.

A desire for worldly society, for instance, is in too strong contrast with the sober reserve characteristic of him throughout his life. The petit-bourgeois' aspiration to penetrate the secrets of an unapproachable superior class can also be only a partial and inadequate explanation, no more satisfactory than the theory advanced by some – so far without proof – that his relations with a distinguished lady of that world had not remained unfruitful.

In order to understand the aspiration towards some sort of political influence, in any case mainly of a local character, one would need to know a good deal more about Ratti's political views at that time, generally presented by his biographers under the somewhat equivocal term of liberalism. It is certainly true that he did not follow the intransigents in their out-and-out defence of temporal power and was opposed to Don Albertario's truculent and unrealistic methods and ideas; but at the same time he also disapproved of the moderates' easygoing readiness to believe the Roman Question had been solved through the wisdom and generosity of the Law of Guarantees. He was, in fact, simply in favour of reconciliation; and his enthusiasm for it led him to take a severe view of the new Archbishop of Milan, Andrea Ferrari, who succeeded Calabiana in 1894 at the early age of forty-four. During the period when the see was vacant, intransigence had gained the upper hand in Milan, and the new Archbishop thought to win the clergy's sympathies by adopting a strongly anti-temporalist line. Whenever the King came to Milan or stayed in the nearby palace of Monza, he at once left the city. Such a gesture admittedly made little difference to the internal life of the diocese, but it was quite another matter when he arbitrarily suppressed the Villoresi Seminary merely because of its tendency towards reconciliation and Rosminianism.

Ratti himself never attempted to conceal his sympathies for everything that might help to improve relations between Church and State. When in July 1901, while on an expedition at Misurina, he heard the news of King Humbert's assassination he at once celebrated a solemn Mass for his intention; similarly, five years later, he did not refuse the Order of Knight of Saints Maurice and Lazzarus, awarded him by Victor Emmanuel III for his research work. But it was a long way from that to sharing a liberal conception of the State and recognizing its claims for autonomy in relation to the Church, and he certainly never went so far. Not for nothing had he been brought up on the *Saggio teoretico di diritto naturale* (Theoretical Study of Natural Law) of the Jesuit Padre Tapparelli D'Azeglio (brother of the statesman Massimo D'Azeglio), well known in Rome during the years of heated political controversy for his studies of canon law. In 1929, in one of his first speeches in defence of the Lateran Pact, his old scorn for secular ways of thinking (promptly condemned, incidentally, in his first encyclical of 1922) came uppermost again in his condemnation of that 'liberal school' which had nurtured

Italian statesmen before Fascism and prevented them from solving the Roman Question.

An episode belonging to this period sheds a significant light on his frame of mind at that time. In 1891 his former fellow-student in Rome, Mgr Radini-Tedeschi, the future Bishop of Bergamo, who was then in the office of the Secretariat of State, was appointed ablegate by Leo XIII to take the cardinal's hat to the Archbishop of Vienna, Mgr Gruscha, and asked permission to take Ratti with him as secretary. The latter, in the course of a conversation with the new Cardinal which touched on the situation of the Church in the Austrian Empire, exclaimed somewhat ingenuously: 'How fortunate your country is, with no anti-clerical liberalism to dominate it, and where the State doesn't try to bind the Church with iron chains!' To which the Cardinal gravely replied: 'You are young, and you have no idea how much heavier are our chains of gold . . .'. Ratti was much impressed but unfortunately not convinced by these words.

Had he been a liberal Catholic and not merely an advocate of reconciliation, there would have been nothing mysterious about his relations with the Milanese upper bourgeoisie and aristocracy; but as it is we cannot but ask what his aim was in maintaining such close contacts with that world over thirty years. As far as is known, he never effected any conversions among his friends, and his influence in the political or civil sphere was confined to two occasions when he played the role of mediator: one in 1895, in helping to solve the question of religious instruction in the schools of Milan, and the other in 1898, in getting the Archbishop, Cardinal Ferrari, to return to Milan after his sudden departure, on the excuse of a pastoral visitation, on the very day when uprisings broke out in the city.[1] All this was the least that could have been expected of someone in Ratti's position.

His conduct in relation to his superior, the Archbishop, raises another delicate question: what was the real reason for his dislike of Ferrari? On the surface there was nothing in it to which exception could be taken: in difficult moments, as we have seen, he used his good offices to some purpose. Even when, in 1907, the Holy Office told Cardinal Ferrari to take a firm line with the

---

[1] General Bava Beccaris, who had assumed full powers in Milan, was so angered by the Archbishop's conduct that he had refused him permission to return until Ratti and others intervened on Ferrari's behalf.

editors of *Rinnovamento,* the well-known review accused of Modernism, he agreed to the Cardinal's request to persuade the editors, Gallarati Scotti among them, to submit. Similarly, he always fell in with the Archbishop's wishes when asked to collaborate over cultural or historical matters, such as the centenary celebrations of SS Ambrogio and Carlo, or the identification of the relics of SS Vittore and Satiro. And he was among those who, in 1911, signed a protest from the upper clergy of the diocese in support of Ferrari when the latter was violently attacked by the *Riscossa.*

All these, however, were really mere formalities. On the other hand it seems certain that he never did anything to facilitate a meeting between the Archbishop and the moderate-liberal members of the aristocracy and upper bourgeoisie, who were hostile to Ferrari because of his intransigence. Nor did his relations with the Archbishop improve after the latter's political change of view and reconciliation with the liberals in 1902. His negative view of the Cardinal extended, indeed, to practically all aspects of his administration, though he recognized the sincerity of his zeal and dedication. He thought him inadequate on the cultural side for so important a diocese; and he did not agree with Ferrari's view of the importance of the pastoral aspect, which caused him to spend most of his time in the outlying parts of the diocese away from the capital. Even when he became Pope this attitude did not change. When the Superior of the Company of St Paul approached him about the cause for Ferrari's beatification, he answered unequivocally that this was something that could wait, at any rate as long as he himself was at the head of the Church. This was confirmed by, among others, Cardinal Schuster when the process for beatification finally got under way. But Schuster's deposition is even more interesting because, while it confirms Ratti's antipathy for Ferrari, it also reveals Ferrari's feeling of discomfort in relation to Ratti. It seems that a Milanese prelate once confided to Schuster that Archbishop Ferrari 'had a certain fear of two people in Milan: one because he talked too much – and this was Mgr Magistretti (one of his ill-fated advisers in 1898, and incidentally a friend of Ratti's); and the other because he talked very little – and this was Mgr Ratti, who at that time lived aloof from any rivalry or priestly party, frequenting instead the houses of the liberal patricians'.

An Unfathomable Vocation

But unfathomable as the enigma of Ratti may seem with regard to his relations with the Milanese patricians and the clergy of the diocese, it appears even more so when we come to consider his attitude towards cultural matters of the day, especially in the ecclesiastical world which at a certain point became involved in the Modernist dispute. The extraordinary thing is that Ratti not only kept aloof, as we have seen, in the political sphere but also took no definite line in cultural matters. There was, indeed, no particular reason why a man in his position should become mixed up in politics; but as a scholar and representative of one of the most distinguished institutions in Milan, the Ambrosian Library, he was professionally involved and could not refuse to declare his standpoint. Yet that is precisely what he did.

As to where his cultural sympathies lay, we are told of only one episode in which he was actually involved, and that does nothing to elucidate the mystery. In 1888 a close friend of his, a certain Giovanni Leoni, chaplain of a church in Milan, died; he was a man of liberal outlook and a follower of Rosmini. Ratti, pursuing, as he said, and in a sense interpreting the dead man's wishes, sent two bronze lamps to the Institute in Stresa to be put on Rosmini's tomb 'when he should be canonized'. This gesture would certainly have been daring and, for us, illuminating, had Ratti acted purely on his own initiative and not largely as interpreter of his friend's wishes. One cannot help wondering if he would have done the same a few months later when Rosmini's 'forty propositions' were condemned. How far, in fact, did his admiration for that great man go? Was it confined to Rosmini the man of God, including at most his political views, or did it extend further, to his philosophy as well?

It is difficult to say, even if we take good care not to over-estimate the influence of Padre Liberatore on Ratti's philosophy – which, in any case, was to become frankly Thomist once he became Pope. It is also a fact that in 1888, when a clergy society of Vigevano invited him to take part in a course on the *Syllabus*, Ratti not only accepted but chose to comment on the fifth paragraph, which condemns dogmatic evolutionism, in other words the doctrine that aroused the greatest disputes during the Modernist period. But apart from these few episodes, Ratti's work as a scholar became increasingly remote from such burning topics. Why was this? In the absence of any evidence of an intellectual crisis in his life, either then or later, one is bound to conclude that he deliberately decided to hold aloof from current controversies, taking refuge in his professional duties as librarian. But that is just what seems so improbable.

Quite apart from the fact that these were the most vital years for the destiny of Catholic culture in Italy, endangered as it was by suffocation from the secular side, the situation in Milan during the thirty-one years (1882 to 1913) of Ratti's work there was certainly not such as to counsel inertia for an intellectual of his calibre. In the last decades of the nineteenth century Milan had become the country's intellectual capital. Immediately after the unification the city, pursuing the teachings of Carlo Cattaneo, had established a Royal Higher Technical Institute (the future Polytechnic) and also, as a temporary substitute for the university that Austria had never granted, a scientific and literary Academy which had offered a chair to, among others, Ausonio Franchi (the ex-priest whose library Ratti took over in 1897 on behalf of the Ambrosiana). In drama, music, and the figurative arts Milan led the whole country; while in the literary sphere new movements developed there, with anti-romanticism succeeded by realism, even during Manzoni's lifetime. Capuana had published *Giacinta*, the movement's novel-manifesto; Verga had moved to Milan from his native Catania and brought out *I Malavoglia* and *Maestro Don Gesualdo*; and Matilde Serao had written her *Leggende Napoletane*, *Il ventre di Napoli* and other works.

In the more strictly religious sphere, in the 1880–90s Milan had become the centre of the Rosminian movement, with Abbot Stoppani and Professor Pestalozza as its ardent champions. In 1888, the year of Ratti's tribute of the lamps, Abbot Stoppani had even dared to publish a review entitled *Rosmini* which, condemned next year by the Holy Office, was revived in 1890 as *Il nuovo Rosmini*. The other side, the Thomists, also had their mouthpieces in Milan in the reviews *Osservatore Cattolico* and *Scuola Cattolica*. During the Modernist period in the early 1900s Milan was the headquarters not only of *Il Rinnovamento* but also of *Letture*, founded by Fogazzaro and with Piero Giacosa, Giacomo Barzellotti, Uberto Pestalozza, and Tommaso Gallarati Scotti among its collaborators. At one point *Rinnovamento* also brought in a group of Florentine intellectuals, among them Giovanni Papini and Giovanni Boine; and the Modernist group in Lugano that published *Coenobium* also had associations with Milan. Among the laity concerned with religious matters an important influence was Gaetano Negri, already mentioned earlier, who, interestingly enough, like Stoppani and Ratti had started out as a geologist but soon devoted himself to analysing the contemporary religious crisis, especially through interpretations of great figures of the past (from St Paul and St Augustine to Julian the Apostate) and the present (Manzoni, Renan, etc.).

Achille Ratti's presence would have been much more natural among those circles than in the drawing-rooms of the patricians. True, he had contacts with Franchi (though after his conversion) and with Negri and the young men of *Rinnovamento*, but these contacts were all of a rather superficial kind, unrelated to the real core of the problems under discussion, and of a strictly private character; so that he would seem to have exercised no positive influence on the Milanese cultural world. Yet no one could have less resembled the usual type of abstract and eccentric intellectual. Almost every town of Italy, great or small, houses some such learned priest, steeped in his musty books, living in a sort of limbo of his own and half-shunned alike by clergy and laity. Their priesthood is more of the study than the altar – and this without disrespect to their religious sentiments, though their ideas are often pretty unorthodox; they are destined to disappear among their parchments and bookshelves, saluted at the last with brief respect by those who in life regarded them as inevitable exceptions to the common rule. But Ratti, despite his isolation from the ecclesiastical world of Milan, which regarded him mainly as an austere scholar of historical records, certainly could not be taken for a passionate devotee of learning terrified of contact with real life. To be an intellectual influence, however, a man must have clearly defined ideas which become widely known and discussed. And though Ratti was by no means lacking in ideas, they were hard to grasp, for he always kept them to himself as something intimate and personal, not to say secret and mysterious. For reasons that have never been revealed, he preferred to shut himself up within the professional limits of his work as librarian, conserving rather than creating the instruments of culture, and with his gaze directed more towards the past than to the present or future.

As librarian, it is true, he undoubtedly had the merit of putting an end, after Ceriani's death, to the old idea till then perpetuated in the Ambrosiana, that the library was the exclusive kingdom and instrument of its own body of learned scholars, rather than a place to be consulted and used by students and outsiders. But though this was the basis of his modernization of the library founded by Cardinal Federico Borromeo, it did little to put Ratti in touch with the intellectuals of the day in Milan or elsewhere. His own studies were chiefly concerned with historical research within the limited sphere of memoirs of the Church in Milan; but that need not have prevented him from taking an active part in contemporary affairs. With his natural versatility that would have been easy for him. The fact that he did not allow himself to do so arouses the suspicion that the real motive might have been some sort of fear or escapism.

This suspicion seems the more justified since certain aspects of his studies might well have directed him towards the present. Apart from history, which naturally has a foot in the present as well as the past, he also carried on liturgical studies, publishing with Magistretti the *Missale Ambrosianum duplex*, besides being a Hebrew expert and still retaining his early interest in the natural sciences. Now liturgical reform, the biblical question, and the problem of the relations between science and faith were probably the most controversial subjects in ecclesiastical studies even before the Modernist crisis. On any of these topics Ratti could have joined in as a specialist, inspired by the example of men like his friend Stoppani, who had made serious efforts to reconcile biblical cosmology with modern scientific ideas. But instead Ratti maintained the most complete reserve and silence.

To what can one attribute behaviour so little in accord with the fighting temperament he was later to display as pontiff? For a man who could inspire fear even in his Archbishop it would be absurd to suggest that he was afraid to compromise himself or his future career. Moreover if one thing is clearly proved today about Ratti, it is the fact that he had no ambitions for a career, not even in his own sphere as librarian. A letter of 1901 to his friend Giovanni Mercati shows with what alarm and dismay he envisaged the possibility of Ceriani's death and his own probable succession to his post as Prefect of the Ambrosiana. Another letter of 1907, also to Mercati, shows that his misgivings when called on to succeed were so great that his friend, to comfort him, even offered to leave the Vatican and take on the post himself or share it with Ratti. Now all this is highly significant when we remember that his appointment as Ceriani's successor in that year, when Ratti himself was just fifty, could be regarded as the crown of all his scholarly aspirations, ensuring him at the same time a privileged position in the Milanese Church. But that is not all. When, three years later, in 1910, it was proposed to transfer him to Rome as Vice-Prefect of the Vatican Library with the right of succession as Prefect, far from being elated at the prospect (though the post normally carried with it a Cardinal's hat), he seemed anxious and alarmed. 'I shall make all the difficulties I have the right and duty to make,' he wrote to Mercati who was trying to persuade him to accept, 'and if nevertheless they still insist I shall submit and accept in penitence for my sins . . . trusting in the help of God.' In fact it took a whole year to reach that conclusion, and it was not until 9 November 1911 that Pius x was able to sign his appointment.

Not only had Ratti no interest in making a career, he was not even particularly enthusiastic about his own profession. His scholarly activities were too sporadic and varied to permit of real specialization; nor did he ever, like so many of his colleagues, make the library his only world. As we have seen, Ratti enjoyed going about in society; and he also took seriously his duties as chaplain, going in for some rather original sidelines such as welfare work among the chimney-sweepers' boys as well as giving religious aid to the German colony in Milan, which all took time from his work in the library. He was also a keen mountaineer, going on long expeditions in his summer holidays as well as shorter excursions during the year; and he loved travelling, particularly abroad (in Italy, while visiting Turin he once went to see Don Bosco, whom he was later to canonize, and on a trip to Mantua was the guest of Mgr Sarto). A number of these journeys abroad were undertaken to visit famous libraries and centres such as Berlin, Munich, Cologne, Dresden, Leipzig, Königsberg, St Gallen, Einsiedeln, Budapest, and Prague; and these contacts with Central Europe undoubtedly influenced his outlook. He also went abroad to congresses (for instance, the congresses of Catholic scholars held in 1897 and 1900 at Fribourg and Munich) or to attend ceremonies (the unveiling of a monument to Roger

Bacon in Oxford) or simply to pursue his own spiritual exercises (for this purpose he stayed three times at the Jesuit monastery at Feldkirch in the Vorarlberg).

Ratti probably first decided to work in the Ambrosiana because he felt greater inclination for research and individual study than for teaching. But he evidently did not feel permanently tied to it, for in 1894 he registered officially with the oblates of SS Ambrogio and Carlo, a special body of priests in the diocese of Milan who offer themselves (hence their name of oblates, i.e. offered) to their bishop with an especial promise of obedience which puts them entirely at his disposal for any task he may wish to give them. In joining this body Ratti abandoned himself to the will of his superiors, thus renouncing any intention of shaping his life and future according to his own preferences or aspirations.

Are we then faced with a man who, beneath a worldly exterior, was really at heart an ascetic? There are a number of pointers in this direction, such as, for example, the fact that as a young seminarist and priest he belonged to a number of devotional societies. The same could, no doubt, be said of most priests but they do not usually continue to cherish these associations in their more advanced years. But in Ratti's case, his secretary Confalonieri was to reveal how right up to the time of his death he preserved in a stout envelope marked 'Devotional Societies' his membership cards going back to more than forty-five years earlier, and to the last remained faithful to the numerous obligations they imposed. The oldest among them were those of the Confraternity of the Immaculate Sacred Heart of Mary for the conversion of sinners, the Franciscan Third Order, and the Angelic Militia of St Thomas Aquinas. Even more significant is his encounter, of later but uncertain date, with the spiritual significance of the complete abandonment to God of St Theresa of the Child Jesus, the young Carmelite who died in 1897 and whose remarkable autobiography was published in the following year. Indeed, despite his discretion and reserve about his own inner life, a number of significant episodes testify to his spiritual leanings: for example, his participation as rapporteur in the second Congress of the Apostolate of prayer and devotion to the Sacred Heart, in 1901; his speech to his former fellow-students at the Sacro Monte in Varese on 7 June 1904, on the twenty-fifth anniversary of their ordination to the priesthood; and even earlier, on 31 December 1899, his midnight vigil with a few friends on the summit of Vesuvius, where they passed in prayer and meditation the last night of the old century and awaited the first dawn of the new. But even if his awareness of the 'Little Way' of St Theresa of Lisieux could be attributed to the same period, it is hard to see how it or any other ascetic standpoint could have inspired his neutrality in relation to the great cultural and religious discussions of that time, or have justified his contacts with the privileged stratum of Milanese society. So it remains only to resign ourselves to accepting the enigma and follow Ratti first to Rome and then in his last moves before the Vatican walls closed around him.

From the Vatican Library to the Banks of the Vistula

The five years that Ratti spent in the Vatican Library are not really very important for an understanding of his character and personality. His habit of life formed in Milan continued in many ways relatively unchanged in Rome, where his work in the Library was varied by occasional contacts with the city's intellectual circles and with friends. He also agreed to be confessor at an institution of nuns, but on one condition – that he should go there only once a week and for not longer than forty minutes (during which he had to hear the confessions of some thirty nuns).

The circles he frequented in Rome could not, naturally, offer him the warm hospitality that he had enjoyed for more than a quarter of a century in Milan. (The farewell dinner in Milan took place in the 'Covo' on 1 December 1913 in the presence of the professors from Ambrosiana, Senator Greppi, Mgrs Nogara and Magistretti, the publisher Ulrico Hoepli, Duke Tommaso Gallarati Scotti, Count Stefano Jacini, and the artists Cavenaghi and Beltrami – in fact the élite of the Milanese intellectual world; and the farewell speech was made by Prince Gilberto Borromeo.) But the new Prefect of the Vatican Library did not have time to exhaust his reserves of nostalgia for the Lombard capital. He believed himself isolated, like his apartment in the Vatican, from the Roman Court and Curia, but watchful eyes kept him under constant observation. Towards the end of February 1918 there passed through Rome on his way to Palestine, where he was serving as envoy to the first section of the French General Staff, an official of the Vatican Library who had been recalled during the war to the service of his own country: Don Eugène Tisserant. Mgr Ratti, who had known him in Milan some years earlier, took him to see the Pope just as he was, in uniform. 'Holy Father,' he said laughingly to Benedict xv, 'here's my military attaché.' The Pope retorted swiftly, 'Clearly, monsignore, you want to go into diplomacy if you've already got yourself a military attaché.' It seemed just a joke, and that is how Ratti took it, but in reality it corresponded to a plan that Benedict xv had been meditating for some time and which had already been put in train by his Secretariat of State. And on 25 April Mgr Ratti was appointed Apostolic Visitor to Poland and Lithuania.

It was the first note of fate sounding to set him on the way towards his great future. Beneath his serious and self-contained exterior, the 'little old man' Ratti had always from his childhood cherished a secret longing for unusual adventures. For a priest, and at a time when mountaineering in Italy was still practically at the pioneering stage, his passion for climbing would suffice to suggest this; but he had also thought of going to the North Pole as a member of the Duke of Abruzzi's expedition, and went to Turin in 1899 specially to talk it over with him. He even managed to introduce an occasional spice of adventure into his activities as librarian, as when, in March 1900, he spent a whole day shut up in a lonely bell-tower at Savona reading the records of a Milanese provincial Council of 1311. On another occasion he actually incurred threat of death. Cardinal Ferrari had charged him, as was mentioned earlier, with the identification of the relics of San Vittore which had just been sent back to Milan, and the problem proved difficult for there turned out to be other saints of the same name, one venerated at Pomarance and another at Volterra, the latter being identified with the Milanese saint. Ratti discovered in Pisa an old record of the Pisan primate's visit to Volterra in 1645 which contradicted that legend. The people of Volterra were so angry that they forbade him to return to their town on pain of death.

But at getting on for sixty years old his time for adventures might have seemed to be over. Instead this totally unexpected chance arrived, which was to lead, though he little knew it then, to the greatest adventure of all. Forty years spent among *in-cunabula* and palimpsests might not seem the best preparation

for the duties of Pope (nor was it so regarded, to judge by past experience, for in nineteen centuries not a single librarian had ever before
become Pope: Gregory II, in the first half of the eighth century,
was a mere archivist in the Lateran). It was not even a particularly suitable background for an Apostolic Visitor in a political
keypoint such as Warsaw at that time. But obviously it was not
just the shortage of available personnel in wartime, nor yet Ratti's
cultural and linguistic qualifications, that drew the attention of
the Pope and the Secretariat of State to the Prefect of the Vatican
Library (Ratti knew no Slav languages, but he was familiar with
German, the language of the two Central Empires which had
allowed Poland to recover a certain degree of autonomy).

Benedict XV must have known Ratti during his studies in Rome,
for they were both at the Gregorian University at the same time,
though Della Chiesa was then living at the Capranica and Ratti
at the Lombard College. He must also have met him and heard
Radini-Tedeschi talk about him at the Secretariat of State when
the latter was appointed to two pontifical missions in 1891 and
1893, to take the cardinal's hat to Mgr Gruscha in Vienna and
later to three French bishops, and chose Ratti to accompany him.[1]
Finally, recent contact with Ratti in Rome must have caused
Benedict XV to reach his decision.

Be all that as it may, Ratti's mission to Poland, though it lasted
only three years, was an exceptional and in some ways decisive
experience for him: so much so, indeed, that it can be regarded as
the mainspring for much of the conduct of his pontificate. It gave
him his first direct experience of command and public responsibilities; it brought him into contact with quite new surroundings;
and he experienced his first encounter with a dictator in the
person of Marshal Pilsudski.

The official aim of Ratti's mission to Warsaw as Apostolic
Visitor was to assist in the reconstruction of the Polish Church.
The partitioning of Poland between Austria, Germany, and
Russia had given rise to three different Polish episcopates which
now strove to impose on each other the attitudes of mind and
traditions under which each had lived, and which each tended to
regard as the ideal to be perpetuated in the new independent State.
To reunite them involved amalgamating not only a few dozen
bishops but three practically separate Churches in each of which

[1] See p. 162.

bishops, clergy, and population formed a compact and independent body. The way in which Ratti set about this task is highly typical of his methods, beginning with a veritable religious exploration of the ex-occupied Polish territories.

His letters of that period give a good idea of the scientific method he used, obviously inspired by his experience as a scholar but flexibly adapted to this particular type of investigation. For example, he paid great attention to the physical and geographical background in order to understand its influence on the inhabitants' religious and spiritual outlook. Writing to Mgr Cerretti[1] he says:

It is a perfectly flat country, always and invariably flat, alternating between extensive (not intensive) cultivation of corn and meadow and, no less extensive forests, and immense stretches of marsh and real steppe. Towns are few, and few places have solidly built houses; more frequent, but lost in the vast plain and almost completely hidden by trees, are the villages where the peasants live, consisting of humble cottages or rather single-storey huts, with a thatched roof and walls of timber. I get the impression that these peasants must live very badly – physically and morally speaking – and that very little has been done for them, I don't mean just by the Russian Government, which purely on the 'divide and rule' principle occasionally hurled the firebrand of land reform into their midst, but also by the great Polish landowners. Only towards Kielce, about 200 kilometres from Warsaw, is there some undulating country with lovely gentle little hills; here, in the south, the corn and meadow lands are less fertile, but beneath the wooded undergrowth the land is rich in minerals . . .

It is a fine literary description, almost in the manner of Stoppani; but it goes on afterwards to give precise and detailed facts about the economic and social life of the inhabitants according to their different categories. But the geologist and sociologist eventually, of course, give way to the priest, whose chief concern is to find out what form religious life takes and the exact size and location of the parishes, carefully comparing the results with the geographical nature of the area, its population density and so forth.

'The religious feeling of this people,' he writes elsewhere, 'is even more apparent than their natural goodness. You have only to see how reverently and devoutly they behave in church, and

[1] See '*Le lettere di Varsavia di mons. Achille Ratti*', by r. m., *L'Osservatore Romano*, 24 July 1960.

to hear with what genuine feeling they pray and sing. The Poles don't like going to church just for a short service; they like long services, and seem never to want to end their slow, solemn, almost lament-like supplications, sung with an almost perpetual expression of sadness and grief. Anyone who knows even a little of the country's history is tempted to believe that these canticles still contain the echo of the sorrow and misfortune recurrent throughout that history.' He mentions with pleasure 'two of the best and most characteristic features' of Polish religious life: 'devotion to the Blessed Virgin and attachment to the Church and the Supreme Pontiff'. But he also notes and criticizes its excesses, such as the way in which religion, rightly or wrongly, invades every activity: even nationalistic processions or political meetings 'always set out from the church and begin with a religious service'. 'A fortnight ago a big procession of peasants, deluded by propagandists, arrived in Warsaw to take part in a Socialist meeting bringing with them their sacred banners and their priest, he no less deluded than they. Indeed everyone here, except perhaps the Bolsheviks, is, or believes he is, or claims to be, a Catholic.'

A few months after his arrival Poland overthrew the tutelage of the Central Empires with their regency council and summoned its own constituent assembly, and on 30 March 1919 the Holy See recognized the new State. By that time it was obvious that Ratti's mission would soon cease to be purely religious and become diplomatic and political as well. On 6 June he was appointed Nuncio and found himself faced with the difficult problem of establishing the foundations for relations between State and Church in a country where virtually no precedent for them existed. The situation was the more delicate since the Poles' strong religious sentiments had in no wise prevented the formation, both among the leading classes and the masses, of political trends similar to those existing in Western democratic countries; and among these trends the strongest were the left-wing movements, which had no intention of seeing their social demands blocked by ecclesiastical conservatism and wanted, among other things, a land reform that would reduce to more acceptable limits the extensive Church ownership of land. Marshal Pilsudski himself, the elected head of the new State and supreme commander of the armed forces, came from a socialist background.

Mgr Ratti therefore had, on the one hand, to persuade the episcopate, bent on retaining Church privileges and property, to moderate their all-embracing and wellnigh medieval claims, and, on the other, to get the Government to accept the two cardinal points of his policy: first, recognition of the unconditional primacy of the Catholic religion in the Polish State, and secondly, the imperative need to reach agreement exclusively with Rome on all questions relating to the Church. The first was an affirmation of all-pervading Catholic confessionalism (justified in the Nuncio's mind by the fear that the quite considerable Orthodox or Jewish minorities might at some future date constitute a serious danger for the Roman Church); while the second strikingly anticipated the concordatory aspect of his future activity as Pontiff (whether on his own personal initiative or at the suggestion of his superiors, will be known only when the Vatican secret archives are opened). From that moment, in fact, he began to think of and work for a concordat, and negotiations were far advanced by the time he left.

But the most influential experience of his time as Nuncio was to find himself face to face for the first time in his life with a dictator – and a dictator *sui generis* who not only fascinated him but also, as it turned out, implanted in the future Pius XI some misleading illusions about the very different dictators he was later to encounter. Pilsudski was a picturesque personification of the old traditional Poland, romantic, quixotic, idealistic, scorning all material considerations. Unlike other and more important contemporary European dictators he was a gentleman of the old style, whom the officials of his entourage never addressed as Marshal but as '*starszy pan*' (venerable sir). He had had an army career, but though a soldier he was no militarist. He had had dealings with the parties but had never become absorbed in them, and above all had taken good care not to form a party himself and make it unique and all-powerful. He enjoyed his own personal power, but for that very reason he took no steps to legalize or institutionalize it in any way, or even to link it with the interests of a particular class or caste; and while he had his own ideals, he was not interested in evolving or trying to impose an ideology. In the twenty years between the two world wars, his was the most anachronistic of the dictatorships, operating in defiance of every rule or definition:

When the Marshal, weakened by age and illness, was near his end, the dictatorship had actually to be 'organized'; for during his lifetime formal organization mattered little, and institutions retained the semblance of parliamentary rule. The development of Polish policy, both domestic and foreign, is completely bound up during the period with the development of the Marshal's ideas.[1]

When, on 19 July 1919, Mgr Ratti went to present his credentials to him, he was living in a small country house at Sulejowek twenty miles outside Warsaw, where he led a modest and frugal life free from outward show and with no tinge of fanaticism about it. At that time, and throughout Ratti's nunciature, he was still regarded as a Socialist and surrounded by his old companions. But Ratti soon realized that he had to deal with him alone, not with a government or parties, and that as this man personified in himself the chivalrous soul of his country, the Church's representative would encounter no serious obstacle in him. He thus discovered for the first time by personal experience how much absolute power of this kind could offer to the Church.

That Ratti himself was influenced by the prestige of the 'old gentleman' of Sulejowek is shown by the fact that he came to share in his far from modest political ambitions. Colonel Beck in his memoirs says that Pilsudski 'throughout his long life strove to adapt Polish policy to Poland's possibilities rather than to the level of his own genius and will'. The Marshal himself is said to have used the telling phrase: 'I have enough ideas for five Polands, but I can only carry them out for one'. But if that was true of the Poland that emerged from the treaty of Brest-Litovsk, it was no longer true of the years 1918–20, when Pilsudski's dreams came up against the realism of Dmowski. Dmowski, who had patiently and scientifically worked out his idea of Polish nationalism, relating it to the national consciousness of the bordering populations, never wanted Poland to push too far eastwards, and saw in Germany the traditional enemy against whom the nation's energies should be concentrated. Pilsudski, on the other hand, thought it necessary for Poland's safety that she should pursue her action against Russia to the limit, uniting in confederation with Poland the Lithuanians, Ukrainians and White Ruthenes. In practice, Dmowski, with his national democratic party and his aim of reconciling his country's interests with those

[1] See J. Beck, *Dernier rapport: Politique polonaise 1926–1939*, Neuchâtel, 1951, p. 95.

Pope Leo XIII (1878–1903) with Prelates of the Anticamera Segreta;
Cardinal Merry del Val on his right

(*above, left*) Pope Pius X (1903–14). A contemporary miniature by Dubrowsky

(*above, right*) Cardinal Rampolla; Secretary of State to Leo XIII

(*below*) Pope Benedict XV (1914–22)

(*above*) Pope Pius XI (1922–39) at the inauguration of the Vatican Wireless Station in 1931

(*below*) Cardinal Gasparri and Mussolini, after the signing of the Lateran Pact, 1929

Pope Pius XII (1939–58) giving his blessing to the crowds in St Peter's Square, 1950

A Canonization ceremony, 1950

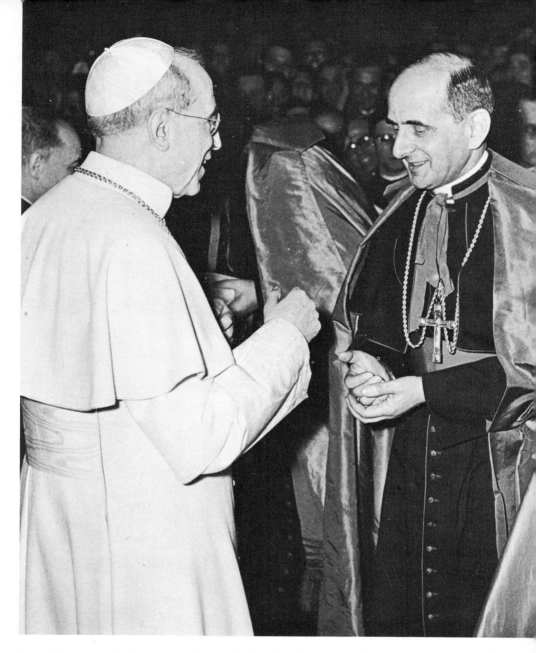

Pope Pius XII, with Monsignor Montini, then Pro-Secretary of State, in 1956

Cardinal Tardini, Pro-Secretary of State under Pius XII

Prince Chigi, Marshall of the Conclave, performing the ceremony of locking the door from the outside at the Conclave of 1963

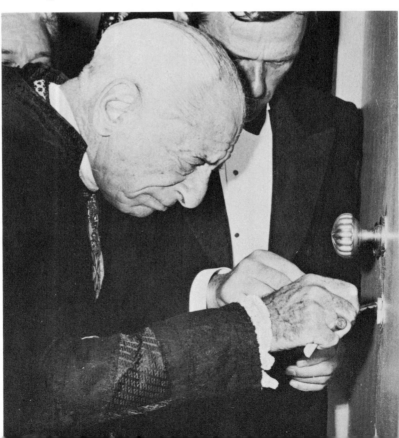

Pope John XXIII (1958–63) speaking at the opening of the Second Vatican Council

The scene in St Peter's at the opening of the Second Vatican Council on 2 October 1962

The crowds in St Peter's Square during the three days (June 1–4, 1963) when Pope John lay dying

of Russia, had no intention of carrying the struggle against Russia through to the end, and demanded merely the annexation of Lithuania to Poland. Pilsudski aimed instead at preventing the restoration of Russian power, and aspired to make Lithuania, the Ukraine, and White Russia into autonomous states confederated with Poland. Between these two statesmen's plans, the Nuncio, Ratti, as can be seen from the reports of the Italian Minister in Warsaw, Tommasini, and General Alberto de Marinis to the Italian Foreign Ministry, favoured those of Marshal Pilsudski, and directed his whole action, especially in Lithuania, towards furthering the Marshal's schemes.

Implicit in this choice was his own twofold aim – that of reducing both Russian political power and the power of the Orthodox Church under the patriarchate in Moscow. Pilsudski's armies would sustain the three new States, while he, the representative of Rome, would contribute to the establishment in each of them of a Slav national Church. In the case of Lithuania, a country which already had a Catholic majority and of Latin rite, it was simply a question of creating an autonomous structure for the local Church with its headquarters at Kovno. The Ukraine, for its part, had set up an independent democratic republic on 22 January 1918 with Kiev as capital and in February 1919 sent a diplomatic mission to the Holy See; it only remained to await its abandonment of Orthodoxy for Catholicism, promised to Ratti in January 1920 by its Foreign Minister Livyckyj: Mgr Szeptyckyj, Metropolitan of Lwow, would then be sent there as Metropolitan. Similar arrangements were planned for White Russia.

These two plans, the political and the religious, seemed to Ratti to embody the realization of a dream that the Roman Church had cherished in vain for centuries and for the furtherance of which the collapse of the Tsarist Empire seemed little short of providential. True, Tsarist rule had been replaced by the Bolshevik régime, but the isolation of that régime by the Western Powers, and its own internal dissensions, made its speedy end seem probable. But Ratti's dreams – the large-scale theorizing of a former librarian – were to be short-lived. Bolshevik Russia, after a series of military defeats, made a successful advance against the rebellious western regions and the Powers supporting them. After a victory at Kiev in the summer of 1920 the Red Armies pushed on into the heart of Poland itself to within a few miles of Warsaw. Most of the diplomatic corps evacuated the capital, but the Nuncio as well as the Italian and American Ministers refused to leave. Ratti, who was not easily intimidated, was even urged to stay by the Archbishop and clergy. The Poles did not forget his courageous behaviour, even when later, largely because of the Silesian question, the episcopate turned against him and sent three representatives to Rome to ask for his withdrawal. By that time he had already been defeated over Lithuania and the Ukraine: his appointment as commissioner for the elections in Upper Silesia proved the last straw. But by then his experience in Poland, the crossroads between the Slav world and the West, had little more to give him. He had penetrated to the furthest frontier of Catholicism and realized the power of Orthodoxy; above all, he had stood at the edge of the Bolshevik crater and had seen, beyond war's curtain of fire and smoke, the tragic future destined for the empire of the 'Third Rome'.

Viewed as a whole, Ratti's mission had failed only on peripheral questions, not as regards relations with the Polish Church and the civil authorities. In what was in any case a highly complicated situation, political factors such as the unexpected recovery of Russia had been largely responsible for the defeat of his dreams – dreams cherished no less in Rome by Benedict xv and his Secretary of State; and they fully recognized the merits of their unfortunate representative. At the end of March 1921, barely two months after Cardinal Ferrari's death, Ratti received the news that he had been appointed Archbishop of Milan. He hoped to stay on in Poland for a few months to complete the negotiations for the Concordat and make a journey to Eastern Galicia. But on 19 May a telegram arrived calling him to Rome for the coming Consistory at which he was to receive the Cardinal's hat.

The Conquest of Rome from Milan

At the back of his mind Ratti had always thought of Warsaw as merely a temporary emergency mission, after which he would go back to his library, no doubt with the recognition of elevation to the purple, but nevertheless still faithful to his books and studies. His appointment as archbishop cut short such hopes and Ratti, resigned to seeing the end of his life as a scholar, distributed his collection of books and scientific material among a few friends and institutions. In returning to Milan he was now to assume openly, with no more enigmas, the kind of role he would have liked to have played there in the past, in patent disagreement with his predecessor's policy. But going back to Milan after three years in Warsaw, though in a way it was like returning home among old friends, was all the same a return to the provinces, a contraction from broad horizons to the familiar and well-loved but undoubtedly modest, if not narrow, horizon of his native region. Nevertheless he took seriously the post that awaited him, which he could not but suppose would be the last of his life. His entry into the city took place on 8 September 1921. After receiving the cardinal's hat, he had gone into retreat for some weeks at the old Benedictine abbey of Monte Cassino to prepare himself in meditation. But neither his first speech in Milan nor his conduct in the early months there did anything to reveal his plan of action. Like the experienced old mountaineer that he was, he would make a beginning only after careful and realistic calculation of the possibilities of success.

He found Milan greatly changed since his last visit before setting out for Poland. The death of Cardinal Ferrari – whose voice had failed some time before owing to illness (he had cancer of the throat) but whose indomitable activity had continued undeterred – had brought a pause of only a few days in the disturbances that now kept the city in constant turmoil. It might have seemed that this holy prelate, with his long-drawn-out agony and painful death in a town agitated by strikes and violence, was expiating the upheavals of 1898; but even the drama of his tragic end failed to restore order or bring reconciliation. The social upheavals had political as well as economic causes; and to someone returning from abroad after a long absence it at once leapt to the eye that the authorities were incapable of dealing with the situation. To make good their shortcomings, a new force had come forward in Milan which, itself appealing to force, promised to guarantee order and social justice: this was Fascism. The leader of the new movement was a former Socialist from Romagna with undoubted personal attraction, who had set up his headquarters, his 'lair' (*covo*) as he called it, in the peaceful Piazza San Sepolcro only a few paces from that quiet retreat, the Ambrosian

Library. The coincidence impressed the Cardinal, aware perhaps of some presentiment as he realized the growing power of this man whose name was increasingly becoming an augury of the country's restoration. That name was heard more and more frequently on the lips of many of the Cardinal's old friends: for such people, law-abiding men by nature of their class, wealth, and privilege, were beginning, despite doubts and hesitations, to turn to him, as too were some among the upper clergy. They inclined towards him the more readily because of a certain 'mystique', not without tinges of evangelism, that Mussolini, the man in question, proclaimed and developed in his speeches and writings. This mystique of renunciation and asceticism, of courage and patriotic fervour, which should have aroused the suspicions of anyone who recalled its author's ideological background, made an impression on quite a number of Catholics. Might not this man be the Man of Destiny who would do away with Italy's old political world, from its presumptuous and inept liberalism to its demagogic, fatuous socialism, and bring to life a new order with which the Church could ally itself?

In his meditations on the hilltop of Monte Cassino, Ratti had frequently found himself thinking that Italy stood at a decisive turning-point. In those cloisters with more than a thousand years of life behind them, he had sometimes felt as if there stood beside him that great apostle of reconciliation, his teacher of ecclesiastical historiography, Luigi Tosti. But the voice that spoke to him, and with a warmth and passion worthy of Tosti himself, belonged to another Benedictine: Abbot Amelli. Amelli believed the hour had come for reconciliation between the Church and Italy: any delay would endanger the very possibility of agreement, for the younger generation no longer understood the ideological causes of the dispute, let alone its practical implications.

To touch on the theme of reconciliation was to set vibrating one of Ratti's most sensitive cords. But to carry it into effect was certainly not the task for an archbishop or a cardinal, even of Milan, and even if the man destined to govern the country's destinies in the near future should be the paladin of Fascist mysticism and action. The new Archbishop's problems were a good deal more modest, even though their solution might have repercussions in religious circles beyond his own diocese.

Ratti was still occupied in assessing the forces at his disposal and deciding on his objectives when, only five months after his assumption of office, on 22 January 1922 the news came of Benedict xv's death. A fortnight later, on 6 February, a little before midday the Cardinal Dean, Bisleti, announced to the crowd in Piazza San Pietro that the Archbishop of Milan was the new Pope. What would have seemed absolutely incredible four years before, most of all to Ratti himself, had come to pass.

What happened within Ratti during the last forty-eight hours of the Conclave will perhaps never be known. But one thing is certain, that those hours decided the fate not only of the man who was to don the tiara but also of the Church for two of the most dramatic decades of its own and the world's history. Those forty-eight hours saw decided not only the succession to Benedict xv but also the basic programme of the new pontificate. The result, as has been said earlier, was largely due to Gasparri's encounters with Ratti during the Conclave. In deciding on a continuation of Benedict xv's line of policy, it was also agreed that the most important aims of the new pontificate would be to end the Roman Question and to establish definitively the international role of the Holy See. The new Pope did an unheard-of thing in announcing this programme at once when, after the canopies above his colleagues' thrones had been lowered and they crowded around him, the Cardinal Dean asked him if he accepted the supreme office and what name he would choose. Replying that he would take the name of Pius, in homage to Pius ix under whose pontificate he had been born and begun his ecclesiastical career and out of gratitude to Pius x who had called him to Rome, he went on to declare that he wished to continue the work of pacification begun by his predecessor Benedict xv and then, after a long pause as was his custom, added solemnly:

I want to say one word more in presence of the members of the Sacred College: I affirm my purpose of safeguarding and defending all the rights of the Church and all the prerogatives of the Holy See. But having said this, I wish my first benediction to go out, as a pledge of that peace for which humanity is yearning, not only to Rome and to Italy, but to the whole Church and the whole world. I will therefore give the benediction from the outer balcony of St Peter's.

Such precipitate action was most unlike Achille Ratti, whose habit it was to take decisions only after prolonged meditation.

Similarly, it was an unheard-of Ratti who with a peremptory 'I wish' imposed his will on men who until a few minutes earlier had been his colleagues. Cardinal Tisserant, speaking of those who were able to approach him in the first hours of his pontificate, was to say later: 'They were struck by his immediate transformation. His consciousness of his new dignity was such that, perhaps without explicitly wishing it, he seemed a different person. To his closest colleagues from the Vatican Library, who were waiting for him at the door of the apartment he had occupied during the Conclave as he came out to visit the pontifical apartment, he gave a cordial blessing, but it seemed to come from the other world. He wished to be Pope and nothing else.' The fact is that there was nothing precipitate about his action, nor had he undergone an instantaneous transformation. Achille Ratti had been Pope incognito from the moment when he accepted the designation offered him by Gasparri. From that moment Pius xi took the place of the man he had been till then.

There can be no doubt, moreover, that by this declaration of his programme, made in the Sistine Chapel while still in his Cardinal's robes, Ratti left no further possibility of choice as to his major objectives. Subsequent events at once confirmed this. Only an hour later he appeared on the outer balcony of St Peter's, as no Pope had done since the election of Pius ix in 1846. On that cold, grey February morning a slow drizzling rain was falling; but the enthusiasm of the crowd, who had hardly dared to hope for that gesture, knew no limits. For the first time since 20 September 1870 Italian troops drawn up before the steps to the basilica presented arms to the Pope.

As if that were not enough, on the following Sunday, 12 February, the day of the Pope's coronation, that inaugural gesture of his pontificate was unexpectedly repeated a second time. While the procession was on its way back, near the chapel of Michelangelo's *Pietà*, Cardinal Gasparri approached the gestatorial chair and exchanged a few words with the Pope. The Pope then signed to the cardinals present to come closer, and those who were near enough to see noticed their perplexed demeanour after he had said a few words to them. Gasparri had told the Pope that the officers responsible for public order had sent word that the faithful outside the Basilica were waiting for the benediction. When the Pope asked the cardinals whether he should agree to give it again, some said yes, others no. Pius XI listened to them tranquilly and then, smiling, settled the question by saying that to satisfy everyone, and especially the faithful, he would adopt a middle course and appear on the balcony to give the benediction '*nihil dicens*', in other words without pronouncing the ritual formula. Which is what he did.

A Hand held out to the 'Man of Destiny'

The history of the Lateran Agreements themselves begins in 1926, but the history of the Reconciliation, at any rate as far as Ratti is concerned, begins on 6 February 1922. And this history provides the key explanation for the most fundamental, contrasting, and disputed feature of Pius XI's whole pontificate. It is pointless to object that one cannot speak of pre-Concordat activities in the spring and summer of 1922 since the Italian 'partner' to such activities did not then exist. For although Pius XI and his Secretariat of State were then occupied with quite different questions, there can be no doubt that they were following Italian developments with the greatest attention and were keeping a watchful eye on the 'new man' whom the whole country now saw as a rising star on the horizon. To confirm this we need only to re-read Gasparri's famous confidences to Buonaiuti, published by the latter in the Rome *Messaggero* of 29 September 1921: 'There are no insuperable difficulties about the longed-for settlement of the Roman Question,' Benedict XV's Secretary of State told his companion, 'It is the particular men concerned that put us in a state of uncertainty. True, we no longer have to deal with that . . . of a Giolitti, but we do not think the other Ministers, Bonomi and Della Torretta, will get as far as a Reconciliation either. We are still waiting for our man.'

But while the Vatican side went no further than watchful waiting or, at most, cautious soundings among Fascist circles in Milan, increasingly insistent recommendations began to percolate among the Black Shirts about the lenient treatment to be accorded to even the most recalcitrant clergy. These recommendations became definite orders on the eve of the March on Rome: Fascists involved in the enterprise were told unequivocally not only to respect the clergy and anyone connected with religion but also to show the deepest consideration towards all sacred things and personalities, especially in the capital. It was highly significant that the plans for manifestations to celebrate the triumph of the Fascist revolution even included a Black Shirt rally in St Peter's Square in homage to the Pope – a plan later abandoned possibly through the intervention, prompted by its customary caution, of the Vatican itself.

What had the Fascist leaders in mind in planning such a manifestation? Was it merely to secure the Pope's sympathies, or to get public opinion, and especially Catholic opinion, on their side by convincing the people that the Pope was with them? Or was the gesture perhaps prompted by reasons of gratitude for the two recent pontifical letters to the Italian episcopate? Those two letters as they stood merely urged concord, but the Fascist leaders interpreted them as a warning to any who might contemplate opposing their revolution by force. They bear the dates of 6 August and 28 October, but it is significant that the *Osservatore Romano* did not publish the second until the afternoon of the following day, by which time the King had not only refused to sign the decree presented to him by the Prime Minister, Facta, proclaiming a state of siege, but had also yielded to all Mussolini's conditions about the formation of the new Government. More serious still, the Vatican daily accompanied the papal letter by a comment from the editor, Giuseppe Dalla Torre, which not only accepted the *fait accompli* but expressed satisfaction at the way in which it had come about:

We note with lively satisfaction how up to the present the aims of the Supreme Powers, the wishes of the leading parties, and those of the man who today is called upon to form the Government have been in keeping with the pious exhortation of Pius XI. For exceptional measures, such as might have degenerated at so perilous a moment into bloody fratricidal strife, were forestalled; the authors of deplored violent acts were recalled to stricter discipline and to respect for all civil rights; and it is announced that Onorevole Mussolini intends to bring men from all sides, whose first concern is the interests of the people, to collaborate in the Government.

With these words the Vatican organ and, indirectly, the Secretariat of State not only unconditionally approved the King's action but also greeted the Fascist revolutionary solution and its leader as giving sure promise of the rebirth and reorganization of the country. A few weeks later, when receiving in audience Count Ambrogio Caccia Dominioni, president of the diocesan board of Catholic Action in Milan and brother of Mgr Camillo, His Holiness's Master of the Chamber, Pius XI after discussing at some length the new situation in Italy said: 'I see that with Mussolini much can be done.'[1]

But by now facts spoke stronger than prophecies. If on the occasion of the March on Rome it was, in a certain sense, the Vatican that took the initiative, on its morrow it was Mussolini who did so. Between November 1922 and January 1923 the new régime took a series of decisions that astounded the Catholic world. It ordered crucifixes to be restored to schoolrooms (and, soon after, to law courts and hospitals), increased the penalties for offences against the Catholic religion and the clergy, re-established military chaplains in the armed forces, promised new rules on duelling in the army, announced improved salaries for the clergy, and made known through the Minister for Public Instruction, Gentile, that religious teaching was to be a basic feature of the educational system; finally, on 13 February, the Grand Council decreed membership of the Fascist Party to be incompatible with membership of Freemasonry. All this came about with such speed that the press began to speak of definite progress towards a solution of the Roman Question.

For once in a way the newspapers' suppositions were not so far from the truth. As a journalist prelate, Mgr Enrico Pucci, equally familiar in Fascist and in Vatican circles, was to reveal some years later in his book *La pace del Laterano* (The Lateran Peace), from the earliest months of the Mussolini régime Cardinal Vincenzo Vannutelli had had a number of conversations with Alfredo Rocco, Under-Secretary for Pensions and later Minister of Justice, on the subject of Reconciliation; and a letter to the Cardinal from Rocco even spoke of the Roman Question as 'pre-eminent among the intentions of the Fascist Government'. Another and much more significant fact to become known only much later was that in the second half of January 1923, probably, around the 20th, the future signatories of the Lateran Pacts, Mussolini and Gasparri, met at the house of Senator Santucci in Palazzo Guglielmi, near the Piazza Venezia. Their long discussion dealt chiefly with the need to settle the Roman Question,

[1] See Enrico Pucci, *La pace del Laterano,* Rome, 1930

a subsidiary topic being the salvaging of the Banco di Roma, whose directors had close links with the Vatican. Mussolini was happy to guarantee this rescue operation as proof of his excellent intentions in relation to Reconciliation.

Mussolini cannot, however, have concealed from his august companion the fact that in order to arrive at the Reconciliation and a concordat his party would need to have an absolute majority in the Chamber; in particular, it would need to secure the unconditional support of the Catholic Partito Popolare and indeed preferably an actual merger of that party with the Fascists, thus bringing about that unity which alone could guarantee the new order in the country. And probably Gasparri with his accustomed bluff frankness did not conceal the Pope's and his own plans, which were to concentrate the whole influence of the Church in Catholic Action, abandoning the Partito Popolare to its fate. As a first step, he was ready to promise Mussolini that he would further his efforts by persuading the Popolari to give up the idea of holding their party congress in Turin in March 1923.

These remarkably sweeping plans of Gasparri's will come as no surprise to anyone conversant with his views, outlined earlier in this book, regarding the Catholic party and its secretary, Don Sturzo. But it was hardheaded calculation, rather than a general antipathy towards that party, that led Gasparri to make his promises to Mussolini. In aiming at the Reconciliation, the Holy See had to put its stakes either on Don Sturzo and the Partito Popolare or on Mussolini and Fascism. Now, in the first post-war elections, of 16 November 1919, the Partito Popolare had secured 103 deputies, thus at once becoming the third strongest party in the country; but in the elections of May 1921 its representation had risen by only five, a fact which suggested that it had reached its limit. It was therefore absurd to hope that, since it accounted for only a quarter of the deputies, it could steer the solution of the Roman Question through Parliament. All the lay parties would have combined to oppose it, or would have yielded their support only if the Church had contented itself with settling the Roman Question proper without trying to achieve an actual concordat. But if the traditional lay parties were recalcitrant and the Partito Popolare impotent, the only hope lay in the new nationalist and totalitarian party, especially seeing that while Sturzo might indeed desire but could not impose Reconciliation,

Mussolini had only to desire it to be able to impose it. And Mussolini could not but desire such a success, which would provide the most striking possible ratification of his conquest of power and consolidate his prestige not only in Italy but throughout the world.

The fact that support for Fascism meant supporting a dictatorship, and hence dealing a mortal blow to Italian democracy, presented no problem to Pius XI or his Secretary of State: both of them disliked and despised democratic forms of government which, by encouraging party rivalry, also encouraged the spread of ideologies largely hostile to the Church and tended to produce weak and frequently changing governments. They could not of course then foresee – or at most only vaguely, given the anti-liberal basis of nationalist governments – the advent of ideological totalitarianisms which would inevitably lead to the elimination of the Church's own influence in the life of the new States; or, if they envisaged any such thing, they believed they could secure exceptional treatment for the Church by means of concordats. Hence the sacrifice of the Partito Popolare was regarded as a modest price in relation to the aims at stake, especially since the Church could always count on the Catholic Action organizations, still completely under the Pope's control.

The first step towards embarrassing the Partito Popolare and creating confusion within its ranks was to deprive it of its founder and secretary. Despite Gasparri's efforts the party held its national congress in Turin, where by a large majority it rejected its right wing's proposal to offer unconditional support to the Mussolini Government, instead approving Don Sturzo's proposal to exact certain conditions. The hopes of Gasparri and Mussolini thus fell to the ground; and Mussolini, angered at this check, accepted the resignation of the Catholic Ministers and soon afterwards gave the word for a revival of nation-wide Fascist violence against the Catholic associations and clergy. This warning spoke for itself, but Mussolini went still further in letting it be known at the Vatican that he would not hesitate to adopt legislation against Church personalities and property if measures were not taken to end the Partito Popolare's intransigence against Fascism and eliminate its leader.

The Secretary of State feigned to submit to this blackmail against his will, and on 25 June the *Corriere d'Italia*, organ of the

Partito Popolare's right wing, published an article by the enterprising Mgr Pucci giving Don Sturzo a clear warning not to create difficulties for the ecclesiastical authorities. At the same time the streets of Rome were suddenly plastered with manifestoes from 'Italian Catholics' proclaiming their support for the Fascist Government and declaring that 'the political function of Italian Catholics should become fused in the new orientation of all the best national forces'. Lastly, a few days later an official emissary of the Vatican came to Don Sturzo to inform him that the Fascist Government was threatening a large scale anticlerical campaign unless the party withdrew its opposition and Sturzo resigned. Naturally, the emissary added, the Vatican wished at all costs to avoid such strife. Sturzo, recognizing that it would be useless to resist, on 10 July 1923 announced his resignation, and on the following day the *Osservatore Romano* assured its readers that his gesture had contributed towards the pacification of Italian hearts, especially 'after the sinister rumours of an imminent offensive against the clergy and Catholic organizations'. Little more than a month later this statement received a bloodstained refutation: on 23 August Don Giovanni Minzoni, Archpriest of Argenta, near Ravenna, was set upon by two assassins and died of a broken skull.

The divergence between Catholic Action and the Partito Popolare could now be openly proclaimed, for Pius XI had lost no time in ensuring the former's neutrality towards Fascism and paving the way for an alliance with it. Catholic Action itself had cherished no particular sympathy for Mussolini's movement before the March on Rome, as was clear from the attitude adopted by young Catholics at its Rome congress of September 1922. The congress not only legalized the formation of 'advance guards' (armed formations designed to oppose Fascist violence) but also approved modifications to the statute in order to give Catholic Action the right to train 'young people to study and solve political problems in accordance with Church directives'. Pius XI did not conceal his irritation when he received the congress members. 'Not politics,' he said coldly and sternly, 'not social economy, not, even, I would say, culture, but first and foremost the individual's personal Christian outlook – that is what the statutes of your organization demand.'

Something more than mere admonition was needed, however.

And after Mussolini came to power Pius XI seized the opportunity of a meeting in Rome of Catholic Action's central committee, on 13 December 1922, to announce through Mgr Pizzardo, its ecclesiastical assistant and also Under-Secretary in the Secretariat of State, the appointment of the organization's new president, Commendatore Luigi Colombo. A Milanese and an old acquaintance of Ratti's, Colombo was eminently suited for the post. Little more than a month later, on 18 January 1923, he made the unheard-of gesture of heading a delegation of his committee to Mussolini to present him with a series of desiderata from the association. A few months later, on 15 May, this time in his capacity of president of the diocesan board in Milan, he signed an agreement with the Milanese Fascist provincial secretary, Signor Maggi, laying down the method of participation of Catholic societies, bearing their banners, in public manifestations. For the first time Catholic Action officially mingled its banners among the Fascist pennants, and the *Osservatore Romano* on 21 May praised the agreement, saying it was 'worthy of consideration and imitation everywhere'.

In making Catholic Action an alternative to the Partito Popolare and according it the confidence it withheld from the Popolari, the Holy See inevitably gave rise to searchings of conscience among the anti-Fascist leaders of the party, thus giving it a further push towards dissolution. The role allotted to Catholic Action, further defined in various official documents of the same year (in which, incidentally, it was given new statutes), was to be non-political, since membership of Catholic Action was regarded as sufficient proof of civic conscience. But, in the circumstances, being non-political did not mean merely refraining from political activity; it also meant pursuing no policy contrary to the régime in power: in other words, it was itself tantamount to a policy and a political action, if only of a negative kind, from which the only possible beneficiary was Fascism. This line continued to be maintained during the 1924 election campaign and was not modified even after the murder of the Socialist deputy Giacomo Matteotti (10 June 1924), an event which aroused indignation and protest throughout the country, or after the secession of the democratic parties to the Aventine. The alliance with a régime that murdered an opponent and was boycotted by all the parties defending civic liberties aroused no qualms in Pius XI and his Secretary of State.

On the contrary, when at the meeting of provincial secretaries of the Partito Popolare in Rome on 16 July 1924 the party's political secretary, De Gasperi, openly declared himself in favour of a Government coalition to include the Socialists, *Civiltà Cattolica* first (2 August) commented adversely and then (16 August), in an article entitled 'The role of Catholics in the present party political struggle in Italy', defended Fascism as the established government and therefore the sole source of authority in the country. Besides recognizing the 'undeniable good service' of Fascism 'particularly with regard to religion' and declaring it unlawful for good citizens, and especially Catholics, to contribute in any way to its downfall, the article also explicitly stated that any collaboration between the Partito Popolare and the Socialist Party would be 'neither suitable nor opportune nor permissible'– because, while the Fascist Party had no specific doctrine, Socialism was in theory and practice irreligious and anti-religious and 'would make use of the power it acquired to undermine the very basis of public morality and the Church and would not even show the same restraint as the liberals'.

The official character of the review left no doubt as to the article's source of inspiration; but on 9 September, in an audience for Catholic university students, Pius xi explicitly stated his own point of view:

Instances are also cited of collaboration between Catholics and Socialists in other countries; but here there is confusion, due perhaps to insufficient experience, between two totally different sets of circumstances. Apart from the differences in environment and historical, political, and religious conditions, it is one thing to find oneself face to face with a party which has already reached power, but quite another thing to open the way and provide the possibility for a party to come to power . . . And it is truly painful to the Pope's heart to see good sons and good Catholics divided and in strife among themselves.

Public opinion against the Fascist régime was so strong as to make any further manifestation of support for the Government inadvisable for the time being. But after Mussolini's speech of 3 January 1925 and the failure of the Opposition parties to react to it, the fate of the Partito Popolare was sealed. Don Sturzo, urged by Cardinal Gasparri himself to take refuge abroad for fear of possible reprisals, had already left for London with a passport from the Vatican on 25 October 1924. The party held its fifth and last congress in Rome in June 1925; its secretary, De Gasperi, resigned in the following December; and it had dwindled and died by the end of 1926.

Thus the way was open for the negotiations with the Government which were to lead to the signature of the Lateran Agreements. In a letter of 18 February 1926 to Cardinal Gasparri, Pius xi declared that the State could not proceed unilaterally to provide a new legal framework for the Catholic Church in Italy, and that this would be possible only by means of negotiations and agreements with the Holy See. This was an indirect but promising invitation. Finally, in the following August, preparations for a Concordat were officially launched.

The agreements, signed on 11 February 1929 in the Lateran Palace from which they took their name, did not achieve the maximum desired by Ratti; but that maximum was so unattainable that it would have been utopian to expect it. The few palaces which he failed to annex to the Vatican City (among them that of the Holy Office and the Villa Doria Pamphili) cost him no sacrifice apart from the difficulty of persuading Cardinal Gasparri, according to whom 'the Vatican, even with its gardens, was a palace, not a State'. Moreover the sum agreed upon to cover once and for all the Holy See's economic claims – 1,750 million lire – was so great as to relieve the Holy See of all material anxieties and provide the basis, as well, for the new Vatican State's finances.

But Pius xi's main aim had always been the Concordat. The real reparation for the wrongs done by the State to the Church in Italy was, as he wanted, in the legal sphere, and it was in this sphere that he succeeded not only in establishing canon law as a counterpart to Italian State law, but also in imposing the supremacy of canon law over the law of the State, or at any rate in inserting it as an element capable of dissolving or overcoming State law. The Concordat, in fact, supported by the Treaty, which in its first article accords to the Catholic religion the position of the sole religion of the State, not only admits the co-existence on national territory of the ecclesiastical society, autonomous and entirely *sui juris*, attributing to it complete freedom in internal relations between its leaders and the faithful and vice versa, but it also at least partially revives old forgotten privileges of the clergy (including special treatment for clergy arraigned on a criminal charge), even going so far as to deprive of certain civil rights any members or former members of the ecclesiastical society under censure by that society. It also removes from the State all jurisdiction over marriages of Catholic citizens contracting a religious marriage; and it imposes teaching of the Christian doctrine according to the form accepted by Catholic tradition as the basis and apex of national education in elementary and secondary schools.

While, therefore, the Treaty on the one hand eliminated the Roman Question as far as temporal power was concerned, on the other hand it revived it in relation to the much more relevant and delicate spheres of the State's jurisdictional rights and the inalienable rights of its citizens; and this at a time when not only had the territorial aspect of the Roman Question ceased to exist and therefore called for no counter-compensation in much more substantial values, but also when the power illegally held by a *de facto* Government naturally inclined it even to sacrifice certain essential prerogatives of the State, provided it could acquire the prestige of a resounding political success both at home and abroad.

The Devil's Pact with Hitler

The extraordinary relationship between Pius xi and Fascism was not, however, an isolated case in Ratti's pontificate. Generally speaking, all the European dictators of the two decades between the World Wars, especially those who were Catholic, either had help from him in their conquest of power (as in the case of Franco) or enjoyed his support in maintaining it (Salazar, Horthy, Dollfuss). The most serious and perturbing case, however, was that of Hitler and Nazism. In Italy there was no organized episcopate with a representative and deliberative body of its own which might have exercised an authoritative and official influence on Church-State relations. This situation had arisen not so much because of the very large number of bishops and dioceses in Italy (there were over three hundred) or because of any special difficulty in creating a national episcopal conference, but rather because of the survival of the Roman Question, which had caused the Popes, from Pius ix onwards, to keep the direct conduct of Church affairs in their own hands. Pius xi was therefore in a position to act directly, without having to take into account the possibly adverse views of the Italian bishops. In Germany, on the other hand, the situation was quite different.

There, an episcopate existed that was highly articulate – partly because it was small – and the German episcopal conference when occasion arose assumed the responsibilities of the Catholic Church in relation to the country; and, generally speaking, the German episcopate had always shown itself opposed to Hitler from the very beginning of his movement's rise to power. When, on 14 September 1930, the National Socialist Party secured six million votes and 107 seats in the elections, the Catholic hierarchy arose as one man and exhorted the faithful to examine their consciences. Similarly, in the following two years the German bishops, whether individually or as a body, continued to issue pronouncements condemning the unacceptable aspects of the Nazi movement. True, in the meantime Hitler's propaganda, skilfully exploiting German nationalist feelings, had succeeded in penetrating Catholic ranks to some extent; but the bishops as a whole did not change their attitude. After 31 January 1933, when the President, Marshal Hindenburg, called on Hitler to assume power, they sided solidly with the *Zentrum*, the Catholic party which refused to accord the new Chancellor full powers for a year, and early in March, when the elections were imminent which were to ratify the *fait accompli*, they recommended people to vote for the Catholic party's candidates.

Yet only two or three weeks later, on 23 March, they allowed the *Zentrum* and the Bavarian Catholic party to vote for Hitler, and on the 28th they themselves took up a position favourable to the dictator. What had caused this sudden volte-face? Certainly not the *fait accompli*, which had already virtually existed for some time. Nor was it any opportunist calculation that by showing forbearance towards Hitler they might later reckon on his gratitude: such forbearance would at once have been interpreted as weakness by the Führer, and moreover the grounds for disagreement with his movement were so substantial and irreconcilable as to rule out any idea of a tactical concession which could only cast confusion among the faithful. The only possible explanation, therefore, is that influence was brought to bear on the bishops and the *Zentrum* by Rome itself. That this is no fantastic supposition is further suggested by the presence in Rome, during the first half of that tragic March, of Cardinal Faulhaber, Archbishop of Munich, who was received in audience by Pius XI on the 12th and the next day was present at a public consistory. On his return to Munich he referred, on the 24th, to his stay in Rome in the following terms:

After my recent experience in Rome in the highest circles, which I cannot reveal here, I must say that I found, despite everything, a greater tolerance with regard to the new Government. It is today, moreover, not only in possession of power – which in itself would not suffice to justify it according to our principles – but it has reached that position by legal methods; indeed it could be said that no revolutionary party has ever come to power in so regular a way. Let us meditate on the words of the Holy Father, who, in a consistory, without mentioning his name, indicated before the whole world in Adolf Hitler the statesman who first, after the Pope himself, has raised his voice against Bolshevism.

This papal eulogy of Hitler was to be later recalled by the German bishops in a collective memorandum to the Führer of 20 August 1935 together with these significant words: 'In the face of this proclamation of the Pope's confidence, millions of men abroad, both Catholics and non-Catholics, have overcome their initial mistrust and accorded credit to your Government.'

In the future, these small rays of light were to serve to illuminate a whole series of much more convincing documents. But for the time being they suffice to explain why, on 23 March, Mgr Kaas, the *Zentrum* leader, persuaded his followers to support Hitler, and also why, on the 28th, the episcopate assembled at Fulda suddenly changed its attitude – a change the more inexplicable because between 1 February and 23 March the Brown Shirts had established a veritable reign of terror in the country. Whatever may have been the reason for Faulhaber's presence in Rome during the troubled days before the voting in Germany, his main aim can certainly not have been to inform the Vatican but to receive instructions; and these, as everything seems to indicate, were to avoid letting the Catholic Church in Germany find itself alone in opposition, since by then nothing seemed likely to halt the advance of Nazism. By allying itself in the last resort with Nazism – so it was thought in Rome – the Church would avoid possibly fatal reprisals.

The conduct of the Holy See can be clearly traced through the course of subsequent events. Mgr Kaas, having convinced his deputies as to the line they should take, left at once for Rome and on his return on 31 March was received by Hitler. On 7 April he went back to Rome, this time accompanied by the German Vice-Chancellor, von Papen, charged by the Führer to take soundings about a concordat with the Holy See. It would seem beyond doubt, therefore, that acceptance of the Concordat was the price paid by Hitler for the adherence of the episcopate and the Catholic party to his cause. Yet his prompt acceptance should have aroused suspicions about the sincerity of his intentions. Von Papen, in his memoirs, admits that he himself was amazed at the ease with which Hitler accepted the proposed arrangements for the Concordat, and in particular at the authorization he received to bypass the normal channels (the Ministry for Foreign Affairs and the German Ambassador to the Holy See) in order to accelerate its conclusion.

As far as is known, on the other hand, no surprise was evinced by the Pope and his collaborators in the Secretariat of State, or if it was, it was soon forgotten. Three years earlier Cardinal Gasparri had been replaced as Secretary of State by the former Nuncio in Berlin, Eugenio Pacelli, who had negotiated two Concordats in Germany, with Bavaria and with Prussia, each of which took him five years of hard work to conclude. But the new and much more important agreement with the Third Reich, which incorporated the earlier Concordats, was ready by 8 July 1933, only three months after negotiations began, and was signed on the 20th at an official ceremony in the pontifical Secretariat. It would even have been signed some weeks earlier if in June the Nazi extremists, headed by Goebbels and Heydrich, had not started a campaign in Germany with the obvious aim of embarrassing the negotiations with the Holy See, violently attacking immorality in German monasteries and demanding the trial of numbers of monks. This naturally caused Pius XI to stiffen, but von Papen, appealing directly to the Führer, got the campaign stopped. Another detail showing the feverish haste, not so much of the Führer but of Pius XI, to conclude the Concordat is provided by the document itself, and concerns the suspension of any decision with regard to Catholic Action or the youth movements which Church and State vied in wishing to control. This is the more striking in view of Pius xi's special interest in this sphere and the importance he had attached to replacing the Partito Popolare by Catholic Action.

Pius xi's conduct in relation to Franco in Spain, on the purely diplomatic plane at any rate, was certainly a good deal more cautious and circumspect. Formal recognition of his Government by the Holy See was delayed until mid-1938, although Franco himself had accorded official rank to his representative at the Vatican in August 1937. On that occasion the Secretariat of State lost no time in issuing a communiqué saying that the Generalis-simo's gesture did not imply recognition of his Government by the Holy See. But this prudence about diplomatic formalities was prompted purely by the desire not to prejudice the future of relations with Spain before the outcome of the civil war, which lasted for three years, ending only on 27 March 1939, was settled. These official precautions were the only ones adopted by the Vatican towards Franco. From beginning to end of the civil war the *Osservatore Romano* was openly and warmly favourable to the dictator. The Spanish war had divided Catholics in Europe, most of those in France siding with the Republicans while all Italian and German Catholics supported Franco; the *Osservatore* did not hesitate to side with the latter (and, in January 1939, even had the authority of Padre Cordovani, Master of the Sacred Palaces, for doing so).

This declared standpoint of the Vatican daily corresponded, moreover, to the attitude publicly and solemnly adopted by the Pope in person in his celebrated speech of 14 September at Castel Gandolfo to five hundred Spanish refugees. In that speech, which the *Osservatore* described as 'suitably helpful', Pius xi incited the whole Catholic world to mobilize against the Spanish Republicans, accepting the slogan of the Fascist press which for some time had been identifying the Spanish Republicans with the Communists, although the Communists in Spain, whether in the Government or as a party, were only a small minority. And it might seem far-fetched to mention the strange coincidence that on the same day Hitler, in Nuremberg, closed his party's annual congress with a vast speech full of attacks on Communism – but for the fact that on 30 August in all the churches of Germany a collective letter had been read, prepared at Fulda by the German bishops at their

annual conference, in which they openly asked Hitler to intervene
on the side of Franco. The disturbing factor in all this is that,
once again, Pius XI had ignored the circumstance that in Spain
the legal government was not the aggressor but the victim of
aggression, and that it was not in the spirit of the Gospel to
encourage a crusade of violence in order to ensure the maintenance of the Spanish Church's feudal privileges.

The Cockade of the Third Republic

Nevertheless it would be lacking in objectivity to suggest that
the Pope combined a *penchant* for the dictatorships with a no less
gratuitous aversion for the democratic régimes. Whatever his
personal predilections might be, he could, on occasion, be
irreproachably realistic. In Spain itself, in 1931, at the highly
delicate juncture of the transition from monarchy to republic, the
Holy See's representative there acted with remarkable skill, not
to say courage. The Nuncio, Mgr Tedeschini – not without the
knowledge and approval of Rome – visited the Spanish Foreign
Minister the very day before the republic was proclaimed on
16 April 1931; indeed it would seem that he had already met
Alcalá Zamora at the house of the German ambassador in the
previous March to discuss with him the ecclesiastical policy of
the new régime.

But the case of France is certainly the most significant and
indicative. From the very beginning of his pontificate, while in
Italy he was preparing cynically to rid himself of the democracy
that impeded his plans, Pius XI (admittedly influenced to some
extent by his Secretary of State) unhesitatingly pursued his predecessor's policy of *ralliement*. Overcoming the opposition of
most of the French bishops, he settled the question of diocesan
associations, even giving them his solemn approval in an encyclical (*Maximam Gravissimamque*, of 18 June 1924); and he
continued to pursue this line of policy even though after the
1924 elections the right-wing and moderate-republican *Bloc
National* was replaced by the Radical-Socialist cartel, which at
once began to threaten the existence of the French Ambassador
to the Vatican and apply more strictly the laws on congregations.

During the election campaign, Pius XI had already intervened
authoritatively to prevent the publication of the pastoral letter

prepared by the Assembly of Cardinals and Archbishops in February 1924, which told Catholics to vote only for candidates prepared to condemn secularism. In March 1925, however, the episcopate returned to the attack, approving a note 'on the so-called secular laws and on measures to combat them' which had been drawn up and issued by the secretary of the Assembly, Père Janvier. This document was so violent as to justify extreme reactions from the Government; and Pius xi demanded its solemn disavowal. On the Sunday after its publication the Archbishop of Paris, Cardinal Dubois, had to give a public assurance in Notre Dame that the Holy See had nothing to do with the document and that it was neither a political act nor a declaration of war, but 'a simple catechism lesson'.

The greatest obstacle to the policy of Pius xi and his Secretary of State in relation to France thus lay in the episcopate, most of whom had been appointed by Pius x. The bishops, however, found a support for their anti-republicanism and integralism in *Action Française*. But Maurras' paper, with its fanatical nationalism, came up against Pius xi's policy not only towards France but in the international sphere. Consequently, when Cardinal Mercier warned the Pope about Maurras' growing influence on Catholic youth even in Belgium, it afforded Pius xi a splendid opportunity to act against the paper, both in order to neutralize its ideological propaganda and to weaken the bishops' resistance and at the same time overcome the French secular government's mistrust of Rome. To this end he skilfully made use of the Holy Office's earlier condemnation of *Action Française*: the condemnation had, indeed, been suspended by Pius x but for reasons which could be represented as temporary. He had no wish to seem to act precipitately. Between 5 September and 29 December 1926, when the decree was published, Maurras and his paper had plenty of time for manoeuvre to ward off the blow; but instead, foolishly egged on by a number of bishops, prelates, and members of the clergy to take up the challenge, they actually dared to answer the warnings about them contained in the Christmas allocution by announcing their positive refusal to submit. Not only that, but after the condemnation they indulged in violent invective reminiscent of the worst kind of demagogic anticlericalism, running the gamut from the Borgias to St Bartholomew's Eve and from Galileo to Bishop Cauchon. The decree condemning them was described as a fake and a lie, the *Osservatore Romano* was called the *'diffamatore romano'*, and the Pope proclaimed victim of a plot concocted by the Nuncio Cerretti, Briand, the police, and the Thoiry and Locarno policy, with the sole object of humiliating France and reconstituting the Holy Roman-Germanic Empire.

All this was eminently calculated to make Pius XI stiffen. On 8 March 1927 he caused the Apostolic Penitentiary to intervene with the sternest possible admonitions: clergy who had absolved readers or supporters of *Action Française* were to be deprived of authority to hear confessions; seminarists who had read or supported the paper were to be judged unsuited for an ecclesiastical career and expelled; the faithful guilty of a similar charge were to be regarded as public sinners, refused the sacraments, and, in cases of extreme rebellion, denied Church burial. At the same time the French episcopate was forced to sign a letter approving the pontifical condemnation which, if not explicitly so, was tantamount to a moral capitulation. A good many bishops prudently hastened to abandon the cause they now realized was irrevocably lost, adopting the standpoint of the Holy See with a zeal proportionate to their earlier weakness. A purge campaign reminiscent of anti-Modernist days was thus let loose, in an atmosphere sharply recalling that of the Dreyfus affair and going to such extremes that the Nuncio himself, Mgr Maglione, at the height of the crisis felt the need to justify himself and assure Cardinal Verdier that he was in no way implicated in the punitive measures inflicted on *Action Française*.

More than once a schism seemed imminent in the French Church, but while some were perplexed, doubting the need to provoke a drama so disproportionate to its cause, and many others were alarmed and anxious, one man alone showed no signs of trouble or doubt: Pius XI. And his early decisiveness and subsequent inexorability brought him victory on all fronts. The steady expansion of *Action Française* was checked, and its following among Catholics, especially among the clergy, seminarists, and monastic cultural institutions, fell sharply. At the same time the French episcopate abandoned its integralist and antirepublican standpoint and passively submitted to Rome's new line of policy. Lastly, the lay world, and in particular the French political leaders, could no longer cherish doubts or find pretexts for rejecting the hand held out to them by the Vatican.

A Twentieth-century 'Unam Sanctam'

Pius xi's conduct in relation to France is decisive for an understanding of the true characteristics of his policy. Sensitive though
he might be to the attractions of the dictators – and here it must
be remembered that he was living in a period in which nearly all
the countries of Europe were either ruled by dictators or under
the threat of dictatorship – his behaviour towards France explodes
any theory that he was exclusively philo-totalitarian. His policy
was inspired, not by sympathy for the régimes, but by the need
for the Church to enter into relations with all States, whatever
their method of government. He himself explicitly admitted this
in one of his numerous polemical speeches after the Reconciliation
with Italy, saying he was ready if need be to make a concordat
with the devil.

His policy was, in fact, determined exclusively by religious and
confessional reasons, even if accompanied by a quite astonishing
impartiality as to the means and methods employed. In its detachment from purely profane objectives he to some extent recalled
Pius x, while he was in direct descent from the most insidious
and machiavellian popes of the Renaissance in his method of
carrying it out. His aim, in any case, was to secure from every
country the greatest possible number of concessions and privileges
concerning ecclesiastical administration, religious teaching, matrimonial legislation, and the economic security of ecclesiastical
institutions. Hence his marked predilection for concordats. The
network of concordatory agreements constituted, in his eyes, the
basis of that world supremacy of the Church of which from the
outset of his pontificate he aspired to be the theoretician and
indeed the theologian.

The key to Ratti's pontificate lies at once concealed and patent
in the two encyclicals in which he announced his programme,
and which are complementary to each other: *Ubi arcano Dei*, of
23 December 1922, and *Quas primas*, of 23 December 1925. In the
first, the new Pope bluntly belittled the effectiveness of any efforts
by the lay world to bring about its own revival and restoration
after the tragic experiences of the war, declaring that the Church
alone could offer the guarantees for the longed-for peace: for it
had been invested by its founder with the office of 'teacher and
guide of all other societies'. The Church, in fact, 'the perfect

society, supreme in its own order, not only symbolizes the definitive reign of God over the universe, but actuates, if by gradual degrees, the sovereignty of Christ in the world, inclining men and peoples to its law of justice and peace'.

There could hardly be a stronger expression of the antithesis between national secular ordinances (further emphasized by a fresh disavowal of the League of Nations in the name of the 'true' community of all peoples) and the theocratic society personified by the Church. But *Quas primas*, intended on the one hand to seal the success of the Holy Year 1925 and, on the other, to establish the feast of the Kingship of Christ, went even further, unravelling with inexorable logic all the consequences of the thesis of the Kingship of Christ the Word incarnate. For the principality of the Redeemer, according to the new Pope, includes not only Catholics but all other men (the former in fact and deed, the latter by right and in potentiality), and not individuals alone but also societies. Governments and rulers, therefore, as well as individuals should be submissive to him. The thesis of the Kingship of Christ further permitted Pius XI to emphasize his struggle against the secession of the civil world from the Church, attacking that 'pest of our age' which, in his view, secularism represented. Humanity, in short, had no other possible choice but to submit anew to the Church and through it to the Pope. In other words, by means of a new and striking argument based on theological foundations, that of the Kingship of Christ, Pius XI was simply reviving the thesis put forward by Boniface VIII in his Bull *Unam sanctam* of 1302 and making it the watchword of modern Catholicism. Not even Leo XIII had dared to advance so frankly medieval a vision of the mission of the papacy in the modern world.

Faced with texts at once so peremptory and positive yet so incredible in content, one is almost tempted to wonder whether this is not a case of simple blackmail, if of a theological order, devised by Pius XI to serve his own aims of power. But there is no doubt that he was profoundly and sincerely convinced of these statements. In this connection one particular episode may be illuminating. At the time of the struggle between Fascism and Catholic Action in 1931, the Rumanian Minister to the Holy See, N. P. Comnène, had been shocked at some of the scenes of violence he witnessed. At a chance meeting with Marchese

Pacelli, brother of the Secretary of State, he said, 'Why don't you submit to arbitration? Give an example to the world.' It was, to say the least, an odd idea. Pacelli, however, did not let it pass, but let the Pope know of it, and Pius xi at once summoned Comnène to see him. Asked what he had meant, the Minister explained his views with some warmth. Pius xi listened to him impatiently and then exploded: 'The rights and prerogatives of which I am the depository,' he said, speaking with barely restrained emotion, 'are of a divine nature. They have been entrusted to me, as Pope, and I cannot depart from them in any way. The essential problem in my divergences with Mussolini concerns, first and foremost, the education of youth. On such a question no compromise is possible. I have been threatened with wrecking and reprisals . . . I am ready for anything. I would even withdraw to a monastery if I was forced, but I will never abandon what I believe to be my mission, never, never, never!'

As he spoke, Comnène relates,[1] the Pope 'became more heated, striking the table with both hands. Finally he rose and continued his protests standing, almost at the top of his voice. He was panting and bursting with indignation until suddenly, probably becoming aware of the impression his excited speech was making on me, he tried to control himself, sat down again and, still panting, added, "But as you see, Minister, I keep calm". When at last he had really calmed down he gave a sad little smile and concluded: "Yes, I can understand if it were merely a question of secular or worldly matters, but not of matters in the spiritual, indeed the divine, sphere." '

To Pius xi the theological thesis of the Kingship of Christ was no mere pretext to justify the disconcertingly dynamic character of his policy but the basic idea inspiring his whole diplomatic action. But having said this, one is bound also to note his profound pessimism about the modern world, which was a direct consequence of that conception; and deriving from it was his conviction that the recovery of the lay world, by now completely separated from the moral directives of the Church in its whole way of living and the organization of its activities, could come about only through the establishment within every State of ever-increasingly powerful Catholic citadels pledged to conquer the

[1] See N. P. Comnène, *Luci e ombre sull'Europa 1914–1950*, Milan, 1955.

leadership of the country and restore it to the Roman obedience. Now it is obvious that, viewed in this light, the function of his concordatory policy was not so much to bring peace and defend the Church's rights as to foster struggle and open rivalry, even if cautiously dissimulated, with the secular forces. In other words, with him the Church became an anti-State in every State, acting on a terrain – that of the so-called *materie miste,* or 'mixed matters', subjects open to the control of either side – that was increasingly fruitful of confusion between the temporal and the spiritual.

The concordats favoured by Pius xi did not confine themselves to safeguarding the cultural and administrative liberties of the Church. They also profited by the weaknesses, due to circumstances, of the contracting States (the new post-war States in need of internal peace and international alliances; the totalitarian régimes anxious for wider support both at home and abroad) to seek privileges for the Church's hierarchies and members, exemption from taxation for its property and institutions, a monopoly in education and social welfare, contributions to its economy, and so on – in short a whole series of concessions which not only gave the Church an exceptional status as to its autonomy and scope but also put it in a position constantly to improve its standing. When the State became worried about the power of the Catholic organization and tried to restrain it, the Church had only to appeal to the written agreements and stiffen its resistance, forcing the State sooner or later to capitulate – at the cost, naturally, of further contributions.

Now, a complicating factor about concordats concluded by the Holy See is that they not only create a legal relationship but also, by the Holy See's express wish, require the prior establishment of regular diplomatic relations with the State concerned. While the Church makes no difficulty about arriving without further conditions at a partial or temporary *modus vivendi,* it never agrees to a real concordat without first insisting on the establishment of regular diplomatic relations, in other words without establishing its presence in the future concordatory State with a representation that in no way differs from that of a normal permanent diplomatic mission between States. And, inevitably, the activities of its ambassador (known as an apostolic nuncio), even if justified by purely religious ends, find expression through virtually the same means and methods as are used by other diplomatic missions.

Thus the effect of this linking of concordats with the instruments of diplomacy is to mix the sacred with the profane in a way that is both ambiguous and liable, as far as religion is concerned, to defeat its own ends.

The disquieting aspect lies not in the concordatory method itself, or the ecclesiastical diplomacy linked with it – though such instruments undoubtedly contain inherent dangers for a religious society – but in the fact that they may be used in a spirit of power rather than of service. And certainly in the concordats of Pius XI (there were eighteen of them in all, including accords and *modus vivendi*), and even more in his whole conception of the Church, the prevailing motive was not service but power. The consequences were to become tragically apparent within his own lifetime and pontificate: for while concordats proved an irresistible temptation even to some of the most anticlerical and violent States in history (such as the Nazi and Fascist régimes), the Church, for its part, had to make bitter expiation for its attempt to seek support for its own freedom among the most inhuman oppressors of fundamental freedoms.

Solitude of Theocracy

An even more serious general effect of concordats and diplomacy has been to cause the Church to act within the limits prescribed by those institutions, preventing it from voicing protests or vindications outside its own particular sphere even when faced with the most inhuman and cruel violations of the fundamental rights of other Churches or religious communities, or of other peoples or States. The most baffling aspect of the dozens of diplomatic Notes sent by the Holy See to the Third Reich during Pius XI's reign in protest against violations of the Concordat is their complete silence about the far more serious violations being perpetrated at the same time in relation to Jews and Protestants.

But was it not, after all, logical that Pius XI's theocratic, anti-State integralism should carry with it intolerance towards other confessions or religions? In relation to the non-Catholic world Pius XI recognized only two possibilities: if Christian to absorb it, if pagan to conquer it. This was what made him one of the great missionary Popes and caused him to cherish for years the dream of bringing the Orthodox Catholics back to unity with

Rome, profiting by the collapse of those political supports which, in his view, had accounted for the centuries-long resistance of Orthodoxy to Catholicism. In particular, he never abandoned the hope of bringing back the Orthodox patriarchate in Moscow, striving first to secure it by alternate threats and blandishments to the Soviet régime at diplomatic level, and then even planning its clandestine conquest by means of missionaries sent in from beyond the confines of the USSR (hence the establishment of the Russicum, the Russian College for the training of priests, in 1929).

If his conduct towards the Protestant world was quite different and in general much less conciliatory, this was because he associated it with the lay world to which it had given rise through its revolt against Rome, and regarded it as quite unready for reabsorption into the Church. Had not one of the major Protestant Churches, the Anglican Church, shown its unpreparedness for a meeting with Catholicism at the famous Malines Conversations[1] in Benedict XV's day and in the early years of his own reign? Hence his lack of understanding for the ecumenical movement which was gradually developing, and which was indubitably one of the most eloquent proofs of the vitality of the Reformation. He made the grave mistake of underestimating the sincerity of these efforts toward union, believing they were merely the customary periodical soul-searchings of Protestantism. This did not, however, prevent him from feeling some alarm at the echo aroused here and there in the Catholic world, if only on a modest scale, by such attempts in the direction of union. His reaction took the form of one of the most unfortunate documents of his pontificate, the encyclical *Mortalium Animos*, of 6 January 1928. In this he first spoke ironically of the various pan-religious experiments that had come into fashion after the First World War ('congresses, meetings, and addresses are arranged, attended by a large concourse of hearers, where all without distinction, unbelievers of every kind as well as Christians, even those who unhappily have rejected Christ and denied His divine nature or mission, are invited to join in the discussion'). He then passed on to the real pan-Christian experiments, denying them any honest or generous aim and indicating instead the snare and

---

[1] Of 1921–5, between Lord Halifax and Cardinal Mercier – see p. 143. *Translator.*

threat which, 'under the appearance of good', they represented to the Catholic faith, and concluding that 'the Apostolic See can by no means take part in these assemblies, nor is it in any way lawful for Catholics to give to such enterprises their encouragement or support', since 'the unity of Christians can come about only by furthering the return to the one true Church of Christ of those who are separated from it'.

If history could be arrested by a pontifical document, the ecumenical movement should have been checked for ever by Pius xi's irony for 'those pan-Christians consumed by zeal to unite Churches'. Fortunately this did not happen: history, if in the course of innumerable errors and horrors, succeeded in surmounting another of the more unhappy effects of Pius xi's theocratic concept: that indifference to human personality and, in general, to natural values, of which, in particular, his encyclicals on marriage (*Casti connubi*) and on the education of youth (*Divini illius Magistri*) afford proof. In the last documents of his pontificate this gap is repaired. Faced with the completely callous attitude of the dictatorships towards individual citizens, even to the point of depriving human beings of their fundamental rights – the rights of life, procreation, property, freedom of thought and of the press, and of free association – the pontifical documents themselves begin to speak of human rights and of their inviolability. Unfortunately, however, this does not imply making the human being the real point of reference in relation to the various basic social entities: the family, the State and the Church. Pius xi was concerned with human beings only indirectly and as pawns, so to speak, in his attack on the States oppressing the Church: he denied them any rights in the family *vis-à-vis* the presumed established ends of marriage or, in the case of children, *vis-à-vis* the wishes of parents, who were forced to decide their religious fate first through baptism and then through their type of education. Similarly, he did not think of defending them against the State, provided the State had a concordat with the Church and was faithful to its agreements with the Church. Finally, he attributed no value to them within the Church itself if they refused to accept its laws and submit themselves completely to it, even making apostasy from the Church, whatever the reason, subject to the same persecutions that the Church reproved in the totalitarian States. The Church's aim was, in fact, in Pius xi's view, to make use of the secular arm to carry out its own sentences against rebellious subjects – an aim impossible of realization in democratic States but not in totalitarian countries: indeed Article V of the Concordat with Italy provided that priests and religious under censure or accused of apostasy should be deprived of all civil rights.

The deplorable aspect of even the most courageous encyclicals of Pius XI against the totalitarian régimes lies in the fact that he never condemned those States for their revolting violations of natural law, their crimes against liberty, their tyranny and oppression of every kind, but confined himself exclusively to denouncing them (for what reasons, has been partly explained earlier) for damage done to ecclesiastical persons and property. As in the past he had been prepared to enter into relations with them, justifying himself by the principle that the Church is not concerned with forms of government, so later he was always ready to resume collaboration with States once they ceased from harming the Church. And this was not simply tactics or political pragmatism on his part, but the result of his overriding concern to safeguard the presumed rights of the supernatural order, which caused him, provided those rights could be guaranteed, to allow the much more fundamental rights of the natural order – which Catholic theology itself does not deny or underestimate – to be trampled on and annulled. This distortion of fundamental values inevitably led to the anomaly – less explicit in his teaching, more apparent in his practice – of his failure to see how, by disregarding the fundamental values of the natural order, supernatural values too became deprived of their very basis.

The favourable treatment accorded to the totalitarian régimes provided they exempted the Church from oppression thus came to seem like the most cynical of bargains, not to say the price paid for silence about their crimes. For example, on the very day on which von Papen, accompanied by Mgr Kaas, left for Rome to prepare the Concordat with the Third Reich, the first two anti-semitic laws, excluding non-Aryans from public office and the legal profession, came out in Germany; but that fact did nothing to check the progress of the Concordat. On 15 September 1935, when the notorious Nuremberg racial laws were published in Germany, among other things forbidding, 'for the protection of German blood and honour', sexual relations between Germans and Jews and thus touching on the sphere of mixed marriages, Pius XI did not condemn the laws, although since 1 July 1933 some fifty thousand Jews had had to leave Germany because of them and many had committed suicide rather than do so. Nor was his voice raised in protest after the night of 9/10 November when reprisals were unleashed against the Jews in Germany for the assassination by a Jewish youth of Ernst von Rath, counsellor at the German Embassy in Paris – reprisals in which 7,500 shops were destroyed and two hundred synagogues burnt down, and as a result of which in four days alone 10,454 Jews were sent to Buchenwald, all non-Aryans were finally eliminated from commercial activities, and a fine of one thousand million Marks was imposed on the Jews. It was not until a few months before his death that he adopted a courageous, if still detached, standpoint against racialism; but even his famous speech on Catholics as spiritual heirs of the Jews was made behind closed doors and was not even mentioned at the time by the *Osservatore Romano*.

A Munificent and Terrible Sovereign

The theocratic conception of the Church that determined Pius XI's relations with the civil and the non-Catholic religious worlds, influencing his conduct of the Church's internal affairs and his own personal attitude, soon found its symbol in the creation of the State of the Vatican City, upon which Pope Pius concentrated detailed and devoted care.

The little State created by the Lateran Agreements in February 1929 on the right bank of the Tiber had, in actual fact, the same area as the Vatican except for the extra-territorial buildings, mostly housing Sacred Congregations, scattered throughout the city. But the new status of those 109 acres of pontifical territory called for the construction of all kinds of public buildings, including government offices, a railway station, a post office, and all kinds of maintenance buildings; and, in addition, seminaries and various other institutions were also envisaged. The area within the confines of the new city-State was turned upside down: not a single wing of the Sacred Palaces escaped restoration or adaptation, hardly an inch of the gardens was left unchanged. Throughout the last ten years of Pius XI's reign the place became a vast workshop under the charge of a big Milanese firm of builders whose head, Leone Castelli, was appointed director-general *ad interim* of the technical and economic services of the Vatican City Government. At peak periods the firm employed fifteen thousand men including those working elsewhere in Rome or other parts of Italy. In Rome itself, one of Pius xi's most ambitious works was the famous Palazzo San Callisto for the Curial departments, erected in the heart of Trastevere to bring under one roof all the Congregations which had no historic or traditional headquarters of their own. At Castel Gandolfo, reconstruction work carried out at the pontifical villa there was almost as extensive and impressive as in the Vatican itself.

Pius xi in fact revived, if on a much more restricted territory, the activity of the great builder-Popes that had been interrupted under Pius ix. But his wish was to resemble not so much Pius ix as the great Popes of the Renaissance and the seventeenth and eighteenth centuries, who had combined with the creation of great public works an ambition for patronage of the arts worthy of the greatest sovereigns. An instance of this ambition is the new Vatican picture gallery constructed under Pius xi; but even more significant, if less well-known, is the almost incredible story of the Vatican astronomical observatory. The creation of the Vatican City raised the question of possibly transferring the observatory because of disturbances due to the increasing illumination of Rome at night. The most obvious plan, which was eventually carried out, was to move it to the Alban hills, to Castel Gandolfo; but for a time Pius xi even had the idea of setting it up no the Ethiopian plateau, where the sky is exceptionally clear. Indeed this plan would almost certainly have been put into effect if the commission set up in 1930 to investigate the possibilities had not been held up in Egypt because of a sudden political crisis in Abyssinia.

Pius xi also allocated large sums towards enriching the Vatican Library, in particular through the purchase of archives belonging to great Roman families – the Chigi, the Caetani, the Rospigliosi, and so on – which were of great value for the reconstruction of Church history; and he set on foot as well fruitful searches for manuscripts abroad through the medium of the future Cardinal Tisserant, then Vice-Prefect of the Vatican Library, and a priest of the Byzantine rite, Cyril Korolevsky, both of them language experts, who, dressed as civilians, scoured the Balkans, Turkey,

Syria, Palestine and Egypt as well as Poland and Hungary. But the climax of his patronage of the arts was the establishment of the Academy of Sciences, planned by Pius x but now open not only to Catholics but to scientists of all faiths, ideologies, and races, for which he reserved that jewel of Renaissance art, the Casina of Pius iv. He regarded this as one of the most significant expressions of the Church's dual aspect, both spiritual and material, for which the new Vatican City State stood.

As a former librarian Pius xi naturally strove to promote Catholic culture, especially in the sphere of ecclesiastical studies. He gave expression to this in the encyclical *Deus scientiarum Dominus*, in which he outlined a reorganization of studies in seminaries and Catholic universities designed among other things to ensure greater strictness in the granting of academic degrees; and he also touched on particular faculties, especially philosophy and biblical studies, in other encyclicals. But these reforms mainly concerned the technical side rather than a genuine liberalization of research and its results; indeed throughout his whole pontificate – and this is another proof of his substantial integralism – Catholic thought remained in the virtual quarantine begun under Pius x even before *Pascendi*. After an almost complete silence during Benedict xv's pontificate, the Holy Office under Pius xi worked with impressive speed, not only striking inexorably at any relics of Modernism but also often inflicting unexpected censorship on the most observant and prudent Catholic writers. This occurred especially towards the end of his reign, when Catholic culture in the Central European countries was becoming increasingly impatient of useless scholarly paraphernalia, and when theology, in particular, was seeking, through a return to biblical and patristic sources, for a new vitality which would be both more original and spontaneous and better adapted to the needs of modern thought and the aspirations of a less formal, more deeply felt spiritual life.

As in his relations with States, Pius xi did not seek any real association between Catholic and secular culture – the kind of relationship that today would be described as a 'dialogue'. He thought, rather, in terms of cultural citadels from which to launch a successful attack on secular culture – with the result that everywhere throughout his reign, with the possible exception of Germany, Catholic culture was confined to a sort of ghetto with no possibility of outlet. Indicative in this connection was his attitude concerning the collaboration of Catholics on the *Italian Encyclopaedia*.[1] Catholic writers represented a most valuable source of knowledge, in a country which had brought about the Reconciliation between Church and State. What, then, could be more natural than to extend that reconciliation from politics to other spheres including culture? But instead, it was only after prolonged discussions, from which it emerged that the Encyclopaedia was not to be regarded as a preserve of Gentile's idealist philosophy (Giovanni Gentile, whose works came *en bloc* under the Index in 1934 together with those of Benedetto Croce, was its editor), that he gave his permission, with the reservation that censorship was not to be withheld if found needful (which fortunately was never the case).

It will be obvious, however, that Pius XI's activities as builder and patron of the arts represented only a part of his work in the many spheres in which he was concerned. The sum total of accomplishment during his pontificate is indeed wellnigh sensational. We have already mentioned, in the diplomatic sphere, the eighteen conventions concluded, to which must be added the arbitration between San Domingo and Tahiti of 31 January 1938. A further catalogue includes his thirty encyclicals (twenty-three letters and seven epistles), the establishment of 128 residential sees, 24 abbeys and prelatures, 116 apostolic vicariats, and 113 apostolic prefectures, the elevation to the glory of the altars of thirty-three saints and some five hundred beatified (not counting saints nominated doctors and patrons), the consecration of three African bishops, the strengthening of various Vatican departments, among them the Eastern Department, the establishment of new pontifical commissions (for sacred art in Italy, for the preservation of the historical and artistic monuments of the Holy See, etc.), and the foundation of new institutes (of Christian archaeology, etc.), ecclesiastical colleges, and special schools (e.g. of librarianship in the Vatican). The list of achievements is even more impressive when we recall the circumstances in which they were carried out; in addition to which, moreover, Pius XI celebrated three jubilee years, besides daily devoting several hours – more indeed, than any other Pope – to public audiences.

[1] See P. P. Trompeo, *Preti,* Caltanisetta-Rome, 1962, p. 270–3.

The objection may be raised that a good deal of this activity can be attributed only nominally to Pius XI himself; but this is far from true. Ratti never wished merely to rule supreme while entrusting to others the responsibilities of government. Right from the beginning he wanted to have direct responsibility for everything, to keep in close touch and take all the decisions himself. As Cardinal Tisserant recently testified, 'in the early days of his pontificate he often asked cardinals at the head of departments or their assistants to leave the papers they had brought to an audience with him for a day or two', and he also took the trouble to read the opinions given by advisers so as to evaluate them and choose the one he preferred. This was one of the reasons why the regular audiences for the prefects and secretaries of the Roman Congregations became such a burden to those who had to attend them. Pius XI, having first informed himself of all the particulars, wanted to discuss everything at length with them and insisted on their having the same grasp of detail as himself.

He would, if he could, have done everything himself. Under the code of canon law the Pope is Prefect of the three most important departments of the Curia: the Holy Office, the Consistorial Congregation, and the Congregation of the Eastern Church. He used to say that he could not but approve of Mussolini's taking on as many Ministries as possible himself: 'In that way everything runs smoothly without strains or disputes.' To some extent he did this himself: for instance, after Cardinal Bisleti's death in 1937 he took over the prefectship of the Congregation of Seminaries and Universities. He even studied building plans in detail both from the aesthetic and functional and the financial angles; indeed he himself suggested the solution for some difficult technical problems, such as the entry into the Vatican through the museums, which involved linking two levels separated by some forty feet: recalling the famous St Patrick's Well at Orvieto, he proposed the magnificent two-spiral staircase now so widely admired.

Before settling the extent of the future Vatican City and deciding what buildings should be included in it, he went up to the balustrade surrounding the dome of St Peter's so as to see with his own eyes what could only be conjectured from the maps. And during the negotiation of the Concordat alone, he was present in person at some two hundred four-hour sittings.

But though he wanted to be first in everything, he wanted others to be there too. The difficulties this caused, in a proverbially indolent city like Rome, can easily be imagined, for it impinged on the whole rhythm of work in the Curia departments and the Vatican itself. He even transferred a number of assistants from Milan in order to galvanize the Romans and arouse them to emulation. It is customary for a Pope to bring in his train some close colleagues who have worked with him in the past, and to give a certain number of posts to trusted or outstanding persons from his native town or previous diocese. Leo XIII, for example, brought in men from Perugia, Pius X from the Veneto. Benedict XV alone showed discretion in this, as in much else. But with Pius XI there were no half measures. The Milanese at his express wish took by storm not only the pontifical apartments but also the Secretariat of State and the various departments and institutions in Rome. The entire episcopate felt the influence of the Ambrosian Library, or at any rate of Lombardy and the North. Catholic Action became another preserve of the Milanese, as did the Vatican City when it came into being, especially with the advent of Castelli and his builders. And in addition to the imported Milanese there were also transitory figures such as the dynamic Franciscan friar Padre Agostino Gemelli, on whom Pius XI relied in all kinds of ways, who as Rector of the Catholic University had his headquarters in Milan.

The Jesuits were not expected to galvanize, but they were, nevertheless, the second group on which Pius XI relied for collaboration. All-powerful under Pius IX, to whom they had suggested the proclamation of the dogma of the Immaculate Conception, the promulgation of the *Syllabus*, and the convocation of the Vatican Council, under Leo XIII they had retained considerable power in the cultural sphere (as witness the Thomist and anti-Rosminian campaigns) but had subsequently gradually lost ground. With Pius XI they came back on the crest of the wave. He owed to Padre Ehrle his appointment as Ehrle's successor at the head of the Vatican Library, and was indebted to Padre Ledokowski, General (i.e. head) of the Jesuits from 1914 onwards, for advice and help during his mission to Poland. He kept both these men, especially the latter, discreetly and unostentatiously close to him. Others more plainly in view were the Jesuit historian Padre Tacchi Venturi, Mussolini's adviser on Church

affairs and his go-between with the Vatican; the German colleagues of Pacelli, the Nuncio, including Bea, Leiber, and others;
and, of course, the whole team of writers on *Civiltà Cattolica*, the
semi-official supporters of pontifical policy.

But the aid of specialist groups could not suffice, and Pius XI
relied most of all on individual action. Hence the unaccustomed
severity he showed towards those in the highest positions in
making an example of them. He made no exception in his dealings
with his own collaborators; and the first to tremble in his anti-
chamber were often the cardinals. Once the details of a particular
task had been laid down, no excuses or hesitations were allowed.
Any evasion or omission roused his wrath and often produced
drastic consequences. When he decided to condemn the *Action
Française* and therefore wished to sign the decree originally
presented to Pius X in 1914, the document seemed to have been
mysteriously mislaid in the archives of the Holy Office; Pius XI
announced that unless it was found and brought to him at once
all the top men in the Supreme Congregation would be sacked.
Needless to say, it was quickly found, and the threat was not
carried out.[1] But soon afterwards, also in the matter of the *Action
Française* affair, an episode occurred which took away the breath
of the whole Curia.

When the paper was condemned, Cardinal Louis Billot was so
unwise as to send a note of sympathy to the editors, who published it. The Cardinal was at once summoned to the Pope's
presence. He was a Jesuit, and thus a member of the Order held
in highest esteem by Pius XI; he was also the greatest theologian
of the day, and had collaborated under Pius X in drawing up the
encyclical *Pascendi*, but everyone in the Vatican knew that neither
these nor any other claims would save him from an apocalyptic
reaction from the Pope. But the event surpassed all expectations.
The meeting was brief and strangely quiet, but when the door of
the Pope's private library opened the man who emerged was no
longer a Cardinal of the Holy Roman Church but a simple
member of the Jesuit Order. Pius XI had confined himself to
asking him to hand back his cardinal's hat; after which Billot
shut himself up in a house of the Order and was heard of no more.

This episode came near to being repeated ten years later in the

---

[1] Related by Mgr Primo Principi in his deposition at the Vatican hearing for the
beatification of Cardinal Merry del Val (p. 146 of the *Summarium*, see Bibliography).

case of Cardinal Innitzer, Archbishop of Vienna. At the time of the *Anschluss* between Germany and Austria a tremendous impression was created in the world by the news that the Austrian Primate had not only been received by Hitler in Vienna immediately after the march-past of troops to celebrate the event, but had also publicly expressed in an interview his satisfaction at the guarantees promised him by Hitler with regard to the Church. This impression was further heightened by a collective declaration from the Austrian episcopate, issued on 18 March 1938 and read in all churches a week later in view of the coming plebiscite of 10 April, which unreservedly praised the achievements of National Socialism in Germany. All this was viewed with grave alarm in the Secretariat of State, especially since it was feared that it might have catastrophic effects on the Pope's already precarious health. Cardinal Innitzer, summoned to Rome for an explanation, made various excuses to delay his departure. Pius xi then took the decision to publish in the *Osservatore Romano* of 1 April a communiqué stating that the declaration of the Austrian bishops had been drawn up and signed without previous agreement or subsequent approval from the Holy See and on the sole responsibility of the Austrian episcopate.

This uncompromising disavowal brought Innitzer rushing to Rome, but now Pius xi refused to receive him. On his arrival at the Vatican on 6 April he was told that the Secretary of State, Pacelli, wished to see him at once. Pacelli had already prepared the draft of a declaration for distribution to the press, which stated that the content of the Austrian bishops' document was to be regarded as subordinate to the free exercise of the rights of the Church in general and the Holy See in particular, especially in all the more delicate concordatory spheres; and the document was not to be regarded as a conscientious obligation for the faithful. Innitzer had no choice but to sign it. The audience with the Pope could therefore take place, but needless to say it was one of the most tempestuous of the whole pontificate. Pius xi did not go so far as to deprive Innitzer of office, but the reason for that is obvious: such a step would have been interpreted by the German Chancellor as a personal insult and a challenge to Nazism, and would have had unfavourable repercussions on the Church in Austria, where a new Primate would inevitably have become the target for reprisals.

These were, of course, exceptional cases; but it was normal routine for even his closest and most trusted collaborators to feel anxiety and trepidation on crossing the threshold into the Pope's private library. His Master of the Chamber, Mgr Arborio Mella di Sant'Elia, in his *Istantanee inedite* (Unpublished Snapshots) on the four Popes he served under, departed from the customary eulogies of his heroes in some of his remarks on Pius XI: 'Even remembering our old friendship [Mella used to visit him in the evenings when he was Prefect at the Vatican], I would never have believed that before Pius XI I would have trembled as never before in my life. He inspired a real feeling of inferiority, which did not accord with the paternal goodness of his heart: he certainly changed from one minute to the next when he became Pope – not from ambition or pride, but because he felt himself to be invested with the divine representation that imposed that change.'

Mgr Mella's comment is no servile justification. True, under Pius XI bishops were at last allowed to sit down in the Pope's presence, both in private and in public audiences. But his courtesy and affability waned when the man he was speaking to revealed weak points in his life or work and was called to account for such failings. Like Mussolini with his famous desk at the far end of the vast Sala del Mappamondo at Palazzo Venezia, he had his writing-table in his private library placed in such a position that, sitting in the window corner and thus hardly visible to his companion, he could himself see his guests in full light. But his table was also famous for the blows he struck on it in moments of anger, which happened quite often at times of political tension or after the onset of the illness that was to bring his end.

Those indignant blows had their forerunner right from the very beginning. On the day after his elevation the pontifical photographer came, as with every Pope, to take the official photographs, and a few hours later the first pictures of the new Pope, in various poses, were going the rounds of the ante-chamber. One of them showed him sitting on the throne with his right arm resting on the arm of the chair and his fist closed. Cardinal Vico was at once struck by this and said to Mella: 'Do you see that, Monsignore? That's a Pope to make men tremble!'

Absolute sovereign as he was, and not only aware of but totally imbued with his own sovereignty, Pius XI made his sovereignty felt in other ways as well as by the imposing solemnity of his own attitude. (That attitude was itself so remarkable as to astound and paralyse even men least prepared to be overawed by a Pope. Such a man was Goering, second in the Nazi hierarchy, who found him standing before his desk waiting to receive him, instead of sitting on his throne as he had expected. Yet he was simply terrified, as he admitted afterwards to the Rumanian Minister, Comnène: 'You know me – you know that I've never in my life lacked courage; but before that little figure robed all in white I felt my heart jump as never before. For the first time in my life I believe I was afraid. It's extraordinary, but that's how it was ...') Pius XI made that sovereignty felt not only by his attitude and his severity but also by isolating himself completely from all others, whoever they might be. Even his relatives had to ask for an audience from the Master of the Chamber just like anyone else, and when they got the card of invitation they had to use their own means of getting to the Vatican and once there wait their turn. Not even during his illness or in the last days of his life were they allowed into his private apartment; and none of them, not even his brother and sister, could be present at his death.

Even the favoured ones were not allowed to go beyond certain limits of intimacy. His wish to keep himself apart and inaccessible also accounts for his dislike of such things as telephones and tape-recorders. He never believed the telephone could guarantee secrecy, and he could not imagine being unable to see the person he was speaking to and study his face and reactions; and it annoyed him, too, to have to make up his mind quickly and speak without his usual long pauses. Consequently, though the latest-style telephone always stood on his desk, he never touched it. He disliked even more the Philips tape-recorder that the firm gave him as a present: when asked to speak into it and listen afterwards to his own voice, he got Pacelli, his Secretary of State, to do it instead; and he eventually gave the machine away to the Academy of Sciences.

For the same reason when Pope he rarely wrote letters in his own hand and took great care to destroy all his hand-written notes and memoranda, as well as the drafts of official documents, encyclicals, or speeches. Once they were typed he would himself tear up the drafts into small pieces. It was only thanks to various wily stratagems that his secretary Confalonieri succeeded in piecing together like a mosaic the complete text, written partly in ink and partly in pencil, of the encyclical *Non abbiamo bisogno*, a polemical masterpiece in the pure style of Manzoni.

But if he refused to allow anyone to become familiar or even to approach him closely, he was even less tolerant of people who presumed to make demands on the Pope. He was very keen on having the actions, works, and events of his reign recorded on suitable stones or tablets. No pope in modern times has scattered so many inscriptions commemorating his deeds throughout the Vatican, Rome, and Italy. Even when he had a simple awning put up over one of the avenues in the Vatican gardens to protect his own walks from the rain, it had to be recorded with an inscription (*Pius XI P.M. ambulationem ab imbribus tutam fieri iussit* – Pius XI ordered the walk to be sheltered from showers). But he could not bear flattery or servility. Incense is inevitably offered pretty freely in a Court and Curia like those of the Vatican. But professional *laudatores* did not have much luck with Pius XI. He would cut short the bows and compliments, so Confalonieri relates, with a curt 'That's enough of play-acting!' and he reduced to a minimum the tedious custom of reading eulogistic addresses in the Pope's presence. His biographers, too, were less fortunate in their careers than those of, for instance, Pius XII: neither Don Francesco Rovelli nor Mgr Fontanelle nor Mgr Galbiati got any special promotion after their books came out. Pius XI was too exalted to be touched by vanity; and with him it was the Pope, rather than himself as an individual, that mattered.

For the same reason he never went in for nepotism. He bowed to accepted tradition in allowing his closest relatives to enter the Roman nobility, but for a long time he delayed giving them a title. Only after the Reconciliation did he accede to frequent promptings and grant his brother Fermo the hereditary title of Count. And when he wanted to make use of his nephew Franco's expertise as a hydraulic engineer and asked for his temporary transfer from the Banca Commerciale in Milan under which he was employed, he made it publicly clear by written agreement that his nephew was going to work free of cost to the Vatican administration.

Unexpected Intimacies

Yet this avowed solitary, who defended his own intimacy even
from close relatives and manifested an exalted, almost disdainful
consciousness of his own sovereignty, had an overriding need to
feel the crowds about him. Perhaps at a certain point in his
pontificate, and especially after the Reconciliation, this desire of
his to see the Vatican daily thronged by the faithful, longing to
meet the Pope at least once in their lives, was prompted by a
spirit of emulation to compete with the mass demonstrations
encouraged by Fascism throughout Italy and particularly in
Rome. Mussolini had his rallies and Pius XI would have his
audiences. But it must not be forgotten that the custom of holding
daily audiences began in the first years of his pontificate, receiving
a special impetus from the jubilee of 1925. Thus it was not a case
of imitation or rivalry but of a need much more stongly felt by
him than by his predecessors from Leo XIII onwards.

Pius IX had, of course, no need to meet the faithful in the
Vatican or at the Quirinal, for he went out almost daily into the
streets of Rome and met them everywhere, especially in churches
and at great religious ceremonies. That high aristocrat Leo XIII
rarely received pilgrimages, particularly in the first half of his
pontificate. It was only later on that he occasionally held audiences
in St Peter's, sometimes of as many as twenty thousand people.
He would appear carried in a litter, advancing slowly between the
ranks of the faithful and conversing with them. Some of these
audiences lasted for as long as six hours, and the prelates in his
train would urge him to make a pause and leave the basilica for a
few minutes' rest. In the end he came to enjoy these occasions,
so much so indeed that before his death he wanted to celebrate a
Mass in St Peter's with open doors. But they were always exceptional affairs. Under Pius X almost the only such manifestation
was the Sunday explanation of the catechism in the courtyard of
St Damian. And then the war came to restrict Benedict XV's
contacts with the faithful, especially from other countries.

Pius XI's predecessors were also no doubt largely influenced
by circumstances in this respect. Journeys were less easy in their
day, and also the atmosphere of relations between the Holy See
and Italy was certainly not best suited to protect pilgrims from
demonstrations of anticlerical intolerance. In any case, under

Pius XI public audiences came to be held not only daily but often twice a day, in the evening as well as the morning. The morning audiences began around midday, after the *tabella*[1] and private audiences, and lasted, according to the numbers attending, until two, three, or four in the afternoon; the evening ones, particularly in jubilee years, went on from six until sometimes as late as 10 pm. They continued at this rate for fifteen whole years with only a single pause during the Pope's illness in the winter of 1936. In addition to all this, from 1932 onwards Pius XI established regular Wednesday audiences for newly-married couples, who came to Rome from all parts of Italy profiting by the special reduced fares offered them by Fascism for reasons of propaganda (the régime was at that time encouraging marriages and population increase).

Naturally the majority of those attending these public audiences were simple, humble people who found it absolutely astounding to see how the usually solemn and severe Pius XI could be so condescending and patient. For private audiences he was rigid in requiring both men and women to wear the prescribed dress, even going so far as to exclude Gandhi from his presence because he insisted on wearing the dhoti; yet he never grudged the time spent in talking to working men and their wives and children.

At the end of each audience he would make an extempore speech. Ratti was not a polished Latin scholar like Leo XIII, who loved to read his speeches in Ciceronian style, nor was he a gesticulating popular preacher like Pius X; still less had he the patience to construct his speeches on classic lines or to write them out, as did Benedict XV, who left behind a mass of manuscripts going back to his days as a deacon. Though once a teacher of oratory, for most of his life his own speech-making had been confined chiefly to the convents of nuns where he was chaplain. Even his time in Poland as apostolic visitor and nuncio did little to make him appreciate sacred oratory as a means of contact with the faithful, for he did not know Polish well enough to speak it extempore or even to read a prepared text. His time in Milan as archbishop certainly gave him a useful training-ground, but he was only there for a few months.

Once he became Pope, however, the need to enter into con-

---

[1] Regular audiences for Heads of Congregations. *Translator.*

versation with the multitudes and smaller groups coming to the Vatican spurred him on to speak more and more frequently. At the audiences he spoke very simply, and most of his ideas might seem commonplace; but anyone who followed the windings of the parenthetical sentences with which, as was his custom, he would revert to his original theme and further develop and shape it without ever losing the thread, could realize how deep his thought went. Occasionally he slipped into these simple, familiar discourses some pungent comments on contemporary events that were troubling the life of the Church or the world. In such cases, when replying to or confuting speeches or decisions of politicians these sentences were most carefully prepared beforehand and the whole speech seemed a mere pretext to include them. But whatever the circumstances, the characteristic tone of these speeches never altered – the tone of a father, not a sovereign. He never wearied of reiterating his joy that his children had come to 'their father's house', and often he did no more than stress this theme before taking leave of them with the kindly cordiality of a father to his sons.

It was, in fact, as if two different personalities coexisted within him and became dissociated from each other at the moment when he left his private library where his real work was done to pass into the rooms in the Vatican palace where the groups of pilgrims awaited him. Obviously it is pointless to ask which of the two personalities was the more authentic: in adapting himself perfectly to the two complementary sides of his office he gave neither the upper hand. Ratti the man surrendered himself to the pontiff in order to realize these two sides while at the same time retaining his own autonomy and individuality. And to anyone near him at the rare moments when he could revert to some sort of private life he could afford some pleasant surprises.

The most unexpected surprise was the affability and sense of humour that quite often provided a link between the two sides of his personality. Majestic wrath might be justifiable at times, but only when occasion made it necessary: characteristics more in tune with the office of Pope as sovereign of the spirit were imperturbability, serenity, a sense of tranquil security and the lasting consolations of faith. This was the countenance he generally displayed at public appearances and mass audiences. But he also showed occasional flashes of humour in dealing with unexpected situations. One day, for instance, at a special audience granted to the family of Marchese Nannerini, a colonel of the Noble Guard, on the occasion of his twenty-fifth wedding anniversary, he found the nobleman's entire progeny, all eighteen of them, drawn up before him. 'What is all this crowd?' he asked with a twinkle in his eye; and when the Marchese began introducing each one separately he interrupted, 'But surely you must have a catalogue'. Another time, visiting the stables, he stopped in front of a splendid Hungarian bay called Ali. 'He's old, but he's still a fine horse,' said Rinaldo, coachman to five Popes (from Pius IX to Ratti); 'Like the coachman,' countered Pius XI in a flash.

Ratti's sayings would make one of the best chapters in a book on papal humour. 'What I like about them,' he said once to a loquacious companion pointing to the fish in his aquarium, 'is that they never speak.' Another time, when visiting the garage for Vatican City cars he noticed the name of a Milan firm of bicycle-manufacturers in the repair-shop; on being told that the head of the firm had been at the Vatican a few days before, he said, 'The next time you see him tell him he's had the honour of making the Pope move about the earth.'

But though Ratti's jokes made him seem less cold and remote, they did little to reveal those more intimate sides of him that only a few were in a position to realize. One such indication was the extraordinary tenderness of his affections. Among his first students in oratory at the seminary in Milan was Eugenio Tosi, for whom he had always had a special fondness because of his simple goodness of heart as well as his gifts of oratory. On his advice Tosi after becoming a priest had joined the oblates of St Charles of Rho, who specialized in popular preaching in the diocese of Milan, and had later been appointed bishop of Adria, a small suffragan diocese of Venice. One of Ratti's first actions on becoming Pope was to make him his successor in Milan. He communicated his decision to him through the normal channels but also on 28 February, only fifteen days after his own coronation, sent him the following note: 'Dear friend, you know how much there is to do. This is the first letter I have written since my election ... I feel I am inspired: I have prayed and prayed again. I want to have your agreement at once: come and give it me yourself, that will be much the best: come and *see Peter*, your old teacher who has always loved you so much ... Pius P.P. XI.'

Such personal relationships were rare with Ratti. His sensitiveness on the human side emerged more frequently in the genuine gratitude he showed, not so much to the great donors, but to the countless humble people who wished to testify their filial love for him. Every day from all parts of the world he received proofs of this affection: modest gifts, holy pictures, brief but moving letters, even post cards from children. Other such gifts were brought in daily during the public audiences. At the Wednesday audiences for newly-married couples there would be whole trays full of wedding *confetti* (the sugared almonds customary at Italian weddings) and family photographs. His secretaries wanted to get rid of these trifles, but he would not hear of it. During the Holy Year of 1925 they overflowed into every room in his apartment. When the situation threatened to become unmanageable the secretaries returned to the attack, but he showed his annoyance and replied that, far from disposing of the things, they must all be listed with the donors' names and preserved 'as a lasting memorial'. 'They give with so much love,' he would repeat over and over again. A whole room in the Vatican Library – the room now called after him – was given up to the collection of gifts presented in his first Jubilee Year. He had splendid bookshelves made to house all the later gifts. They were put in the main room of his private apartment, and every day as he went by to the lift on his way to the audience chamber he would pause for a few minutes to examine some of these modest offerings. The more valuable gifts he listed in special notebooks with the date and the name of the donor.

So behind the majestic attitudes and solemn gestures, behind the impetuous reactions of indignation and severity, a simple and touching sensibility lay concealed. But the least known and least suspected Pius XI belongs to a different sphere, the spiritual. Reference has already been made to certain characteristics of his piety which reveal the kind of simple, ingenuous faith found in quite humble people, such as his lasting loyalty to the 'Devotional Societies' he had joined in youth. But who would ever expect to find him, even as Pope, having faith in the visionary powers of certain monks and nuns? For instance, on 3 April 1929 a Portuguese nun wrote to him with the permission of her spiritual director asking him to make his first appearance outside his new Vatican City State on the occasion of the Corpus Christi procession, ten days after Whit Sunday, to carry the Saviour of the World in triumph at the eucharist. Far from disregarding this strange communication, Pius xi ordered inquiries to be made about the nun, and when the answers proved satisfactory he accepted the suggestion, only carrying it out with a few weeks' delay (on 25 July, on the occasion of the international pilgrimage of seminarists).

Such regard for the message of a visionary nun was doubtless a rare occurrence. But Pius xi's permanent relations with certain religious communities were not without some influence on his actions as Pope. An example of this is revealed by Charles Maurras in his book *Le Bienheureux Pie X sauveur de la France*,[1] where he says that Ratti asked the Carmelites of Lisieux for special prayers and penitences for the Church of France during the dispute with *Action Française*. Around 1936 one of these nuns whose family knew Maurras, and who had offered her life to the cause the Pope had at heart, wrote to Maurras, then in prison in the Santé, urging him to send a message to Pius xi. The message, transmitted by the Carmelite of Lisieux, arrived safely at its destination, as did a reply in the Pope's own hand. Encouraged by this seemingly incredible fact, Maurras wrote again to Pius xi through the same medium, stressing 'the inoffensive nature of his paper's political doctrines' and their spiritual and moral efficacy, though admitting that some of his own personal ideas might be heterodox. After he left prison he made a pilgrimage to Lisieux every year for the next three years (1937–9) on the anniversary of St Theresa's death (13 July), sending a telegram to the Pope. But by the time of his third pilgrimage the miracle that the nuns of Lisieux sought on his behalf had become a reality; three days earlier the Congregation of the Holy Office had issued the decree, published in the *Osservatore Romano* of the 16th, removing the *Action Française* from the Index. By that time Pius xi had been dead some months, but the document was the outcome of measures initiated by him.

It took a St Theresa to induce a man of Pius xi's iron will to countermand one of the most notorious actions of his whole pontificate. But it is precisely at this point that the borderline between an ingenuous faith and a courageous and magnanimous faith vanishes, producing a whole transcending either. As far as

[1] Paris, Plon, 1953.

the nuns of Lisieux are concerned, Pius XI's boundless devotion to their saint is well known. The cause for the young Carmelite's beatification was already in progress when he became Pope. It is nevertheless striking that little more than a year after his election, on 29 April 1923, he proceeded to her beatification and only two years later, on 27 May 1925, decided to raise her to the honour of the altars and make her a saint. He later also made her the patron saint of missions as well as of Russia. He hesitated and refused only when urged to make her the first woman to be given the title of 'doctor of the Church'. And he was wrong, for of all the names that might be given to her that was undoubtedly the most fitting: after St Francis – for whom Pius XI had a special devotion – no one so reached the core and essence of the gospel message as did little Thérèse Martin. To have understood this and personally embraced the way of self-abandonment to God is astonishing, even taking into account the attraction of opposites, in a man of Pius XI's authoritarian and totalitarian temperament. The only cause for regret is that his discovery was confined to his own abandonment of self, instead of extending to a revolutionary conception of the Church which would have put to rout once for all, anticipating John XXIII's pontificate by decades, that neo-temporalism that spurred him on into repugnant and dangerous alliances.

A Prophet Disarmed on the Threshold of Eternity

This intimate and secret Pius XI remained almost unknown up to the time of his death. But some two-and-a-half years before then a change was observed both in his pontificate and in his person which startled and impressed many of his sternest opponents and critics. The change came towards the end of 1936, significantly coinciding with the serious illness that struck him then. Most men who are rather inhuman in relations with their subordinates are people who have not suffered much, at least in the physical sense. Ratti used to boast that in all his eighty years he had never had a headache or visited a dentist. As Pope, when his predecessor's doctor died, the office of archiater, or papal physician, was left vacant. But for the illness of one of his secretaries it would not have been filled for years.

The first warnings of illness came some months before the

Osservatore Romano announced, on 5 December 1936, that he was much fatigued and would be unable to continue attending the sermons of the spiritual exercises then going on in the Vatican. Towards the end of August, at Castel Gandolfo, he had felt giddy and fainted, but had got over it in a few hours. Then on the night of 23 October as he was leaving his study to go to bed he fainted again, falling and banging his head against a wooden pillar. On both occasions he obstinately refused to see a doctor. But in December he had to give in. The diagnosis was myocarditis and diffused arteriosclerosis with varicose swellings which subsequently caused oedema of the lower joints and ulceration.

Despite all his protests he had to stay in bed, and although the main audiences continued to take place in his bedroom there were long hours of silence and solitude each day. And it was in those hours of meditation on the borderline between life and death, in an atmosphere already redolent of eternity, that he passed in review all the vicissitudes of the world that he had witnessed during his long life. He was to do the same later, on 3 February 1939, a week before his death, with Duke Tommaso Gallarati Scotti in an audience that was more of a prolonged soliloquy:[1]

A glance back to the days when he began to be aware of things going on around him as a small bystander of thirteen or fourteen sufficed to show how fragile is what we call power with all its fluctuations. What was left of the Europe shaken by the great Franco-Prussian war of 1870? Empires shattered, régimes fallen like the old curtains in a theatre, though in the past they had known hours of splendour, pomp, and glory: Napoleon III, the Tuileries in flames; the Empress Eugénie fleeing from the throne she had ascended as if in a dream. Conquered, fallen among the imprecations of France . . . And Germany the conqueror? . . .

So the soliloquy went on right down to recent times, while his companion 'listened overawed to the meditation of a Pope who reviewed the fate of the proud in the twilight of his last hours'.

But those hours of meditation also brought the indomitable Pope to a detached and rigorous re-examination of his pontificate, especially the things in it which had been his own work or the

---

[1] See Tommaso Gallarati Scotti, *Interpretazioni e Memorie*, Milan, 1960, pp. 308–313.

result of his initiative. He had latterly been conscious of rising perplexities and doubts, especially in view of the increasing tension in Europe and the Nazis' persecution of the Church. That year of 1936 had been particularly crucial, with the anxieties arising first from the Abyssinian war and then from the outbreak of the civil war in Spain. That last episode, in particular, seemed in his eyes to raise the question of the future of Europe, threatened in one of its most traditionally Catholic strongholds by that Communism that the West had till then succeeded in isolating in Soviet Russia, but which now had managed to break out of encirclement and set up at the opposite end of the continent a State that promised to be its ally. To make the situation worse, France now had a Popular Front Government which was also, out of reaction to Germany's growing military power, favourable to Moscow. True, Italy and Germany supported Franco and were even sending him men and arms; but Hitler was proving increasingly inexorable towards the Catholic Church, and Mussolini had further strengthened his own position in Italy since the establishment of the empire in Africa. The balance of power was insidiously changing as alliances altered, and the increasing intimidations of the two Axis dictators confirmed fears that their aims were anything but peaceful. Concordatory policy still stood the test, if precariously, in Italy, but in Germany it had been a resounding failure. And, worse still, the most serious damage was not on the level of official relations, though there it was bad enough, but at a lower, more basic level, in the Church's inability to protect the masses from the steadily increasing influence of a propaganda subservient to radically anti-Christian ideologies.

What remedy could there be, the old Pope asked himself, for a situation which was daily becoming more dangerous because of the Church's failure to react adequately? What use was it to place one's hopes in a policy of legal agreements and diplomatic relations that were constantly evaded, if not shamelessly mocked and trampled on? Might not the Church's salvation lie, rather, in a policy of denunciation and in breaking off relations? One day, looking at a Latin inscription referring to himself as '*Sedente Pio XI P.P.*' he burst out, '*Sedente,* indeed! Standing upright!' He had always stood upright from the first day of his election: omnipresent and dynamic, farsighted and imperious. But now that he was confined to his bed, he grasped that what was really needed to set upright his pontificate and his figure as pontiff in the face of history and above all of God was not to treat with but to challenge the ephemeral leaders of his day. So, even while the press was gradually preparing public opinion, if not for the Pope's death, at least for his playing a much smaller part, in March 1937 within a few days of each other the three most explosive encyclicals of his whole pontificate came out: *Mit brennender Sorge* on 14 March, *Divini Redemptoris* on the 19th, and *Nos es muy conocida* on the 28th. The sub-title of the first encyclical was 'On the situation of the Catholic Church in the German Reich', that of the second 'Against atheist Communism', while the third dealt with religious persecution in Mexico.

Details of the background and drafting of the anti-Nazi encyclical have only recently become known. In August 1936 the German episcopate, assembled at Fulda for its annual conference, asked Pius XI for an encyclical on the situation of Catholicism in Germany. On 4 November Hitler requested a meeting at Obersalzburg with Cardinal Faulhaber, Archbishop of Munich, at which he left no room for doubt about his intention to put pressure on the Catholic Church in Germany if it did not collaborate more zealously with the régime. On 21 December, and thus a few days after the seriousness of the Pope's illness had become evident, the Secretary of State, Cardinal Pacelli, invited in his name the highest representatives of the German Church – the president of the episcopal conference, Cardinal Bertram, Cardinals Faulhaber and Schulte, and two bishops, von Galen of Münster and von Preysing of Berlin – to an emergency meeting in Rome to take place on the day after an extraordinary conference of the German episcopate at Fulda.

The five German prelates met Pacelli on the evening of 16 January 1937 and unanimously gave it as their opinion that the time had come for a public act on the part of the Holy See. Next day they, together with Pacelli, were received by Pius XI in his sickroom. The Pope was almost unrecognizable, pale, emaciated, his face deeply lined and his eyes swollen and half-closed: nevertheless he listened to them and then talked to them at some length. He told them he had learnt a great deal from his recent weeks of illness. His sufferings, so he said (what follows is a literal transcription of a recently authorized report of the episode), had made him understand as never before the sufferings of Christ and the Church; especially had he understood the mysterious law of the Cross, which brings salvation through suffering, in union with the sacrifice of the Redeemer, to the benefit of the mystical Body which is the Church. It seemed to him, he added, that till then he had been an ignoramus in the great and holy science of suffering. Now he daily offered his sufferings for Germany, Russia, Spain, Mexico and all the countries whose faith was being tested by persecution. He then said he was convinced of the need to publish as soon as possible an encyclical about the situation in Germany, and he asked those present to collaborate with him in preparing it. It was therefore decided that Cardinal Faulhaber should draw up a draft of the document. Faulhaber's draft, composed in three nights, consisted of eleven large single sheets written in his own hand, which he brought to Cardinal Pacelli on the morning of the 21st.

These details are important because they explain the more surprising aspects of the pontifical document that saw the light a few weeks later. That document is not so much an amplification of Faulhaber's draft as a faithful and even literal transcription of it (even the encyclical's opening words echo those of the draft, which began '*Mit grosser Sorge*'). Cardinal Pacelli, at Pius XI's request, merely added a full historical introduction on the background of the Concordat with the Third Reich. It is of course difficult to say whether, had he been in better health, less pressed by the urgent need to publish the document together with the other encyclicals, and working on a draft of his own. Pius XI might not have gone much further than the German bishops and Faulhaber in the attack on Nazism. What is, in any case, beyond doubt is that the encyclical that came out on 14 March certainly cannot be described as an anti-Nazi encyclical.

So little anti-Nazi is it that it does not even attribute to the régime as such, but only to certain trends within it, the dogmatic and moral errors widespread in Germany. And while the errors indicated are carefully diagnosed and refuted, complete silence surrounds the much more serious and fundamental errors associated with Nazi political ideology, corresponding to the principles most subversive of natural law that are characteristic of absolute totalitarianisms. The encyclical is in fact concerned purely with the Catholic Church in Germany and its rights and privileges, on the basis of the concordatory contracts of 1933.

Moreover the form given to it by Cardinal Faulhaber, even more of a super-nationalist than the majority of his most ardent colleagues, was essentially dictated by tactics and aimed at avoiding a definite breach with the régime, even to the point of offering in conclusion a conciliatory olive branch to Hitler if he would restore the tranquil prosperity of the Catholic Church in Germany. But that was the very thing to deprive the document of its noble and exemplary intransigence.

Nevertheless, even with these limitations, the pontifical letter still remains the first great official public document to dare to confront and criticize Nazism, and the Pope's courage astonished the world. It was, indeed, the encyclical's fate to be credited with a greater significance and content than it possessed. But when one recalls that only five days later it was to be followed by the much more radical condemnation of atheist Soviet Communism and the protest against persecution in Mexico, it is easy to imagine the impression made by the unexpected change of attitude of the Holy See and its head. The Pope himself, in the meantime, seemed almost to have gained strength from his resolute and vigorous gestures and was gradually resuming his usual work. In August 1937, as was mentioned earlier, he even took on the personal direction of the Department of Seminaries and Universities. Then in 1938, in a rising crescendo in tune with the impression of his increasing stature, came his reactions to Hitler's annexation of Austria (the Innitzer episode) and to Hitler's arrival in Rome (Pius XI was prepared to meet him face to face, but Hitler evaded it), his speech of 28 July against Nazism and exaggerated nationalism, and lastly his great appeal for peace on the eve of the Munich meeting, culminating in the final offering of his life by the 'sorrowful and weary labourer'.

These final gestures of his pontificate do not mean that Pius XI, like Penelope, was undoing the web of his own making: anyone who suggested such a thing would have seen him rise at once in defence of all his past work, which he could not but regard as in the main positive and constructive. Prisoner of his own theological and legal view of relations between the Church and the world, when things went badly he looked on it as merely the inevitable alternation between periods of darkness and of light and also, of course, as the logical consequence of those errors, attributed to secularism, that he never wearied of denouncing, even if only in the abstract and from the narrow perspective of his own clericalism. But his resolute conduct in turning his back on those whom he had believed in as men of destiny when he unwisely offered them his support, and confronting and challenging them – and the constant pinpricks he gave them through his kindly, paternal talks with visiting pilgrims, which also amounted to quite considerable gestures – all this sufficed to arouse the astonishment and admiration of his contemporaries.

Those near him, however, were not only overwhelmed at the behaviour of this indomitable old man, who seemed from his very infirmity to draw new strength to meet the situation, but were also deeply impressed by the external transformation in his attitude. The one-time sovereign, powerful and sure of himself, magnificent and imperturbable, still seemed sometimes, if ever more rarely, to rouse at the sound of the horse-hooves of the Apocalypse galloping before him. But the visibly wearying man borne in the gestatorial chair or sitting on the throne before the crowds was a man who no longer saw the world or heard its applause and execration. His little gold spectacles seemed almost useless before those lowered eyelids which, even when raised for an instant, veiled eyes that no longer wished to see. His words, becoming ever fewer and more difficult to follow, were barely murmured, as if he hardly cared whether they were heard or not. For this man's speech and gaze were now turned towards another world, or rather they came from another world. The too-temporal sovereign had given place at the last to the spiritual sovereign, the prophet, the pontiff in the original meaning of the word, a bridge-builder to the infinite. This was the authentic man that had lain hidden in potentiality from the beginning of his reign and now finally revealed himself: the real man from whom came at the last words that were ever greater, more abstract, and more eternal, and those last gestures that were to perpetuate him in the memory of the world.

On 18 December 1938, when at the appointed hour the Master of the Chamber entered his study to accompany him to the Casina of Pius IV for the inauguration of the third year of the Academy of Sciences, he found him much perturbed: the Pope had not had a single free minute to prepare the important speech expected of him, and now he was so tired he could hardly think. He asked him to wait a few minutes. 'He thought and thought,' wrote the witness of this scene afterwards, 'stretched out his hand, took the breviary from his desk, turned the pages, searched and finally seemed to find the cue he needed . . . He nodded in satisfaction . . . but then his face clouded. That was not what he wanted, and he put down the breviary still wrapped in thought. Then suddenly, as if he had just remembered something, he put out his hand again, took up the breviary, turned at once to the psalm he was looking for, and re-read it with obvious signs of satisfaction. Then he closed the book, reflected again and calmly handed it to me saying, "You'll give it to me when we get there". The speech was ready!' And it was the most inspired speech of his whole pontificate: the speech of the *Logos Creatore*, the Word of Life, built up on a brilliant counterpoint between the two famous passages in Proverbs and in the Gospel according to St John (these, and not a psalm, were the passages he had been looking for). 'He spoke like one who was seeing . . . It was a real feat of theological mountaineering' were among the most fitting tributes on this amazing contemplative commentary, his real swan-song.

The new year 1939, whose threshold he was barely to cross, brought the imminent prospect of the tenth anniversary celebrations of the Lateran Agreements. Recent controversies with the régime in Italy over its adoption of Nazi anti-semitism, by no means the only sign of Hitler's growing anticlerical pressure on Mussolini, had strained relations between the two Romes. Vatican circles were not alone in believing that the Pope was determined on a gesture regarded by many as irrevocable. Some even thought the Agreements might be broken. When it became known that for the first time in history he had summoned the entire Italian episcopate to Rome catastrophic rumours began to circulate. No less anxiety was felt in Fascist circles, for a breach of the Concordat was something they were bound to fear.

All was set ready for 11 February, and on the night of 31 January Pius XI had begun to draft the first of the two speeches he was to make, when on the following day rumours began to circulate that his condition had suddenly worsened. Alas, the rumours had some foundation. His heart had shown signs of weakening. Nevertheless for some days his normal vitality remained unimpaired, and on 6 February there even seemed to be some improvement. But the next day he was worse again, and from then onwards there was very little hope. Yet Ratti would not give in: to die mattered nothing to him, but he wanted first at all costs to reach the 11th for the anniversary and the 12th for his meeting with the Italian bishops, and he kept on insistently asking his doctors to make every effort and use every means to keep him alive till then. They did all they could, but in vain. On the afternoon of the 9th the final crisis banished the last remaining hopes. Pius XI died at 5.31 am on the 10th.

The man who had said, 'Mountains are not to be looked at, they are to be climbed', had failed by a hair's-breadth to reach his ultimate peak. He had always wanted to die on his feet and without warning, like St Andrew Avellino whose effigy he kept before him in his bedroom, and to whom he had always prayed for that favour. Perhaps in the last days he had dreamed of dying in St Peter's before all his bishops, immediately after his second speech. But the dream had not come true. He had wanted to pass his Rubicon and an invisible hand had stopped him just too soon. Not even the partial publication of the one speech he had prepared for 11 February, issued by John XXIII on the thirtieth anniversary of the Lateran Agreements,[1] has cleared up the mystery of its real contents, which soon became legendary. One of the most widespread rumours on the morrow of his death was that it had mysteriously been spirited away by Fascist spies. But in Palazzo Venezia the incubus of that unmade speech lasted long, for the fear that it might be revived by the indomitable Pope's successor. Mussolini, on learning the news of his death, strove to take comfort saying, 'At last that stiff-necked man is dead'; unaware, perhaps, that it was the greatest compliment he could have paid him.

[1] In a letter to the Italian episcopate, 6 February 1959 (*L'Osservatore Romano*, 9/10 February 1959).

Pius XII: Eugenio Pacelli

2 March 1939 – 9 October 1958

The Heir Apparent

The news of Pius XI's death came upon an astonished world in the early hours of 10 February 1939. Up till then it had not been generally known how serious his condition was. The Pope, who was particularly anxious not to disturb the Italian bishops on their way to Rome or already there, had insisted on absolute secrecy. After seeing his doctor he even tried to do some work: he glanced at the list of audiences that his Master of the Chamber had drawn up to satisfy him, and then sent for his Secretary of State to hand him some files.

But things could not go on like that. On leaving the sickroom Cardinal Pacelli discussed with the Under-Secretary Montini, who was waiting for him in the next room, how best to prepare the public for the news without alarming them too much. In the end they decided to compromise: no communiqué would be issued from the Vatican, but the Vicariate of Rome should order three days of prayer in all the city's churches for the happy outcome of the imminent festivities commemorating the Reconciliation and for the Pope's health.

This news was naturally given a pessimistic interpretation but, all the same, when early next morning the wireless and special editions of the newspapers announced the Pope's death, it came as a shock to the whole world. Yet this was the first time in recent history that among the speculations about his probable successor practically no one, either in Church circles or in the world at large, had any doubt of the answer. His name, of course, was never actually mentioned in any official or semi-official communiqué or in any of the declarations issued by Vatican personalities and the hierarchies throughout the world after

Ratti's death. But everyone with merely a superficial familiarity with Vatican affairs of recent years had become accustomed to finding him always in the forefront there like the Pope's shadow, and not a shadow that astutely contrived to overwhelm him, but one to which the Pope himself drew attention so insistently as to leave no room for doubt of his intention. The missions he entrusted to him, the praise he accorded him in public, went far beyond mere satisfaction at having a loyal collaborator and faithful interpreter: they amounted to an indication of what should happen when he himself was gone. There was, of course, nothing formal in all this: anything of the kind would have been both inadmissible and illegal, as well as being bound to produce a contrary effect among the members of the College of Cardinals, justly jealous of their own autonomy and their inalienable right. It was only a paternal, discreet insinuation – which did not pass unobserved.

The first episodes of the kind were naturally of a private, almost intimate nature. For example, on his patron saint's day in 1935 Pius XI sent him a fine reproduction of the conferment of the primacy on St Peter. The news was reported in the *Osservatore Romano*, but without mentioning the more interesting detail of the Pope's accompanying words: 'Also as an augury for Your Eminence.' Then, little by little, the indiscretions became more explicit, though still only to isolated individuals, in such phrases as, for example, that Cardinal Pacelli would have made 'a fine Pope'. He once confided that if he could have taken part in the Conclave for his successor he would certainly have voted for his Secretary of State. And on another occasion, probably after his illness, he went so far as to say: 'If I were sure that the Sacred College would elect Cardinal Pacelli, I would resign at once.'

At his last consistory for the appointment of new Cardinals, on 13 December 1937, he came within an ace of mentioning his name in public. '*Medius vestrum*,' he pronounced solemnly, quoting the famous words of John the Baptist to his disciples, '*stat quem vos nescitis*' (he is among you, but you do not know him). Then, to break the tense, expectant silence in the hall, he added as if in reproof to himself Christ's words to Peter: '*Quid ad te? Tu me sequere*' (What is it to you? You think only to follow me . . .). But when, back in his apartment, some of his companions dared to ask to whom he had alluded, he answered without more ado, 'To Cardinal Pacelli'.

But the facts counted for more than allusions, and they showed his clear intention to bring him forward at all costs and reveal him to the world. In the autumn of 1936 when his chosen heir was travelling about in the United States he said at an audience to the Secretary of Extraordinary Ecclesiastical Affairs, Mgr Domenico Tardini: 'I make him travel so that he may get to know the world and the world may get to know him'; and then, after one of his usual pauses, in a particularly solemn and assured tone of voice he added: 'He will be a splendid Pope . . .'

A Travelling Secretary of State

He had begun to make him travel as early as 1934, without bothering about whether the official reasons for his missions had much to do with his office as Secretary of State. In that year he appointed him Papal Legate to the Eucharistic Congress in Buenos Aires, and the year after he sent him in the same capacity to Lourdes for the close of the Jubilee of the Redemption. Except for the visit to the United States in 1936, the other journeys on which he was sent as Legate had to do with purely religious events: the benediction and inauguration of the Basilica of St Theresa of the Infant Jesus at Lisieux in 1937, and the International Eucharistic Congress at Budapest in 1938.

Needless to say, these journeys were a quite unusual and daring innovation. Ever since the occupation of Rome in 1870, and indeed going even further back to the days of Consalvi,[1] it had never been known for a Secretary of State to leave the Vatican and cross the Alps for an official visit to a foreign capital; and certainly no prelate holding that office had ever crossed the Atlantic, which Pacelli did twice over, going to both South and North America.

These journeys were a success both in themselves and in preparing the world to welcome the future Pope. This emerges clearly from the visits to France, especially the second one, which took place in particularly favourable political circumstances. In

---

[1] Secretary of State under Pius VII; he negotiated the Concordat with Napoleon. *Translator.*

1937 France had a Popular Front Government, supported from outside by a rapidly advancing Communist Party. But when a rumour spread that the Pope in person, known for his devotion to the 'little saint of the roses', planned to come to Lisieux, the incredible happened. At first, as was to be expected, no one believed it, if for no other reason because for more than a century no Pope had ever left Italy; moreover, only four months before, Pius xi in his encyclical *Divini Redemptoris* had both condemned Communism and forbidden any alliance between Catholics and Socialists. How could anyone imagine, then, that his first journey abroad would be, of all places, to France? But there was some foundation for the report, and when Léon Blum, the Prime Minister, heard it was true he hastened to let the Vatican know that he would put the palace of Versailles at the Pope's disposal. However, Pius xi had to abandon the idea because of his precarious state of health which forbade his travelling even by air, and the choice of his representative naturally fell on his Secretary of State. A burst of enthusiasm greeted this news in France. Pacelli had already won the sympathies of the French in 1935 during his mission to Lourdes. On that occasion his meetings with the political authorities had been extremely cordial, and his cry of protest against 'the superstition of race and blood' was also remembered as a courageous and clear warning directed against the eternal enemy of the French.

In the meantime France's relations with Hitler's Germany had become further strained; and the Government hoped for an even stronger stand from the Legate of the Pope of *Mit brennender Sorge*. Some of the country's most famous writers – Mauriac, Guyau, Gillet, Vladimir d'Ormesson, Pichon, Bidault – were recruited as special correspondents for the visit; the Havas Agency laid on Maurice Schumann to report the pontifical mission; and radio and cinema were fully mobilized. Faced with such preparations of welcome, the Vatican could not refuse to expand the programme to include an official visit to Paris as well, either before or after the ceremonies at Lisieux, to allow the Legate to have meetings of a political nature at the Elysée and the Quai d'Orsay. It seemed as if a second reconciliation was about to be launched between separatist France and the Holy See. Nor were these expectations disappointed. At Lisieux the Pope's representative made some transparent allusions to happenings beyond the

Rhine, to 'all the iniquitous violence' and 'all the vile criminal actions' committed in the name of the new idolatry of race whose 'bad shepherds' were leading astray 'a noble nation'. Later, at Notre Dame, from the pulpit where, in the century before, Lacordaire had preached, he praised 'the first-born daughter of the Church', vindicating before the whole world the significance and prestige of the 'historic mission entrusted to it'. One needs only to read the French press of the day, with its exaggerated eulogies of the papal delegate's eloquence, to have an idea of the personal success he achieved.

What counted most in these journeys at the Conclave of 1939, however, was the contacts he had established with the leading religious authorities in the countries he visited. At that time all the members of the Sacred College, except for Tappouni from Lebanon, came either from Europe or the American Continent: fifty-seven from Europe, of whom thirty-five were Italian, and six from North and South America. Though travel was then much more difficult, all these cardinals had naturally had occasion to meet and get to know the Secretary of State at some time in his official capacity in the Vatican. But an official visit with a fixed time-table and conducted on regular preordained lines does not provide the ideal conditions for establishing human contacts. It was quite another matter to meet the Secretary of State on one's home ground, away from all the paralysing inhibitions of protocol, especially when the guest was somewhat relaxed from the duties of his office.

Thus the ecclesiastical authorities in the various countries he visited discovered an unknown and unsuspected Pacelli, or rather the complete Pacelli, who combined at the same time a detailed knowledge of their countries' internal problems and Churches, and a remarkable feeling of religious concentration; the customary aristocratic isolation, and the most approachable kindliness; hieratic bearing, and affability to humble people; the elaborately framed speech of the orator, and the cautious and prudent but nevertheless warm, frank, and familiar comments of the conversationalist.

Even those who accompanied him, who had been near him for years and imagined they knew him, constantly found surprises in him, as can be seen from the following ingenuous account in the *Osservatore Romano* of his visit to the United States:

What had first been thought of as an ordinary period of leave became transformed into a journey with a truly American rate of progress. Instead of travelling by car or train, it was found necessary to have recourse to the aeroplane to enable the Cardinal, who had often made use of aviation before during his nunciature in Germany, to cover great distances – some 15,000 kilometres, from the Atlantic to the Pacific – in a relatively short time. During these flights all the many beauties of that country, with its inexhaustible natural riches, passed before his gaze like an immense kaleidoscope: superb mountains, limitless deserts, immense tracts of land cultivated by the most modern methods, oil- and mineral-bearing regions, vast forests like giants stretched out upon the ground, wonderful seashores in the paradise of California. In addition, to a mind like his, so versatile and open to all the valuable conquests of science, always eager to keep abreast of technical developments and improvements, visits to important industrial centres and their imposing factories were also of real interest; while the immensely tall buildings, the giant shapes with their harmonious lines, the vast schemes for the production of electrical power and for irrigation like the Boulder Dam, all afford reasons to strengthen the special esteem accorded to the daring practical genius of the American people.

One evening at Buenos Aires during the World Eucharistic Congress, he failed to turn up at a performance of Refice's *Cecilia* at the Colon theatre. Knowing his fondness for music, everyone supposed that he must have been either too tired to come or else held up by important duties connected with the Secretariat of State. But instead he had chosen to make a nocturnal flight over the city. And since the machine put at his disposal was only a passenger plane and unsuited for great speeds, he insisted on going back again the next night in a military plane where there was only himself and the pilot.

But the thing that most struck Pacelli's hosts during these famous missions abroad was his general bearing, compounded of asceticism and religious inspiration. Even today, turning over the photographs of these visits where he appears among groups of the local, civil or ecclesiastical authorities, one is struck by his invariable pose, his hands joined as if taking part in a liturgical ceremony. During his visit to Lourdes in 1935 two things made a particular impression: first, that he always ate alone and his meals never changed (invariably ending with three stewed plums); and secondly, that he spent a large part of the night in prayer or study before lying down to sleep, not on a bed, but on a chaise longue.

One afternoon, however, it seemed he was going to allow himself a break: he asked to visit the valley of Labigorre, near Saint Savin, and its monumental fortress-church. A two-horse carriage was brought out, and a priest from the sanctuary accompanied him as guide. But once out of the town, the Cardinal took no notice of the view but opened his breviary and began to read the office. This went on for an hour, after which he said: 'And now, Monsignore, let us go back.' The carriage turned round, and Cardinal Pacelli closed his eyes and became immersed in meditation. Back at his lodging, he got out of the carriage, turned to his companion saying 'Excuse me', and went into the house.

That he was the most widely known among all his colleagues at the Conclave of 1939, from personal contacts as well as by reason of his reputation and office, can be demonstrated by mathematical proof. For the number of cardinals he met as Nuncio in Germany, on his visits to the United States and France, and at Buenos Aires, Montevideo, and Budapest, adds up to a figure not far off the total of those present at the Conclave. A few of the cardinals had died in the meantime, but he must have been seen by hundreds of bishops on those occasions (there were three hundred at Budapest alone). Not since the Conclave of 1878, when Pecci was elected, had the future Pope been so familiar a figure to the rest of his colleagues. In that case, the future electors of Pius ix's successor had had an opportunity to get to know each other during the Vatican Council of 1870, which brought most of the leading churchmen to Rome for eight months. By contrast, Sarto, Giacomo Della Chiesa, and Ratti were all, with the possible exception of Della Chiesa, illustrious unknowns to almost all the non-Italian cardinals.

A Fabulous Career

Nevertheless the fact that Pius xi's Secretary of State had won the sympathy of the Catholic world abroad and of its episcopate did not suffice to guarantee him a majority among the College of Cardinals, for the determining factor there and at the Conclave was the Italian group. Moreover twenty-six of the thirty-five Italians were Curia Cardinals, and that could prove a further obstacle if it be true that no one is a prophet in his own country.

At the same time some of them were Romans, and there had been no Roman-born Pope since Emilio Altieri, Clement x, in the seventeenth century – 1670–76 – (not, as was sometimes supposed, since Innocent XIII, Michelangelo Conti, for he was born at Pola); so to be a 'Roman of Rome' might prove an advantage, especially in view of the irritation aroused in Vatican and Curial circles by the recent supremacy of the Milanese in many of the top posts. If under Pius x Mgr Duchesne could say of the influx of Venetians: '*De la barque de Saint Pierre ils ont fait une gondole*' They've made the barque of St Peter into a gondola), the immigrant Milanese might be said to have transformed it into a shipyard. A Roman Pope would at least readjust the balance and restore the traditional predominance of his fellow-citizens, and especially of the Curia.

Moreover, though the Pacelli family was Roman only in the last three generations and was certainly no Almanach de Gotha family (Marcantonio, the future Pope's grandfather and founder of its fortunes, came from Acquapendente, in Latium, and received a minor title in 1853 for having followed Pius ix into exile at Gaeta), it had rendered exemplary service. Besides being on the purge commission to weed out supporters of the Republic of 1849, Marcantonio was Under-Secretary in the Ministry of the Interior and co-operated in the foundation of the *Osservatore Romano*; his son Ernesto did good service for the Vatican's finances, especially at the time of the Libyan war, when he was at the head of the Banco di Roma; and his grandson Francesco (brother of the Secretary of State), carrying on his father's and grandfather's legal tradition, had further raised the Pacellis' prestige by collaborating with Pius xi in the drafting of the Italian Concordat and the laws of the new Vatican State, for which the King of Italy gave him the hereditary title of prince. Indeed, on the family side the only thing against Pacelli's candidature for the Papacy was that his ancestors appeared to be a long-lived stock. His grandfather Marcantonio lived to 102, his great-uncle Felice to 103, covering three centuries (1799–1902). Now, Eugenio Pacelli himself was only sixty-three, and a forty-year-long pontificate was really too much to contemplate. But was anyone likely to remember those details?

As to his own personal career, none of the Curia Cardinals about to be shut up in the Sistine Chapel under the eyes of

Michelangelo's tempestuous Christ as Judge could presume to equal it. Entering the Secretariat of State in 1901 at the lowest grade, by the time he left it sixteen years later to become nuncio in Munich he had been through all the stages, ending up with three years as head of the first section, being under-secretary of the Sacred Congregation for Extraordinary Ecclesiastical Affairs. At the same time he had held other positions of trust, from his collaboration with Cardinal Gasparri in drafting the White Book on the antecedents of France's breach of relations with the Holy See and in the codification of canon law, to his mission to the Austrian Emperor in January 1915. His appointment to Munich, significant enough in itself for Munich was at that time the most important nunciature in Europe, also had a further importance as the prelude to Benedict XV's approach to the Kaiser, effected at the young Nuncio's meeting with Wilhelm II at Kreuznach on 29 June 1917. And what other nuncio could boast two concordats to his credit? – with Bavaria in 1924, regarded as the ideal prototype for such conventions, and with Prussia in 1929. Diplomatists such as Maglione, Marmaggi, Pellegrinetti, Pizzardo, and Tedeschini, and also Fumasconi-Biondi and Massimi in other branches of the Curia, were doubtless considerable personalities, and one or other among them might certainly have been found worthy to assume the tiara – but only provided there was no Pacelli in the running.

It had always been his fate to cause even the most outstanding men to lose stature once they fell beneath his shadow. When he first came into the Secretariat of State all his colleagues felt he was the predestined one among them, that his calm, sure steps would carry him far, that he would be second to none and nothing would stop him till he reached the summit. Everything about him foretold this: his intellectual capabilities, his methodical, tenacious industry, his punctilious exactness and precision, and most of all his serious gravity and that courteous but inexorable reserve that set him almost magically apart in an inviolable solitude.

An old photograph of him as a child shows him among his companions on an excursion, sitting at the feet of Padre Lais, a learned Filipino priest: his gaze, already deep and serious, expresses both detachment from his surroundings and also a surprising self-awareness and control. In later years he showed a

remarkable capacity for keeping his own superiority in the background while still letting it be felt, maintaining cordial relations
with everyone yet intimate with none and, though more at home
with his superiors, showing every consideration to his equals
and inferiors.

The secret of this capacity lay not in pride but in a certain
withdrawn shyness; and this helped, in the long run, towards his
success. For an imperious, dominating character, unable to dis-
regard or endure hostility and dissension, would inevitably have
made enemies; whereas his shyness helped him to ignore and even
to forget such opposition. Thus if he had enemies they were few
in number, and even those few were denied the satisfaction of
declaring themselves as such.

Moreover once arrived at the headship of the Secretariat of
State he could allow himself to unbend a little, especially since by
then to indulge in a few friendships could even be of assistance
to him without weakening his iron rigidity. An aspirant to the
Papacy is not like an aspirant to the French Academy, forced to
make a humiliating round of visits among his electors. He must
not fawn, but must rather ensure his supremacy by a cautious
distribution of honours and powers. The few but trusted friends
of Pacelli the Secretary of State later proved, in fact, to be those
who benefited most. The war years at first obscured this fact;
but when peace returned the full significance was soon realized
of certain appointments that had seemed surprising or inopportune when announced by the new Pope within a few weeks
of his election. Canali, Pizzardo, and Piazza were then seen to be
the triumvirate of the curial electors of Pacelli, which was soon
to be expanded into the famous 'Vatican Pentagon'.[1]

All this does not mean, however, that even before Pius xi's
death all the eligible candidates for the tiara had voluntarily
abandoned the field to Pacelli. It was, rather, the case that Pacelli's
prospects inexorably improved by force of circumstances. Two
main reasons combined gradually to concentrate universal attention on this man with the brilliant past career and the magical
touch in diplomacy: first, the exasperating and provocative
behaviour of the Axis Powers towards the Church, and secondly,

---

[1] The five Pacellian Curial Cardinals, all-powerful in Pius xii's last decade, included
also Cardinals Micara and Ottaviani. See note in Bibliography, p.377. *Translator.*

the mounting pressure of international problems as the prospect of war drew ever nearer.

A Day-Long Conclave

But was it really a diplomatic Pope that the Church needed in such an emergency? And was it really inevitable that the choice must lie between a political and a religious Pope? Judging by the results of the 1939 Conclave, that choice was undoubtedly the main question in the minds of the electors, and the majority opted for a political Pope – a majority so strong, indeed, as to make short work of the traditional opposition to choosing a Secretary of State to be Pope. But was there really any such opposition in this case? On due reflection it seems unlikely. Pacelli's own personality ruled out anything of the kind. True, the remarkable qualities he had shown as papal legate might themselves suggest the doubt that he had been less fitted for the day-to-day life of the Curia; but even that is refuted, and by no less a witness than Ernesto Buonaiuti. That leader of Modernism in Italy, strongly hostile to Pacelli as diplomat and member of the Curia, in a critical work on him which appeared at the end of the war[1] nevertheless shows no hesitation in praising his personal virtues. 'His whole career,' he writes, 'is characterized by a rigid sense of ascetic piety and exemplary morality. A fine figure of a priest, imbued with a sense of his mission and the holiness of his office, Eugenio Pacelli cannot but arouse honest and sympathetic admiration for the dignified moral figure he presents and his proud composure as a prelate.' And again: 'He is undoubtedly one of the most eminent figures among the Roman clergy of the past fifty years. His personal piety, his exemplary apostolic zeal, the religious sensibility of his temperament, are all qualities that commend him to universal respect and consideration.'

In the laborious preparatory encounters of the Conclave when the various groups of cardinals met during the nine days after Pius xi's death, Pacelli's religious and pastoral attitude must have been discussed down to the last little-known detail. Someone, for example, revealed that as a seminarist and neophyte priest his

[1] *Pio XII*, Rome, 1946.

cherished aim was not a diplomatic or curial career but the care of souls, and only on the insistence of Cardinal Serafino Vannutelli, a friend of the family, was he persuaded to enter the Secretariat of State. It was, indeed, no secret to his colleagues that at least for a time he was not much attracted to politics and at a certain point, but for Cardinal Gasparri's veto, would have left the Secretariat and accepted a chair of canon law at Washington University. Later on, as nuncio in Germany, he had given convincing proof of pastoral zeal. And after his return to Rome, despite all the duties of his office had he not, unlike his more inarticulate colleagues (except for Cardinal Salotti's outbursts), shown constant willingness as a preacher? – a preacher, maybe, too clipped in speech and too much given to gesture, but all the same of great dignity and religious inspiration.

So though a struggle was anticipated between the majority, consisting of curial and non-Italian cardinals favouring Pacelli, and the minority, mostly cardinals from Italian sees determined to keep politics out of it and therefore to block the candidature of the ascetic and supposedly anti-Fascist Archbishop of Florence, Elio Dalla Costa, that struggle evaporated before it even began. Nor was it the only one to be avoided: for the supporters – Curialists for the most part – of a pro-totalitarian Pope friendly to the Axis Powers failed to cross swords with those who wanted a pro-democratic Pope. The latter, mostly foreigners, recalling Pacelli's travels in France and the United States, believed that in backing him they would be backing the man who, as they saw it, had brought about Pius xi's final *volte-face*, and one who, moreover, had no special leanings towards either totalitarianism or democracy since his real care was for one thing alone: the power of the Roman Church. The Curialists, on the other hand, who cherished fewer illusions about him, reckoned that his weakness for Germany would prevent him from dissociating the Church from the régime that was now all-powerful there, and hence from opposing the Axis policy.

Small wonder, then, that the Conclave lasted barely a day. It opened on the evening of 1 March; balloting began on the morning of the 2nd; and at 5.25 pm that same day the white smoke announcing that the Pope had been chosen proclaimed at the same time that it could be none other than Eugenio Pacelli. This was confirmed an hour later from the balcony of St Peter's by the

Cardinal Dean, Camillo Caccia-Dominioni; and a few minutes afterwards the new Pope, who had announced his name
as Pius XII, showed himself for the first benediction 'Urbi et
Orbi'. On 12 March the silver trumpets gave the first greeting
in the Vatican basilica to the 261st successor of St Peter as he
advanced between the feathered fans in his gestatorial
chair with a hieratical solemnity that already seemed completely
habitual.

Beneath the mitre and the ample ceremonial vestments only
his head and his long, nervous, aristocratic hands emerged. Seen
either in profile or front-view, that long pale face with deep
hollows round the eye-sockets and the prominent aquiline nose,
the skin riddled with wrinkles and shadows except where the
bones projected, and with those sharp but surprised-looking eyes,
could not be described as beautiful. Yet the intense, mysterious
concentration emanating from it was so strong as to produce an
irresistible impression, especially when the frail, tall figure rose
and held his arms wide open as in the form of a cross. 'He is like
someone in an El Greco painting,' a French writer said of him.
'It is the outward elongation of the emaciated, almost translucent
body, as if made only to be a refuge for the soul: it is the fine-
drawn face, as in Pascal or the Grand Condé, and most of all the
spiritual vitality concentrated in his extraordinary, almost supernatural gaze, unfortunately half-hidden by his spectacles.' Among
all the figures of great statesmen and soldiers of his day, that
diaphanous image of a bitter prophet and conscious sovereign,
seen in the press or on television screens, was to be the most
familiar to his contemporaries for the next twenty years: but that
first impression was ineradicable.

In the basilica, to the right of the shrine of St Peter where the
papal cortège was about to arrive, the tribunes of the sovereigns
and diplomatists (thirty-six special missions) were packed as never
before for a coronation. The Roman crowd, familiar with their
faces, ran over their names: Queen Elizabeth of the Belgians,
ex-King Alfonso XIII of Spain and his wife, King Ferdinand of
Bulgaria, Prince Umberto of Piedmont and Princess José, the
Duke of Norfolk, Count Ciano, Prince Charles Count of Flanders,
De Valera the Prime Minister of the Irish Republic, the princes of
Liechtenstein and Luxemburg, and so on.

At that moment few perhaps foresaw that the cameras focused

on those stalls were capturing the last shots of a world on the threshold of upheaval, or realized the symbolic significance of this assembly of potentates gathered around a man upon whose words or silences, in the tragic years to come, a large portion of humanity would wait with bated breath. Few of those present had grasped in the previous days the pregnant import of the new Pope's words to his electors on the morrow of his designation: 'We see before Us the vision of the immense ills that afflict the world, to whose succour the Blessed Lord sends Us, defenceless but trusting', almost as if the happiness or misery of the world depended henceforth on a sign from him. Just as no one thought to attribute any meaning beyond the customary ritual to those other statements he made during that same ceremony: 'The office of Supreme Pontiff throughout the course of the centuries aims at nothing but the service of the truth; of the truth, we say, that it may be complete and sincere, not obscured by any cloud or subject to any weakness, nor may ever depart from the charity of Jesus Christ.'

Of all the great sovereigns and representatives there present, only a minority believed that the religious realities represented by that man really constitute one of the poles of human history; most of them merely had a sceptical belief in the wisdom of putting to good use the aura of mystery of which he was the focus, and some even allowed themselves an ironical comment on the episode they were compelled to witness, convinced that in a few years the world would be freed for ever from such anachronistic superstitions.

Thus, between the shortsightedness of his own entourage who counted chiefly on his diplomatic gifts, and the incredulity of the powerful temporal personages come to satisfy their curiosity about him, the new Pope was indeed alone. Alone beside those men of the Church who asked nothing more of him than that he should bear the heritage of his predecessors intact across the Red Sea of the world war to come, and alone beside those statesmen who each proffered inducements to secure his support for their own cause, regardless of compromising that role of pre-eminent moral arbitrator which constitutes the true strength of every authentic religious power in the world.

How did the new Pope answer the great and diverse expectations placed in him in that dramatic spring of 1939?

There is no mystery about the fact that one of the great strengths of the Catholic Church is its feeling and respect for tradition – and tradition not only in matters of faith, rites and discipline but also in curial practice, and especially in the continuity between one pontificate and another. A history of the Popes could even be written based on the thesis that their own personal contribution was irrelevant in comparison with the coherent development of the Holy See's activity as ensured by the organs of the Curia. It would, of course, be a paradoxical and largely unacceptable method of treatment, but it could be supported by quite a number of arguments. In the same way, a history of the Church could be written interpreted solely in the light of the personalities and decisions of its Popes. The truth lies probably midway between the two. The affairs of the Church, at the summit at least, are in fact conditioned simultaneously by the two complementary forces of the Curia's routine conservatism and the Pope's personal initiative; and while it is true that the former nearly always ends by reabsorbing sooner or later all the innovations arising from the different psychological and circumstantial situations in which the Popes find themselves, it is equally true that a good many papal decisions or innovations, though they may become gradually absorbed in this way, nevertheless retain their originator's personal imprint.

Did Pius xii's reign follow the usual course and become absorbed in curial routine, or did it receive the unmistakable stamp of his own personality? And if the latter, in which direction did its originality chiefly lie, in internal Church affairs or in the Church's relations with the world? His reign coincided with three exceptional periods in world affairs, the Second World War, the Cold War, and the beginning of the thaw in East-West relations; and it also coincided with changes in the centres of power, and in social structure and habits, such as would normally occupy decades or centuries. What was his attitude towards a world undergoing such radical changes? Did he adapt himself passively to it, or react intolerantly, or come to it with intelligent understanding and stimulus? And, above all, what were the effects of his actions in the sphere of religion?

His admirers think to provide an exhaustive and convincing answer by presenting Pius xii as the personified synthesis of all his predecessors. According to them, he was at one and the same time a statesman of genius and a great teacher like Leo XIII, a standard-bearer of doctrinal integralism like Pius X, a champion of neutrality and pacifying internationalism like Benedict XV, and a direct follower of Pius XI's policy of concordatory relations and, above all, of anti-Communism. His detractors, on the other hand, maintain that he was no more than a high-level curialist who strove with remarkable skill to adapt all the traditional curial practices to the new circumstances in the belief that that would suffice, whereas in fact he was merely temporizing and covering up the lack of real answers in a flood of oratory.

The only way to arrive at a true estimate is to turn to the facts in a spirit of dispassionate inquiry and follow Pacelli through the various stages of his pontificate, beginning with the war, which conditioned not only the early but also the subsequent years of his reign.

Diplomacy as a Bulwark against the Threat of War

During and immediately after the war, there were some who, partly because of his lack of bold religious fervours – of which more later – but mainly from indiscriminate dislike, actually accused Pius XII of having wanted or at least supported the war; though they failed to produce a shred of documentary proof. Now, in the absence of documents, it is certainly possible to support a thesis by deductions, provided they are not reached from simple *a priori* – and especially *a priori* anticlerical – hypotheses. In the case in question one would need to bring forward convincing reasons for Pius XII's interest in fomenting a conflict of world proportions. This was never done; on the contrary, the documents so far available in the various countries' official publications (including, as this book was being written, those of the Holy See itself[1]) and the memoirs of contemporary statesmen all go to prove the exact opposite, in other words Pacelli's genuine and zealous intervention to prevent and confine the conflict.

True, certain steps he took were remarkably ingenuous – such as the proposal for an international conference early in May 1939, just after Hitler had rejected a similar suggestion from Roosevelt; but that cannot be taken as proof that he wanted to sabotage real

[1] See Bibliography, p. 376.

peace initiatives. His Secretary of State's later diplomatic activities were a good deal more adroit. As to the instructions given to the nuncio in Warsaw, Mgr Cortesi, they were certainly not such as to prevent a stiffening on the part of the Polish Government, but it was at least a legitimate opinion to believe, as Pius XII did, that resistance to Germany over Danzig and the Corridor was not necessarily bound to lead to a second world war. And when he heard in the middle of August 1939 of Germany's military preparations on the Polish frontier, Pius XII reacted on 24 August from Castel Gandolfo with the famous appeal for peace which includes his well-known and possibly his only aphorism: 'Nothing is lost with peace: everything may be lost with war,' and on the 31st with the diplomatic Note in which he asked Germany and Poland for a truce in order to summon an international conference.

It would, indeed, have been surprising had he behaved in any other way. The war was beginning with an attack on the most important Catholic State in Eastern Europe, by a Power which for years had shown fanatical intolerance in its ideological opposition to the Church: that alone would suffice to make the Holy See inevitably hostile to a conflict that could only damage even further the already unstable balance in Europe, especially since the Molotov-Ribbentrop pact had opened the gates of the continent to Soviet influence.

To adduce Pacelli's sympathies for the German people in support of the interventionist thesis is not only absurd but grossly misleading. There is no denying, of course, that he had such sympathies. They had matured during his long period as nuncio in Germany, for eight years in Munich and five in Berlin. In a certain sense, indeed, his own temperament and his methodical, punctilious habit of life could be said to have predisposed him towards the Germans and them to him. His departure from Berlin and Germany was almost an occasion for national mourning. Yet it was perhaps he himself who had gained most from his sojourn there, for in Germany he had found his ideal of order, discipline and scientific seriousness, as well as a group of colleagues whom he left behind only temporarily, to gather several of them round him again later as Secretary of State. As Pope, too, after the war and the defeat of Germany he still continued to keep Germans around him as his closest collaborators – the Jesuits Leiber, Grisar, Hendrich and Bea – and he always spoke German with them, and with the German nuns in charge of his household. One reason that doubtless influenced his special feeling for the German people was that his first and longest contacts with them were in Bavaria, a region by temperament, tradition, and religion, as well as by reason of its political autonomy, profoundly different from North Germany or Prussia. Moreover in the years after the First World War he had witnessed the shining and vigorous revival of German Catholicism, the more impressive by contrast with the moral and civil crisis the country was undergoing after its defeat. Guided by an intellectual leadership unequalled in any other European country (such names as Guardini, Adam, Herwegen, Scheler, Przywara, Lippert, and Haecker come to mind), German Catholicism was for long in the forefront of Catholicism on the Continent. What more natural, then, than for Pacelli to think of Germany, where he was both guest and Rome's official representative to the Government and the episcopate, as the key country in the new European conformation, and above all as the bulwark of the Christian West against the threats of Slav Bolshevism – all this, of course, within the framework of a Christian and European order in which Germany should collaborate, gradually redeeming itself from the heritage of the Protestant Reformation and becoming once more a part of the old Catholic continental unity.

But Pius XII's incontestable sympathies for the German people must in no way be confused with a penchant for Nazism or its ideology. It would be no less facile and absurd to call Pius XI a pro-Nazi because he appreciated the German cultural world. Indeed Pius XI's sympathies for Germany went even further back than those of Pacelli. A year before he was ordained priest, he had translated from German a study on sacred music. His pupils in the seminary in Milan used to notice how many German books were included in the bibliographies he gave them, and he even followed German authors in his lessons on oratory. He had the opportunity, without ever leaving Milan, to get to know the German people better than he could when travelling there, for throughout the 1890s he was chaplain to the German colony in Milan, holding regular services for them and also occasionally lecturing and preaching. He was also concerned with the care of children of the German workers in the Kolping factory, and even founded a *Mädchenheim* for the girls which was later taken over by the Grey Sisters of Breslau. We have seen how as nuncio in Poland he was accused of favouring the Germans in the elections in Upper Silesia. When he became Pope someone even claimed to have discovered German blood in his ancestry. But though all this may have had some influence on his decision speedily to secure a concordat with the Reich in 1933, he was certainly never a pro-Nazi or in favour of Hitler; indeed no contemporary statesman showed more open repugnance than he for the ideology of the new régime in Germany.

Throughout the long resistance to Nazism which began virtually on the morrow of the Concordat's signature, and to which dozens of protest Notes, now made available, bear witness, Pacelli was constantly at Pius xi's side. He stood there not only from duty but also from profound conviction, for while the Nazi ideology was in violent contradiction to that of Catholicism, being second in this only to Communism, its incarnation in the Third Reich constituted a permanent and possibly decisive challenge to the future of the Church. It is quite absurd, therefore, to imagine that he could welcome with enthusiasm a war which threatened to bring a further extension of Nazi influence on the European continent. The efforts he made during and after the conflict to preserve Germany from total catastrophe (as implied, for instance, in the Allies' insistence on unconditional surrender) are not to be confused with any attempt to save the Nazi régime. And though he waited – always with the idea of not involving the fate of Germany with that of National Socialism – until after the war was over to express, on 2 June 1945, his public condemnation of the régime, it is nevertheless beyond dispute that he did everything possible to free the Germans from its yoke and paralyse its plans.

To that first end, in the spring of 1940 he even went so far beyond the limits of his pontifical office as to support a *coup d'état* aimed at causing Hitler's fall. Earlier, his determination to check the conflict had led him to try to split the Axis and make the Pact of Steel inoperative by persuading Italy and Spain to remain neutral. That he succeeded only with Spain does not diminish the merits of his effort.

His first attempt in relation to Italy was aimed at exploiting the differences separating the Quirinal from Palazzo Venezia, and above all from the German ally. After long and careful diplomatic preparation there seemed some hope of success. On 21 and 27 December 1939, in Mussolini's absence, an exchange of courtesy visits took place between the King and Queen and the Pontiff. On 27 December, for the first time in the history of Italian unity a Pope crossed the threshold of the Quirinal, now the palace of the one-time Italian 'usurper'. On both occasions, Pius XII insisted on dominating the situation with the baroque rhetoric of his addresses. Apart from their irritating form, however, what struck everyone was his emphatic praise of the Italian people's will for peace and the 'political wisdom of its illustrious leaders' which had kept them out of the conflict. But unfortunately Victor Emmanuel III was not the most easily malleable person in clerical hands, even in the pontifical and diplomatic hands of Pope Pacelli; and by June 1940, when Italy entered the war, it was all too apparent that the attempt had failed.

Pius XII had tried in the meantime to act directly on Mussolini as well, profiting by an event which took place just before his first meeting with the Royal family. This was the friendly and sympathetic message he received from President Roosevelt containing the news that he was sending Myron Taylor as his personal representative to the Vatican. The most important fruit of his journey to the United States in 1936 as Secretary of State thus fell into Pius XII's hands just at the most propitious moment, both giving the Roman Church a new political and religious prestige through this eloquent recognition of its moral influence, and offering him a strong ally in his efforts towards political mediation.

At the end of January 1940 Myron Taylor and the American Secretary of State Sumner Welles landed within a few days of each other at Naples. Myron Taylor was at once received by Pius XII, while Sumner Welles set out on a tour of European capitals to examine the possibility of efforts for conciliation. Pius XII saw him at the end of his mission, and they then agreed that the Pope and Roosevelt should both exercise pressure to try to keep Mussolini at least to non-belligerency. Pius XII's personal letter to Mussolini of 24 April was followed by two letters from Roosevelt, but Mussolini's answers were far from reassuring. On 13 May, angered by the Vatican's pacificism, he ordered Dino Alfieri, who was being transferred from the Italian Embassy to the Holy See to be Ambassador in Berlin, to give Pacelli a stern warning when taking his farewell. Less than a month later Italy had entered the war.

The Temptations of Impartiality

But though Pius xii neither desired nor supported the Second World War, and indeed did all he could to prevent it, his conduct in relation to the individual belligerents was nevertheless both puzzling and disturbing. He should, according to his own principles, have shown complete neutrality, or rather impartiality; but in fact he did so only when it was a question of avoiding taking a solemn and public stand such as would imply the explicit denunciation of definite responsibilities incurred by one or other of the belligerents. This attitude is apparent from his various speeches and messages, especially the Christmas Eve broadcasts which were soon to become famous. Any attempt at objective analysis is defeated by these carefully calculated and extremely skilful texts, in which both sides always contrived to find support for their own cause and blame for the other, believing themselves immune. But the unfortunate part of it was that this carefully poised impartiality in the long run benefited the guilty rather than the innocent and so ceased to be impartial.

This is not to deny that Pius xii at times expressed sympathy with the victims, but such expressions of sympathy fell short of precise and formal denunciation of the guilty (the most striking case is the audience given to the Poles on 30 September 1939, after the fall of their country) and were, moreover, distributed in a far from convincing manner. When Germany violated the neutrality of Belgium, Holland, and Luxemburg, invading all three countries without prior ultimatum or declaration of war, Pius xii sent telegrams in warm if not precisely fervid terms to their respective sovereigns, rejecting the more incisive texts prepared in the Secretariat of State; but there was no shadow of such sympathy when Denmark, Norway, Yugoslavia, or Greece were invaded. Yet the Holy See was in diplomatic relations with Yugoslavia, and even if the other three countries were mainly either Protestant or Orthodox, the same applied to Finland: nevertheless only in Finland's case did he allow himself to make an exception and mention it by name in the Christmas broadcast of 1939.

The case of Finland, indeed, brings out the most serious contradiction of Pius XII's policy of impartiality. For whereas in speaking of Germany he always, up to the end of the war, avoided making any direct or indirect condemnation, he lost no time in insinuating it where Russia was concerned. The Red Army had barely crossed the Polish frontier and occupied the eastern regions of Poland when he told the new Lithuanian Ambassador, presenting his credentials on 18 September 1939, of his fears about the 'new and incalculable dangers' arising from the 'sinister shadow, daily closer and more threatening, of the ideology and actions of the enemies of God' (yet in what sense were the Nazis less enemies of God than the Communists?).

True, when the Soviet Union in turn was attacked by Germany, he resisted pressure from all sides – from the German and Italian Governments and their allies (Italians, Rumanians, Hungarians, Croats, Slovaks, Bulgars, and Spaniards were fighting beside the Germans on the Russian front) as well as from their respective clergy and episcopates – to transform the anti-Communist war into a religious crusade. But such a gesture would have been both dangerous (implying open support of the Axis countries against the Western Powers) and also superfluous, for the war had already begun and the episcopates, especially those attached to the forces, and most of the Catholic press were openly describing it as an anti-Communist crusade. In addition, by keeping the Holy See officially out of it Pius XII hoped to earn the gratitude of the Soviet Union should it succeed in withstanding its enemies; while in the event of a German victory he would have secured all the benefits hoped for, while justifying his reserve on the customary principle of pontifical neutrality.

The fact remains, however, that behind this seeming impartiality he not only anxiously awaited the success of the German armies in the East but also prepared for the advance of Catholic propaganda into Orthodox Russia, mobilizing priests trained in the Russicum and other groups of German and Polish Jesuits who were to follow the Nazi armies and organize the first advance bases for a conquest of the country. This was a perfectly legitimate attempt – though it was naturally boycotted by Hitler, who, having failed to get the war proclaimed a crusade, saw no point in complicating the Russian situation by the introduction of a religious war, for it suited him far better to present himself as the liberator of Orthodoxy from the Communist yoke. But if it was difficult enough to justify a departure from impartiality on such a ground, it could never justify the fact that in order not to compromise the German advance in the East Pius XII kept silence about all the crimes committed against civilians by the Nazis and their allies behind the screen of their own so-called crusade.

Drama and Capitulation of the Threefold Silence

This point marks the borderline between an admissible and possibly unavoidable silence about responsibility for the war as such, and an inadmissible silence about gratuitous crimes committed in the name of erroneous ideologies such as racialism. There are limits, of course, even to the first kind of silence: for while it is certainly not within the competence – or even the technical possibilities – of a Pope to decide where the moral responsibility for the outbreak of a war lies unless the guilt of one side is proved beyond all doubt, there are nevertheless certain ethical rules of international law which cannot be brushed aside with impunity. Pacelli himself recognized this over the violation of the Low Countries' neutrality (though unfortunately, as we said earlier, in their case alone). When Alfieri, at his farewell audience with him on 13 May 1940 before leaving for Berlin, conveyed Mussolini's message of annoyance about the telegrams of sympathy sent to those countries, Pius XII replied (we quote from the account of the audience given by Montini, then Under-Secretary of State):

In certain circumstances the Pope cannot keep silence. Governments put political and military considerations first . . .; for the Pope, on the other hand, that consideration [i.e. his duty to speak out – *trans.*] is the first, and it is one that he absolutely cannot ignore. His Holiness said in this connection that he had recently had occasion to read the letters of St Catherine of Siena who, writing to the Pope,[1] warned him that God would subject him to the most severe judgement if he did not react against evil or fulfil what he believed to be his duty. How could the Pope in the present instance make himself guilty of so serious an omission as to stand by indifferent to events of such importance, when the whole world awaits a word from him?

When advantage is taken of a wartime state of emergency to

[1] Pope Gregory XI, 1370–8. *Translator.*

commit crimes against humanity which are totally unjustified by
any necessity of war, the duty of a religious leader to denounce
those crimes can admit of no exception, and there can be no
mitigating circumstances for his silence. Pius XII, however, not
only abandoned his own principles in failing, as has been shown,
to maintain impartiality between the contestants, but he also was
guilty of inadmissible silence about the millions of civilian victims
of Nazism – Jews, Poles, Serbs, Russians, gypsies, and others.

When the accusation was raised (in the first instance crudely
and inaccurately by Hochhuth in his play *The Representative*, of
1963, which dealt only with the Jews), it seemed so incredible
that people tended to believe the defence officially put forward by
the Holy See, which hastened to explain that if Pius XII had not
spoken, or had spoken inadequately, this was because he was not
fully aware of the facts. But that too-simple defence was quickly
refuted. With regard to the extermination of six million Jews of
all nationalities, the action he himself took to protect the lives
of Jews outside the Reich and Poland – chiefly in Rumania,
Hungary, and Czechoslovakia, but also in France and Belgium –
is itself sufficient refutation. In any case he had from the very
beginning full and accurate knowledge of the slaughter of the
Poles and their forced migrations, and he also knew all about the
massacre of Orthodox Serbs in Croatia under the Ustashi. The
present writer was able to discover, as a result of researches on
the spot, what methods of communication the Vatican had in both
those countries and what information it received from them.

In the case of Poland, for instance, the local underground
government communicated uninterruptedly between 1942 and
late in 1944 (i.e. right up to the time of the Soviet occupation) with
the Holy See through the government in exile quartered first in
France and later in London, which had its own official representative at the Vatican, Ambassador Casimir Papée. Papée
received full information about the situation in Poland through
secret messengers or the radio, and regularly passed it on to the
Secretariat of State. He himself published after the war some
official letters from the President of the Polish Republic to Pius XII
and from Pius XII to the President and to several members of the
episcopate, adding some interesting comments based on his own
diplomatic activities. Scanty though this correspondence is, its
particular value lies in the proof it affords, through the Pope's own

words, of Pius XII's knowledge, even down to details, of the situation in Poland, and of how throughout the war the Polish Government kept on insistently asking the Pope to denounce the violence inflicted on the Poles by the Germans.

Writing, for example, to the Polish Cardinal Primate, Augustus Hlond, on 30 May 1942, Pius XII stated: 'We are fully aware, and grievously feel the repercussions, of the present deplorable situation of Poland, stricken by so many terrible misfortunes . . .'; and to the President of the Republic on 16 February 1943: 'In the message you have sent Us through your Ambassador, you have again drawn Our attention to the situation in which Our dear sons in Poland find themselves through the present circumstances, although you know well that of the facts you lay before Us and the grievous sentiments you express, not one is unknown to Us. In this grievous general situation every day a sorrowful echo comes to Our ears of all the ills afflicting humanity . . .'

The Polish President sent an appeal to Pius XII on 2 January 1943, ten days after the Christmas broadcast in which Pius XII had seen fit to abandon reticence and refer less vaguely than hitherto to the crimes against civilians committed under the pretext of the war. Avoiding any reference to that broadcast (and thereby showing that he regarded it as too generalized to be taken into account), he wrote:

Holy Father, divine laws trampled upon, human dignity humiliated, hundreds of thousands of men murdered without trial, families separated, churches profaned and closed, religion forced into the catacombs – this is the picture of Poland as shown in the reports we receive from the country.

In this tragic moment my people are fighting not only for their existence, but for everything they hold sacred. They do not want vengeance but justice, they do not ask for material or diplomatic aid – for they know that such aid cannot reach them except on the very smallest scale – but they implore a voice which will clearly and definitely indicate the evil and condemn those who collaborate in it.

I am convinced that if the people can be strengthened in their belief that divine law knows no compromise and is above all human considerations of the present, the Polish people will find the strength to resist . . .

In the past, in Poland's times of difficulty, though times less fraught with tears and blood than the present, Your Holiness's great predecessors addressed fatherly words to the Poles. Today, when in the greater part of our country men can neither preach nor pray in Polish, the silence must be broken by a voice from the Apostolic See, and those who die with the consolation of religion, defending their faith and their traditions, must be able to count on the blessing of the Vicar of Christ.

From the beginning of 1942 the Vatican was able to profit by another more direct method of communication with Poland: the so-called 'way of the bishops' or 'of the clergy'. The information offices of the clandestine Polish Government received the order to pass on everything to do with the situation in Poland, especially the religious situation, to the head chaplain of the clandestine army, who would arrange for it to be conveyed regularly to Rome through his courier service. The State Archives in Warsaw contain vast quantities of such material, salvaged from destruction in the war, including often very detailed new reports, analytical studies regularly produced by experts, and files and official documents or copies of documents from the German occupation authorities. There also existed a whole network of private individuals, members of the diplomatic corps, or chaplains and officers of the ARMIR (the Italian expeditionary corps in Russia) who offered their services to the Holy See, going back and forth more or less regularly between Poland (and other countries) and Rome.

As to Croatia, that state was set up under Ante Pavelić in April 1941, following the occupation of Yugoslavia by Italian and German forces. It soon established a *de facto* exchange of representatives with the Holy See, receiving Abbot Ramiro Marcone as Papal Legate in Zagreb and sending to the Legation at the Quirinal in Rome emissaries charged to maintain contacts with the Vatican (for at the Vatican itself there were still members of the Royal Yugoslav Legation to the Holy See). Those emissaries' reports, restored to Zagreb in 1945, besides providing an unexpected and original glimpse of the Roman Curia and the Secretariat of State at that time, show how through the Yugoslav Legation and the Allies' ambassadors the Vatican knew all about the campaign of forced rebaptism promoted by the Ustashi Government with a view to Croatizing the 2,200,000 Orthodox Serbs in Croatia. If the latter refused to embrace Catholicism, and sometimes even when they did, they were massacred, especially in the villages, in the most brutal way. The most conservative estimates indicate that at least half a million Serbs fell victim to this policy of religious racialism pursued by Pavelić at Hitler's behest. According to the reports of the Ustashi representatives in Rome, neither Pius XII nor any member of the Secretariat of State dared to reproach them for these horrible deeds. At most, Mgr Montini and Mgr Tardini alluded cautiously to them, showing themselves convinced and relieved by the denials they received. Among all the leaders of the Curia, one alone had stormy encounters with the Ustashi representatives and dared to accuse their government of these medieval crimes that marked Catholic Croatia with an indelible stain, even confronting them, in June 1942, with the appalling number of victims, 350,000 – and that was Cardinal Tisserant.

Immediately after the war, at the time of the trial of Mgr Ludwig Stepinac, Archbishop of Zagreb, by the Tito Government's authorities, Pius XII defended himself against accusations made in the tribunal against himself and the Croat episcopate, who were alleged to have collaborated in the forced baptism of Serbs. He then recalled a reply given by his Secretariat of State to the head of the Yugoslav Legation to the Holy See on 25 January 1942, which promised Vatican intervention with the Croat episcopate and cited measures taken by the episcopate to cope with the situation. The official records of the Croat episcopate certainly appear to be unexceptionable, whereas Pius XII's own conduct in this connection is not so clear. But in any case there is no doubt about the fact that no organ of the Holy See, still less Pius XII himself, ever made any public stand in the face of such serious misdeeds.

When lack of information failed as a line of defence for Pacelli's silence about the Nazis' illegal crimes, his apologists fell back on even weaker arguments. First they maintained that if he had kept silence, it was largely out of consideration for the victims, who would have been subjected to still worse reprisals had he denounced the crimes, and also in the hope of preserving the Church and the millions of Catholics under the administration of the Reich from further persecution. It is quite true that Pius XII several times said as much himself. But how far was this argument really valid? It was not difficult to establish that the great majority of victims of Nazi extermination had insistently urged that he should speak out, rightly thinking that no fate could be worse than the one that awaited them, whereas a resounding protest would probably lead eventually to an end of the atrocities (as in fact it did in the case of euthanasia), even if some fatal reprisals took place first. The second argument used was really in itself a flagrant accusation, for it invoked reasons of (ecclesiastical) State to justify permitting a mad act of wholesale slaughter. But as everyone knows, the task of a religious leader is to defend the moral rather than the material foundations of his Church, and his mission is not to preserve his faithful from the trials sent by Providence, but to help and sustain them to withstand those trials.

That last unfortunate attempt at defence brings us up against the third and not the least serious 'silence' of Pius xii: his apostolic silence. It was this silence that Cardinal Tisserant reproached him with, in the famous letter discovered and made public early in 1964, but which in fact goes back to 11 June 1940, the day after Italy declared war on France. Cardinal Tisserant, then Prefect of the Eastern Congregation, confided to his colleague and fellow-Frenchman Cardinal Suhard, Archbishop of Paris, that since December 1939 he had 'insistently' asked the Pope to issue 'an encyclical on the duty of the individual to obey the dictates of his conscience, for that is the most vital point of Christianity'. And he added: 'I fear that history will tomorrow have to reproach the Holy See with having pursued a policy of convenience to its own exclusive benefit, and little more. And this is a terribly sad thing, especially when one has lived under Pius xi.'

If Pius xii had followed Cardinal Tisserant's advice in 1939 and early 1940, he would probably have made a political rather than a religious or moral choice. But in 1942, when crimes against civilians were at their height, it was no longer just a question of repudiating war, as Benedict xv had so emphatically done, but of repudiating sheer insane and sadistic crime and if need be exhorting its perpetrators to civil and military disobedience. That Pius xii never did this understandably shocked the world.

But the first duty of history is not so much to act as a tribunal as to attempt to explain men's actions and events. And there is certainly an explanation which may help us to understand the conduct of Pius xii, whose loftiness and strictness of conscience cannot in all honesty be denied. Many convincing testimonies exist to the fact that the dilemma of whether to speak or keep silence constituted, especially in the war's middle years, a genuine crisis for him. It even affected him physically. In his commemorative speech about Pius XII, Cardinal Tardini recalls how during the war years he restricted his meals to a bare minimum and refused to have his apartment heated; but it was probably his own inner conflict, at least as much as such penitences, that reduced his weight at the end of the war to under nine stone despite his six-foot height.

If in the end Pius XII elected to keep silence rather than speak, this was undoubtedly a result of his bureaucratic and legalistic mentality, which caused him to have an over-temporalistic conception of the Church even while fully recognizing its super-terrestrial ends. Hence his preference for the art and machinery of diplomacy, and his tendency to regard the Church as a Power, if *sui generis*, involved in the inter-play of other Powers. Purely religious or revolutionary aims seemed to him possibly appealing but certainly utopian. He did not, indeed, reckon the power of Catholicism with the military yardstick of a Stalin, but he attached too much importance to the physical aspects of its structure and the numbers of its adherents. It was a power, if on a higher plane, to be expressed in concrete terms of numbers and quantity, rather than a moral and spiritual power. So when the Archbishop of Canterbury, speaking in the House of Lords on 20 March 1939, proposed an alliance to transcend political alliances against the perils of war, a common front of all who believed in the Gospel, and offered the newly-elected Pius XII the presidency of a 'Christian Conference' consisting of Catholics, Protestants, and Orthodox, he refused for the usual 'theological reasons'. The juridical traditions of 'splendid isolation' adopted from time immemorial by the Church in relation to schismatic communities fully account for his decision, but that does not alter the fact that this restricted outlook caused him to prevent a stout bulwark against war from being built, and the Church from acquiring unprecedented moral and political as well as religious prestige.

The Victory of Charity

The only really indisputable victory secured by Pius XII during the war and the immediate post-war period was in the sphere of charity; and although it was made financially possible through contributions from Governments and various organizations (Catholic, Jewish, etc.), he must be given full credit for it. It began with the establishment of the Vatican Information Service, at first housed in rooms in the Secretariat of State; these quarters soon proved too small, and it was then transferred to the San Carlo palace, where it had room to expand into various sections, dealing with prisoners, missing persons, refugees, deportees, the sick, orphans, relief work, medical supplies, clothing, and food. Letters asking for help came from all over the world, sometimes as many as 1,800 a day. The Vatican radio also helped in tracing prisoners and missing people by sending out messages almost uninterruptedly – 27,000 in a peak month – to Cairo for the Middle Eastern countries, Mombasa for Kenya and Tanganyika, Bangkok for Indochina, Leopoldville for the Congo and Equatorial Africa, as well as to the capitals of London, Ottawa, Addis Ababa, Tokyo, and Washington for their respective countries. Food and medical supplies were dispatched to Finland, Norway, Greece, France, Belgium, Holland, Ethiopia, Malaya, and other countries. As well as parcels for prisoners, supplies were also sent to refugees and the wounded, and even the burial of the dead was looked after.

But perhaps even more important than those activities was the protection afforded to victims of civil strife. One of the most tragic aspects of the Second World War was the fact that it was fought not only between countries but between peoples of the same nationality. This meant that in the course of its changing vicissitudes persecutions and purges were carried out not only by the victorious foreign army in an occupied territory but also by collaborating local elements. Almost every country in Europe in those bitter years experienced the ebb and flow of invading armies and the downfall and restoration of their supporters. Thus in addition to political prisoners and refugees from destruction there were also refugees from persecution, and beside hospitals overflowing with wounded the prisons were also packed with opponents of the victorious side. The victors hunted the vanquished and gave them short shrift when captured. Factional hatred in those years accounted for almost as many victims as the actual fighting.

In such conditions, an outside Power could be of inestimable help in intervening to protect the vanquished from being unjustly sacrificed. Giving them temporary protection did not imply sharing their political responsibilities, let alone their moral errors, but merely defending them from further injustice. The shelter afforded in those days, with the example and secret encouragement of the Vatican, by bishops and priests, monasteries and religious institutions of all kinds at great risk to themselves constitutes one of the finest examples of Christian charity in the whole war.

And it must also be said that Pius XII's charity, especially during the war itself (for later on it deteriorated into an instrument of personal propaganda either on behalf of the Church or for all too obvious political ends), was not merely charity of an official or bureaucratic kind but something that involved him so directly and personally that the effects were visible in his drawn face and emaciated frame. It was especially moving to see him bowed down in sympathy at the evidences of misery thronging around him at his audiences and to hear his simple and truly heartfelt words on those occasions. People were deeply touched by his visits to the scene of the two bombardments of Rome in the summer of 1943; but perhaps even more convincing was his participation in certain ceremonies in St Peter's when he insisted on going on foot, not in the gestatorial chair or accompanied by any pomp or ceremony, and in distributions of food which brought him into humble contact with the harassed populace.

The Anti-Communist Crusade

But Pius XII's valuable work in the realm of charity and the efforts he made to confine the conflict cannot outweigh the accumulated responsibilities of his threefold silence and his partiality towards certain of the contestants. Unfortunately that partiality persisted after the war and ended by colouring his whole international policy.

His correspondence with Roosevelt, published in 1947, showed his constant effort to isolate Russia from the Allies, and in particular to moderate the American President's undoubtedly excessive optimism with regard to Stalin. But relations between Pius XII and Roosevelt became distinctly cooler after the bombardment of Rome in 1943, and this influenced the Holy See in its critical attitude towards the Allies' plan, decided on at Yalta, for a World Organization based on the principle of the 'Grand Alliance' of the Great Powers. The *Osservatore Romano*, for example, wrote that the decision taken at Yalta did not tally with the principles of equality in mutual co-operation, and that 'it would mean a return to the distinction between great and small, strong and weak, rich and poor, victors and vanquished, thus classified in perpetuity according to the systems of the Holy Alliances and Leagues of Nations based on these fatal discriminations'. Almost the same words had been used by the Vatican daily a quarter of a century earlier: with the difference, however, that while Benedict XV was enunciating a principle of undeniable universal validity, Pius XII and his propaganda organs were using it as a shield for opposing the key position that Yalta accorded to the Russians.

After Roosevelt's death the Holy See's criticisms and reserves increased and became more explicit, significantly coinciding with the approaching end of the war and, more particularly, with the advance of the Red Army into the heart of the continent. The Vatican's chief mouthpiece in this connection was the United States episcopate, which issued a first and extremely forthright declaration on the organization of world peace on 16 April 1945 in view of the San Francisco conference, and another on the same lines in November after the Potsdam conference. In the latter declaration ('Between War and Peace') the American bishops stated explicitly that acceptance of co-operation with the Soviet Union was too onerous for American democracy. 'We must face the facts,' they said. 'There are profound divergences of thought and political aims between Russia and the Western democracies; Russia has acted unilaterally in many important decisions ... There is a clash of ideologies. Frank recognition of these divergences must precede any sincere effort for realistic world co-operation for peace.'

The American episcopate would never have dared to adopt so positive a stand without explicit authorization from Rome. But its attitude, which received regular approval and support from the Vatican daily, saved the Vatican from having to expose itself too dangerously. Pius XII's own personal pronouncements also became increasingly explicit as the breach between East and West widened and the opposing blocs built up. True, in his Christmas message of 1947 – that of the so-called 'Pacifying Impartiality' – he simply stated:

> Our position between the two opposing camps is exempt from any prejudice, from any preference for this or that people, for this or that bloc of nations, as it is foreign to any sort of temporal consideration. To be with Christ or against Christ: that is the whole question.

But in thus transferring the problem from the political to the religious sphere there is an obvious equivocation and, in a certain sense, an exercise of pressure: for, in the name of the inaccept-ability of atheism and the irreligion inseparably linked with Communist ideology, Pius XII was proclaiming anew, and with the added motive force of religious passion, the opposition between the two political camps. In the same speech, in fact, he qualifies as 'a deserter and traitor anyone who lends his material support, his services, his talents, aid or vote to parties and to forces that deny God, that put might in place of right, and threats and terror in place of liberty, that make lying, opposition, and incitement of the masses to revolt so many weapons of their policy, thus rendering national and international peace im-possible.'

The serious aspect of these words lies in their mixture of the sacred and the profane, confounding the two spheres of religion and politics and enabling the Powers concerned to make use of the alternative 'with Christ or against Christ' in order to justify a crusade against the Eastern bloc. It is, of course, entirely legiti-mate for a religious authority, and particularly a spiritual head, to take up a definite standpoint against an ideology that involves religion itself and to give guidance to his followers about their own responsibilities; but the danger that their words may be misunderstood or wrongly exploited should make responsible religious leaders especially careful not to lay themselves open to any such misconception. Failure in this constitutes a responsi-bility that brings its own consequences.

Pius XII, however, did not wait long before acting more openly and speaking more explicitly. In May 1948, for example, he allowed the Nuncio in Belgium and Holland to be present officially in the name of the Holy See at the Congress of Europe promoted by Churchill and the Movement for European Union and held at The Hague, and in his allocution of 2 June 1948 he

stressed the significance of the presence there of a 'Roman Nuncio
. . . representative of that papacy that baptized Europe', saying
that the unexpected appearance of an 'irreligious, pagan, anti-
Christian' Europe made necessary the cohesion of the divided
spiritual unity of Western Europe around the vivifying nucleus
of an identical Christian faith.

But it was above all in his broadcast Christmas message of
1948 that he for the first time took up a clear and definite position
in favour of a strategic conception of international solidarity and
asked European Governments to join in a system of exclusive
security. Among the fundamental ideas he advanced were the
impossibility of remaining neutral in the face of a threat of
aggression – from what source was not stated; rejection of the
principle of Great Power unanimity, with the object of cancel-
ling from the United Nations 'every trace of its origin, which was
necessarily a wartime solidarity'; and exclusive security, which
consisted in 'improving on' the old dictum, *si vis pacem para
bellum*.

The general lines of what the editor of the *Osservatore Romano*
described as 'the great strategic theme of the Church', in other
words mobilization against the atheists, were now clear. It
remained only to fill in the details on the religious and political
planes. One of Pius XII's measures in this direction was to issue,
on 1 July 1949, a decree of the Holy Office against Catholics who
were registered members of the Communist Party; and he
resisted all efforts towards détente not only after Stalin's death
in March 1953 but right to the end of his own life. The obvious
aim of the decree was to bring back the Catholic masses attracted
by Communism, thus leading to the disintegration of Communist
Parties in the democratic countries and the concentration of
opposition in the Socialist Parties. At the same time resistance to
détente would exacerbate the tension of the Cold War between
the two blocs, thus leading to the explosion, at the first suitable
opportunity, of that preventive war which in his view offered the
only chance of eliminating atheist Communism from the world.

That Pius XII's pontificate was constantly on the watch for
this war of 'liberation' from Communism to break out, was
clearly shown in the tragic days of the Hungarian insurrection of
October-November 1956. Nothing could more openly have
revealed his own hopes than the insistent messages he then sent

to the Hungarian people, and nothing disappointed him more than the inert attitude of the Western world standing by powerless to avert the end of the revolution and the unimpeded return of Russian domination. Yet the outcome of the Hungarian episode, in contrast with the positive results of the Polish rising, should have opened his eyes to two facts: first, that the West was not to be relied on to take part in his crusade, and secondly, that there were possibilities for the Eastern European countries drawn into the Soviet orbit to progress towards a better future, even from the religious angle, by following a less rigid and intolerant course. But he continued to maintain his own rigid attitude, showing his preference for the extreme line adopted by Cardinal Mindszenty and his disagreement with Cardinal Wyszynski's more cautious policy in Poland. Cardinal Wyszynski had to wait three days for an audience when he came to Rome in April 1957, and the demonstrations prepared to greet his arrival were banned. Such gestures were clear proof of Pius XII's intention to remain firm upon his rock regardless of American advances towards a thaw.

The most serious aspect of Pius XII's anti-Communist policy, indeed, was not so much that it was extreme but that it was quite unrealistic. He seemed unable to grasp how situations are constantly changing, especially at times of deep and profound transition, and how inopportune it was for the Church to adopt an absolutely intransigent attitude. Such an attitude not only made him cling to his belief in the increasingly unlikely possibility of armed intervention against the Communist bloc, but it also forced the Churches in the Eastern European countries towards progressive extinction. It was obvious after October 1956 that insistence on intransigence no longer made sense but would merely jeopardize the new possibilities arising for a relative improvement in their situation. By his unwillingness or inability to recognize this fact, Pius XII became the unwitting accomplice of his own enemies in undermining the various national Catholic communities in Eastern Europe (except for Poland), and virtually responsible for the state of affairs that he himself named the 'Church of Silence'.

It would obviously be absurd to criticize Pius XII's initial encouragement of opposition to Communism in the countries that fell under Soviet influence, either during the period when some vestiges of democratic liberties still survived or in the early days of the régime's establishment there. He had an indisputable right to do this, just as Catholics in those countries had the right to react against the progressive erosion of their civil and religious liberties. But once the new order appeared to be irrevocable, he should, without in any way abandoning his ideological stand-point, have disengaged himself from a rigid policy now become sterile and stressed instead at an international level his own autonomy *vis-à-vis* the two blocs of East and West. A Church's task, as Karl Barth has said in one of his lectures, is not so much to choose between different political blocs as to vindicate its own autonomy in relation to them. The conflict between East and West was essentially a power conflict, and only in the second place a conflict of ideologies, neither of which was evangelical; the Catholic Church, therefore, like every other Church, should have resisted all pressure to associate it with one bloc rather than the other. Even if at first sight the cause of the West might seem to be its own cause, that did not make it the cause of God.

To quote Karl Barth again, 'the future of the Christian cause in no wise depends on its adopting a standpoint against the East, with all that that would imply in the way of agitation, propaganda, and machinations. The Christian faith, its solidity, and its future have nothing to do with crusades. It is not a crusade that the Church of the West should preach against the atheism of the East, but the word of the Cross, that word which the Church should rather first of all proclaim here, in the West, and through which it itself should first submit to a complete self-renewal . . . The Christian Church, in short, cannot be against either West or East. It can only intervene between West and East . . .', taking its adversaries at their word by proclaiming and carrying into effect the justice of God against the capitalism of the West and defend-ing freedom against the absolutism of the East. Then alone can reconciliation come about between the two contestants and form the stable bond of peace.

By favouring one of the two blocs instead of acting as an intermediary between them from a higher level, Pius XII un-happily frustrated his own desire to serve the cause of the Church and of world peace. Within the Catholic community itself, he cast confusion among the consciences of believers by urging on some towards absurd crusades contrary to the spirit of the Gospel and

restraining others from prudent but opportune attempts at dignified and useful collaboration. Nevertheless, though he definitely
favoured the Western bloc, his international policy cannot really
be called pro-American. He never felt any particular attraction
towards the United States, and he certainly never regarded it as
representing the ideal way of life. His respect for tradition and
his humanistic background, such as it was, prevented any feeling
of kinship with so young a country. He recognized and appreciated the positive good qualities of the American people, but
taken in combination with all the other manifestations of the
American view of life they could not command his enthusiasm.
He regarded the United States mainly as a source of defence and
preservation for Europe, which to him was the one true cradle
of civilization and the natural meeting-point of Christianity
with Greco-Roman culture. In relation to the old continent, in
short, he saw America largely as a colony called upon to
help and sustain the mother-country in times of difficulty and
danger.

An example of this attitude can be seen in the way he defended
the Curia from American influence and intrusion. Immediately
after the war, the presence of numerous American prelates among
the ranks of the Holy See's active diplomacy (as Nuncios or with
equivalent functions in various countries of Europe, Africa, and
Asia), and of other Americans then in positions of some power
in Rome in connection with rehabilitation work, seemed to
suggest that some of the key posts in the Roman Church's
departments might soon be swallowed up by Americans. But
instead within a few years the situation quietly reverted to normal
with the return of all those persons to their native land. This
naturally led to complaints and pressure from the American side,
but only towards the end of his pontificate, in 1957, and then
only in the case of the Propaganda Fide (where it was especially
useful from the financial point of view) did Pius XII allow an
American to join the Curia; this was Cardinal Stritch, Archbishop of Chicago, who, however, died of an infection only a
few months later.

Europeanism and Christian Democracy

It was very natural that close relations should exist between the

Vatican and the United States in Pius xii's day, given the USA's outstanding role in the Western world. American economic power alone was in a position to provide the world, and Europe in particular, with the means for reconstruction and defence. But that did not mean that pro-Americanism was ever a ruling influence with Pius xii in the way that anti-Communism was. It was anti-Communism alone, not pro-Americanism, that paralysed him on the international plane to the point where he was unable to appreciate the importance of the 'Third World' – the non-aligned nations – and it alone inspired his continental policy in Europe and elsewhere and the policy he desired to see in the individual States, whether Catholic or otherwise.

Pius xii certainly had not a colonialist mentality. Though he may have been rather reticent in showing his own sympathies for autonomist movements in the colonies, he left the individual local episcopates (which still consisted of elements brought in from outside) perfectly free to support their cause. There was no contradiction in this, for his personal reticence, while it was partly due to his awareness of the Church's responsibilities in the past in having supported the colonial system and profited by it to secure privileges for missionary activities, was mainly caused by his fear of weakening the colonial Powers at a time when they had to face the Soviet menace. This motive was so strong that in order to avoid giving impetus to the anti-colonialist movement he even delayed replacing the white hierarchies by native elements, thus seriously endangering the position of the ecclesiastical communities in countries aspiring to autonomy, which might easily have been led to attack those communities as off-shoots of Western power. That was precisely what happened in the former Belgian Congo, once the most Catholic country in Africa with five million Catholics (baptized or under instruction) out of a population of thirteen million, which at Pius xii's death had not yet achieved an autonomous hierarchy (two years before one native bishop had been appointed, but even he was only the auxiliary of a white colleague).

How superficially the first efforts of the 'Third World' to constitute an autonomous non-aligned entity, independent of the two great blocs, was regarded in Vatican circles and by the *Osservatore Romano,* can be seen from their treatment of the Bandung Conference of 1955, which was actually interpreted as an attempt by the Communist world to influence the new States against the Western Powers. Pius XII held the over-simplified view that the economic situation of those underdeveloped countries must inevitably make them a prey to one of the two blocs and prevent them from forming a self-sufficient force capable of standing midway between the two and making its own political ideas prevail.

His enthusiasm for the European idea was of a quite different order, indeed he was one of the first and most consistent apostles of a United Europe. Yet his open championship of it was directed much more towards defending Europe – from Communism, of course – than towards giving it genuine unity and effectiveness. In the early days, too, it was not yet possible to foresee how the balance in it between Catholics and Protestants would work out: in the event, it proved such as to come near justifying his hopes about the possibility of reconstituting a Europe which would be not only Christian but also, if not actually Catholic, at least under strongly Catholic influence. There was even a moment when the presence at the head of the European movement of three out-standing Catholic statesmen – Adenauer, De Gasperi, and Schuman – made him believe that his dream might be near to being realized.

But even when that Utopia dissolved, Europeanism and anti-Communism continued to be his watchwords for the States of the old continent, and especially for the Catholic parties in each State. Generally speaking, in Italy, Germany, Austria, France, Belgium, Holland, and Luxemburg the Catholic parties that came to the fore after the Second World War, broadly described as Christian Democrat parties, either had no precedent or were only tenuously related to the pre-war or pre-dictatorship Catholic parties. This made it easier for the Holy See to exert influence on them.

The degree of dependence on Rome varied according to each country's past traditions of autonomy. Italy was thus an extreme case, but none the less instructive for that in affording an idea of the curious methods adopted by Pius XII, especially in relation to States with a Catholic majority. The Holy See, situated in the heart of Rome, has always regarded Italy as its own strategic and demographic hinterland, essential to ensure the physical and moral preservation of its own central organs: a country entitled of course to have a government of its own to administer its own needs, but on condition that the government adjusts its autonomy to the requirements of the Vatican, whose chief concern is to keep the Italians as a people ready to serve the Church's needs. Was it not this that Pius xi aimed to achieve with the Concordat?

Pius xii, however, after the war, found himself operating in much more favourable conditions. He no longer had to deal with an intransigent totalitarian régime; and in addition he had the possibility of filling the power vacuum caused by the defeat – a vacuum especially dangerous for the Church because of the rising Communist Party – by exerting pressure both on the recently-founded Christian Democrat party and on Catholic Action. In this way a Catholic majority was ensured within the Constituent Assembly, and after that it was relatively easy for him to secure that the Constitution of the new Republican State should not only contain nothing contrary to the ethical and social principles of Catholicism but should also fully recognize, under its Article 7, the Lateran Pacts, with all their provisions about marriage and religious teaching in State schools. Less than a year later, the elections of 18 April 1948, carried out under the slogan of 'Rome or Moscow', gave the Christian Democrats an absolute majority in both Houses, thus ensuring a series of governments docile towards the Church's directives. But despite all this the 'party of Moscow', encamped, so to speak, at the very gates of the Vatican City, continued to be the largest and most compact of all the Communist Parties in Western Europe. This fact determined the Holy See to maintain and even increase its pressure on the young democratic State in order to keep its hold on it and be able to manoeuvre it at will against the supreme enemy.

Pius xii had already, in the spring of 1947, got the Prime Minister, De Gasperi, head of the Christian Democratic party, to dismiss the Communists from the Government, and in the summer of 1948 he encouraged the rupture of the post-war combine which had till then united all brands of trade-unionism. But those steps he regarded as merely the prelude to the establishment of an out-and-out Catholic régime in the country. He therefore exerted all his efforts towards securing an even wider abdication of power by the State *vis-à-vis* the Church, obtaining outstanding successes in legislation in favour of the clergy and the Catholic organizations; in the sphere of education, where Catholic private schools profited from exceptional treatment; and in that of welfare, where the *Pontificia Operad' Assistenza* (Pontifical Aid Organization) expanded and spread throughout the peninsula to become almost like a department of the Church on a par with the State's own departments. Nevertheless, especially in his frequent interventions in State affairs on the more purely political plane – for instance in his efforts to get the Communist Party banned – he constantly came up against resistance from De Gasperi, who, trained in the liberal Austrian school, was deeply averse to any form of clericalization of the country and the government.

One of the most unpleasant episodes in De Gasperi's career as a statesman, an episode highly typical of Pius XII's efforts at intervention, occurred in the spring of 1952 on the eve of the municipal elections in Rome. The Communists, acting in combination with the other left-wing groupings, had drawn up an immense neutral list of candidates headed by the veteran statesman F. S. Nitti, which because of its seemingly moderate character seemed likely at one stage to compete with and even possibly beat the Christian Democrats, who had recently suffered considerable losses on the Right as a result of their social policy. Interested parties, eager for their own ends to show up Christian Democracy in a bad light, hastened to inform Pius XII of the danger that the Red Flag might soon fly over the seat of Rome's municipal Government, the Campidoglio, in direct challenge to the Vatican. The Pope lost no time: he allowed the head of Catholic Action and of the Civic Committees, Luigi Gedda, to prepare a 'civic list' of his own, composed of elements outside Christian Democracy and formally supported by the *Osservatore Romano*; and at the same time he informed the Christian Democrats that he thought it advisable that their list should be laid open to include all forces of the Right, not omitting the neo-Fascists. He even tried to get the backing of the veteran anti-Fascist Don Sturzo (who had returned to Italy after the war) for this list. De Gasperi and the Catholic party were thus faced with the dilemma of having to go against all their past traditions and ally themselves with the most reactionary elements of the Right or else find themselves ousted by Gedda's supporters.

This manoeuvre was clearly directed not so much against Christian Democracy as against De Gasperi's own person, for whether he accepted or refused he was bound in either case to emerge compromised and discredited, and refusal would mean rebellion against the Pope's wishes. That the real target was De Gasperi is confirmed by the mission entrusted to Padre Lombardi, perhaps the man closest to the Pope at that time, whom Pius XII a few weeks earlier had made leader of the 'Movement for a Better World'. This famous Jesuit, manoeuvring with all the subtlety of the inquisitors, did not tackle De Gasperi direct but sought an interview with his wife. 'In the course of an hour and a half', related De Gasperi's daughter Maria later,[1] 'he went from flattery to threats . . . He said things like: "The Pope would rather see Stalin and his Cossacks in St Peter's Square than the Communists victorious in the elections at the Campidoglio. Take care, for if the elections go badly we shall make him (i.e. my father) resign." '

Fortunately a combination of technical rather than political circumstances, and the Pope's own hesitation about the unknown factors involved, brought the scheme to nothing: Gedda's civic list was abandoned and the Christian Democrat list, left in its original form, won the day. But thereafter De Gasperi was regarded as a rebel in the Sacred Palaces, and when he asked for an audience for himself and his family on the thirtieth anniversary of his wedding, which was also the anniversary of his daughter Lucia's becoming a nun, Pius XII refused although De Gasperi was then still Prime Minister.

Aftermath of the Spartacist Revolt

The conclusion to be drawn from all this is that Pius XII's anti-Communism did much to prevent him from serenely evaluating the situation around him; it paralysed his action and caused him to adopt attitudes that retarded rather than promoted world peace – with the results we have seen for the Church, both as a whole and in individual countries, especially those beyond the Iron Curtain. No one will attempt to deny his contribution, in the power vacuum left at the end of the war, in restraining the

---

[1] Maria Romana De Gasperi, *De Gasperi uomo solo*, Milan, 1964.

countries of Europe from the chaos into which they might have been thrown by revolutionary elements. But it would have been much more useful if he had appeared as a peacemaker between the victors, already disputing among themselves, and the vanquished, and as the bearer of a truly universal message. True, his too-diplomatic silence during the war about matters that called for open denunciation, and particularly his ambiguous conduct in relation to the Soviet Union, might have prejudiced success; but a decisive and clarifying stand on his part would probably have commanded a hearing. Disillusionment had already set in with the collapse of high hopes and ideals, and a disinterested, loftily inspired message might have struck home. But Pius XII failed to find the words, or else he believed it more important to mobilize the world against the danger of Communism, thus ending by himself aggravating that danger. What was the reason for this tragic inadequacy at so vital a moment?

One main cause was undoubtedly the unexpected development of Communism immediately after the war. His worst fears proved true. If the Cossacks were not actually encamped in St Peter's Square, the Red Army had nevertheless brought the frontiers of the Communist world into the heart of the continent, and where it stopped short the local Communist parties threatened to secure power either by armed force, as in Yugoslavia and Greece, or by means of skilful propaganda, as in Italy. In the States controlled by the Soviet army the democratic parties were quickly neutralized, and once popular governments were established relations with the Vatican were suspended and the Concordats declared obsolete, while at the same time attempts were made to create autonomous national Churches or minor schisms between the clergy and the laity. Land was expropriated under the land reform decrees, Church-owned educational and welfare establishments were confiscated, the religious orders and Catholic Action associations dissolved, and all this often under threat of drastic reprisals in the event of resistance. The higher ranks of the clergy came under especial attack, bishops and other dignitaries being suspended from office with a view to spreading confusion at lower levels; or the Catholic Church, like all the other religious denominations, was given statutes ensuring full control by the State. Must not all this mean that the eventual aim was completely to dismantle the national Catholic communities in obedience to the demands of Marxist atheism? And could Pius XII be blamed for thinking so?

But to Pius XII's mind religious persecution in the Communist-controlled countries was not the worst of it. Persecution always ends by reinforcing faith, at any rate among the best elements, and preparing the way for return. But the stifling of the Churches beyond the Iron Curtain disrupted his own plans, destroying the patient long-term work of all the war years, the aim of which had been to preserve at all costs the ecclesiastical structure in each country so that when peace came the Church would be in a position to assume the moral leadership there. And now he had to admit not only the dissolution of his great dream of reconquering Orthodox Russia but also the fact that even the countries forming the eastern rampart of Catholicism had fallen into the enemy's hands.

This meant the collapse of a policy pursued by his predecessors as well as himself. It was Pius IX, in the previous century, who first cherished, if only in a superficial and romantic way, the dream of a reconciliation with the Church of Moscow. Leo XIII had gone so far as to formulate a plan of action, and it was in this atmosphere of attempts at union with Russian Orthodoxy that Pacelli had begun to prepare for his mission in the Church. He was still at the Secretariat of State, and about to go to Germany, when Benedict XV, undeterred by the Russian Revolution and indeed hoping that Catholicism's great new venture might find a place in it, was laying the groundwork for his plans in the Curia itself. Subsequently Pacelli was not in a position to follow at close quarters the adventurous vicissitudes of the relations between the Holy See and the Soviet Union during the first years of Pius XI's reign; but as Secretary of State he was in at the final phase of complete rupture, culminating in the outbreak of the Spanish civil war and the promulgation of the encyclical *Divini Redemptoris* against atheist Communism.

But at the root of Pacelli's anti-Communism there was a deeper and more intimate, indeed almost a personal cause. None of his predecessors had witnessed at close hand the volcanic eruption of revolution. Not even Pius XI had come near the edge of the crater. When he had written to Lenin asking permission to stay in Moscow in his capacity of Apostolic Visitor to Russia, the answer he received convinced him that any such attempt would be useless. But Pacelli had been caught in the blast of revolution at risk of his life. That was in 1919, in Munich, during the famous Red Days of the Spartacist rising. The outer walls of the nunciature were riddled with bullets from a shooting affray in the street, but then the shouts and singing died away in the distance and the nunciature was left to deal with endless telephone calls, telegrams, and visits from diplomatic colleagues and the higher clergy. It seemed an invulnerable oasis in the midst of the city's turmoil. But suddenly a group of Spartacist Guards burst in, rifle in hand, to violate its extraterritoriality. Pacelli insisted on confronting them alone. His solemn, unarmed figure overawed them, and they left the house without committing any violence. But the shock was such that for years after, even to the last years of his life, as he told his doctor, he often dreamt of it. This psychological complex may well account for the irrational and fanatical features that characterized his anti-Communist policy in later years, putting to flight the calm determination that he otherwise habitually displayed at times of serious and difficult decisions.

Triumphalism and the Sense of Power

It would, however, be a complete misrepresentation of Pius XII's pontificate to portray it, even in regard to its outer aspect of relations with the world, purely in the light of the Communist incubus. While the danger of Communism undoubtedly, to his mind, represented a psychological, religious, and political incubus, it was nevertheless also a cause for fanatical exaltation in as much as he felt himself to be invested with the historic mission of leader of the anti-Bolshevik crusade.

But even stronger and more exalted than this consciousness, and even more typical of the outer characteristics of his pontificate, was his unshaken certainty of the irresistible ascent of the Church's fortunes, in other words his 'triumphalism'. The Jesuit Father Leiber, who was his secretary and close collaborator for thirty-four years, said of him in a profile written shortly after his death that among his chief characteristics were an acute sense of 'power' and an instinctive repugnance for any form of exaggerated spiritualism or isolation in the purely religious. This was true of him even before he became Pope. During his pontificate three particular occasions contributed to reinforce his sense of exaltation: the end of the war, which saw him acclaimed as the most inspired moral prophet of victory and brought before his throne in the Vatican an uninterrupted sequence of all the great figures of the contemporary world; the Italian elections of April 1948, which by guaranteeing an absolute majority for the Catholic party removed all risk of further harm to the Holy See itself; and lastly the unbelievable success of the Holy Year of 1950, when millions of pilgrims flocked to Rome. He did not wait till then, however, to express his triumphalist conception of the Church; in his celebrated speech to the consistory of 1946 for the creation of thirty-two cardinals he had already expounded it in substance, if with some slight toning-down to meet spiritual claims. Even that, however, was soon abandoned, and his words, already compromising enough, were followed by deeds. Nothing, as we know, is further from the spirit of the Gospel than a theocratic Church: the beatitudes of the Sermon on the Mount are the beatitudes of the vanquished, not the victors. But nothing could prevent the explosion of that phenomenon, which became increasingly exaggerated throughout the last ten years of his reign.

Its visible expression was naturally most apparent in the political sphere. Reference has already been made to Pius XII's particular conception of relations between Church and State, especially as shown in his attitude towards Catholic parties. Italy was of course an exceptional case, but in his eyes it pretty closely resembled the ideal situation. It was no chance policy on his part that in this as in much else he faithfully pursued Pius XI's line, defending to the limit the Concordats signed with the Fascist and Nazi Governments and their allies (including the Austrian Concordat of 1933); just as it was no mere chance that the three further Concordats he signed were all with totalitarian States – with Salazar's Portugal (1940), Franco's Spain (1953), and the Dominican Republic under Trujillo (1954). Of these the Spanish Concordat best conveys the ideal conception of Church-State relations cherished by Pius XII on the hypothesis of a revived *Civitas christiana*.

Nevertheless his 'triumphalism' as applied within the Church itself is even more startling, when one reflects how the Church emerged from it paralysed on the more purely spiritual sides and extended to exaggerated limits on the temporal – beginning with its very centre. From the Holy Year 1950 onwards, in fact, the

Vatican – and not only the Sacred Palace or the basilica of St Peter's, but even Bernini's square – became a permanent stage, with almost daily spectacles and mammoth assemblies. Even the audiences lost their natural spiritual atmosphere and became more and more of a show for the curious or the worldly – at public audiences the Pope was even called on to witness gymnastic displays and ball games, while private audiences were attended by sports champions, film stars, offshoots of the aristocracy, captains of industry, and so on.

But pomp and colour were only the most visible and ephemeral aspect of the 'new' Catholic power. These jarringly theatrical displays of triumph went side by side with an increasingly un-believable ostentation of wealth and an unbridled commercial activity. It was not without significance that halfway through the war, in 1942, Pius XII had decided to found the Vatican City's first bank (under the pious nomenclature of 'Institute for the Works of Religion'). What happened during the rest of the war, with or without this organization's support, was revealed once it was over both in various scandals – such as the Cippico affair, which involved some high prelates of the Vatican – and in the sudden and almost inconceivable manifestation of the Vatican's economic power as shown in investments in real property and shareholdings. The boom in land and building speculation of which Rome became the theatre, carried out by various eccle-siastical organizations and by companies supported by Vatican capital, was the eloquent symbol of a flourishing economic situa-tion such as the Holy See had not known since time immemorial – a situation further confirmed, if more vaguely and mysteriously, by increasing investment of Vatican capital in the most solid financial institutions and in important companies both in Italy and abroad.

The contagion soon spread beyond Rome, helped by the success of that American style of apostolate popular in the States, carried out through literature and films—such films as *La mia via* (My Way), *Città dei ragazzi* (Boys' Town—and *Le campane di Santa Maria* (The Bells of St Mary's) had an immense success), and also by the example of commercial and financial enterprise shown by the American representatives of various charitable organizations under the National Catholic Welfare Conference, whose activities extended throughout Italy and the rest of Europe. The lean post-war years of poverty and reconstruction had to be overcome before its full effects could be seen. But once a certain prosperity was established, with the start of the economic 'miracle', the building craze, and the general fever of business activity they exploded to the accompaniment of scandals and excesses, the most typical of which was the Giuffrè scandal, so called after its central figure, a banker of Imola nicknamed 'God's Banker', which involved bishops, priests, and religious orders throughout several regions of Italy.

The most harmful effects of this 'Americanization' of the apostolate, dominated as it was by feverish activity and the search for visible, material, self-advertising achievement, by the cult, in a word, of quantity and of financial power, lay in the belief it instilled in the power of technical means, organization, and propaganda. In Italy, Catholic Action, especially after the electoral success achieved by Gedda's Civic Committees in 1948, was contaminated and sterilized throughout Pius XII's pontificate by methods of operation based on the psychological techniques of publicity, which it employed – with small success – not only in the big national campaigns to win back Communists or push the Catholic trades union, but also in local missions to arouse the parishes from apathy.

These manifestations affected Italy much more than any other country. But what mattered was that Pius XII had the Italian situation constantly before his eyes and that, except for the most obvious excesses, he gave his unreserved approval to what was going on there, honouring with his trust and friendship the men actively concerned in it and supporting and defending them when need arose against all their adversaries.

Conservatism

But the worst effects of the spirit of power or neo-temporalism introduced by Pius XII into the internal life of the Church lay less in what it produced than in what it prevented. For it prevented the Church from devoting its attention to social problems, and inhibited the progress of the various movements towards renovation (in theology, biblical studies, liturgy, catechistic instruction, etc.) which only succeeded in making real headway after his death. How serious this paralysis was, will be realized when we recall the profound need for modernization felt within Catholicism, especially in the European countries, in the last years of Pius xi's pontificate. The majority of the initiatives for renovation that arose within the Church after the war had a history going back, whether publicly or in secret, to the war years themselves and often earlier.

Pius xi had used a heavy hand to suppress some of these stirrings, especially those of a theological nature. Pius xii, on the other hand, seemed at first to understand and approve them. Of particular significance in this connection are the two encyclicals of 1943, on the Church as the Body of Christ (*Mystici Corporis*) and on biblical studies (*Divino Afflante Spiritu*), and also the *Mediator Dei*, of 1947, on the liturgy. The biblical encyclical owed its origin to the fiftieth anniversary of Leo xiii's *Providentissimus Deus*, on the same subject; while the other two arose out of a memorandum to Pius xii from Mgr Konrad Grueber, Archbishop of Freiburg-in-Breisgau, on the errors spread abroad in Germany by certain theologians about the doctrine of the Mystical Body and on some unacceptable ideas advanced by the local liturgical movement. Nevertheless the character of all these texts was positive rather than negative – an attitude subsequently contradicted and refuted in the second, triumphalist, phase of Pacelli's pontificate.

It took a time of trial like the war to inspire such an encyclical as *Mystici Corporis* on the spiritual nature of the Church, and a common need like that of liturgical spirituality to inspire *Mediator Dei* and the reforms arising out of it. The first encyclical foreshadowed a more exalted and mystical conception of the Church, while the second pointed the way towards a profounder and simpler religious experience. As for *Divino Afflante*, it was the first document to surmount anti-Modernism, restoring confidence to scholars and giving hope of a more genuine return of theology to biblical sources.

But at the climax of the Holy Year 1950 Pius xii quite unexpectedly issued what might be described as his *Pascendi*,[1] the encyclical *Humani Generis*, in which he cut short any attempt at 'new theology' and even revoked some concessions made in the sphere of biblical studies, thus returning to the intransigent

---

[1] Pius x's encyclical of 1907 on Modernism – see above, pp. 37 ff.

standpoint of Pius x and Pius xi. This measure was quite serious enough in itself, but it was rendered more so by the over-zealous and intemperate way in which its originators, the conservatives in the Curia, applied it. The 'new theologists', who advocated a return of theology to scriptural and traditional sources, in other words to the Bible and the patristic writings, were removed from their professorial chairs, prevented from upholding their views in lectures or writings, condemned to silence and inactivity, and Thomism – the ratiocinative and legalistic school of theology – regained the upper hand.

It was not until years to come that the full effects of the new *Pascendi* came to be felt. But only two months later, when Pius xii proclaimed the dogma of the Assumption, an inkling was given of the ultimate aims. One passage in the encyclical stated that 'theology, even when positive, cannot be equated with a purely historical science, since God has given His Church, together with these sacred sources, the Living Teacher to illustrate and develop those truths which are contained only obscurely and as it were by implication in the storehouse of faith'. The precepts of *Humani Generis* were therefore intended to prepare the way for the new fact that even theological 'intuitions' or 'discoveries' that are quite unsupported by the sources of revelation can be the subject of dogmatic definition, provided the Church recognizes them as commonly accepted and believed at a given point in its history. This was a dangerous claim, destined to open the gates to an increasingly alarming extent to the irrational and the sentimental. For the scientific advance of theology will always be slower than the fable-spinning advances of intuitional and popular faith, which will always find it only too easy to forestall the theologians by anticipating not only their hard-won conquests but also those they fail to achieve. Hence the success of the 'intuitional theologians' who began to lay down the law, especially in the sphere of Mariology.

At first sight it may seem surprising that Pius xii could put himself in the ambiguous position of condemning the rebellious anti-Thomism of certain theological trends and at the same time fomenting the sentimental irrationality which is at the basis of the increasingly extravagant success of Mariology. But the reason is quite simple, being closely connected with the urgent need to reconquer or retain the masses at a critical moment for the

Church such as that which arose after the Second World War. In the early stages he had recourse to intensified manifestations of Marian devotion (pilgrim Madonnas, etc.); and later on he made the culminating point of the Holy Year the solemn proclamation of the dogma of the Assumption (1 November 1950) and promulgated the Marian Year of 1954.

It would be easy to demonstrate how the fundamental characteristics of the Marian cult practised under Pius XII, and especially the mass manifestations which became such a feature of it, were profoundly at odds with the need for a reform of piety felt by more thoughtful Catholics after the war. That reform visualized as its starting point the return to liturgical piety, in terms of a communitarian rather than an individualistic piety, imbued with biblical and patristic content rather than inclined to sentimentality, essentially theocentric and christocentric, in accordance with the spirit of the liturgical year. Pius XII did, it is true, permit and introduce certain modernizations of the liturgy, some of which, such as the reform of Holy Week, were relatively unimportant, while others, more daring if less well known, concerned privileges granted to native peoples in the use of the vernacular and of local customs in their church services, especially in the Mass. Of greater importance were certain innovations aimed at facilitating the fulfilment of the fundamental religious practices in the changed circumstances of modern times. The new and more reasonable conditions for fasting before the Eucharist, and the institution of evening Mass on feast days, met with great and well-deserved success; but their aim was rather to check the exodus from the Church than to initiate the faithful more closely into liturgical practice.

These were Pius XII's only reforms of a popular nature. The others, of a more external and superficial kind, were concerned solely with the College of Cardinals and the organization of the religious families. The first secured a quite disproportionate publicity. As Cardinal Tardini, second after Mgr Montini in the Secretariat of State, has revealed, Pius XII greatly disliked having to make appointments and promotions: for that reason he held only two consistories in seventeen years for the creation of new cardinals, which was why the number of appointments made at each was so large – thirty-two at the first, in 1946, and twenty-four at the second, in 1953. A feature of both was the increase in international representation in the Sacred College. 'We wanted,' Pius XII said, 'the largest possible number of peoples and backgrounds to be represented, so that it may be a living image of the Church's universality.' The most obvious characteristic of this huge 'intake' was the representation accorded, for the first time, to non-Western civilizations – Africa (in the person of a Portuguese missionary bishop), China (now receiving its first native cardinal), and increased representation for Latin America. But the most surprising and revolutionary fact was that, for the first time in the whole history of the College of Cardinals, there were now fewer Italians than non-Italians, thus making possible the election some day of a non-Italian Pope. The internationalization of the Curia was acclaimed as an accomplished fact, although nearly all the foreign cardinals either were, or were destined to remain, residential bishops, thus leaving the Roman Departments to their Italian colleagues. Pius XII himself, in his second and last consistory, restored the balance of Italians in the Sacred College, for of the twenty-four promotions ten were Italians, most of them from the Curia. In short, under him the international character of the Church's Senate remained nominal rather than real, and that of the Curia only potential.

It is not surprising that a life-long Curialist like himself should not have dared to touch the closely preserved caste character of the Curia except to make a largely symbolic reduction in the excessive pomp of the cardinals' vestments (by a *Motu proprio* of December 1952). Still less would he be likely to reduce in any way its often despotic powers over the whole world. True, he permitted the formation or re-formation of national episcopal conferences in many countries, and he even allowed a continental episcopal conference to be founded in Latin America (the CELAM). But these conferences enjoyed no legal recognition or power, and the effect was merely to increase still further the authority of the nuncios and the Curia itself. The CELAM, for instance, was actually officially controlled by a Pontifical Commission for Latin America.

In the last years of his life, especially after his illness at the end of 1954, Pius XII concentrated in the Secretariat of State, with the additional aid of a titular theologian and jurist (posts created for the first time by him), many of the powers hitherto belonging by right to the other Vatican Ministries, reserving to the Secretariat

a large number of the special cases falling within their competence. In the end he virtually ceased to hold regular audiences for
the prefects and secretaries of Congregations, but in the long run
this gave an even freer hand to the Departments of the Curia, while
it also accentuated the division of command at the Church's apex.
The real victims of this state of affairs were the bishops, who were
ignored by the Pope and humiliated by the Departments (as can
be seen from their reactions later on, in the Vatican Council of
1962-5). As for the priests, Pius xii did not even accord them the
reforms relating to ecclesiastical studies about which his predecessors had been concerned. Little or nothing, and that largely
on the initiative of individual bishops, was done under him to
bring about greater social justice for the lower clergy, among
whom flagrant inequalities persisted.

The only Ministry to show unusual vitality under Pius xii was
the Congregation of the Religious, which from 1950 onwards
promoted the first world congresses of religious Orders recorded
in the Church's history. The most important outcome of these
congresses was the formation of central co-ordinating bodies,
consisting of the Superiors General of the various Orders, whose
aim was to promote collaboration and organize a better distribution of effort, and also to assist the more needy Orders. The
women's Orders were now for the first time organized in cross-
sections according to their specialization (teaching sisters, nursing
sisters, etc.) and a secretariat was established to provide economic
aid for enclosed nuns. For the latter, Pius xii himself took steps
to absolve them from the vow of seclusion and give them some
possibility for external apostolate through the apostolic constitution *Sponsa Christi* (21 November 1950). At the congress of nuns
of September 1952, which among other things decided on the
establishment of the Pontifical University for Nuns, he recognized
the need to modify antiquated customs and traditions, including
their forms of dress, and adapt them to apostolic activities.

This meagre list of reforms fell far short of the hopes and needs
corresponding to the current climate of opinion. (In France, for
example, the experiment of the worker-priests was regarded by
the whole country, laymen included, as a wonderful venture in
the rediscovery of a religious meaning for life; journalists, writers,
sociologists, and politicians all took sides passionately in the
dispute which developed when Rome ordered the suppression of

the experiment, treating it as a national affair involving the country's honour and prestige.) Pius XII was in the best position of all to realize the need for swift action in a radically changed and changing world, and to calculate what prestige would accrue to the papacy and to himself from a courageous adaptation of Catholicism to meet the situation. It can only be concluded that he found it wiser to wait and postpone more far-reaching reforms until the world had reached a more stable state, so as to avoid involving the Church in a tangle of provisional changes that might prove more harmful than useful.

But if that was his reason, it is hard to say how far it was prompted by wisdom and how far by fear of risk and lack of enthusiasm. For if clergy and laymen alike sometimes took too resolute a tone in demanding reforms, that happened only in the immediate post-war days. Afterwards, discipline coupled with a fainthearted desire to conform gained the upper hand. And if certain communities like the French showed a ferment of initiative that did not call for encouragement, the courage needed to challenge their loyalty might have been much more suitably employed to moderate rather than to suffocate their ardour. Mistakes made in the course of new experiments ought not to cause more anxiety than the oft-repeated mistakes of old, tired methods. The series of repulses administered to the official Church of France, and hence to its episcopate, in reaction against almost every attempt at pastoral modernization (from the worker-priests to the progressive catechism), thus remains one of the most obscure pages of Pius XII's pontificate.

The view that the blame for these refusals rests largely on Pius XII's advisers cannot be rejected out of hand. But he had, after all, chosen those advisers himself, picking men of tastes and mentality resembling his own. So, once again, the root of the problem must lie in Pacelli himself and in his own psychology, part that of a bureaucrat, part that of a man of natural rather than supernatural faith. It must never be forgotten that Pacelli was by origin a Roman, reared in the curial tradition that permeated his own family, consisting as it did of minor but faithful members of the 'black' aristocracy. Growing up in the first decades of the Roman Question, he breathed in the atmosphere of firm and dignified opposition which those surrounding him continued to maintain towards the State in which the pontiff and the Church's supreme hierarchy had to live. His faith was not so much an abstract ideology located in the pure world of reason and sentiment, but rather an almost physical and tangible experience of a transcendent reality localized in that city of Rome 'whence Christ is Roman', the meeting-place of its dazzling pagan past and its no less mysterious and prodigious later vicissitudes. For a Roman of the Rome of the emperors and popes, at once the civil and the religious capital, faith is not only an inner but also an outer experience, not only hope but also certainty, the breath of tradition, the sense of solidity and immutability, the undisputed acceptance of an evident and essential reality inherited in time and yet beyond all time, in a word the living contact with the very substance through which Rome is by definition the eternal city.

His ecclesiology therefore signified cult and exaltation, not criticism or debate, and above all it implied vision from the centre and the apex in the light of the *romanitas* of Catholicity. The body of the Church, discussed by his theologians in the encyclical on the Mystical Body, was for him no more than a projection of the Head, in the sense that, being shaped and conditioned by it, it can admit of but one manner of thinking, feeling, and acting. Hence his lack of understanding for any kind of pluralism, whether theological or disciplinary. The one possible theology was Thomist theology, the one discipline the Code of Canon Law. True, he did not exclude some varieties of manifestation, as in the rites and the laws, but only if they were superficial and temporary and, above all, mere stages towards final unification and identity. Did not the Code of Canon Law itself, which he promulgated partly with the Eastern Churches in mind, aim at the eventual Latinization of those Churches – so much so that it provoked protests from the Uniates and had to be suspended?

For the same reason, he regarded relations with other faiths, even with separated Christians, as a dangerous source of contamination and corruption rather than an opportunity for meeting and reconciliation. We have already mentioned how in March 1939 he let slip the offer to preside over a conference of all the Christian Churches which was to launch a world appeal for the defence of the supreme values of the individual and humanity against totalitarianism. After the war, despite the solidarity that peace established between Catholics and Protestants, he only partially mitigated the rigid rules hitherto imposed on Catholics in their contacts with schismatic Christians; and that was largely because, after the world assembly in Amsterdam in 1948, the Protestant-Orthodox ecumenical movement had become a reality which the Roman Church could no longer ignore.

Unique and Unapproachable

If these were the reasons for Pius XII's conservatism and isolationism, it is obvious that within such a framework the Church would tend to call for isolation rather than reform, immunization rather than innovation, exaltation rather than corrective intervention. And it is equally obvious that the exaltation of the Church would tend to culminate in exaltation of its visible and symbolical centre, Rome and the papacy, and especially the latter. The main instruments used to accomplish this were speeches and propaganda. The Holy See itself published a handsome monthly review, *Ecclesia*, and an even more massive annual volume illustrating 'The activities of the Holy See'. One of Pius XII's cherished projects was to rediscover the tomb of St Peter beneath the Vatican basilica, so as to end once for all the dispute concerning the apostle Peter's coming to Rome and his martyrdom in the capital of the Empire. Pius XII also aspired to be the first pontiff to make use of the infallibility solemnly recognized by the first Vatican Council in 1870, with his proclamation of the new dogma of the Assumption. But where he showed inexhaustible zeal was in the canonization of his predecessors. Before him, Pius IX and Leo XIII had permitted themselves only a passing recognition of the existing cult of certain beatified Popes. Since 1588, when Sixtus V founded the Congregation of Rites to deal with the canonization of saints, only one Pope, Pius V, had been canonized. Pius XII alone, however, elevated to the solemnity of the altars Pius X (beatified in 1951 and canonized in 1954) and Innocent I (beatified in 1956), revived the cause for the sanctification of the Blessed Innocent V (1943) and Gregory X (1944), and initiated the cause of Pius IX (1954).

Having reached this point, Pius XII did not shrink from passing on from exaltation of the papacy and his predecessors to exaltation of his own person. Every Pope, of course, accepts in some way the worship of his faithful, but with many of them that worship bypasses their own person to centre on the dignity and office they represent. With others, however, the distinction is tenuous, and worship becomes directed less towards their official actions and duties than towards their own personal gifts and characteristics. This was particularly true of Pius XII, of whom someone even dared to say that he aspired to canonization in his lifetime. The reason for this lay in the fact that no other Pope within recorded memory had ever so insistently and provocatively laid claim to having been granted supernatural experiences.

In October 1951, for example, no less a person than the Cardinal and Papal Legate Federico Tedeschini revealed in Portugal to a vast crowd of hearers that between the end of October and the beginning of November 1950 the Pope while walking in the Vatican gardens had on four separate occasions seen astronomical phenomena in the skies. In December 1954, it was the heads of the Secretariat of State and the enterprising Jesuits of the '*Mondo Migliore*' who published in the press the report that Christ had appeared at dawn at the bedside of the sick Pope on 2 December. Pius XII gave his support to even more romanticized episodes such as the conversion of a Roman tram-conductor following the alleged appearance of the Virgin in the Tre Fontane neighbourhood. The man in question had previously belonged to a Protestant community and had conceived such a hatred for the Vicar of Christ that he determined to make an attempt on his life. One of the Jesuits who launched the publicity about the earlier apparition arranged for the converted tram-conductor to be present at a Vatican Radio broadcast when the Pope recited the rosary, after which the new convert offered the Pope the dagger with which he had proposed to kill him.

Mythical exaltation of the Pope has gone beyond all reasonable limits if it has to rely on such questionable incentives, for there is no need of such phenomena to surround him with an aura of sanctity. Catholic theology itself denies that the heroic nature of virtues need necessarily be linked with charismatic gifts, and even the canonization of saints does not in itself imply recognition of their visions or prophecies. But to give publicity to such episodes in the lifetime of the protagonist becomes an even more serious matter when it is done with his own approval, if not at his own instigation. Leo XIII was said to have had a vision, in the summer of 1887, of the Archangel Michael descending in flames from the skies to defend the Church ensnared by the dragon from hell;

indeed this apparition was said to have been the reason for inserting at the end of the Mass a special prayer to the Archangel, which
has recently been abolished. But Leo xiii only told his intimate
circle of the vision.

According to some reports, the manifestations of self-exaltation
on Pius xii's part, especially in the last years of his pontificate,
reached positively morbid limits; though this is difficult to confirm. In normal circumstances it would be easy to tell, but
religious experience clouds, not to say cancels, any sharp line
between the pathological and the supernatural. In any case, the
secret, if it ever existed, was confined to a few intimates who
would be unwilling to reveal it. But whatever the truth of the
matter, the fact remains that the effects of Pius xii's self-exaltation
can be seen both in his extraordinary isolation and in his partial
renunciation of active government of the Church.

His isolation is not to be confused with that of his predecessors.
With Leo xiii, for instance, the need for solitude was largely the
expression and characteristic of his own regality, while with the
absolute theocrat Pius xi it emerged in his contacts with his
collaborators, in the exercise of power, initiative in action, and
the magic of authority behind his commands. And theirs was, in
any case, only a relative isolation. With Pius xii, on the other
hand, it was something much more concrete, more nearly resembling the isolation typical of the seer, the prophet, or the oracle.
As the mouthpiece of the Godhead in his messages, it was inevitable that he should stand apart absorbed in contemplation of
it, foreseeing in private what he later testified to in public.

Few people realized it in the early stages, but he undoubtedly
began to give up certain of his activities in government quite
some time before he got rid of his most authoritative collaborators.
Pius xii must early have decided that he wanted merely simple
executives around him, and in 1944, when his Secretary of State,
Cardinal Maglione, died, he did not appoint a successor. Later,
when he became aware of the growing influence of the Under-
Secretary, Montini, he first thought of getting rid of him by
offering him a cardinal's hat but then instead appointed him Archbishop of Milan. His abandonment of the direction of the Court
and the Curia, however, goes back to the early days of his pontificate, when he virtually discharged the Governor of the Vatican
City, replacing him by a committee of cardinals with his trusted

henchman, the civil engineer Pietro Galeazzi, as secretary. Within a few months all his former colleagues who were destined to take on the central management of the Church were already at their posts: Cardinal Canali at the head of the Vatican City, Cardinal Marchetti-Selvaggiani at the Vicariate of Rome, Cardinal Pizzardo at the Holy Office and the Congregation of Seminaries, and so on. But for the war, which delayed for years their full exploitation of their positions, it would much sooner have been realized that the consignment of nearly all the positions of power in the Curia into the hands of his 'great electors' was the root cause both of a serious crisis in the Church's central Departments and of that form of shadow government which fostered the most resounding scandals of his pontificate.

Thus this totalitarian absolutism resolved itself into a strangely variegated oligarchy in which the purple of the Pentagon Cardinals mingled with the court dress of the Pope's nephews, Pietro Galeazzi, and Professor Gedda and, if at a discreet but dominating distance, the nun's coif of his housekeeper, Sister Pasqualina.

The presence of this nun in charge of Pius XII's household was not really such a novelty as the more malicious chroniclers strove to suggest. Even Pius XI had had a woman, and not even a nun, at his side, if only in the first years of his pontificate – Teodolinda Banfi, his old housekeeper from Brianza, an orphan whom the Pope's mother had taken from an institution forty years earlier and put in charge of his household in Via Moneta in Milan when he was Librarian at the Ambrosiana. Ratti sent for her as soon as he became Pope, thereby casting the Court, which had never known the like before, into confusion. To begin with, no title existed to describe the duties of a woman in the Pope's apartment, and they had to think up that of 'Mistress of the Wardrobe'. However, to the relief of all those who found the situation unorthodox, the despotic character of the Pope's Perpetua compelled him to retire her on a pension after three years and provide her with a little flat of her own in Piazza Santa Marta.

Pius X provides an even remoter precedent. This time, it is true, it was not a question of a woman living in the pontifical apartments, but all the same she was a permanent guest of the Vatican and, like Sister Pasqualina, a nun as well, the founder of the Sisters of St Anne who ran the college of that name within the territory of the Sacred Palaces. Like Sister Pasqualina, too, she was a German, by name Teresa Bong, from an old Catholic family of Cologne which included a prelate, her brother; she died in 1922. Cardinal Agliardi told the well-known scholar Mgr Faloci-Pulignani that if he wanted to enter Pius x's good graces he should try to secure the protection of Sister Teresa, who had free access to the Pope and for that privilege was maliciously known in the Vatican as 'the cardinal'.

Nevertheless by comparison with these rather mild precedents the affair of Sister Pasqualina Lenhart has some extraordinary sides, suggesting surmises not particularly suitable for an ecclesiastic. A Bavarian by birth, born at Ebersberg in 1894, she worked in a house of her Order, the 'Stella Maris', near Lorschach in Switzerland, which gave hospitality to priests in need of rest, and she looked after the Nuncio Mgr Pacelli when he came there from Munich in 1918. It so happened that the representative of the Holy See was at that time in the midst of a domestic crisis in his own residence. His two lay servants there, whether from rivalry or incompatibility of character, had frequent arguments, and he once heard them exchanging every epithet under the sun. He complained of this to Archbishop Faulhaber, who suggested that he should ask for a nun from the Institute of teaching sisters of the Holy Cross at Menzingen, the Order to which Sister Pasqualina belonged. As he had been very satisfied with his stay at 'Stella Maris', and especially with the attentions of the young nun who had looked after him (Sister Pasqualina was then twenty-four and Pacelli forty-two), the Nuncio took the necessary steps to find out from the Order's main house if she could come to Munich together with another colleague. The Superior General was naturally much flattered at the request and a few weeks later Sister Pasqualina and a companion came to the nunciature in Munich. In the ordinary course of events such an appointment would have been purely temporary, for a few years at most: but instead it lasted for forty years, right up to Pacelli's death.

Sister Pasqualina's position was exceptional both because she spent the rest of her life in the service of the same prelate and because she followed him throughout all his moves, from Munich to Berlin and then to Rome, whereas her accompanying companions changed frequently. Moreover, once installed in the Vatican in the Secretary of State's apartment she achieved another unique record – that of being probably the only woman and nun ever to be admitted within the bounds of the Conclave; for Cardinal Pacelli was able to remain in his apartment throughout the Conclave of 1939, and Sister Pasqualina with him. When he became Pope, far from discharging her, he had a special part of the pontifical apartment prepared for her and her fellow-nuns. And in her case there was no question of her being retired like Teodolinda Banfi.

The little German sister was, in truth, ever more energetic and despotic than Ratti's Mistress of the Wardrobe, but her ascendency over her Pope was of a quite different order, and she had no need to fear being got rid of through her victims' dislike. The officials of the Pope's household, the old majordomo Stefanori and the various monsignori who served as chamberlains, grasped at once what she meant to Pius XII. He reposed complete confidence in her, but he also obeyed her so docilely that he lived under her continuous, discreet, and sometimes inexorable control. The little nun with the typical square face of her compatriots, her rosy complexion and her grey-blue eyes, went in and out of his study moving about in her felt slippers with a silent yet almost martial step, sensitive to the slightest change of atmosphere or alteration in the Pope's state of mind, without his even being aware of her.

When a private audience was due to end, especially when the Pope was in poor health, it was she who inexorably cut it short, whoever the visitor might be, whether Foster Dulles or anyone else. When the Pope came out of a general audience, it was she who disinfected his hands and ring with cotton-wool soaked in spirit, and whenever she noticed a spot on the white half-sleeves he wore at his desk she brought him a fresh pair. She was in charge of the kitchens as well as the wardrobe, but she also acted as his secretary as well. Particularly in the last years, she used to type to his dictation the drafts of quite important documents.

To read into all this an intimacy of another kind would be a futile irreverence – and that not necessarily because Pacelli's temperament inclined him to feel no need of the needs of the heart. If shyness inevitably tends towards isolation and self-sufficiency, it nevertheless has need to take refuge in friendship or in genuine love. This is just what might have happened with Pacelli, at least in his earliest youth. Giovanni Papini relates in his *Diary* under the date of 18 May 1948 how Piero Bargellini, a Catholic Florentine writer who was then preparing a biography of Pius XII, told him that at Onano (a mountain hamlet where the young Pacelli used often to stay with relatives) there were still old people who said, 'If Lucia had said yes he would never have become Pope'. The phrase leaves one to suppose that the girl turned down a more or less formal proposal of marriage, and its rejection may well have left a void and a regret difficult to eradicate.

That void and regret may have opened up again after the meeting with the young nun from Lorschach, though no longer in an amorous context but rather as an appeal for a sort of maternal protection. No one ever gives his heart to a woman, even purely platonically, without putting himself to some extent in her power. This is especially true of a shy and sentimental man like Pacelli faced with a vigorous and managing German peasant girl. Sister Pasqualina in fact ended by exercising over him, even as Pope, a mysterious and despotic power certainly not envisaged by the sacred canons, especially when it was directed towards questions relating to the government of the Church itself, even if mainly in a personal connection. Quite a number of prelates, it would seem, owed their promotion to her intervention, and certainly many petitions and not a few decisions of Pius XII's found their real arbiter in her. For that reason Sister Pasqualina was alluded to in the Vatican, to avoid mentioning her by name, under the malicious epithet of '*virgo potens*'.

The Oracle

Pius XII unquestionably made mistakes in giving too little of his attention to the government of the Church, confining himself almost exclusively to the political and diplomatic side of affairs and to cases of exceptional gravity, and in neglecting to foster relations between himself and the Vatican Departments and the episcopate. But there can be no doubt that the best of himself came out in his remarkable teaching through the spoken word.

At bottom he was an intellectual, a man interested in systems and abstract ideas, indeed a utopian in the best sense of the term – but not a man of action. A man of action and a statesman is someone who can recognize his peers for better or worse and make use of them for his own ends, exploiting their gifts and abilities – not a man who draws back from contacts with them and fears their reactions. But Pius XII was paralysed by his fear of contact with other men: their cleverness and shrewdness disarmed him, their vanity and passions bewildered him. Hence the doubts that assailed him whenever he had to make new appointments to vacant posts.

For the same reason, he was not a politician but merely a first-class diplomatist. A politician dominates a situation at the same time that he manipulates it for his own ends. In him the inspiration and imagination behind his schemes are perfectly balanced by the realism with which he controls and keeps contact with the circumstances in which he has to operate. But in Pius XII's case, in his internal policy the whole force of his prestige was directed towards conservation, towards preventing or delaying innovations; and in his foreign policy all his courage was expended on a single great but negative programme: the struggle against Communism.

As an intellectual, too, he was something of a lightweight. The most striking things about him at first sight were his technical and natural gifts – his memory, knowledge of languages, sense of order and method, and so on. He had little feeling for poetry or for art in general (as a young priest his taste in religious music ran to the rather meretricious type of works banned by Pius X's reforms) or for philosophical or theological speculation. His bent was for law and moral philosophy, in which he was really outstanding, while for scientific subjects he had only a dilettante's interest.

Even as an orator he was really not much more than an amateur. Only his courtiers' enthusiasm could have given him the illusion that he had a genuine gift for oratory. (One of his biographers went so far as to write that 'the sacred orator Pacelli has no precedent in Italy except for Segneri'.) His oratorical gifts – of voice, diction, and gesture – in truth existed only in the imagination of his interested flatterers. His delivery lacked verve, his voice was metallic and without inflexion, his tone monotonous, his gestures stiff and mechanical. It could hardly be otherwise, for instead of delivering his speeches spontaneously or at least partly extempore, reacting quickly to his own state of mind and that of his audience, he behaved as if he was reading them, following line by line the carefully prepared text he had memorized. This method produced a stereotyped style of delivery fatal to oratory, in addition to which when his excellent memory occasionally failed him long pauses ensued that were highly embarrassing for his audience.

The form of his speeches also left much to be desired. Pacelli's humanistic studies had followed a too archaic and aridly academic pattern lacking in inspiration or spontaneity. The style and prose of the early speeches of his pontificate can be very irritating. Practically all of them sound like scholarly compositions, highly polished and precise but cold and artificial. The structure of the most important speeches closely imitates that of the classic orators of modern times such as Bossuet and the great French orators, the sentences are constructed like Latin periods, with subordinate and co-ordinate clauses, insertions, and even latinized terminology, the use of adjectives is stereotyped and cloying. There is never a clear-cut, incisive phrase, never a pungent sentence, never a striking or original simile. However, little by little, except for the more technical and legal parts of the wartime Christmas messages, these defects become less marked. For as time went on the Pope had to make speeches almost daily, and this made it impossible to indulge in literary effects or constant polishing. The result was that his speeches became simpler and more flowing in style, besides keeping more closely to the point.

A defect he never succeeded in correcting, and which indeed got worse rather than better, was the parade of up-to-date knowledge of all sorts and kinds. A catalogue of the subjects he treated, ranging from the simplest and most banal to the most complex and sublime, would fill dozens of pages. The *Indice delle materie contenute nei primi quindici volumi dei discorsi e radio-messaggi di Sua Santità Pio XII* (Index of Subject-Matter contained in the first fifteen volumes of the Speeches and Broadcasts of His Holiness Pope Pius XII), published by the Poliglotta Vaticana in 1956, runs to 627 pages: if all eighteen volumes of speeches were covered it would be about a thousand pages long. But the extraordinary thing about this list is not so much the number and variety of subjects dealt with but their heterogeneous nature in relation to what one imagines to be the normal field of competence of a churchman, however broadminded in his interests. There are little up-to-date treatises about sport and various kinds of sporting events, private and public systems of communication, types of footwear through the ages, the history of mineral extraction, recent progress in surgery or pharmacy, disquisitions on nuclear physics, cinema techniques, newspaper production, the functioning of press and information agencies, or the most up-to-date methods of animal slaughter in public slaughter-houses, surveys of the hotel and tourist industries or the personnel situation in the railways and postal services, and hundreds of other such subjects.

To deal with topics of this kind, it was obviously not enough just to consult encyclopaedias, however specialized. Pius XII used first to consult the necessary specialists either directly or indirectly, and then sent for manuals, tomes, parliamentary reports, etc., in every language and from all sorts of countries, which he would read as far as possible himself. This was an old method he had adopted in Germany and as Secretary of State in Rome when called on to make some special speech or deliver a panegyric about a new saint. Cardinal Tardini, recalling Pius XII in the presence of John XXIII, described how one day at Castel Gandolfo in the summer of 1958 he noticed a huge pile of books. The Pope, observing his curious glances, said, 'You know, all those books are about gas'; and, sure enough, on 28 September he addressed a congress of the gas industry.

All this effort was certainly unnecessary and quite out of proportion, for none of the specialized groups that came to call on him expected to find the Pope so astonishingly competent in their own particular field or to get technical advice from him. But Pius XII with his improvised knowledge of a problem not only strove to give an impression of genuine competence but also made the ingenuous mistake of trying to produce real discoveries and give professional advice. His encyclopaedic knowledge included a preference for certain branches, those of medicine and astronomy. Foraging among his speeches on medical matters one comes on a curious little treatise on descriptive anatomy. He was especially interested in the organs of sight and hearing, but most of all – as an orator, perhaps – in the mouth. To take a random example, in a speech to dentists on 9 September 1957 he described the latest advances in facial and dental surgery and various other specialized branches of dentistry, going into minute detail over the abnormally precocious development of the tongue as compared with the jaws, resulting in 'deforming pressures tending to excessive enlargement of the upper jaw so that the

teeth close badly', and even suggesting ways of correcting
children who 'go on sucking their thumbs beyond their early
years'.

On 20 May 1957, receiving scientists attending a study week
on stellar problems, he felt it his duty to admonish his illustrious
guests that 'the sun deserves not to be neglected, for besides the
influence it exercises on the earth and its inhabitants, it also by
reason of its nearness more readily reveals the secret of its
behaviour; thus study of the sun will never cease to be an essential
branch of astronomy'.

As can readily be imagined, in speeches framed on this sort of
basis there was little room for discussion of spiritual and religious
matters, which was reduced to a few brief remarks at the end that
generally had only a casual connection with the earlier exhibition
of encyclopaedic knowledge. The speech just mentioned, for
example, one of his most pretentious, known as the 'galaxies'
speech, touched only near the end on the reasons for the credi-
bility of divine existence, and then in such general terms that the
Osservatore Romano felt called upon to comment that the dis-
proportion between the scientific and the religious parts of the
speech was, contrary to appearances, quite fitting and 'functional',
since the Pope had wished to review 'the state of the question'
especially fully in order to bring out more clearly the convincing
nature of the concluding application.

Passing on from this rather baroque and unpleasing outer
framework to the religious content of his speeches, and disregarding the texts concerned with ordinary administrative
matters, there still remains a considerable nucleus worthy of the
highest consideration. This includes chiefly speeches on problems
of medical ethics or international law. An anthology of his
speeches on these themes would certainly contain the best of
Pius XII's thinking: the best both in choice and originality of
treatment and in the topicality and modernity of the problems
discussed. Such a collection would also be useful for an evaluation
of his attitude on these questions, which, especially in the matters
of sexual and matrimonial morality, was, once again, far from
revolutionary.

His early speeches on medical ethics, on the other hand, were
really daring, so daring as to cause bewilderment in the Vatican
and the Curia and astound both believers and non-believers who

learnt of them through the press. On 29 October 1951, at an audience arranged for some thousands of members of the Italian Catholic Obstetric Union, he gave a real lecture both on the limitation of births and on periodical continence, touching also on sterilization and artificial insemination. No Pope had ever dared to do anything of the kind. On certain aspects of morality reserve, even in written documents, had always been considered *de rigueur*. If they had to be mentioned aloud, no one ever went beyond the most cautious allusions; and it was customary, even in modern-language works on Catholic morality, to treat the more delicate subjects in Latin.

In substance the speech contained nothing exciting. Yet this would have been an ideal opportunity to remodernize, for example, the Catholic Church's view of sex, still closely linked with its Augustinian-Manichean origins, or to modify the traditional doctrine on procreation as the primary end of marriage, profiting by the recent increasingly vigorous assertion of the personalistic trends among theologians. Be that as it may, the publicity the speech received prompted Pius XII to continue in the same direction. In the following year he addressed the members of the First International Histopathological Congress on the moral limits of medical methods of investigation and treatment. But 1953 proved the most fruitful year in this field: on three separate occasions he expressed his views on psychoanalysis, on the doctor's relations with the patient and with public authorities both in peacetime and wartime, and on the principles and application of genetics. To the accompaniment of a rising crescendo of publicity, on 8 January 1956 he recognized painless birth as permissible, and on 23 February, though without of course admitting actual euthanasic practices, he countenanced an extensive use of analgesics.

As is well known, the first and most lasting assertion of Pius XII's teaching came in his wartime broadcast messages, especially the Christmas messages. His habit was to introduce, sandwiched between a somewhat exuberant and rhetorical beginning and ending, programme points for a solution of the major problems of war and peace. In 1939 he dealt with the prerequisites for a new order in Europe, in 1941 with those for a new international order, in 1942 with international relations and the countries' internal order, and in 1944 with democracy. Similar subjects were covered in the post-war Christmas messages: prerequisites for a new peace (1945), a recommendation to national rulers to reach speedy agreement (1946), insincerity as the root of present evils (1947), and so forth down to the last messages on the dangers of technocracy and on coexistence. It is a fact, however, that, re-read at a distance, the first messages seem distinctly disappointing. The principles enunciated were, to say the least, obvious, or so generic and colourless as to be quite inapplicable. And there was something very irritating about that 'Solomon-like carefulness to establish in advance a line of conduct of impartial and imperturbable objectivity between the parties at war'.[1] But, all in all, the impression left on the public in general was one of great zeal and inspired wisdom. What counted most was that the Pope should speak, and speak often, even if his words were not always quite clear. The tone of his voice, the photographs of him as he read, the propaganda use made of the speeches by friends and enemies alike, did the rest. And in this connection it must not be forgotten that it was Pius XII's great good fortune to be able to have his speeches broadcast (the Vatican station inaugurated by Pius XI in 1931 transmitted his speeches over and over again in all the principal languages of the world). The press, given the length of his appeals, could only give résumés of them, whereas the radio gave them in full in the authentic text and with subsequent commentaries. Benedict XV would not have been half-suffocated and blotted out by the events of the First World War if he could have profited by such a medium.

After the war, the possibility of speaking without his earlier fear of harming or seeming to favour one side or the other enabled Pius XII to develop in an impressive, if somewhat fragmentary, way his conception of an ideal international order which, though never fully synthesized, undoubtedly constitutes one of his most appreciable and original contributions. But by that time he had come increasingly to prefer direct contact with the crowds to the indirect contact of radio or television, in the sure belief that his colloquy with the different audiences coming before him was incomparably more fruitful. He was doubtless

[1] E. Buonaiuti, *Pio XII*, Rome, 1946.

quite right in finding speech-making a method more fitted for the day-by-day treatment of topical subjects. But his very insistence on making the effort to show himself and hold forth every day proclaimed the ephemeral effect of all these appearances. His speeches sought in vain for the essential words amid the stream of words pouring out upon the world. Possibly the secret of his uninterrupted flow of oratory lay in an attempt to make up for his failures as a world political leader. Having compromised his influence as arbiter between the two blocs by incautiously coming down on one side, and taken unawares by the unexpected appearance of an uncommitted 'Third World' that he had always resolutely denied, Pius xii sought to replace action by preaching. But though the messages multiplied he never succeeded in finding the right message. Politically, they lacked sufficient realism; and as sermons, they lacked real prophetic inspiration and genuine intuition. Standing on the shores of the Red Sea of a new era again and again he raised his wand but the waters refused to divide.

Death in Silence and Exile

Nevertheless the strength of his legend survived to the last. It seemed, in spite of all, impervious to attack: but a crack sufficed to cause it to collapse and vanish in a moment. The crack came on 3 October 1958, when the first official news of his illness appeared. Eight days later Pius xii was no more and his legend had dissolved in silence as if by magic. His body was hardly cold before the first critical assessments began in the press, till then so faithful in its homage and servility to him: and suddenly his swift and tragic end assumed a symbolic significance.

When his illness was announced the newspapers were in the midst of denouncing under banner headlines the latest scandals of the Vatican shadow-government, in connection with which the names were being mentioned of the Pope's own nephews and of one of the most publicized and unpleasantly intrusive organizations of his pontificate, the *Pontificia Opera d'Assistenza* (Pontifical Aid Organization). Then followed in dramatic sequence the bewildering circumstances of his death. First, that it happened at his villa at Castel Gandolfo, away, if only a few miles, from the city of his birth and his too easy triumphs, as if a mysterious vengeful power had banished him and death had struck him encamped outside its walls like a deposed king. Then, that he was completely unconscious when he died: the pentecostal Pope, the pontiff of the crowds and gatherings, the hundreds and hundreds of speeches, unable to pronounce a single word on his deathbed, a single phrase to be handed down about his pontificate or his approach to the judgement-seat of God – this seemed the most impossible and unbelievable of paradoxes, the most disturbing sign of a mysterious intervention from on high, whether in punishment or in readjustment of the balance. Lastly, the irreverent throng of journalists and press-photographers encamped outside his villa throughout the night of his death-agony, the wanton intrusion of television cameras into his sickroom, the Court physician's vulgar speculations about the details of his end, the humiliations inflicted on his dead body in St Peter's to try out new methods of embalming . . .

With the end of a man came the end of a reign and a whole system of government. But none could yet foretell that, for the Church and the world, it was something much more, the irrevocable end of an epoch.

John XXIII : Angelo Giuseppe Roncalli

28 October 1958 – 3 June 1963

Search for a Harmless Old Man as Transitional Pope

Pius xii's death at Castel Gandolfo, rather than in the Vatican, was a quite unanticipated feature of his end. Cardinals, courtiers, and papal officials found themselves faced with an involved series of contretemps and unexpected situations which greatly complicated their work and responsibilities.

The first thing they realized was that, among many other vacancies, the post of Cardinal Chamberlain – *Camerarius,* in the Latin of the Curia – had never been filled. This is the Cardinal who, during the interregnum between one pontiff and the next, is called upon to fulfil the duties of handing over intact the properties and rights of the Church from the defunct Pope to his successor. His first symbolical action is therefore to take possession of the Apostolic Palaces of the Vatican, the Lateran, and Castel Gandolfo. According to an official description of 1846 of the ceremonies preceding and following the Conclave, the Chamberlain's chief duty was to guard against possible intervention in their own interests by the Secretary of State and the Pope's relatives: 'The *Cardinale Padrone* (as the Secretary of State was called in those days), if there is one, and the Pope's nephews must leave the Palace, whether at the Vatican or Monte Cavallo (the Quirinal), the Pope's usual residences; the aforesaid Cardinal Chamberlain takes possession of them in the name of the Apostolic Chamber, and one of the clerks allotted for this task assists at the inventory of everything found there'. In those days the Cardinal Chamberlain, who as a mark of distinction for his position was constantly escorted by the Swiss Guard (a privilege he still retains), was even empowered to strike coins.

In the absence of a Cardinal Chamberlain in those early days

of October 1958, it fell to the Dean of the Sacred College, Cardinal
Eugène Tisserant, to carry out the first and most urgent duties.
Foremost among them was the official recognition of Pius XII's
death. Up to Benedict XV this rite had been accompanied by the
famous striking of the dead man's forehead with a silver hammer.
In the case of Pius XI, the Chamberlain Pacelli when the master
of the ceremonies presented him with the hammer was visibly
embarrassed. 'Do you really think one must?' he asked, and
confined himself to calling on the dead man by name. This time
there was no sign of the hammer.

Next the question of embalming the body had to be settled.
The pontifical physician, Dr Galeazzi-Lisi, proposed a new
method which would obviate removing the entrails. In this way
it would be possible to omit the embarrassing and unpleasant
formality of transporting them from Castel Gandolfo to Rome
('the Entrails,' said the description already quoted, 'when the
Pope dies in his Palace of Monte Cavallo, are enclosed in an urn
and borne in a Carriage accompanied by one of the Secret Chaplains of the Palace to the Church of Sts Vincent and Anastasius
near the Pontifical Palace with four lighted Torches'). Otherwise,
of course, they would have to go by car; but would it be possible
to conceal this macabre journey from the vigilance of the
journalists and press-photographers perpetually lurking round
the entrances to the villa? These arguments convinced Cardinal
Tisserant and, little foreseeing the dramatic consequences of his
decision, he agreed. To his great relief, on the morning of
Friday the 10th the first general congregation of the Cardinals
present in Rome proceeded to appoint the seventy-nine-year-old
Cardinal Benedetto Aloisi Masella as Chamberlain. From that
moment the Cardinals as a body also assumed responsibility for
all the provisions and decisions arising from the state of 'Sede
Vacante'.

Another new and quite different feature of the election of
Pius XII's successor was the brevity of the pre-Conclave period,
resulting from the speed of modern methods of communication.
Some Cardinals set out for Rome on the very day of Pacelli's
death. Tisserant, who was in France, had only to get into an
aeroplane; but even Cardinal Spellman, who was in mid-Atlantic
on the way to New York, had no difficulty in getting the ship
diverted to the Azores, where he got a plane that brought him to

Rome on the evening of the 10th. At the election of 1939 the most anxiously awaited arrival had been that of the Cardinal Archbishop of Sydney. But this time Cardinal Gilroy left Sydney on the evening of the 9th and was in Rome on the 12th. At the general congregation on the 11th, Cardinal Betancourt, Archbishop of San Cristobal de Havana (Cuba), was already present; by the 12th all three Spanish Cardinals were in Rome, by the 13th the two Argentinians, and a few days later all the others had arrived except for those prevented from coming by age or political reasons (such as Cardinal Stepinac of Zagreb and Cardinal Mindszenty, Primate of Hungary).

In 1939 the Cardinals attending the Conclave numbered sixty-six. In 1958, two sudden deaths – those of Cardinal Costantini, Chancellor of the Holy Roman Church, and Cardinal Mooney, Archbishop of Detroit – reduced their already smaller numbers to fifty-two (Pius XII had held his second and last Consistory in 1953). This fact, however, did nothing to simplify the difficulties of the election. When Pius XI died the Italian Cardinals formed a clear majority, so that the Conclave had, so to speak, a definite geographical centre of gravity. At Pius XII's death, on the other hand, the fact that the majority was no longer Italian but European made the choice no easier (there were thirty-six from Europe, or thirty-eight taking into account the Eastern Patriarchs of Syria and of Cilicia of the Armenians). The number of Cardinals from the other continents was far from negligible (nine from South America, five from North America, and one each from India, Australia, and China), and alliances might always arise between some of them (for instance, the Latin-American Cardinals) and various groups of the Europeans. In short, the unknown factor of the Conclave lay in its divisions along lines of nationality and origin.

Pius XII may perhaps have supposed that in broadening the basis of the Sacred College he would make it a supra-national assembly. As far as its external representative character was concerned he achieved his aim. But an assembly of co-opted members does not become a living and operative entity, let alone a homogeneous one, unless its members meet frequently and collaborate effectively. The Senate of Cardinals, however, though some of its meetings were well attended, had never met in full, and, moreover, had never met to discuss or deliberate, but simply to listen to and approve their sovereign, lending their presence to his majesty. They now did so for the first time, and for a matter so serious as the election of a new Head of the Church; yet they were given no time to discuss officially, but had to pass on at once to the ballots and voting.

Above and beyond the somewhat inhibiting divisions on national lines, however, ideological considerations tended to catalyse, so to speak, the future Pope's election around the two opposite poles of sympathy or antipathy for Pacelli's line of policy. The sympathizers, notoriously led by the members of the 'Pentagon' (Canali, Pizzardo, Micara, Ottaviani, and Mimmi) who up to Pius XII's death had enjoyed his full favour and had completely dominated the Curia, consisted of the Americans, Canadians, Spanish, Portuguese, Irish, and Latin Americans.

Their only opponents in the Vatican had been Cardinals Costantini and Valeri (Tisserant for personal reasons preferred to remain in the background), both of them elderly and in poor health; but until a few years before the opposition had been able to count on the authority and dynamic energy of the Pope's closest and most powerful collaborator, the Under-Secretary and later Pro-Secretary of State, Mgr Giovanni Battista Montini. After Montini's transfer from Rome to Milan at the end of 1954, the anti-'Pentagon' and progressive trend had gravitated towards the Milan-Bologna-Venice triangle, the sees respectively of Mgr Montini and Cardinals Lercaro and Roncalli. In Rome, the group's minor supporters were led by the new Under-Secretary, Dell'Acqua; while abroad it had the support of the French Cardinals, the Polish Primate Wyszynski, the Indian Cardinal Gracias, and a few others (in recent years it had made some inroads into the Latin American front but without having much effect on its position as a whole).

But for Pius XII's death and the reaction it produced, nothing could have caused the balance to veer in favour of the second group. But more than one Cardinal on arriving in Rome for the Conclave became aware almost at once of the atmosphere of decomposition and decay surrounding not only the dead Pope's ill-embalmed corpse but his whole pontificate. This prompted the conviction that Pacelli's prestige and personality alone had succeeded in concealing the incredible gaps in a reign which had failed in most of its basic aims, remaining fixed in a sterile rut of

anti-Communist crusading even after the post-Stalin 'thaw' and
the Soviet Communist Party's Twentieth Congress, while combining, in the Church's internal administration, a tendency to
over-centralize with delay in dealing with problems and unwillingness to undertake reforms.

The younger Cardinals could do no more than register the
shortcomings of the late pontificate; but the older ones who had
taken part in the previous Conclave could not but recall Pacelli's
unfulfilled promises of the days before his election in March 1939.
One such, for example, concerned a proposal made by the French
Cardinals, asking (according to the former Ambassador to the
Holy See, Charles-Roux, who revealed the episode in his memoirs)
for 'a moderation of the excessive centralization, which hampered
the bishops' initiative and even their authority in their respective
dioceses'.

Nevertheless despite all this the 'Pentagon' group appeared to
be invincible. Objective estimates gave them some thirty supporters. Moreover Pius XII's protégé, Archbishop Siri of Genoa,
seemed to be endowed with all the gifts calculated to ensure his
becoming a second Pacelli, whereas the opposition's own candidate, Montini, was not to be reckoned on as a starter since he
was excluded from the Conclave, not having yet been raised to
the purple. True, the Pope does not necessarily have to be chosen
from among the members of the Sacred College, but the minority
certainly could not add to their troubles by advancing his cause.
It was also obvious that the 'Pentagon' followers were not going
to rest passively on their laurels: like Spellman they had all come
rushing to Rome, and in the first congregation had secured the
election of the Chamberlain and of two of their leaders, Canali
and Pizzardo, in the interim government of the Vatican City.

Compared with their activity the calm demeanour of the anti-
Pacelli group seemed almost an admission of defeat. How else,
for instance, could one account for the French Cardinals' delay in
not reaching Rome until a week after Pius XII's death? And
could they and their colleagues really expect to reverse the
situation largely on the basis of pressure of public opinion, even
though there could be no doubt about the rising hostility in both
ecclesiastical and lay quarters to the recent pontificate, and the
desire for a change? Within the enclosed walls of the Conclave,
newspaper comments and rumblings in the outer world would

certainly have no influence whatever on the two sides' attitudes.

A new factor, however, seemed to enter in with the advent of Cardinal Wyszynski, Primate of Poland. Wyszynski uttered not one word, but the mere sight of him on arrival at the Termini station in Rome was like a call to arms. Many saw in him, the only Cardinal from a Communist country to reach the Conclave, the champion of a courageous experiment insufficiently recognized, indeed half-disowned, by Pius XII, the personification of the hopes of a whole segment of the Catholic world, the voice of those 'Churches of Silence' deprived of speech by Communism but almost as much by Curial integralism. Conservatism suddenly revealed itself as the other face of ideological persecution, and now the only talk was of a Pope determined to make an end of both. In a few days the feeling grew that the little anti-'Pentagon' party was slowly but surely gaining ground not only among the few hitherto uncommitted members of the Sacred College but also among some who up to the last minute had sided with the majority; this impression gained strength and reached its climax on the day the Conclave opened.

That morning, in accordance with tradition, the Cardinals met for the Mass *de Spiritu Sancto*, designed to invoke divine aid for their coming deliberations, and to hear the customary speech of the Secretary of Briefs to Princes – a speech (known as '*de eligendo pontifice*') that is nearly always very general and rhetorical, interspersed with the usual commonplace descriptions of the duties of the Head of the Catholic Church. That morning, however, Mgr Antonio Bacci read an oration that was certainly fluent but which chiefly impressed its hearers by its daring, even including some controversial references to the pontificate, if not the person, of Pius XII. After saying, for instance, that the new Pope should have the gifts of a teacher, he laid even greater stress on his capacity as 'pastor of souls'. As such, he said, in the first place 'he will be ready to receive and welcome the bishops as his collaborators in the government of the Church of God; he will be ready to give them counsel in their doubts, to listen to and comfort their anxieties, and to encourage their plans'. Going on to present him also as a father, he continued:

... his heart will feel movements of particular tenderness for peoples oppressed by an absolute, tyrannical, and persecuting power; and equally, too, for those social classes that still find themselves in

such straitened conditions and poverty that not even by the sweat of
their brows can they procure for themselves and their children sufficient food and a sheltering roof. He will take to heart, like Jesus Christ
Himself, the cause of the poor and the disinherited. The rights of
human toil will certainly be safeguarded by him by every possible
means . . . May the new Vicar of Christ be like a bridge between
heaven and earth; may he recall the wrongdoers and the errant to the
right way. May he be as a bridge between the various social classes . . .
A bridge between nations, even between those that reject, rebuff, and
persecute the Christian religion, and may he seek to rebuild between
them that true peace which is the only source of prosperity, tranquillity,
and progress.

It was like throwing up a rainbow between East and West; but
the end was even more impressive:

It is not enough to have a learned pontiff, a pontiff endowed with
human and divine knowledge, who has explored and tried out the
subtle reasonings of diplomacy and politics. That too is certainly
necessary, but it is not enough. What is needed above all, Most
Eminent Fathers, is a holy pontiff; for a holy pontiff can obtain from
God what natural gifts cannot confer.

The impression was tremendous. Many thought that if a Curialist
like Mgr Bacci had dared to speak in this way there must be some
reason for it. Something must be brewing. Perhaps all the discussions in private groups before the Conclave had produced
definite results: probably neither more nor less than the choice of
a progressive Pope. But the more prudent observed that it was
ingenuous to go by a purely oratorical forecast. Besides, Mgr
Bacci himself, closely linked as he had been till then with the
heads of the 'Pentagon', was hardly the person to justify such
excessive optimism. The probability that it was a manoeuvre of
the conservatives was suggested, too, by the fact that the picture
of a Pope described by the Secretary of Briefs coincided perfectly
with that of a compromise Pope. And, given the circumstances,
a compromise Pope might be just what the conservatives were
realistically aiming at.

For a Pope who, being inhibited from planning changes and
innovations, would alter nothing in the *status quo* of the Holy See
in particular and the Church in general, would in the long run
behave as the embalmer and hence the continuer of the Pacellian

line of policy, postponing indefinitely the confrontation between the two programmes dividing the Sacred College. Only in theory, in short, would a transitional-seeming Pope appear to keep things in suspense: in practice he would merely continue the past, thereby aggravating its defects.

But if that was really how matters stood, and if the progressives could not succeed – and how could they? – in reaching a majority, the only way of solving the impasse in their favour must be through the choice of the candidate. In other words, their only chance of outwitting their opponents was to put up a seemingly peaceable and noncommital candidate who in fact had ideas and plans similar to their own. But could they succeed, especially since they had to do with such extremely subtle adversaries?

The 'Transitional' Pope is Chosen and Enjoys his New Realm

The explanation of the three long days of the Conclave and its eleven ballots may perhaps lie in the unremitting struggle that went on to achieve this end. Or perhaps the secrecy of the Conclave also concealed other attempts, such as to divert the choice towards a non-Italian Cardinal. But if that was so, it must have petered out quickly. For the election of a foreigner involved insuperable difficulties, since cardinals from both the Great Powers and the Communist countries were virtually excluded, as well as those from countries under totalitarian Catholic governments; and that really exhausted the possibilities. The only way out would have been to back a candidate of Eastern rite. In that case the Conclave offered the choice between the unbending Tappouni, Patriarch of Antioch of the Syrians, and the gentle and flexible Agagianian, Patriarch of Cilicia of the Armenians and Prefect of the Propaganda Fide. But the fact that they belonged to a minority of the Catholic community which, though negligible in numbers, was notoriously a restless and uncertain quantity, effectively ruled out their candidature.

Thus the choice came back to the Italian Cardinals: and excluding those of the Curia and those from residential sees who had no chance of being elected (such as Siri and Ruffini among the conservatives and Lercaro among the progressives) or were too old (like Fossati of Turin and Dalla Costa of Florence), the only remaining possibilities were Roncalli and Valeri. And at that point the choice became difficult. We do not yet know, and perhaps we never shall, why the one was preferred to the other. Valeri was at that time Prefect of the Congregation of Religious Orders, having reached that office after a long period during which he had held no important post since his eventful nunciature in Vichy. His piety, intelligence, and character, gentle but also capable of unsuspected strength, undoubtedly made of him a worthy successor to Pacelli. Was he really turned down purely for the reasons of health that he himself invoked? If so, it was an over-pessimistic estimate, as it turned out, for though his colleague and friend Roncalli then seemed in much better condition, Valeri survived him, if only by a few months.

On the other hand, while there were no doubts about the moderation and conciliatory good-nature of the Patriarch of Venice, there was no denying that during his brief term of office in Venice he had sometimes shown a disconcerting broad-mindedness (besides being the first Patriarch to remove the ban which since Sarto's day had prevented priests from visiting the Biennale art exhibition, he had consented to receive delegates from the Communist women's organization, and had even extended a warm welcome to the Socialist Party Congress, held in Venice in 1957). True, he had also disowned in unmistakable terms a group of progressive Catholics; but his actions as a whole gave one to think. In any case, to guard against all possibilities, both sides decided that the new Pope should have a Secretary of State satisfactory to the Pacellians (this was carried into effect with the immediate appointment of Tardini).

But, in the end, which of the two sides thought it had won in choosing the Patriarch of Venice? Almost certainly both of them. So it would seem, at least, from the unfeigned exultation shown alike by 'Pentagon' members such as Ottaviani and Micara and progressive leaders such as Wyszynski and Feltin. Words can be deceptive, but not tears, especially from one so little of an actor as Ottaviani; and both he and Micara were moved to tears. Wyszynski's exultation, on the other hand, arose largely from his certainty that the question of the Church's relations with the East European countries was now entering a new phase; while the French cardinals felt sure that the modernization of their Church would no longer incur the obstacles put in its way under Pius XII. Apart from these particular reactions, certainly no one had the slightest suspicion of the real personality of the man they had chosen, or of what his coming was to mean for Catholicism and the world as a whole.

He himself up to that moment had simply not believed in the likelihood of his election: so much so, indeed, that he had brought with him to Rome the purple cloak to wear at the receptions and the red cope for the 'third adoration' of the Cardinals for the new Pope, and did not leave out his Will, as he had always done before when setting out on an important journey (for instance to Lebanon or Spain). Three years later, in August 1961, he reflected in his *Diary*:

When on 28 October 1958 the Cardinals of the Holy Roman Church designated me for the supreme responsibility of governing the universal flock of Jesus Christ, there was a widespread belief that I would be a provisional, transitional Pope. But instead, here I am on the eve of the pontificate's fourth year, with an immense programme of work in front of me to be carried out before the whole watching, waiting world. As for me, I am like St Martin: *nec mori timuit, nec vivere recusavit* (he neither feared to die nor spurned to live).

What wonder, then, that his advent was not only unexpected but also, for some time, misunderstood? The most obvious misunderstandings were among the general public. For them it began with the ambiguous puff of smoke that emerged at 5.07 pm from the absurd little chimney in the Sistine Chapel. The radio and television reporters, while taking every possible precaution to protect themselves should they prove wrong, were nevertheless at one in declaring that they must wait for the next ballot, for another hour or so. But they had only just begun to calm down and half believe in their prevarications, when increasing animation in the Sacred Palaces, followed by official confirmation over the radio, spread the certainty that, despite the ambiguous smoke, the Pope had been well and truly chosen.

More and more prelates and lay dignitaries were crowding into the Bernini galleries. After a further half-hour's wait all doubts were set at rest when the retainers came to open the big central window of the Loggia of Benedictions, looking on to St Peter's Square, and hang out the large strip of red velvet. But when, at 6.02 pm, the Cardinal Dean, Ottaviani, came to the balcony to announce the name of the new Pope, the crowd knew a moment

of uncertainty. They had, of course, seen Roncalli's name
mentioned in the papers of the past few days as one of the
probable candidates, but on the whole they had paid little attention to what they regarded – with some justification – as the
machinations of pseudo-experts or initiates. What they had learnt
of him personally, moreover, was too sketchy to give them any
idea of what the chosen Pope was really like. Hence their first
instinctive hesitation, which quickly gave way to the knowledge
that, come what might, this was the new Pope. Then faith,
coupled with the hope that he would correspond to expectations,
prevailed over all their doubts.

But perplexity revived when, at 6.16 pm, the new Pope
appeared on the balcony in a simple surplice and stole for the
first benediction *Urbi et Orbi*. Despite the glare from dozens of
arc-lamps directed on him, seen in the growing twilight his figure
was little more than a black-and-white blur. All that could be
made out was a thickset, massive frame with a powerful head
above it. The contrast was striking between these clumsily
spherical contours and the tall hieratical figure of his predecessor,
with his unforgettable gesture of the arms held out like a cross
before the benediction. So the applause broke out uncertainly at
first, only gradually gaining ground and becoming more resolute.
Only after the deep, calm, modulated voice of the new Pope had
pronounced, not without a tremor of emotion, the ritual formula,
did the crowd become more nearly convinced. But to anyone
moving about among them as they dispersed after the ceremony,
it was not difficult to discern a state of mind still half divided
between the fear of admitting disappointment and the need to
abandon themselves to faith and confidence.

Yet only forty-eight hours later the image of the new Pope had
moved beyond the sight of their eyes into the hearts of the
multitude. What had brought about this miracle? Partly, of
course, the gentle, bewitching magic of his face and his whole
appearance. That broad, calm, luminous countenance emanated
only serenity and cordiality. The powerful nose, the big ears set
flat against the head, the strong jaw all contributed to his unmistakable personality; but if the little twinkling eyes indicated
intelligence and guaranteed wisdom and experience, there also
welled forth from them a compelling flow of simple goodness.
In that face and those eyes there was something at once childlike

and mature, roguish and disciplined, that delighted by reason of its contrast.

His figure, too, of medium height but sturdy, indeed stout like a lively old grandfather still in the prime, created around him an atmosphere of confidence and familiarity never felt before in relation to a Pope. Soon every gesture, every attitude of his became common knowledge. People took eager note of how he walked, how he sat, how he gesticulated, how he spoke. In conversation, they noticed, he caressed his pectoral cross with one hand, with the other taking off and putting on the *zucchetto* at frequent intervals; sometimes he would hold his bent thumb enclosed in the palm of his left hand; when he sat, his left leg always seemed restless, and when searching for a word he would tap on the ground with his red and gold slipper; and just as he never bothered in the least about rearranging his dress in public, so too when speaking in French, the only foreign language he could manage without too much difficulty, it never worried him at all to insert an occasional word in Italian or Latin when the word he wanted escaped him – indeed he would sometimes apologize for his improvisations *'comme ci comme ça'*.

Looking at him, in short, one felt that everything about him was authentic and spontaneous, his looks, his words, his smiles and gestures: that he was transparency and naturalness personified. That, though he wore the dress of a Pope, he still remained the good country priest, with whom everyone, even the unbeliever, was glad and honoured to gossip for a few minutes in the churchyard. A man of God, yes, but first and foremost a man in the truest sense of the word, knowing life and its laws, its values and its shortcomings. More a friend than a judge, more ready to counsel and comfort than to censor or rebuke. In the improvised biographies hastily put together in the newspapers, what most struck the popular imagination was his peasant origin and his stubborn, lasting affection for his own countryside. People found it touching that he still had brothers working in the fields and byres, that he could count dozens of relatives like the patriarchs in the Bible, that they could easily imagine him dressed not in his white robe but in well-worn trousers and jacket, against a background of the Brianza, in his farmyard, on the threshing floor, or among the farm implements.

They liked to hear that journalists, even famous ones, had been invited to interview his relatives and had approached them as if they were princes though they still had their baskets on their backs or their forks stuck in the hay. Their answers were more vivid and full-flavoured than those of any politician or film star, and they had all kinds of interesting things to tell about the new Pope's childhood. Like the story, for instance, of his father's reaction when the fourteen-year-old boy asked if he could enter the seminary. Angelo had gone to talk to his father in the fields. Battista Roncalli stopped his work to listen and stood there thinking for a few minutes; then he turned his spade upside down and stuck it in the furrow by the handle, so that the blade shone in the sun, and answered: 'If only I could see you like that one day, with this spade on your head!' (in other words a bishop with a mitre on his head). As it turned out, paternal pride proved too modest in its hopes. And then there was his mother's diplomatic answer when a neighbour exclaimed in amazement at seeing Don Angelo, who had recently become a monsignore, dressed all in purple: 'What can you expect? These are just things that priests arrange among themselves!'

In point of fact, it was not so much ambition as poverty that prompted his father's forecast. In the Roncalli household when Angelo was a little boy, and even later when he was growing up, there were over thirty mouths to feed, and sometimes there simply wasn't enough. One day the future Pope had to share an egg with his brother. At home on holiday from the seminary, he sometimes could not write his diary at nights for lack of ink or a candle. But fate was kind to him, and the boy who saw the up-turned spade shining in his father's hands had not only attained the mitre but, after distant sojourns in the Balkans and on the Bosphorus, had finally arrived in the halls of the Quai d'Orsay and the Elysée in Paris, there succeeding to many a famous nuncio; and later still, when promoted to be patriarch, he had lived in one of the most sumptuous palaces of the city of the Doges; until finally he reached the Vatican.

It was like a legend, an incredible fairy-tale become true. But the legend of the past was not the only one to make the new Pope popular. Forty-eight hours had sufficed to give birth to another one, even more fascinating and incredible: a legend that had blossomed half a century before, with Pope Sarto, but had swiftly faded even as its hero languished and became suffocated in the unreal setting that surrounded him. In the long run Pius x had become a pathetic figure who ended by disappointing and under-mining the sympathies that his unusual situation had aroused. Nothing of the sort, however, happened with Roncalli, a genuine peasant and therefore simple but provident, versed from child-hood in the wonders of nature rather than the petty stratagems of men, and therefore accustomed to find nothing in the works of man superior to the works of God, yet none the less prepared to appreciate and find honest enjoyment in them. From the very first day he could be found, happy as a child with an unexpected treat, wandering about all over the place, escorted only by a private secretary even less at home than himself in the corridors of the Vatican, intent on finding out all about his surroundings. He went without warning into the garden, walked about the passages of the Sacred Palaces which until a few days before had inspired him with genuine fear, drank toasts with the carpenters in the apostolic workshop, and chatted and joked with whomever he met.

Everyone had expected that he would find it embarrassing to follow a predecessor so aristocratic, so solemn even in the most normal actions, so deeply convinced that his simplest word and act made history; and that he would be at a loss how to behave in a palace and court that he had always visited unwillingly and judged severely from his years of experience, in a humble situation far away, of its inhuman cruelty. But not in the least. From the first day, in the most natural way possible he brought revolution into the somewhat lazy, somnolent habits of the Apostolic Palace. He continued his custom of rising early, between three and four in the morning; but while he spent the first hours in the solitude of his apartment without disturbing anyone, he woke them all up after that. At six or seven he welcomed whole groups of people for his first Mass, or else left the Vatican to go out to them. And after the normal routine of public and private audiences, in the afternoons he was liable to make improvised sorties to the most unexpected places.

These sorties were for a long time the most exciting novelty provided by the new Pope, especially because of the escapade-like flavour which the press took a friendly delight in accentuating. Had he not himself, in the first days, laughingly complained of his confinement and invited all and sundry (like the clowns from the Orfei Circus) to come and visit him? And since the sorties happened quite without warning, in the most private and informal way and often in extraordinary circumstances – for instance, he would sometimes stop his car and proceed on foot through the city streets or the country lanes – it was natural that the public should view them as whimsical escapades, conducted with a spice of delight at the shocks they caused among the starchy officials of the pontifical Court. Quite a number of people even thought that at last the Vatican had got a Pope free from all the paraphernalia of mysticism and ritualism, who made no secret of the fact that he loved life, who wanted to keep contact with men and was determined not to deprive himself of any legitimate satisfaction existence could afford. They talked of his enjoyment of good food in the company of his friends, so unlike the customary rigid etiquette of the Popes, and of his delight in going to all the concerts and shows to which he was invited.

Some time passed before people realized that these interpretations were completely mistaken; and they were never at any time tinged with vulgar malice, but tempered always with a reverential sympathy. At bottom they were an almost inevitable overflow of the attraction he aroused. The first true inklings about the new Pope dawned gradually. The key lay in his look of overwhelming concentration when at prayer or celebrating Mass. Then his face seemed stern and severe, but with a gravity that held nothing of sadness. Immersion in the sacred, contact with the divine, seemed with him to carry gravity but also a revealing naturalness. And anyone who saw how, soon afterwards, in contact with the crowd, he would resume his easy, happy demeanour could realize that in that too there remained something of the supernatural. Thus little by little people came to understand that the urge that took him out of the Vatican was prompted not so much by personal restlessness or a need for distraction or to satisfy his curiosity, but rather by the desire to establish living, direct contacts outside the bounds of officialdom and etiquette, like those of every good parish priest in his care of souls.

Only during the pontifical ceremonies, sitting on his throne or carried in the gestatorial chair, was his face seen to cloud and contract as if in some interior conflict. People believed they had found the reason for this when he himself mentioned his distaste at having to appear in the centre of glittering manifestations whose outdated pomp and artificiality annoyed him. This was true, but only in part, for he did not, as many had expected, proceed drastically to suppress display in pontifical ceremonies; what mattered to him a good deal more than his own discomfort was to draw the spiritual moral from the situation. 'It is better to be borne by the Father, by the Lord, than on the shoulders of men,' he told the bearers from his native Bergamo who carried him in the gestatorial chair. He believed that there were things in the Church that stood in much greater need of change than the gestatorial chair or the feathered fans, and that in any case a true Pope could awaken the feeling for that need more effectively by making use of those adjuncts than by abolishing them. In the words of a remarkable priest and prophet, Don Primo Mazzolari, writing of the coronation ceremony,[1] by his whole attitude he brought that too-majestic rite, with its overtones of imperial display, back to its Christian confines, distilling 'the human and divine from a stupendous but too choreographic ceremony that bears the same relation to Holy Mass as the tiara does to the crown of thorns'. Or, in the words of the speech he himself made that day, 'What matters even more than what we do is the spirit in which we do it' – thus revealing the secret of his revolution.

In that same homily he made clear what were to be the characteristics of his pontificate, and in so doing harked back, obviously intentionally, to the words of Mgr Bacci's oration *'de eligendo pontifice'*. In the Pope, he said, people must not look for 'the statesman, the diplomatist, the scholar, the organizer of collective life, or someone with a mind open to all forms of progress in modern life, with no exception'. The true ideal of a Pope is to 'realize first and foremost in himself the splendid image of the Good Shepherd'. Therefore, he added, 'especially close to Our heart is the task of shepherd of the whole flock. All the other human qualities – knowledge, perception, diplomatic tact, organizing ability – can serve as embellishments and completions of pontifical rule, but they can be no substitute for it'.

Those who had still not understood came at last to understand him at his first Christmas, two months after his election, when they saw him make a lengthy visit to the children's Hospital of the Infant Jesus, going on afterwards to the general Hospital of

[1] *'Una parola paterna'*, *Adesso*, 15 November 1958.

the Holy Spirit and in the afternoon receiving in the Vatican the boys from Cardinal Tardini's Villa Nazareth and Don Gnocchi's little cripples. At eight in the morning next day he was at the gates of the Regina Coeli prison to visit the prisoners. In the days of temporal dominion the Pope-Kings had doubtless done the same; but no one could remember that, and in any case this time the Pope was visiting the hospitals and prison of a friendly but foreign State, doing so simply in the name of his faith and his paternal and pastoral mission. Pius XI had visited in great secrecy a sick prelate in hospital, but that was an exception; and the only time he visited the Vatican prison was to inspect the new premises, still unoccupied. The visit ended with a joke: 'We wanted to make sure there were no instruments of torture.'

There was a reason for Pope John's perpetual gaiety and cordiality which only became known much later. As the young secretary of the Bishop of Bergamo, Radini-Tedeschi, he had been deeply disillusioned, during an audience with Pius X, by the Pope's remoteness and lack of interest; when receiving the Bishop together with others from the diocese, he had not even bothered to thank them for the handsome gift they brought. Roncalli had commented on this afterwards to the Bishop, saying that he thought the Pope, whatever his anxieties or worries might be, should always show a kindly, smiling face to the faithful. He was putting that idea of long ago into practice now, and if he seemed to love popularity it was not because it pleased him personally, but so that he might give more than he received. So little, indeed, did he care about popularity as such that when someone tried to attribute to him a vision of Pius X, he brusquely and unequivocally denied it. He might admit popularity when it meant being ready to understand and be understood, to speak and be listened to, but he firmly rejected any ridiculous or meaningless cult attaching to it.

At a distance of two months from the election of John XXIII, however, it was not only the faithful from every rank and region of the world who were pleased with the new Pope. His electors, too, were well satisfied. The Pacellian cardinals had known a moment of alarm immediately after the election and his pronouncement of the word '*accepto*'. When the Cardinal Dean asked him by what name he would be known, he answered at once, as if

no choice could be more natural, '*Vocabor Joannes*'. Now, for the
past five-and-a-half centuries, since the disaster of Baldassarre
Cossa, the Neapolitan made anti-Pope in opposition to the
Venetian Gregory XII, no Pope had taken that name. More than
one cardinal thought he had misunderstood and asked his neighbour for confirmation. Roncalli meanwhile went on unper-
turbed: 'John, a name dear to Us, because it is the name of Our
father; a name sweet-sounding to Us, because it is that of the
saint of the humble parish in which We were baptized; a name,
lastly, solemnized by its countless cathedrals scattered throughout
the world, first among them Our own, the sacrosanct Church of
St John Lateran.'

A publication presented to Roncalli early in 1959 by the Archpriest and the Mayor of Riese revealed the fact that the Patriarch
of Venice, Sarto, when leaving for the Conclave of 1903 had
jestingly said he might call himself John XXIII. When Saccardo,
the editor of the Venetian daily *La Difesa*, approached him and
asked what name he would take if elected, the Patriarch with his
usual good humour replied: 'Oh, if that's all you want to know,
I can satisfy you: I'll call myself John XXIII.'[1] And, as Saccardo
related at Riese in 1928, commemorating the 25th anniversary of
Pius x's election, there were people in Venice in August 1903
who actually sent a telegram to the new Pope, Leo XIII's successor,
addressed to 'His Holiness John XXIII'.

The difference between the two Patriarchs of Venice lies in the
fact that while Sarto was just making a joke, Roncalli really did
take that name, thereby breaking with the two-centuries-old
tradition that Popes should choose their name from a very limited
list – always either Pius or Benedict, Leo or Gregory, or, at most,
Clement. But it seems unthinkable that he should have done so
by chance, with no deeper reason than the purely sentimental
ones just quoted. A Protestant admirer of John XXIII, Jean
Jacques von Allmen,[2] thought up a very subtle reason. Baldassarre
Cossa had been deposed by the Council of Constance: in choosing
the name of John XXIII, Roncalli wished to signify his 'approval
of the act whereby the Council of Constance had put itself above
the Pope'. But that is obviously too far-fetched. There is a much

---

[1] See *Sua Santità Giovanni XXIII nei ricordi di Riese – Pio X*, 1959.
[2] In *Il Mulino* (Bologna), 1964, no. 6.

simpler but none the less significant explanation: namely, his intention to detach himself from all his immediate predecessors and their complex heritage, even the best-loved among them, and revert to an ancient tradition initiated by a saint and martyr in the golden age of the papacy – the period between the pontificates of St Leo the Great, in the fifth century, and St Gregory the Great, in the sixth, which included the first three Pope Johns.

Another unexpected feature of the outset of John XXIII's pontificate was the giving of the Cardinal's hat to the Secretary of the Conclave, Mgr Alberto di Jorio, immediately after the Pope assumed his name; this was a revival of an old custom interrupted under Leo XIII. Further appointments followed that same evening, including those of Majordomo, vacant for some time, and Master of the Chamber. Such an unusual beginning was bound to make some people wonder, especially those who thought they had backed a shy and inexperienced man as Pope, expected to take months to find his way about. But no further alarming innovations followed; such as there were, if sometimes slightly fantastic, proved in general more acceptable. Any excesses of the kind were, in the Pacellians' view, strictly to be avoided in order not to compromise the dignity of the office till recently sustained with such incomparable aristocracy of bearing by Pius XII. Similarly, they could not but regret that on the most solemn occasions the new Pope's speeches were of a different kind from his predecessor's magisterial pronouncements. However, on the whole and for the time being, everything went on according to their expectations: the only cause for worry might be what would happen to this parochial and popular Pope when the fascination of his rather unorthodox whims and deeds began to wear off.

As for the progressive Cardinals, though they may have shared some of their colleagues' surprise and apprehension they were nevertheless daily more satisfied with their choice. For them, the chief surprise about the new Pope lay not in his popular side-lines but in the discovery that his attitude and actions revealed a quite unexpected decisiveness and sureness of touch. If his unusual actions and excursions outside the Vatican might seem to suggest an exuberant confusion, there was nothing confused or fortuitous about his actions as head of the universal Church.

His sure eye and step showed that he knew what he wanted. Had he not within a few weeks set in order the Secretariat of State without making a single change of personnel, providing it once more with its legitimate head (the Secretary of State, vacant since 1944) and restoring it to the sphere of its true functions? And had not relations with the Curia – whose several Departments he visited at once – been completely regularized, with the restoration of the Prefects' audiences and the reduction in the number of offices held by one person? All this implied a wise internal policy, but no less hopeful was the respect he had hastened to show for the individual episcopates and their organizations. Thus he had enthusiastically agreed that the third meeting of the Latin American Episcopal Council (CELAM) should be held in Rome, under his very eyes, and he approved its results. Still more important was his proposal to the Italian episcopate that they should discard the old statutes of their episcopal conference and create new ones more favourable to its autonomy. In the pastoral sphere, he gave unmistakable proof of his personal interest by his decision to visit as many parishes as possible in his diocese of Rome. As for foreign policy, his intention to work for a détente with the Communist-controlled countries, thus putting an end to the dangerous and sterile state of cold war, was at once apparent from the prolonged two-month stay in Rome of the Polish Primate, Wyszynski.

But the new Pope did not merely show that he had definite ideas and meant to pursue them firmly; he also knew how to go straight ahead undeterred by those who tried to oppose or sabotage his plans. Some among his entourage were worried because he would not agree politely to eliminate such people. But his wish was not to make victims but to secure loyal and enthusiastic collaborators: as for his opponents, they too, so he said, fulfilled a useful function in acting as a brake, and if left to themselves they might change their views for the better. There were, in fact, very few dismissals, and none of them total, under his pontificate. Such as there were were delayed as long as possible so as to avoid giving any impression of vendetta or reprisal. A typical case was that of the President of Catholic Action in Italy, Pius xii's *homme de confiance* Luigi Gedda, who was retained in office for nine months and then relieved of the presidency of the association but not of his rather more insidious post as head of the Civic Committees. Among the other dubious personalities of the previous pontificate, the only one to vanish at once was the pontifical physician, Dr Galeazzo-Lisi, who resigned of his own accord. His half-brother, the civil engineer Pietro Galeazzi, hitherto all-powerful in the Vatican City, remained at his post, and so did Pius XII's nephews. Higher up in the scale, not one of the 'Pentagon' Cardinals was relieved of any of his high offices except at his own request. And when Cardinal Pizzardo offered his resignation as Secretary of the Holy Office since he was also Prefect of the Congregation of Seminaries, no objection was raised to Ottaviani's succeeding him. On the contrary, right from the beginning there were many promotions and marks of recognition. Only two months after he became Pope, at his first consistory for the election of new Cardinals – when, incidentally, he took another revolutionary step in increasing the number beyond the seventy established by Sixtus V – John XXIII raised twenty-four prelates to the purple, a good proportion of them being from the Curia. Heading the list was the Archbishop of Milan, Mgr Montini, in reparation both for the wrong done him by his removal from Rome in 1954 and for the unjust delay in elevating him to the cardinalate.

After only two months at the helm the new Pope had not only reorganized the top-level administration of the Church, remedying its earlier gaps and favouritisms, but he had also definitely banished from its government the whole paternalist and absolutist style of relations. The Vatican had ceased to be a palace and become a house: the 'house of the Father'; and the new Pope's behaviour demonstrated that in order to be Pope and exert authority there was no need to establish a cold, forbidding etiquette or, worse still, to isolate oneself to the point of inaccessibility. Which was quite a good deal for any Pope to have done, especially for one regarded as merely 'transitional'.

The Pope Shows his True Mettle and Announces the Council

A single day sufficed to prove that if till then Pope John XXIII had shown himself no transitional Pope, he was even less likely to accept any semblance of that role in future. That day was 25 January 1959. According to the programme for the day, he was to go in the afternoon to the basilica of St Paul's Without the Walls to be present at the pontifical vespers commemorating the apostle's conversion and to conclude the octave of prayers for unity. This was his tenth official appearance outside the Vatican in ninety days, and it involved no further engagement. Or, at least, everyone supposed that the visit announced immediately afterwards, with the attendant cardinals, to the nearby historic monastery of the Benedictines would be a purely routine affair. But instead, John XXIII not only received the homage of the monks in the chapter-house but also assembled there in extraordinary congregation the seventeen cardinals then present in Rome, who had been summoned by an 'intimation' from the Master of Ceremonies. There and then in a short speech he made an announcement which came as a thunderbolt: his decision to summon an ecumenical council to promote the unity of all the Christian communities; to hold a synod for the city and diocese of Rome; and to proceed to a general reform of the Code of Canon Law.

A few days before, as he himself was to reveal (and as was also later confirmed by the Secretary of the Congregation for Extraordinary Ecclesiastical Affairs, Mgr Antonio Samoré, who published an extract from his superior's diary about the event), John XXIII had already made known these plans to his Secretary of State, Cardinal Tardini, who, though astounded at their scale, had expressed his unconditional agreement. Strangely enough, Tardini had also received a confidence about his future plans from Pius XII shortly after his election. As Tardini mentioned in his official speech on Pacelli in the Vatican on 20 October 1959, the latter had then revealed the three main points of his programme for his pontificate: 'First, a new translation of the Psalter, so that the clergy may better understand and enjoy the beauties of the daily liturgical prayer; secondly, the definition of the dogma of the Assumption; thirdly, the excavation of the tomb of St Peter.'

'Three truly daring decisions' – so Tardini described them:

The first modified a tradition going back for centuries. The second involved serious and lengthy researches of a patristic, liturgical, and theological nature, and presupposed (such was Pius XII's intention, which was carried out) consultation of the whole episcopate. The third presented enormous technical as well as historical, topographical, and archaeological difficulties, for it involved complicated and dangerous work under the main altar of the basilica of St Peter's and in proximity to Michelangelo's great pillars. The revised Psalter was published on

24 March 1945. The definition of the dogma of the Assumption was solemnly promulgated on 1 November 1950. The valuable results of the Vatican excavations were announced by the Pope himself in his Christmas message of 23 December 1950. In conclusion, three great objectives, three great victories.

And though Cardinal Tardini added that 'The Lord permitted Pius XII to go far beyond his initial programme', that statement was modified by the following sentence: 'He nevertheless continued to move along the luminous path of his three great ideals.'

On 21 January 1959, when he took note of the remarkable revelations made to him by Pope John, Tardini did not recall what had happened twenty years before, or, if he remembered it, he took good care not to make any written comparison between the two Pope's programmes. Such a comparison would have been annihilating to Pius XII. For his three proposals not only revealed an almost incredibly limited imagination but they lacked homogeneity, having no common denominator beyond that of superfluity. Two of the three were of a definitely controversial nature – the excavations in St Peter's were bound to be so interpreted by the separated Christian Churches, while the dogmatic definition of the Assumption proved highly provocative. But in addition to this they were not calculated to make more than the most superficial impact on the life of the Church, and thus would ill support the definition of 'programme points for a pontificate'. The situation is not altered if the comparison is extended to all the other main achievements of the Pacellian reign. Even in the liturgical sphere, where it is less striking, there is still a considerable difference of proportion between Pius XII's translation of the Psalter and his other liturgical reforms, and the great liturgical revolution carried out under John XXIII at the first session of the Vatican Council. And what possible comparison can there be between Pope Pius's 'week of faith' in Rome in 1952 and Pope John's Roman Synod, still less between the launching of an equivocal movement like Padre Lombardi's 'Better World' and the convocation of the Second Vatican Council?

John XXIII's programme was highly organic and close-knit, the Roman Synod being visualized as a precursor and curtain-raiser for the Council, and the reform of the Code of Canon Law as an application of the Council's decisions. Within that programme the most modest point was undoubtedly the Synod, but it was all the same an unprecedented step, for the holy city of the Popes had never, so far as is known, had such a thing since medieval times. As for the summoning of an Ecumenical Council and the bringing up to date of the Code of Canon Law, either of these would alone suffice to establish a pontificate's place in history. The true significance of the announcement made on 25 January 1959 can, in any case, be fully appreciated only by taking into account the accompanying circumstances. For there was nothing fortuitous about the choice of St Paul's Without the Walls for its setting. A remote predecessor of the same name, John VIII (872–82) eleven centuries earlier had linked his own name with the '*castrum sancti Pauli*', whose walls he had erected to protect it against attack and pillage by the Saracens, and for centuries afterwards this appendage of Rome was known as Giovannipoli.[1] But John VIII had no idea of contrasting in any way the Pauline *castrum* with that of St Peter. John XXIII, on the other hand, aimed at emphasizing a certain antithesis between the two.

As Mgr Pericle Felici revealed some weeks after the end of Vatican II, John XXIII had for some time cherished the project of celebrating his Council in the basilica of St Paul's and calling it 'Ostiense I'. Pope John's exclusion of St Peter's from both the announcement and the celebration of the ecumenical assembly is highly significant, not only because it emphasizes his intention to distinguish between the new Council and that held under Pius IX in 1869–70, known as the Vatican Council, but also because it characterizes beyond all doubt the objective he had in mind, of relaunching a movement for unity between the Christian Churches. Viewed in this light, the basilica of St Peter's, reconstructed with the proceeds of the unhappily notorious campaign for indulgences which was not the least significant cause of the Reformation, was, to say the least, an unpropitious meeting place. Not to mention the fact that in the basilica of St Peter's, above the apostle's shrine vainly ransacked by Pius XII's excavations, the Council of 1870 had promulgated the dogmatic definition so blasphemous to Protestant and Orthodox sensibilities: that of papal primacy and infallibility. To Pope John's mind it seemed impossible to con-voke in council the separated brethren in surroundings which

[1] See I. Tassi, '*Giovannipoli, la città fortificata a difesa della basilica di san Paolo*', *L'Osservatore Romano*, 27 January 1966.

historically were the living testimony to Rome's intolerance and hegemonic presumption.

All these circumstances, of course, could not be guessed at by the seventeen members of the Sacred College as they heard the Pope read his sensational announcement. But the very words 'ecumenical council' were enough to make them start and remain paralysed in astonishment. Was this the man upon whom only three months before they had caused their votes to converge in the confidence that they would secure a transitional Pope? The man who had delighted the world with his spontaneous personification of the good old country priest, satisfied with his jokes and picturesque sorties from the Vatican? Could he really imagine he could turn the Church upside down and give a voice and power to the world episcopate, after Pius XII had brought the papacy to the apex of its fortunes and omnipotence? Could he dare to pitchfork the Church into the venture of promoting the reunion of all Christians, when not a single new fact had emerged for centuries in favour of a solution of this most intricate problem – indeed everything suggested, rather, that the political and religious disputes undermining the other communities would sooner or later bring about their unconditional return to the rock of Peter?

Sitting rather uncomfortably on his too rigid throne, Pope John had read his message a little breathlessly and, as he later confided, with a beating heart, but from joy rather than anxiety, though there was some of that too. Expecting to be interrupted once or twice by applause, he paused here and there to leave opportunity for it. Instead, to his amazement there was no applause even at the end. Drawn up in a semi-circle before him, at once close and remote, the seventeen princes of the Church remained stiff and motionless as statues in their purple cloaks. He then passed on quickly to the benediction, and after almost shyly expressing the wish to meet them privately one by one to hear their respective views, he withdrew.

Even after his black Mercedes had carried him back to the Vatican, John XXIII could not bring himself to understand his hierarchs' strange behaviour. He kept on telling himself that the shock of his announcement must have left them speechless, but he was not quite convinced. He was still absorbed in these thoughts when the Secretary of State urgently asked to see him, saying that he must speak to him, in the name of the majority of the cardinals who had been present at St Paul's, about the publication of the text of his speech. His colleagues of the Sacred College felt that the decisions announced by the Pope were of too serious portent for the Church to be made known thus abruptly without previous preparation. A carefully-worded communiqué would secure more notice and interest.

Arrived in the Pope's private library, Cardinal Tardini, still acting as his colleagues' ambassador, explained that they had nothing to object to in John XXIII's decision to mobilize the whole Church to review its situation. But they were troubled about the possible consequences that might arise from the forces that the convocation of the ecumenical assembly might set in motion both within the Catholic Church and outside it. In particular, quite apart from the fact that the daring attempt at union broke with the tradition of intransigence hitherto maintained by the Roman hierarchies, was it not perhaps to be feared that, if the separated Churches gave the same answer that they did to Pius IX at the time of the Vatican Council, the isolation of the Holy See would be intensified through the loss of prestige incurred from such a rebuff?

At a distance of eight years from what the conservative wing of the Senate of cardinals described as the *coup d'état* of 25 January 1959, the revolutionary character of that event is apparent to all. With it, in fact, Pope John put an end to his predecessors' authoritarian monologue and gave the word to the whole Church, bishops, priests, and laymen included; he dealt a blow at Roman centralization and at the privileges of the Curia, opening the way to recognition of the pluralism and federalism of the national and continental Churches; he reconsecrated the primacy of the Church's spiritual mission, subordinating to its pastoral ends the legalism of its lawyers and the temporalism of its diplomatists; he gave an impulse to the progressive secularization of the ecclesiastical community by extending greater responsibilities to laymen; and, finally, he brought the Catholic Church in a certain sense into the vanguard of ecumenism, thrusting it towards an embrace not only with other Christian communities but even with other faiths.

Now all these goals of John XXIII's revolution might not be clear to the public in general immediately after 25 January 1959, but they were clear as day to the heads of the Curia, with their senses sharpened by the feeling that they were becoming involved in uncontrollable events. It was quite natural, therefore, that they should almost spontaneously find themselves at the head of the resistance and opposition aimed against the Council. Moreover, since the Council constituted a threat to the stratified interests, the outworn beliefs, and the prejudices of Roman circles, their action inevitably became catalysed around the Curia leaders.

Vain Siege by the Pacellian Old Guard

In a courageous essay published in the spring of 1965,[1] Cardinal Lercaro somewhat euphemistically defined the situation that now developed around John XXIII as 'the great institutional solitude'. This euphemism, however, did not attempt to conceal the dramatic reality of Pope John's isolation '*vis-à-vis* those organs of the Church which should be the instruments of his government and teaching, embrace his prophetic intuitions, and by cordial and active collaboration translate them into concrete measures'. According to Lercaro, the 'great institutional solitude' lasted throughout Pope John's pontifical life, 'at least up to 11 October 1962 (the day the Council opened), and to some extent even afterwards'. What is beyond doubt is that the prologue to this silent, defensive, but implacable struggle was Cardinal Tardini's audience with the Pope on that evening of 25 January.

Pope John, while agreeing to defer the publication of his speech, not only wished the communiqué to be explicit about the three points of his programme but also insisted that, with the obvious precautions, it should be explicit about the unionistic aims he had decided to assign to the Council. In the following months, however, he agreed to cut down references to the realization of his great plan and even forced himself to let the Church's modernization appear to be the Council's main aim. This was certainly something: but the Curia's aims went a good deal further. Its programme was in fact to monopolize the Council by securing the control of all its organs; then to inflate it by giving it a positive encyclopaedia of draft *schemi* to digest; and lastly, by carefully omitting to give it a pre-arranged organic plan, to avoid giving it a definite character. By monopolizing the

[1] See Bibliography, p.378.

Council the Curia leaders would be able not only to eliminate any unpleasant surprises for themselves but also to manoeuvre it against their opponents, and by inflating it and at the same time depriving it of a definite character they would make it into an apparently solemn and imposing but actually cumbersome and unwieldy machine which would eventually collapse under its own weight. Appearances, in other words the honour of the Church, would be saved; but at the same time the Curia would ensure its ability to continue as undisturbed ruler and sole arbiter of the Church's life for at least a few more decades.

This might seem a presumptuous and excessive programme, as of course it was; but the extraordinary thing is that every point of it was carried out. When, on 5 June 1960, the list of chairmen of the Council's Commissions was published (together with the *motu proprio, Superno Dei nutu*, which established as the Council's preparatory structure ten Commissions and two Secretariats), everyone realized that the Curia had won the first round. The chosen chairmen were all Curia Cardinals and were, moreover, respectively put in charge, in the new organization, of the same subjects they already dealt with as Heads of Congregation. In the following weeks the appointment of members and advisers of the individual Commissions only served to confirm the Curia's supremacy, for the majority of them came from among the officials of the sacred Departments or their list of advisers. As for the great theologians and foreign experts, especially if progressive by repute, there was a repetition of what happened at Vatican I, for the national episcopates concerned found themselves forced to use all kinds of pressure to launch their candidates, and even then with only partial success.

With regard to the Council's unionistic aim, the same *motu proprio* registered another obvious success for the Curia, for the *ad hoc* organ which it created had merely the subordinate role of a secretariat. All this, however, was merely, so to speak, the logistic preparation for the *coup*. Its execution proved equally triumphant. Between the autumn of 1960 and the autumn of 1961 the ten Commissions and two Secretariats produced seventy *schemi*, or drafts (of decrees or dogmatic constitutions) on a wide variety of subjects, several of them obviously marginal. In the previous year, the pre-preparatory commission (also, needless to say, one hundred per cent curial: it was presided over by Cardinal Tardini and had as its members the under-secretaries of all the Roman Congregations) had asked for advice and opinions from the bishops of all countries. The huge dossier collected, which when printed filled eight volumes, was laboriously catalogued; but only some vestiges of it passed into the *schemi* drawn up by the Commissions, later defined by the Dominican theologian Père Chanu as veritable systematic theses, framed at a level of timeless, abstract objectivity, the fruit of pure syllogistic deductions, 'conscientiously illustrated here and there by references to Holy Writ and its historical perspectives, but without any reference to the needs of the contemporary world'.

The farce reached its climax, however, with the work of overall control carried out by the central preparatory Commission, which began to function in June 1961. Between November of that year and the following June, in six sessions of forty-four meetings, each lasting from three to four hours, the Commission discussed and approved (or sent back for further modifications) all seventy *schemi*, thus dealing with an average of about two at each sitting.

Nevertheless despite all this John XXIII was not overwhelmed by pessimism, and for fairly obvious reasons. First and foremost, the Council was going ahead at the rate envisaged and would open on time. The Curia could therefore do as it pleased, for when the Council met the assembly itself would decide about both the elected membership of the Commissions and the programme of work to be carried out. As for the *schemi* drawn up with such zealous care, the precedent of Vatican I showed just how much the Council members need stand in awe of them, for it had spared not a single one of them but had effected the most exterminating decimation in conciliar history.

The 'great institutional solitude', on the other hand, was compensated for by the increasingly frank and generous welcome given to the Council by certain episcopates, especially those of Western Europe (the French, Belgian, Dutch, German, and Austrian), which included some of the most dynamic and enthusiastic leaders of the pro-conciliar movement such as Cardinals Koenig, Archbishop of Vienna, Suenens of Malines and Brussels, Alfrink of Utrecht, Feltin of Paris, Bishops Jaeger of Paderborn and Bekkers of 's-Hertogenbosch, and others. Outside Europe other members of the Sacred College or the episcopate stood out, such as Cardinals Léger of Montreal and Cushing of Boston.

And the young native bishops from the Afro-Asian countries also showed promising signs of interest.

The most impressive and decisive help for John XXIII, how-ever, came from some of the separated Churches or Christian communities, who did not conceal their emotion at the sensa-tional announcement of a unionistic council promoted by Rome. Foremost and most assiduous in praising John XXIII's action was the Orthodox Patriarch of Constantinople, Athenagoras. True, deeds were slow to follow words, but the emphasis and exuberance of his words made an impression even on secular public opinion. Dr Fisher, Archbishop of Canterbury and head of the Anglican Church, did almost the reverse of his Orthodox colleague. Instead of indulging in rhetorical and high-sounding messages, he chose to have a direct meeting with the Pope which, when the fact became known, astonished many of his co-religionists. On 2 December 1960, on his way back from the Middle East where he had met the religious heads of the ancient Christian Churches, he stopped in Rome and went to the Vatican to pay what he described as a 'courtesy' visit to the Pope.

For the past four centuries, ever since the schism under Henry VIII, no heads of the Catholic and Anglican Churches had ever met; and the two Churches had repeatedly indulged in violent anathemas against each other. Little more than a century earlier, the reconstitution of the Catholic hierarchy in England by Pius IX in 1850 had aroused violent anti-papist reactions there. At the end of the century Leo XIII's pronouncement on the invalidity of Anglican ordinations had threatened to produce a similar outburst. Later, indeed, there had been the Malines Con-versations of 1921–5 and, at the beginning of Pius XII's pontifi-cate, the somewhat more significant offer to the new Pope from Dr Fisher's predecessor Dr Lang, to preside over a conference on Christianity. But there was nothing in this to foreshadow so dramatic a step as this visit. On that afternoon of 2 December the Vatican was almost deserted and strangely quiet, but behind the scenes the eyes of all the Court, and especially of the Curia, were fixed on this sprightly old gentleman in his strange half-lay half-clerical dress who moved with a small following towards the Pope's apartment, and whom John XXIII left his throne to greet with open arms and with all the warmth of an old friend who had constantly awaited the day and hour of this meeting.

The Secretariat of Christian Union, planned by John XXIII as one of the preparatory organs of the Council, had been set up only in the previous June and had not yet finished settling into its provisional quarters in the Palazzo dei Convertendi in Via Serristori; its membership was not complete and it had barely started on its programme. But that was no obstacle to Dr Fisher, and his gesture, as was to be expected, opened the doors of the various Churches to the intrepid Cardinal Bea and proved the forerunner of an almost uninterrupted stream of visits to Rome by representatives of the separated communities, mainly American and English. The Curia feigned indifference, but it was obvious that if the siege still held out at the top, its outer defences had been broken.

Little by little, moreover, John XXIII's hitherto largely popular prestige extended more widely through the attention attracted by his official pronouncements. His first encyclical, *Ad Petri Cathedram*, of 29 June 1959, straightforward in content and simple in form, might have been likened to a modest pastoral; but the *Princeps Pastorum*, of the following November, on missions, though it passed unnoticed by most of the press, was a great document worthy of, and even superior to, *Maximum illud*, which it was designed to commemorate. Then on 15 July 1961 (ante-dated 15 May) appeared the long-awaited social encyclical, *Mater et magistra*, which impressively surpassed the by now too restricted view of the working-class question so commendably treated in his day by Leo XIII in *Rerum Novarum* and again later by Pius X in *Quadragesimo anno*. John XXIII daringly set this problem in the wider framework of relations between individuals, intermediate societies, and the State, leading up to the even vaster question of social justice in the international sphere, especially in relation to the need for balance between rapidly developing and backward communities. Not the least merit of this encyclical was its simple, technical, up-to-date language which made it, unlike most pontifical documents, easily understandable to non-ecclesiastical circles and the masses. The encyclical thus aroused exceptional, indeed perhaps slightly exaggerated, interest both in the Catholic and the secular worlds and particularly – a new sign of the times and one favourable to John XXIII – in the Communist world.

As the Council's opening drew near, even within the Curia, or, more precisely, within the world of the Council controlled by the Curia, increasing importance gradually came to be attached to the Secretariat for Christian Union, despite the attempts to boycott it. Its dynamic character, the publicity surrounding its undertakings, and the personal successes of its chairman, Cardinal Bea, absorbed the attention of the public, enhancing the impression of the Council's largely unionist aims, but also encouraging them to believe in the mirage that a modernized, up-to-date Curia might emerge from the reform of the Church.

The Council is Saved

All these hopeful prospects, however, seemed suddenly jeopardized when, in June 1962, the first warnings came of the illness which was to hasten the end of Pope John's pontificate. Had the old Pope agreed to an operation, as some advised, everything hitherto achieved might have hung in the balance. But he did not hesitate to challenge his malady unarmed, though he had no illusions about the consequences of his refusal. 'Once the Council has begun,' he said to Cardinal Suenens as he took leave of him after the close of the central preparatory Commission's labours, 'I know well what I shall still have left to do. My part, then, will be to suffer.'

But Pope John did not content himself with accepting the suffering he was destined to endure. It was time now for him to take the helm of the Council resolutely in his hands, show it its course, and yield responsibility only to those truly responsible: the bishops of the world. This he did, to the astonishment of the whole world, in two great speeches, of 11 September and 11 October 1962. These, much more than the Bull of Indiction of Christmas 1961, mark the date of Vatican II's birth. Significantly, he made no reference whatever to the vast amount of preparatory work done. By his complete silence John XXIII meant to do it summary justice. His view of the Curia's labours was clear enough, if indirectly, from the context of the two speeches: in the first he virtually revealed what the preparatory Commissions had failed to do, and that was pretty well everything essential; in the second he denounced what they had done badly, and that was practically everything.

The subject of the broadcast message of 11 September was the

relations between the Church and the world, relations visualized
not in the form of fresh interference in politics but as a voluntary
and disinterested collaboration for the solution of its problems.
At the centre of everything Pope John put the problem of peace,
not so much in the negative sense of excluding war, but in the
positive sense; but he did not, either, forget to speak of the
'fundamental equality of all peoples in the exercise of their rights
and duties', or the position of underdeveloped countries to which
'the Church presents herself as she is . . . the Church of the poor',
or the 'miseries of social life which cry out for vengeance in the
sight of God'. To all these urgent and topical questions the
famous Commissions had not dedicated a single one of their
seventy *schemi*.

In the official opening speech of 11 October 1962, on the other
hand, John XXIII spoke of what the Council should resolutely
and unreservedly accomplish for the benefit of the Church itself.
There were, even at the apex of the Church, those who thought
that all the evil lay outside and that little or nothing in it needed
to be changed or modernized, as if the tides of time washing
against it washed against eternity, and as if the Church were not,
instead, herself the daughter of time, to say the least in her most
external and visible aspect. With unexpected sternness and vigour
the gentle Pope John declared he could not agree with these
embalmers of the past:

In the daily exercise of Our pastoral ministry Our ear is sometimes
offended by comments from persons full of ardent zeal but not over-
endowed with a sense of discretion and moderation. In our modern
times they discern only prevarication and decay; they maintain that
our era, by comparison with the past, is deteriorating; and they
behave as if they had learnt nothing from history, which nevertheless
is the teacher of life, and as if at the time of earlier Ecumenical Councils
everything had proceeded under the triumphant auspices of the
Christian idea and way of life and of due religious freedom. To Us it
seems that We must dissent from these prophets of misfortune who
continually announce baleful events as if the end of the world were
impending . . . At the present moment in history, Providence is leading
us towards a new order in human relations, which, through the
operation of men and largely beyond men's expectations, are tending
towards the accomplishment of higher and unlooked-for designs; and
everything, even human adversity, is disposed for the greater good of
the Church . . .

The twenty-first Ecumenical Council wishes to transmit pure and entire, without attenuation or distortion, that doctrine which throughout twenty centuries, and not without difficulties and disputes, has become the common patrimony of men . . . [Nevertheless] Our duty is not only to guard this precious treasure as if our sole concern were with our ancient heritage, but also to dedicate ourselves readily and willingly and without fear to that work which our era demands, so continuing along the road the Church has pursued for twenty centuries.

The salient point of this Council is therefore not the discussion of this or that theme of the Church's fundamental doctrine, repeating over and over again the teaching of the Fathers and the ancient and modern theologians which is supposed to be constantly present and familiar to our minds. There is no need of a Council for that. But, setting out from a renewed, serene, and tranquil adherence to all the teaching of the Church in all its entirety, such as still shines forth from the Councils' records from Trent down to the First Vatican Council, the Catholic and apostolic Christian spirit of the whole world now awaits a leap forward towards a doctrinal penetration and a formation of consciences corresponding more completely and faithfully to the authentic doctrine, which itself should be explained and elucidated in accordance with the methods of research and literary formulation familiar to modern thought. It is one thing to have the substance of the ancient doctrine of the *depositum fidei* but quite another to formulate and reclothe it: and it is this that must – if need be with patience – be held of great importance, measuring everything according to the forms and proportions of a teaching of pre-eminently pastoral character.

This resolute adoption of a standpoint in a certain sense burnt the Council's boats, steering it towards objectives which, while precise in themselves, also clearly typified the spirit that was to govern it. Thereafter the Council reverted to being what John XXIII had always wanted it to be, and he could, so to speak stand aside as a simple spectator. It was now the turn of the Fathers, and of them alone, to move on to action.

Less than forty-eight hours later, frantic dispatches from the press agencies, excited comment on the radio, and full-page headlines in the special editions announced the Curia's first serious setback. The General Congregation's first sitting, on 13 October, was supposed to deal with the election of members

of the Council's Commissions, a complicated technical operation
which was expected to occupy the whole morning. Apart from
the religious ceremonies, however, the sitting lasted only ten
minutes and twenty seconds. Cardinal Liénart, Archbishop of
Lille, having obtained permission to speak, and speaking in the
name of the French episcopate, had pointed out that it was
impossible for the bishops to proceed at once to so important
an act, for to do so would mean leaving the election to chance
or weighting it heavily towards the re-election *en bloc* of the
members of the preparatory Commissions (which was just what
the Curia wanted). He therefore suggested that the sitting should
be suspended for some days to give time for the various national
or continental episcopal conferences, whether already in being
or about to be formed, to consult about the persons to be
elected.

Loud applause from the Assembly greeted the Archbishop of
Lille's intervention. But when Cardinal Frings, associating himself and his German-speaking colleagues, Doepfner and Koenig,
with Liénart's proposal, received a similar prolonged ovation,
there could be no doubt about what the presiding board's
decision must be. Cardinal Tisserant, after briefly consulting with
his colleagues, announced that the motion was approved. Thus
the assembly of the Council both rejected the self-interested
tutelage of the Curia and asserted its own fundamental autonomy.

Subsequently, the debate on the first *schema*, about the liturgy,
besides revealing the tremendous technical difficulties of functioning for a parliament of some 2,500 members, brought out
clearly the two main trends in the Council, the curial and conservative, and the episcopal and progressive. Disagreements on
practical matters proved much easier to settle than those on
questions of theory or principle. Discussion of the second
schema, on the sources of revelation, produced some dramatic
and discouraging moments and even at one point threatened to
bring about a complete impasse. In order to surmount it, it was
necessary to know the precise strength of the two trends. A vote
was therefore taken, which resulted in 1,368 for the progressives
and only 821 for the conservatives. But this majority, impressive
though it was, was still not decisive, for the rejection of a *schema*
required a two-thirds majority. Only the intervention of the Pope
as arbiter could prevent the Council from foundering at its outset,

and on a fundamental question too. John XXIII did intervene, and sent the *schema* back not to the doctrinal Commission, which should by rights have revised it, but to a mixed Commission specially formed for the purpose, which included among its members representatives of the Secretariat for Union.

The Council was saved, but the serious nature of the split within it continued to paralyse its work. The *schemi* on means of social communication and on the Eastern Churches received summary treatment, and the session seemed to be drawing to a close in minor key, even though the *schema* on the Church was still on the agenda. Most of the Council Fathers seemed reluctant to embark on a top-level debate such as this subject demanded. But when Cardinal Ottaviani proposed substituting *De Beata Maria Vergine* for *De Ecclesia* the progressives jibbed. It had, moreover, become increasingly obvious from all the pre-ceding debates that the *schema* on the Church was the central and most important topic of the Council. All the threads led out from it or were entangled around it. It was therefore decided to discuss that *schema*. And it was in its final week, when the Council seemed irretrievably endangered by a serious crisis in Pope John's health, that it discovered its true self and acquired its definitive structure.

The determining support came this time from the Belgian Primate, Cardinal Suenens. He proposed that the Fathers of the Council should 'consider with great attention what should be the primordial objective of the Council, so that: (i) the work of the first session, like that of the subsequent sessions, can be ordered around a central theme which will effectively govern its develop-ment; (ii) the activities of every Commission may be seen as the activities of a part of the whole, all directed towards the same common end'. Recalling how John XXIII, in his broadcast mes-sage of 11 September, had presented the Church as '*lumen gentium*' – the light of the peoples – he suggested that the central theme and axis around which the Council's labours should develop should be the *schema* under discussion, suitably recast. The Church should be considered first of all *ad intra*, in rela-tion to its need for internal modernization, and then *ad extra,* in relation to its dialogue with the separated brethren and the world. Cardinal Montini, whose influence on the Council had till then been largely indirect, warmly agreed with the Belgian Cardinal's proposals.

Two days later, on 6 December, John XXIII, still convalescent from his attack, caused the significant and timely announcement to be made in St Peter's that a special Co-ordinating Commission (better known under its subsequent name of Super-Commission) was to be set up to co-ordinate and control the work of all the other Commissions; and that two governing principles should inspire the work in connection with the Council during the interim period between the first and second sessions: first, a definite reduction in the number of *schemi*, and secondly, the close relation of the *schemi* themselves to the aims set out in the Pope's opening speech.

The running-in process had been laborious and even at times dramatic, but the Council had won through at the last. First and foremost, it had affirmed its own autonomy *vis-à-vis* the Curia's attempts to monopolize it; it had clearly defined its own character and aims; it had decided on a logical agenda, an organic plan for its work; it had adapted its own structure and organization to meet the needs of that overall task; it proposed drastically to prune its programme of superfluous undertakings; and it had ensured for itself a secure majority determined to carry out the Pope's hoped-for 'leap forward'.

When they met together around him on 7 and 8 December, the Fathers could be proud of their work. If a shadow clouded their satisfaction, it was caused mainly by the question in the background in each prelate's mind as he observed the alarming pallor and emaciated features of the Pope: would John XXIII survive to the second session, originally fixed for 12 May 1963 and then postponed to 8 September?

'Why should a Pope not die in the street?'

Had the first of those dates been adhered to, the Council would have found itself meeting for the great Pope's funeral. It would have been the most sensational funeral of any Pope in the Church's history. But there is no cause to regret that matters fell out otherwise. The presence of 2,500 prelates in Rome, and all the paraphernalia of the Council, would have distracted people's attention from that great rite, the death-agony of the most evangelical of all the Popes. But as the Council was not to reopen so soon, Pope John had still several precious months left in which to expend not so much his remaining strength – which indeed seemed to be acquiring fresh vigour – but the best of his heart and spirit. He, for his part, threw himself at once into an activity regarded by many as rash and unwise for a man of over eighty who had just narrowly escaped death.

He resumed both the Prefects' and special audiences and the general audiences; received various ambassadors presenting credentials and top-rank politicians and statesmen, among them the Mwami of Burunda, Mr Macmillan, President Segni, and the Turkish Foreign Minister; conducted services in the chapels of the Sacred Palaces and in St Peter's; carried out another canonization and two separate beatifications; prepared and read broadcast messages, among them those for Christmas and Easter; made a score of speeches to various groups of specialists; and, beginning with Christmas when he went back again to visit the sick children in the Hospital of the Infant Jesus, he made eleven visits outside the Vatican.

The first three visits were to the Church of Santa Maria in Trivio to do homage to the tomb of St Gaspare of Bufalo, and to two ecclesiastical institutions, the Roman Seminary and the Pontificio Ateneo Angelicum, recently renamed the University of St Thomas Aquinas; but later, when Lent came, after taking part in the first Lenten visit, to Santa Sabina, he dedicated each Sunday to visiting various parishes in the outskirts of Rome, once even going so far as Ostia Lido. The last time he went out was on 11 May 1963, for the Balzan Prize presentation ceremony in the Quirinal.

All this prodigality of effort was watched with the most lively anxiety: at every general audience or public appearance, especially when outside the Vatican, people studied his face, noted his pallor and his strained smile, listened to his tone of voice, and drew their various conclusions, whether pessimistic or hopefully optimistic. In the end everyone became accustomed to these alternating hopes and fears, and when one day he stumbled while mounting his throne and nearly fell, nobody dramatized the event. In the same way, no one made much of it when on arriving at the Quirinal for the Balzan presentation he asked, with his usual gentle courtesy that always made hay of ceremony, to be allowed to rest a while.

His secretary, Mgr Capovilla, was later to tell how he often tried to persuade the Pope to give up an audience or a visit outside the Vatican. 'My son,' was Pope John's invariable answer, 'what could be better than for a father to die with his sons assembled around him?' But John XXIII's dynamic energy in outward affairs during the last six months of his life is as nothing by comparison with his activity in the more delicate and, so to speak, newer spheres of his office as Head of the Church. Throughout this period, needless to say, he maintained his relations with the separated Christian confessions (receiving among others the head of the Methodist Church in Great Britain, the Prior of the Protestant community in Taizé, and the Canadian Anglican Bishop Luxton). He also went some way towards satisfying the claims of the Catholic Uniates (the former schismatic group in the Near East which in recent centuries had returned to Rome) by promoting their six Patriarchs to be 'associated members' of the Congregation for the Eastern Church, thus recognizing their status as practically that of a cardinal.

The most important events of this last period of his pontificate are, however, of a different kind. First among them was undoubtedly the issue of the encyclical *Pacem in terris*, which he signed on 9 April 1963 at a ceremony which, for the first time in history, was televised. The encyclical rightly aroused tremendous interest, while at the same time evoking some absurd attacks from right-wing extremists. Another event which attracted less notice than it deserved was the appointment, on 29 March, of a Commission of thirty Cardinals to revise the Code of Canon Law. As will be recalled, the third point of the programme that John XXIII had announced at St Paul's Without the Walls on 25 January 1959, after those about the Roman Synod and Vatican II, was the modernization of the Code, decided on by Pius X and promulgated by Benedict XV as long ago as 1917. It is significant that John XXIII did not wish to await the end of the Council before beginning to put this last point of his programme into effect.

The most important and unremitting of Pope John's activities in those last six months were concerned with the Council and with the establishment of new political and diplomatic relations with the countries of the Communist world. His activity in those two spheres seemed almost frenzied, as if prompted by the fear that he might not have time to make the most of the exceptional possibilities that he himself had largely created.

As far as the Council is concerned, this is not the place to give a detailed record of the work of the various Commissions, especially the Super-Commission. Here it must suffice to say that John xxiii followed all this work closely through discussions with the leaders responsible and perusal of the records, received the members of the Super-Commission on 28 January 1963 at the end of its first session (21–27 January), and presided over one of its meetings on 28 March. He also sent an important letter to the bishops of the world, *Mirabilis ille,* published on 8 February, on the work of the Council and the responsibilities of the episcopate in collaborating with it during the current interim period.

John xxiii's thoughts were constantly fixed on this great goal of his pontificate. But towards the end of his life he showed almost the same sense of urgency about translating into practice the famous principle affirmed in the fifth part of *Pacem in terris,* on the Church's relations with States governed by anti-Catholic ideologies, with a view to establishing the basis for new relations with the Communist countries. Without in any way deviating from doctrinal intransigence, he had from the outset of his pontificate striven ardently to establish coexistence and if possible a feasible form of cohabitation with them, with a view to ending oppression of the Catholic communities there, and to initiate a dialogue within the limits of possibility. His efforts had been crowned with success on the very eve of the Council's opening, with the unhoped-for arrival in Rome of delegations or representatives of all the episcopates (of Poland, Hungary, Czechoslovakia, etc.) hitherto prevented from leaving their countries. The Council's abstention from any anti-Communist manifestation did the rest; and at the beginning of 1963 the astonished world witnessed not only various indications of the new relations now possible between Rome and the Churches beyond the Iron Curtain (the sending of blessed candles, letters, and gifts, the encyclical on Sts Cyril and Methodius, etc.) but also more significant episodes such as the return of Mgr Slipyi, Archbishop of Lwow in the Ukraine, from a Soviet prison, the amnesty extended to the whole Hungarian episcopate and practically all Hungarian priests under ban or imprisonment, and, in particular, the meeting in Rome of Khrushchev's son-in-law, Adjubei, with John xxiii himself.

Nevertheless the exceptional feature of the last phase of

John xxiii's life is not his heroism or his limitless personal dedication. Other Popes may have equalled or even surpassed, in their secret consciences or their concealed actions, the generosity of his self-offering. The most completely typical feature of this last period was the 'choral' character, if one may so express it, that his existence took on. In the last weeks he spent not one day in solitary isolation, not a single gesture of his went unobserved, not a word unheard. What happened on a small scale in Rome – when he went out on a Sunday afternoon to a chapel or church in the suburbs, finding the way lined by hundreds of thousands of people, and the political parties mutely agreed to cover up their manifestoes, the cinemas took down their placards, and men and women of all sorts and stations mingled in the crowd to greet him – was only a symbolical fraction of the sympathy accorded him by the whole world. A smile from him, the sight of his picture, sufficed to bring peace and brotherly fellow-feeling. In his presence there was no longer any difference between Catholics and Protestants, Orthodox and Jews, pagans and atheists. He was the Pope of all, the man most loved by all humanity, and all men vied with each other to do him honour (as with the Balzan Prize for Peace), erect monuments to him, and praise his efforts (as with *Pacem in terris*) even before they came to realization; and beyond the crowds, the great men of politics and art, philosophy and learning – from Kennedy to Khrushchev, from Stravinsky to Milhaud and Manzu – joined in admiration and support for him.

This universal crescendo of love and enthusiasm is the only possible explanation of the atmosphere prevailing in the last week of his life, when his illness and death came to be felt not as some remote, half-mythological happening but as something personal to everyone. In those days of a sorrow at once incredulous yet serene, bitterly felt yet tempered with resignation, one deeply moving episode followed another. A young Muslim woman from Istanbul sent him by air an amphora of miraculous water from Ephesus; a fugitive priest in Denver telephoned several times from America to let him know of his repentance; pilgrims from far-off countries walked barefoot to Rome, sometimes carrying heavy wooden crosses. His agony lasted three days and nights, and throughout those days and nights he was watched over like some old patriarch surrounded by his sons silently encamped outside his tent. His bedroom – this altar, as he called it, the altar of his last Mass – was, so to speak, thrown wide open on to St Peter's Square. That last general audience, the longest of all, was also the most moving. Never had his words attained a more majestic simplicity, or a more magical efficacy. The miracle was prolonged over the days when, as broadcasts described, his body, carried by bearers on a simple litter through the Bernini colonnades, lay exposed, first in the basilica of the Council, and then lowered into the crypt of St Peter's for burial.

'I have never chosen anything' . . . *'It is better to be borne by God than by men'*

Obviously the key to the secret of John xxiii's revolution is to be found in his own person alone. Fortunately for us, there are ample sources and testimonies available to enable us to reconstruct the events of his life and the development of his ideas. Nevertheless they confront us with a further enigma that calls for an answer. The ideas and programme that characterized John xxiii's pontificate and changed the face of the Catholic Church were no sudden development, for he had cherished them all along; but he never thought of putting them into practice or making them public until he became Pope. How was this, seeing that he was clearly persuaded of their importance and the urgent need for their application?

There can be no doubt about the fact itself. A whole series of statements and attitudes, anticipating by decades what he was to say and do as Pope, go to prove it. He already had an extraordinarily clear conception of social problems, for instance, at the time of the strike at Ranica in 1909,[1] when he was still secretary to Mgr Radini-Tedeschi at Bergamo. His views on war were equally clear when the First World War broke out. His severe views on the dangers of nationalism can be seen in a letter from Bulgaria of 4 January 1926. His conception of Church-State relations, based on the apolitical nature of episcopal, and hence also of papal, action goes back many years, to the lesson he learnt at length from Radini-Tedeschi. Coming to matters more nearly

---

[1] When workers at a factory at Ranica, near Bergamo, went on strike, with the official support of the Bishop and clergy. This was the first time that such a thing had happened in Italy.

concerning the problems of faith and particularly of the Church, a summary programme for them already appears in the legend beneath the picture commemorating his first Mass, *Ecclesiae libertatem – unitatem – et pacem – adprecatus* (In prayer for the freedom, unity, and peace of the Church). In particular, his anxiety for union, especially with regard to the Eastern Churches, seems to have been nourished by his student years in Rome under Leo XIII's pontificate. His best pages on the ideal bishop were written in 1916, when drawing a profile of his spiritual father and benefactor, Radini-Tedeschi, who had recently died. His commemoration of Pius XI at Istanbul in 1939 anticipates word for word the description of the ideal Pope that he was to give in his speech at his own coronation twenty years later. In the same text of 1939 he makes a suggestive analysis of the Church's catholicity, described as 'in depth, in breadth, and in unity'; while in 1935, in another speech in Istanbul, he had already defined his anti-structural views. Lastly, going through his diaries the origins of the image so dear to him, of the Church likened to a village fountain, can be found far back. In 1958, the year he was to be elected Pope, he spoke prophetically in Venice of the collegial character of the episcopate.

In short Roncalli, long before he became the 261st successor of Peter, was already in full possession of the ideological explosive to which he was to put the match, so to speak, only in the last years of his life. Why, then, did his peaceful revolution not break out earlier? Obviously, up to 1953 there were difficulties in the way because of the highly delicate offices he held. An apostolic delegate and nuncio is inexorably circumscribed in his possibilities for action. But after he was transferred to the patriarchal see of Venice, and was, moreover, covered by the powerful immunity of the purple, why did he not pass over to the attack? The stand he took over certain things was, as we have shown earlier, courageous; but when he encountered hostile reactions in Rome, why, for instance, did he not entrust his message of freedom to the written word? Even if he was not cut out for theoretical treatises, he was still, given the impetus, a fine writer, and could certainly have found the right words. Moreover the essential thing for him was not how he expressed himself but what he said. Why, then, did he keep silence?

The answer, disconcerting though it may seem, admits of no

alternative: because he awaited his hour; or, truer still, because he was waiting until God, should it please Him, caused the hour to sound. This is the gist of the revelation entrusted by Pope John in indirect but unmistakable fashion to his *Giornale dell'anima (Journal of a Soul)*.[1] In other words, he wanted the seal of God upon his work before he could attribute it to Him with certainty. And it is thus that the secret of his revolution in the end coincides with the secret of his deeply religious soul. For John XXIII, with all his intuitive, almost mediumistic capacity for sensing historical needs and popular aspirations, his genius for communication, his marvellous flair for contacts at all levels, was nevertheless first and foremost a man of God. Whoever rejects this key will never open the door to a real knowledge of him. The *Journal of a Soul* has destroyed the whole basis of the legend, once regarded by many as incontestable, of his natural, virgin, spontaneous goodness. The truth is quite different, indeed almost the reverse: that the future Pope attained by conquest, through bitter, unremitting effort, all those natural virtues which in the end reached such irresistible perfection of flowering in him. Were it not so, the word 'effort' would not be among those most frequently met with in his diaries. But the greatest effort of all, in which he concentrated his whole self, was the effort to seek no other thing but the will of God, and to abandon himself utterly to it.

The reason why too many religious spirits wander endlessly along mistaken paths, victims of the most colossal and monstrous delusions, is that they choose to confuse, or confuse despite themselves, their desires and aspirations with the desires and aspirations of God. True religiousness, instead, consists essentially in putting oneself in the right place in relation to God, transforming one's own life into utterly selfless service of Him. John XXIII, one may say, did nothing else but understand and practise to the point of heroism this truth. 'One must let oneself be borne by God,' he told himself constantly. 'God knows I am there, and that is enough for me' was his greatest comfort in the bitterest hours of loneliness and misunderstanding, until he was able to give himself this, the supreme testimony: 'I have never chosen anything.' The first part of the *Journal of a Soul* is quite

---

[1] *Giovanni XXIII Il Giornale dell'Anima*, Edizioni di Storia e Letteratura, 1964; complete English translation, *Journal of a Soul*, The New English Library Limited in association with Geoffrey Chapman Limited, 1965; Four Square Edition, 1966.

simply the story of the discovery of this fundamental rule of life, and the rest is the story of its heroic application.

That there were in him natural predispositions to set him on the road towards this discovery, seems beyond doubt. It was little Angelo Roncalli's good fortune that he grew up in a peasant family, and though he early showed inclination for study and the priesthood, he remained stubbornly attached to the soil. Which, from the religious point of view, meant that he found himself breathing in God like the air and light, and perceived His will in relation to his own spirit just as he recognized it outside himself in the rhythm of the seasons, the fertility of the land and the animals, and in every law of nature. This he owed to the atmosphere of faith and practical Christianity that surrounded him, and in which the dominant and venerated figure was his great-uncle Zaverio, the only bachelor in the family and for that reason regarded by his relatives as a sort of lay priest and an oracle of wisdom and faith. In an autobiographical sketch, the future Pope described him as 'a most pious and devout man, well instructed in things pertaining to God and religion'; and he even went so far as to add that he gave his great-nephew a preparation in spiritual matters worthy 'not of a simple priest but of a bishop and a Pope'.

A similar influence came from his first parish priest, Don Francesco Rebuzzini. But when, at the age of fourteen, he entered the seminary he encountered a different attitude which came near to changing completely, if not destroying, his spiritual outlook. This arose from the Ignatian methods of spiritual teaching traditional in the seminary for the past century, which had been more strictly applied of late following upheavals caused by a school of thought headed by a Bergamo priest, Don Angelo Berzi, who had attracted attention both by his saintliness and gifts as a preacher and by the interventions he evoked from the Holy Office. The fundamental characteristic of Ignatian spiritual teaching is the just balance between passivity in relation to the will of God and activity in personal initiative towards putting its precepts into practice. But the militant tradition associated with the Society of Jesus leads, despite the precept of obedience *perinde ad cadaver* (even unto death), to accentuating the side of ascetic practice, nourishing it by means of the many and detailed observances, the perpetual reminder, reinforced by exhortation, of the presence of God, constant and intensive mortification of every kind, frequent and methodical examination of conscience, and so on – with results profoundly affecting the spontaneity of the soul's religious aspiration.

The seminary at Bergamo, like many other seminaries at the end of the nineteenth century, had both resident and external students and was therefore like a college as well; and the Superior, in order to further the vocations of both categories of students, had evolved the idea of creating a 'Congregation of the Annunciation of the Immaculate Conception' whose aim was to bring together all the most promising students who felt themselves called to the priesthood. The Congregation and the names of its members were secret, and it had a secret statute entitled 'Rules of Life', which carefully subdivided 'practices and observances' into those for each day, week, month or year as well as those for all times.

The aim of the Congregation was to separate the 'called' from those destined to remain in the world. It therefore prescribed complete isolation from evil companions, from those who 'use bad, cynical or Lombard dialect (*sic*) words . . . who cultivate the company of the other sex, discuss flirtations, frequent inns, have a reputation for violence or for carrying weapons, stroll or loiter in the piazza, or frequent gaming houses'. This species of white freemasonry with its atmosphere of secrecy appealed to the youths' imaginations and pride, giving them the feeling of being pure, predestined, and preserved, provided they were imbued with punctilious, wellnigh fanatical strivings towards asceticism. Optimism and serenity were, in fact, the last characteristics of the spiritual attitude it encouraged, as can be seen from such passages in young Roncalli's diary as: 'Of ourselves, we have only corruption, as to the body; ignorance and sins, as to the mind.' Moreover the strict account kept of practices and observances, regularly checked through frequent examinations of conscience, far from fostering the purity of the students' inner dispositions, caused them to seek concrete proof of God's love and so to be more active in doing than in being.

Spiritual teaching of this kind was obviously ill suited to a temperament like young Roncalli's, by nature more inclined to contemplation than to action. Fortunately this experience came to an end with the completion of his philosophical studies and his transfer from Bergamo to Rome, where he was to study theology. At the Roman Seminary his new spiritual director was a Redemptorist and thus a son of St Alfonso Maria de Liguori, Padre Francesco Pitocchi. Imbued with the spirit of his founder, he gradually and imperceptibly weaned the young student away from the unnatural exaggerations of Ignatian spiritual teaching, immersing him instead in the Alfonsine atmosphere ('which better corresponds,' so the future Pope wrote later, 'to our Italian genius, open, perceptive, filled with a sense of balance and also of liberty, steadfastness, and poetry'). The good father's constant refrain was: 'Obedience always, with simplicity and goodness – and leave it to the Lord.'

In his notes on his spiritual exercises in December 1902, when the seminarist from Sotto di Monte was just twenty-one, we encounter the first open acceptance of the spiritual attitude of abandonment to God which he was henceforth to follow and strive to perfect throughout his life. The terms in which he expresses himself are still in part Ignatian ('holy indifference'), but beneath the old terminology a new conception emerges:

I like to enjoy good health, and God sends me sickness. Well, blessed be this sickness! Here starts the practice of that holy indifference that made the saints what they were . . . Poor or rich, honoured or despised, poor priest of a mountain parish or Bishop of a vast diocese, it must be all the same to me, as long as in this way I do the will of my Master, fulfil my duty as a faithful servant and save my soul . . . Suppose I should wish to take up some special course of study: my Superiors will not allow it. Very well, then no special study, but cheerfulness always. I would like to be ordained subdeacon at Easter: my Superiors will not hear of it. Then let us wait in the same cheerful spirit. I would like to be left as I am. Instead my Superiors wish to give me a task [as sick-room attendant] which I find humiliating, and which offends my pride. It costs me an enormous sacrifice to obey. Well then, let us obey.

Two months later, on 6 February 1903, his new attitude is given decisive expression as follows:

My real greatness lies in doing the will of God, entirely and perfectly. If God required me to burn my books or to become a poor lay brother, set to do the most humiliating tasks in some out-of-the-way and despised monastery, my heart would bleed but I should have to do it, and in so doing I should become really great.

In December of that year, during spiritual exercises in preparation for the diaconate, he again confirms his new attitude:

No anxiety then, no castles in the air; few ideas, but they must be sound and serious, and fewer desires. 'One thing is needful.' Golden dreams of working in one way rather than another, highly coloured plans of what I hope to be able to do tomorrow or next year or later: away with all these! I shall be what the Lord wants me to be. It is hard for me to think of a hidden life, neglected, perhaps despised by all, known to God alone; this is repugnant to my pride. And yet, until I succeed in doing such violence to my own likes and dislikes that this obscurity becomes not only indifferent but welcome and enjoyable, I shall never do what God wants from me.

The renunciation of an active part, and the acceptance of abandonment to God, advanced here largely as a programme for living, were to be henceforth put into practice with a fidelity often approaching heroism. He never again deviated from his chosen course, however strong might be the influence of other indubitable examples of holiness he encountered. Almost certainly the strongest temptation to return to the Ignatian and post-Trentine formula arose during the ten years when as a young priest Roncalli was secretary to his bishop, Radini-Tedeschi, a military, authoritarian character whom someone once termed 'tsarist' but who could better have been described as a Jesuit outside the Order. No man left a deeper trace on Roncalli; yet on 10 August 1914, only a few days before the great bishop died, he confided to his diary this significant confession:

My own natural disposition, my experience and my present circumstances all indicate calm peaceful work for me, far removed from the field of battle, rather than controversial action, polemics and conflict. Ah well, if this is the case I will not try to save my soul by defacing an original painting, which has its own merits, in order to become an unsuccessful copy of somone else whose character is entirely different from mine. But this peaceful disposition does not mean pampering my self-love, seeking my own comfort, or mere acquiescence in thoughts, principles and attitudes. The habitual smile must know how to conceal the inner conflict with selfishness, which is sometimes tremendous . . . so that my better side may always be shown to God and my neighbour.

From that moment the ever more heroic practice of the programme for living he had laid down can be said to have begun.

With his bishop gone, he was called up for service as a military chaplain, and on his return to his diocese was given teaching and pastoral duties, gradually becoming accustomed to the idea of spending his whole life in the priesthood there. To check any further aspirations, he had joined, in 1911, as an external member the diocesan Congregation of Priests of the Sacred Heart: a sort of 'oblates' such as were described earlier in connection with Pius xi. He did not, however, merely confine himself to the tasks given him but voluntarily took on others; for instance, he devoted a good deal of time and energy to a sort of college hostel he started for university students. But he had no hesitation when, in January 1921, at the suggestion of Benedict xv, who was a great friend of Radini-Tedeschi, Cardinal Van Rossum called him to Rome.

His new task was to organize a central Council for Italy of the *Pontificie opere missionarie* (Papal Missions), of which he became president. This was a post of trust but a modest one, causing more worries than satisfaction; but it was the Pope's will, and he readily obeyed. When the work was done and he was about to enjoy its fruits, he was moved again. He had also latterly been asked to take a course in patrology at the Lateran Seminary which had been much appreciated by his students. But this too he had to give up when, on 3 March 1925, he was appointed Apostolic Visitor in Bulgaria. The new post carried with it promotion to the episcopate and even a titular archbishopric, but Roncalli did not allow himself to be unduly dazzled by the splendour of the mitre. He went into retreat, meditating on the ideal characteristics for a bishop listed in the *Pontificale Romano*, and wrote in his diary:

I have not sought or desired this new ministry, but the Lord has chosen me . . . So it will be for Him to cover up my failings and supply my insufficiencies. This comforts me and gives me tranquillity and confidence . . . The world has no longer any fascination for me. I want to be all and wholly for God, penetrated with His light, shining with love for God and the souls of men . . . I insert in my coat of arms the words *Oboedientia et pax* (Obedience and Peace) which Padre Baronio used to say every day, when he kissed the Apostle's foot in St Peter's. These words are in a way my own history and my life.

He had even fewer illusions about his destination, Bulgaria: 'Perhaps I shall find many tribulations awaiting me. With the

Lord's help, I feel ready for everything. I do not seek, I do not desire the glory of this world.' What he did not expect, however, was what he had to admit twenty months later:

As I clearly foresaw, my ministry has brought me many trials. But, and this is strange, these are not caused by the Bulgarians for whom I work but by the central organs of ecclesiastical administration. This is a form of mortification and humiliation that I did not expect and which hurts me deeply. '*Domine, tu omnia nosti*' (Lord, you know all) . . . I must, I will accustom myself to bearing this cross with more patience, calm and inner peace than I have so far shown. I shall be particularly careful in what I say to anyone about this. Every time I speak my mind about it I take away from the merit of my patience. I shall make this silence – which must be, according to the teaching of St Francis of Sales, meek and without bitterness – an object of my self-examination.

On 30 October 1929 he noted:

Last July I was so discouraged that I wanted to ask the Holy Father to relieve me of the burden of this Apostolic Visit. It was a moment of weakness, I must and will stay at my post of obedience to the end. Now after the festivals, after the holidays, where I savoured with my good Bergamaschi the delights of the pastoral ministry, after the comforting words of the Holy Father, I feel more and more fortified to continue calmly and serenely along my way, here, whatever the cost and the situation. I do not think of or desire or long for anything else in the world for myself but to do my duty day by day, for the love and glory of Jesus my Lord and for the Holy Church.

Six months later his notes on a retreat begin '*Fac me cruce inebriari* . . . ' (Make me love Thy Cross) and go on:

The trials, with which in recent months the Lord has tested my patience, have been many: anxieties concerning the arrangements for founding the Bulgarian seminary; the uncertainty which has now lasted for more than five years about the exact scope of my mission in this country; my frustrations and disappointments at not being able to do more, and my enforced restriction to my life of a complete hermit, in opposition to my longing for work directly ministering to souls; my interior discontent with what is left of my natural human inclinations, even if until now I have succeeded in holding this under control: all this makes it easier for me to enjoy this sense of trust and abandonment, which contains also the longing for a more perfect imitation of my divine Model.

With the grace of God, I feel, I want to feel, truly indifferent to all that the Lord may decide for me, as regards my future. Worldly gossip about my affairs makes no impression on me. I am willing to live like this even if the present state of things were to remain unchanged for years and years. I will never express the desire or the slightest inclination to change, however much this may cost me in my heart. *Oboedientia et pax.* That is my episcopal motto. I want to die with the satisfaction of having always, even in the smallest things, honoured my obligation . . . The difficulties and trials of my ministry in Bulgaria during these five years as Apostolic Visitor, without any consolation save that of a good conscience, and the rather sombre prospect for the future, convince me that the Lord wants me all for Himself along the *regia via sanctae crucis* [the royal road of the holy Cross], and it is along this way and none other that I wish to follow Him . . .

One of the similes used by St Francis de Sales, which I love to repeat, is: 'I am like a bird singing in a thicket of thorns'; this must be a continual inspiration to me. So I must say very little to anyone about the things that hurt me. Great discretion and forbearance in my judgements of men and situations: willingness to pray particularly for those who may cause me suffering, and in everything great kindness and endless patience . . .

The Bulgarian diaries are such a fascinating mine that it is impossible to resist including one or two more extracts from them. In that spiritual desert the future Pope reached perhaps the highest point of heroism in his life. On 25 November 1930 he noted:

No thought for my future. Many interest themselves superficially on my behalf, and destine me for Milan or Turin or elsewhere. I have no thought for anything, for I do not believe that the Holy Father can seriously think of me for offices so important and so superior to my small attainments. These things *nec habeo, nec careo, nec egeo, nec curo* [I neither have, nor lack, nor need, nor care about]. And therefore I continue to live content and tranquil.

On the same date three years later he wrote:

According to the insinuations of so-called human reason I might be tempted to think that this *incolatus* in Bulgaria *nimis prolongatus est* [that this stay in Bulgaria has been too prolonged]. But that does not depreciate my ministry, my service; it makes it more precious and meritorious before the Lord. My wish is to continue to study always to remain serene and imperturbable at my post. I am not worthy, I say this and I write it, that the Holy Father should concern himself with me. I am here and here I wish to stay, cost what it may. That other I who is always within me though enchained would sometimes try to make me sorry for myself and rattle its fetters and murmur and cry out. Let it stay there in its prison *usque ad mortem et ultra*. I bear my banner ever high and unabased with its motto: '*Oboedientia et Pax*'.

The long and bitter exile in Bulgaria terminated only at the end of 1934. On 4 January 1935 Roncalli took leave of Sofia and arrived next day at the Apostolic Delegation in Istanbul. In October 1936 in his notes during a retreat he said:

I feel quite detached from everything, from all thought of advancement or anything else. I know I deserve nothing and I do not feel any impatience. It is true, however, that the difference between my way of seeing situations on the spot and certain ways of judging the same things in Rome hurts me considerably: it is my only real cross. I want to bear it humbly, with great willingness to please my principal Superiors, because this and nothing else is what I desire. I shall always speak the truth, but with mildness, keeping silence about what might seem a wrong or injury done to myself, ready to sacrifice myself or be sacrificed. The Lord sees everything and will deal justly with me. Above all, I wish to continue always to render good for evil, and in all things to endeavour to prefer the Gospel truth to the wiles of human politics.

Little by little the Curia's hostility died down, though it did not disappear altogether. But the hair-shirt became more supportable, and whereas in Bulgaria the most serious temptation was to despair because of outer circumstances, the temptation that most troubled him now came from within, for the honours and career he saw inevitably opening up before him. In December 1937 the snare still had little strength: 'Honours and promotion in this world,' he wrote, 'do not much affect me; and I think I keep the thought of them in check. But help me, Lord, because the temptation of them may easily arise, and I am weak. The Church has already done too much for me. I am "the last of all".' Two years later it had become more subtle and encroaching:

There is no lack of rumour around me, murmurs that 'greater things are in store'. I am not so foolish as to listen to this flattery, which is, yes, I admit it, for me too a temptation. I try very hard to ignore these rumours which speak of deceit and spite. I treat them as a joke: I smile and pass on. For the little, or nothing, that I am worth to Holy

Church, I have already my purple mantle, my blushes of shame at finding myself in this position of honour and responsibility when I know I am worth so little. Oh what a comfort it is to me to feel free from these longings for changes and promotion! I consider this freedom a great gift of God. May the Lord preserve me always in this state of mind.

After his unexpected transfer to Paris his language is no different. He writes in December 1947:

No temptation of honours in the world or in the Church can now affect me. I am still covered with confusion when I think of what the Holy Father has done for me, sending me to Paris. Whether I shall receive further promotion in the hierarchy or not is a matter of complete indifference to me. This gives me great peace of mind and makes it easier for me to do what I must do here, at all costs and at any risk. It will be wise for me to prepare myself for some great mortification.

He stayed in Paris eight years, and though no one could complain of his work there, not many, especially among the episcopate and clergy, went out of their way to praise his gifts as diplomatist and statesman. As always, he concealed and disguised himself, so to speak, from men's eyes so as to be openly revealed only to the eyes of God.

It was the same again in Venice. Two months after his solemn entry into the city he commented: 'I do not want to set myself any new precepts. I shall continue on my own way and according to my own temperament. Humility, simplicity, fidelity to the Gospel in word and works, with unfaltering gentleness, inexhaustible patience, and fatherly, insatiable enthusiasm for the welfare of souls.' We may wonder that he made no reference to what he might do for the renewal of the Church and the good of the world. Could he possibly not have realized that he harboured within himself revolutionary truths and ideas? But if he knew it, how could he accept with indifference that they should be buried with him at his not too distant death? The thought of death had been long familiar to him. He first referred to it in his *Journal* in 1937, and thereafter it became a recurrent theme – though not a subject for fear, but for a dignified, virile serenity: 'At this thought' (of death), he wrote in April 1945, 'Hezekiah turned to the wall and wept. I do not weep.' In 1953, when he was seventy-two and about to become Patriarch of Venice, he wrote: 'The arc of my humble life, honoured far beyond my deserts by the Holy See, rose in my native village and now curves over the domes and pinnacles of St Mark's. I want to add to my will the request that I should have a resting place reserved for me in the crypt of the basilica near the tomb of the Evangelist . . . Mark, son to St Peter, and his disciple and interpreter.'

But by now the secret of this indifference is clear. He has abandoned himself completely to the will of God. If in truth God has plans for him, He will bring him out from concealment at the right time. Thus, and thus only, God's time will be his time too, and not the reverse. Not even as Pope, when he can no longer be in doubt about God's intentions, does he take it on himself to hurry things. He might believe himself destined to purify God's house with fire and sword, to take a scourge to drive out the traders from the temple. Instead, he still waits calmly for the signs from Providence. At seventy-eight years old there is no time to lose if one has boundless ambitions and tremendous tasks before one. But he knows that God can accomplish everything in a moment, even if it be his own last moment on earth, and he refuses to anticipate God's time by a fraction of a second. After presenting himself on the balcony of St Peter's for the first benediction to Rome and the world, he finds himself at last alone with his secretary in the cell in the quarters of the noble guards where he had spent the three dramatic days of the Conclave. Mgr Capovilla busies himself about him, asking him what he wants to do, whether he wishes to dictate an address, dispatch a telegram, or send him on some message. 'For the present, my son,' he answers, 'we will do the simplest thing: we will take the breviary and recite Vespers and Compline . . .' A few days later he tells journalists: 'Let me carry out my novitiate.' But just for that reason, because he has known how to wait, because he has never forced things but has let himself be borne along by God until the appointed time, when the hour strikes he has no hesitations; and he speaks of divine inspiration in a very different sense from that in which his predecessor spoke of apparitions or visions. Then he has no more doubts: it is no longer he himself who thinks or wishes, but God who commands and he who obeys. From this faith is born the miracle of his pontificate.

This interpretation can, no doubt, be described in more natural terms, indeed in ordinary secular language; but purely natural and secular (if by secular we mean non-religious) John XXIII's experience certainly was not, and the story of his life would be inevitably falsified if it were expressed in terms other than those he used. This, it must be repeated, is the key that he himself has offered us for an understanding of his secret. Up tilll now no Pope's spiritual diary had ever been published. But this is not the only original feature about John XXIII's *Journal*: the deeper originality lies in the fact that its publication was permitted, and therefore desired, by him, after he had re-read it all and had even occasionally quoted from it in his speeches at Wednesday general audiences. He was convinced, in fact, that in it he offered not only the most complete explanation of himself, his life and work, but also the secret of the true religious life, reduced to its simplest and most sublime focal point: abandonment into the hands of God. From this discovery, he believed, would come not only fruits of peace and individual and social happiness but also a new way of regarding religion and its various institutionalized forms, beginning with the Catholic Church.

This key, moreover, besides providing the secret of John XXIII's life and work, also reveals the secret of all the other aspects of his exceptional personality, from its simplicity to its poetry. Simplicity with him was not a form of poverty but a manifestation of richness and power. It served not to eliminate but to unify, allowing no experience or knowledge to remain abstract or isolated, but fusing everything into a single whole. And just as his thought, theological thought included (he used to smile gently but with a touch of malice over professional theologians), went straight to the point, so, too his action was a remarkable combination of audacious daring and controlled pragmatism. There was no dualism between his life and his teaching; and his experience and knowledge combined to strike off those sparks of intuition that enabled him to overleap the gradual stages and reach at once the heart of the matter. One evening at Castel Gandolfo he made a remarkably self-revealing comment to a guest, Jean Guitton. Pointing to the cupola of the pontifical observatory visible on the horizon, he said: 'Look there, you see, to guide men these learned astronomers use the most complicated instruments. As for me, I ignore them. I content myself, like Abraham, with going forward step by step through my night by the light of the stars.'

His simplicity was also, at the same time, a triumph of truth. Speaking of his experiences as a diplomatist, Pope John used to say that the sole secret of his success lay in always telling the truth, so that there was never a savour of diplomacy about what he said. In all his relations and attitudes, indeed, truth was so patent, so tangible, that no one could doubt it. No one ever dared to accuse him of cunning or duplicity. When he walked among the crowds in the streets not even the most fanatical anticlerical thought he was courting popularity. When he first visited the hospitals and prisons, it never occurred to anyone that he might be doing it just for show. For in him simplicity was transparency: the transparency of sincerity and honesty.

Himself in the line of the biblical patriarchs, Pope John's soul and life were steeped in a poetry worthy to be found in the pages of the Book of books: a poetry that emerged sometimes in the written word, but much more constantly in the whole atmosphere and transfiguration of daily life. His life was poetry and – with no play on words – his poetry was life. As in his famous farewell to the Bulgarians, inspired by the recollection of a touching Irish tradition:

On Christmas Eve a light is put in the window of every house, so that Joseph and Mary, passing by on that night in search of refuge, may know that within it there is a family awaiting them round the fire and at the table spread with the good things given by God. Dear brethren, no one knows the ways of the future. Wherever I may go in the world, if anyone from Bulgaria passes by my house at night in distress, he will find a light in my window. Knock, knock! I shall not ask you whether or not you are a Catholic, my Bulgarian brother. Enter! Two fraternal arms will welcome you, the warm heart of a friend will rejoice at your coming.

Or as in this page from the *Journal of a Soul*, which dates back to November 1939:

Every evening from the window of my room, here in the Residence of the Jesuit Fathers, I see an assemblage of boats on the Bosphorus; they come round from the Golden Horn in tens and hundreds; they gather at a given rendezvous and then they light up, some more brilliantly than others, offering a most impressive spectacle of colours and lights. I thought it was a festival on the sea for Bairam which occurs just about now. But it is the organized fleet fishing for bonito, large fish which are said to come from far away in the Black Sea.

These lights glow all night and one can hear the cheerful voices of the fishermen. I find the sight very moving. The other night, towards one o'clock, it was pouring with rain but the fishermen were still there, undeterred from their heavy toil.

Oh how ashamed we should feel, we priests, *piscatores hominum* (fishers of men), before such an example! To pass from the illustration to the lesson illustrated, what a vision of work, zeal and labour for the souls of men to set before our eyes! Very little is left in this land of the kingdom of Jesus Christ. Debris and seeds. But innumerable souls to be won for Christ, lost in this weltering mass of Moslems, Jews and Orthodox. We must do as the fishermen of the Bosphorus do, work night and day with our torches lit, each in his own little boat, at the orders of our spiritual leaders: that is our grave and solemn duty.

Or as in this episode of his daily life as Pope, told by his secretary:

A spring morning; at first light the Pope has recited the Angelus. In the piazza, the splash of the fountains mingles with the greeting of the bells . . . The Pope goes to the window and looking out thoughtfully observes with a smile a youth and a girl mounting the steps side by side to the Basilica. A young married couple? Or an engaged couple? Lost in the vastness of the piazza, they do not know that at that moment the eyes of the most loved and venerated Father on earth are upon them. Nor can they imagine the comment of his heart: 'There go two souls: a feeling of love, which is natural, which is good, has drawn them together; the design of the Lord has been accomplished, or is about to be accomplished. This ascending together, led by the hand of God's law, is like the synthesis of human life.'

The New Church of Pope John's Revolution

But it cannot and must not be forgotten that if John XXIII was loved as a person and a man – for the sympathy he inspired, for the genuine goodness that made his genius for communication irresistible, for the shining example of his life as priest – he was loved still more, and most of all, as Pope. Not, however, as a traditional Pope, but as an exceptional Pope, a completely unheard-of and revolutionary Pope. To be still more precise, as a Pope who repudiated in his own person that disputed and disputable facet of the Papacy that his predecessors, despite schisms and rebellions, had assumed in the name of a primacy and infallibility distorted to connote unheard-of privileges – and this at a time when the original image of the successor of Peter was becoming

ever more disfigured and corrupted. In short the first real anti-
Pope, in a profoundly orthodox sense, in history.

Among the Popes of classic stamp, Pius XII was not only the
latest but also the ultimate, most complete and insuperable personification. Hence John XXIII was the most violent antithesis,
the most inexorable de-mystificator of what had gone before. A
Catholic writer and priest dear to John XXIII, Don Giuseppe de
Luca, who wrote several sketches of Roncalli,[1] almost invariably
portrayed him, whether consciously or not, as the living opposite
of Pacelli – though without, of course, mentioning the latter by
name:

> No infatuation, no exalted gesture: he seems if anything to apologize
> and say that it can't be denied that he is Pope, but it was not his doing,
> or done on purpose . . . There is no separation in him, no putting
> himself on the one hand and his authority on the other . . . He talks
> simply with everyone about the most ordinary, least sublime things:
> he does not argue, or make pronouncements or responses, or pontifi-
> cate all the time . . . He does not investigate, or make disquisitions, or
> even indulge in talk about all those different current topics that make
> up the sound of passing time . . . He has really *met* with those he meets
> and seen what he has seen. He has lived and lives . . . When he prays,
> he does not compose himself but rather abandons himself; he does not
> stiffen, he relaxes.

This might seem a mere contrasting of attitudes or characteristics;
but it is much more than that. For if Pius XII was the Pope who
reigned at the summit of the Church, John XXIII was, and wished
to be, the Pope who is the servant of all, down to the humblest
believer. And the way in which he carried out such a reversal of
the 'idolatrous' idea of the Pope (the definition comes from some
Fathers of the Second Vatican Council) is the more astounding
since he did not bother in the least about abolishing all the
oriental flummery that had for centuries surrounded the person
of the Roman Pontiff. He did not relegate the gestatorial chair
to the Vatican attics, or bring down the feather fans, or silence
the silver trumpets. He even retained the tiara and continued to
mount his throne, to cover himself with gold-woven brocades,
and to speak with the majestic 'We'. He did not wish to create
the slightest suspicion that his reform might be confined to such

[1] See Bibliography, p. 377.

purely symbolical gestures. Only for his funeral he requested
that the obsequies should be of the simplest kind, that his body
should be carried into St Peter's on the shoulders of bearers just
like any poor man's, and that in the bier the only ornament
should be a little metal cross. And yet it was with him alone that,
for the first time since the days of early Christianity, the Pope
reverted to being, if indeed he had ever been, 'the servant of the
servants of God'.

He had begun to reflect on the profound significance of that
title when he was only nineteen years old, a modest seminarist
with no remote idea of the career for which he was destined.
'Servant of God! What a proud title, what a wonderful service
this is!' he wrote then with youthful ingenuousness in his *Journal*,
and with the expansiveness of his years went on:

> Did You not say, O Lord, that Your yoke is easy and Your burden
> is light? Is it not written in Your Scriptures that to serve You is to
> reign? Is it not the greatest honour for a holy man if people say of
> him that he is the servant of God? Surely Your Pontiff, Your Vicar on
> earth, is proud to be called by this name: *Servus servorum Dei*, the
> servant of the servants of God!

After having learnt so young to appreciate the inspiring meaning
of that biblical term, 'Servant of God', and of all its derivatives,
'divine service' and so on, it is not surprising that he should
always have regarded the Pope and the Papacy in a way that
could only be inspired by an exceptional vision of faith, and that
later he should have seized the first moment to translate it into
reality.

If, in a certain sense, Pope John's whole revolution can be
said to lie in this, its consequences inevitably went much further,
extending to a Kingdom in which the sovereign accepts a constitution. The first repercussion was in fact within the Catholic
Church itself. For in overturning the classic pyramid of the legal
conception of the Church, it was inevitable that while the apex
was lowered the basis should be propelled upwards – that, in
fact, the oppressed flock of the faithful should be transmuted into
the biblical 'people of God', an elect, sacred people, the object of
celestial choice and of the care and service of its terrestrial pastors.
Thus all the old, outworn ideas of hierarchy as signifying jurisdiction and power, of authority as teaching and rule, were over-

turned, or rather were seen in their true light and significance, thus making possible a re-evaluation of the laity itself and its function in relation to the Church, a revival of episcopal collegiality to counterbalance pontifical monarchy, communitarian pluralism as against the centralization and bureaucratic dominance of the Curia.

All this came about before the 'new theology', which had been suffocated under Pius XII, was in a position adequately to tackle this problem of ecclesiology. Researches into the background of the veritable Copernican revolution effected in Vatican II's *schema* on the Church all show with what eager haste it followed, developed, and interpreted the intuitions of Pope John's disconcerting simplicity, and never, or only rarely and partially, preceded them.

Before Pope John's coming, deeply-felt aspiration towards an urgent reform of the Church had existed only on a relative scale, centring round the return to the supremacy of spiritual over temporal values and the abandonment of old-fashioned temporalism in relations with the secular world. That particular aspiration was naturally one of the first to be satisfied under the new Pope. His whole life was, indeed, a preparation for this regeneration of the Church. After the valuable lessons he learnt under Radini-Tedeschi, it seems that the time when his mind turned most decisively towards reflection on the Church's historic destiny was while he was in Turkey. It was there, in any case, that he clearly demonstrated how he had moved beyond the structuralism that was one of the most rigid and dangerous limiting factors of Pius XII. Speaking to his small flock at Epiphany 1938, he said:

Observe this land of Turkey. Here was the theatre of the Church's eventful life for many generations; here the early dioceses were numerous as the stars in heaven. Today everything has vanished, it is difficult to identify the ancient places or even to be certain of their names. Now, in the designs of the Lord what is material and by nature mutable is unimportant. We may feel attached to it because of the link it has with what is higher and more sure. Let us therefore venerate these ravaged places, these monuments of the past, even if in ruins, these illustrious remains; but let us not stop at that. The Kingdom of Jesus is all for the benefit of humanity: but it is not subordinate to the material, outer, transitory aspects of true religion. Jesus of Nazareth laid down the basic lines of ecclesiastical organization, but he did not link it to considerations of place or circumstances. A whirlwind comes; it shatters the stoutest buildings and devastates and transforms every thing. No matter. In the designs of the Lord everything tends to His glory, everything corresponds to His teaching, which purifies and renews human generations: everything is put to the service of His grace, which can overthrow and raise up again, can trouble and console . . .

Two and a half years before, at Whitsun 1935, after a moving apostrophe to the Church ('Oh! holy Church of ours . . . the world, the whole modern world, belongs to you. Your heralds are scattered everywhere. Sometimes they bow beneath the storm. But then fair weather comes again. The Church asks only for freedom, and that suffices for her peaceful victories'), he said:

It often happens that I hear from the lips of our separated brethren words of admiration for the Catholic Church, for its good organization, for the sound structure of its framework. People prefer to ignore the real reason for the Catholic Church's continued vigour amid the collapse of institutions, the dispersal of peoples, the fall and rise of dynasties, governments, generations. We believe in the Holy Spirit, Lord and giver of life . . .

This conception, so open-minded when we recall the Roman Catholic tradition, found its most striking corollary in Pope John's opposition to the Constantine, or imperial, tradition. 'We must shake off the imperial dust that has accumulated on the throne of Peter since Constantine,' he once said to an ambassador. But deeds count for more than words – such things as, for example, the new style pervading his relations with Italy, or the abandonment of strong-arm tactics and of anathemas even in relation to persecuting States (e.g. Cuba). But perhaps the most eloquent witness comes from a page in his *Journal* of 13 August 1961:

The sublime work, holy and divine, which the Pope must do for the whole Church, and which the Bishops must do each in his own diocese, is to preach the Gospel and guide men to their eternal salvation, and all must take care not to let any other earthly business prevent or impede or disturb this primary task. The impediment may most easily arise from human judgements in the political sphere, which are diverse and contradictory according to the various ways of thinking and feeling. The Gospel is far above these opinions and parties, which agitate and disturb social life and all mankind. The Pope reads it and with his Bishops comments on it; and all, without trying to further any worldly interests, must inhabit that city of peace, undisturbed and blessed, whence descends the divine law which can rule in wisdom over the earthly city and the whole world. In fact, this is what men expect from the Church, this and nothing else.

My conscience is tranquil about my conduct as newly elected Pope during these first three years, and so my mind is at peace, and I beg the Lord always to help me to keep faith with this good beginning.

It is very important to insist that all the Bishops should act in the same way: may the Pope's example be a lesson and an encouragement to them all. They are to preach to all alike, and in general terms, justice, charity, humility, meekness, gentleness and the other evangelical virtues, courteously defending the rights of the Church when these are violated or compromised.

The Pope of Everyone

But detachment from worldly things, and especially from politics, did not mean for Pope John detachment from the world or from men. All humanity, in his way of thinking, as in that of every truly religious spirit, was, as we have seen, viewed as being on the road to God, its natural and inevitable goal. Even unbelievers journey by irresistible attraction towards Him. Sinners and saints, the indifferent and the rebellious all flow into this great sea. Even stagnation and deviation do not radically separate men from Him. But that is not all. For Pope John, man is journeying towards God not only when he holds more or less supernatural beliefs but also when he functions at a purely natural level. Does not the Gospel say that God's sun rises on the just and on the unjust, on those conscious of their eternal destiny and on those unmindful of it? And the 'sun of God' naturally signifies His loving-kindness, His love.

Hence Pope John's fundamental optimism (so different, we cannot help stressing, from the tactical optimism of his predecessor) about everything in the world, everything human, even to wrong-doing when to err is not confused with error and real sin. Hence, in particular, his enormous respect for natural values and his unprecedented re-evaluation of them, which was to become one of the leitmotives of the Council's texts. Hence, in a word, his optimistic 'Yes' to life and progress, always conceived of by him as being completely and insolubly united with faith. In his greatest encyclicals, *Mater et Magistra* and *Pacem in terris*, he goes so far as to make no explicit reference to the supernatural until the final conclusions. The laws and rules to which he referred were almost exclusively those of nature, behind which he of course implied the presence of the Creator. Hence the fundamentally natural – one is almost tempted to say naturalistic – character of his religious outlook. It is no mere chance that those encyclicals, or more specifically the latter, for the first time in the history of pontifical documents are addressed not only to Catholics but 'to all men of good will'.

His daring initiation of an ecumenical dialogue with the separated brethren will certainly stand as one of the most sensational events of his pontificate, marking a definite turning-point in the history of Catholicism, which till then had remained rigidly fixed on post-Council of Trent and Counter-Reformation lines. But ecumenism is only the first and the innermost of the three rings or circles of the unity he pursued. The dialogues with Christians, with other believers, and with unbelievers in fact represent the three aspects of the single dialogue with the world which he offered on his own behalf and even more on that of his Church. A dialogue, be it noted, not conceived in the partly equivocal, partly adulterated forms in which it confusedly appears in his successor's first encyclical (*Ecclesiam suam*), where it seems to be largely reduced to a propagandist monologue embellished with skilfully framed precepts. The dialogue that John XXIII desired was a loving coming-together, a trusting collaboration in the work of building a better world to unite all men in common, and only at the last, and indirectly, a testimony or proclamation of faith. For this reason his preoccupation with anti-temporalism and with peace were not so much prior conditions but all part of the same pattern.

Significant of this is the way in which, in the drafts for three lectures he gave in Venice in 1954 on relations between Catholicism and Orthodoxy,[1] his anti-temporalist conception of the Church and his dislike of every form of violence converge when he deals with unionism. He did not hesitate, for example, in dis-

[1] Unpublished until they appeared in *L'Avvenire d'Italia*, 3 June 1965.

cussing the reasons for the schism between East and West, to give more importance to the coronation of Charlemagne in St Peter's by Pope Hadrian III than to theological debates and the dissenting opinions advanced by the Patriarchs of Constantinople, Photius and Cerularius.[1] Nothing afterwards, he thought, had done more to worsen the situation than the Crusades, especially the fourth Crusade, owing to the 'horrors' perpetrated in it. As for the abortive attempts at union made at Lyons in 1274 and at Florence in 1489, he uncompromisingly averred that they could have had no other outcome because 'they were not inspired by transcendent ideals but by the desire, prompted by fears of Turkish power, to conserve terrestrial kingdoms'.

As for peace, it would be in the worst possible taste to suggest that his attitude towards it might have been in any way actuated by demagogic considerations such as those which inspired Communist propaganda; moreover documentation going back to the First World War, and especially decisive in relation to the War of 1939–45, eloquently refutes any such idea. Horror of war and the longing for peace were so strong in John XXIII that he even avoided certain words such as 'crusade', and re-christened the 'Eucharistic Crusade' the 'Eucharistic Movement'. But in his conception the elimination of war in international relations was a problem to be solved on a much vaster and higher plane than that of disarmament conferences: on the plane of active solidarity between all peoples above and beyond the intransigence of the ideological systems that might separate them. For this reason his encyclical *Pacem in terris* is only indirectly and in a subsidiary sense an encyclical against war, for its real subject is international order. In this order religions too can and must collaborate in the front line, coming together on the basis of what unites them and disregarding what may separate them. Secular ideologies, in their turn, must not be regarded as an obstacle to coexistence, because their abstract unassailability is virtually contradicted by the concrete compromises forced on them by circumstances (the reference here is to the concluding passages of the encyclical, where historical and sociological arguments are adduced in connection with the possibility of a détente between the Catholic Church and the Communist world).

[1] In the ninth and eleventh centuries – Photius *c.* 810–95 AD, Cerularius 1043–58. *Translator.*

It is impossible adequately to express the depth and extent of the revolution effected by John XXIII within his Church and in the relations of Catholicism with the world. With him and through him the Catholic Church literally rediscovered itself, repudiating, at least potentially, all the deformations accrued in the course of its two-thousand-year-long history and thus striving to recapture the essence and original purity that had seemed irremediably lost. It would therefore be no exaggeration to say that he subjected it to a process of de-catholicization.

It has sometimes been said that whereas in the Church institution and charisma are usually separated, in Pope John they appeared to be exceptionally reunited; but the truth of the matter is rather different. For there is an objective but insuperable hiatus between Pope John's personal religious attitude and the institutionalized religiosity of Catholicism. In a certain sense, as we have seen, it can and must even be admitted that Pope John put himself outside orthodoxy: but in withdrawing himself from Catholic orthodoxy (in the more pejorative sense of the term) he put himself at the heart of the essential orthodoxy of humanity, which not only is in no wise contrary to the deepest nucleus of primitive Christianity, but is also in conformity with all that is deepest and truest in naturalism itself. It is for this reason, even more than for the sympathy aroused by his warm, irradiating humanity, that Pope John has become the Pope of everyone.

A Catholic biographer[1] has said of him that even the secular world was surprised and fascinated and conquered by Pope John because for the first time it found itself loved by a Pope. That is a somewhat ingenuous view. The secular world certainly did not worry itself about not being loved by the heads of the Catholic Church. On the contrary, it would have been surprised and embarrassed to be so loved. The secular world has always mistrusted modernizing advances by the Popes. Pope John alone contrived to conquer that mistrust. How did he do it? Certainly not because he was modern ('rather was he archaic, both in language and in psychology'), but 'he became modern because he was a man, without reserves, and did not impose many conditions on the world for it to be worthy of the peace of God; the only condition was authenticity, fidelity of nature to itself, in

---

[1] Ernesto Balducci, *Papa Giovanni*, Florence, 1964.

short life, which, when it does not deny its own profound urge, is always on the line of moral law'. Beyond the regalia of the Pope the world thus found only a reflection of itself. But precisely this is the most obvious proof that it was not the world that was converted but if anything the Church, even if only for a fleeting instant that might never return. The world has registered not its defeat but its own victory: its ideal – pure humanity, life believing in life, in progress and – why not? – in God – had descended to become flesh and blood in none other than a Pope. It was not the natural that was submerged by the supernatural, but the supernatural that flowed back from the natural and allowed it to re-emerge as undisputed victor. With the apparition of the man called John, in short, a symbol of reconciliation in humanity shone forth. It is no mere chance that his last testament, *Pacem in terris,* is and remains a courageous document of lay thought, endorsed by the most lay – and least clerical – of Popes.

Bibliographical Notes

(a) General Bibliography

Reserved official sources

The following published volumes, containing the Proceedings for the introduction or the development of the causes for the beatification and canonization of Pius x, Cardinal Merry del Val and Cardinal Andrea Ferrari, have been consulted in the archives of the Sacred Congregation of Rites in Rome:

Romana Beatificationis et Canonisationis Servi Dei Pii Papae X: Disquisitio circa quasdam obiectiones modum agendi Servi Dei respicientes in modernismi debellatione, una cum *Summario Additionali* ex officio compilato, Typis Polyglottis Vaticanis, 1950, pp. xxxii–304. (The *Disquisitio* occupies pp. iii to xxxii; the *Summarium Additionale* contains (pp. 1–52) the *Excerpta ex Processibus* and (pp. 53 ff.) the *Documenta* relating to (i) Pius x's attitude to Catholic journalism, (ii) the controversy between the Scotton brothers and Cardinal Ferrari on Modernism in Milan, and (iii) Mgr Umberto Benigni's organization, the *Sodalitium Pianum*. This volume, compiled by the Historical Section of the Sacred Congregation of Rites, is extensively quoted in Maria Torresin, *Il cardinal Andrea C. Ferrari arcivescovo di Milano e San Pio X*, published in Vol. X of the *Memorie storiche della Diocesi di Milano* (Milan 1963), pp. 37-305.

Romana: Beatificationis et Canonisationis Servi Dei Raphaelis card. Merry del Val, secretarii Status Sancti Pii Papae X, Typis Polyglottis Vaticanis, 1957. (After the *Informatio*, pp. 1–69, the most important part of the volume is the *Summarium*, pp. 1–442, which, as regards the ordinary Vatican hearing, gives seventy-four testimonies.)

Mediolanen: Beatificationis et Canonisationis Servi Dei Andrea Caroli Ferrari S.R.E. Cardinalis Archiepiscopi Mediolanensis – Positio super

Causae introductione, Roma, Tipografia Guerra e Belli, p. di Porta Maggiore n. 2, 1963. (After the *Informatio*, pp. 1–51, the most important parts of the book are the *Summarium* (pp. 1–353) and the *Vota Theologorum Censorum super scriptis* (pp. 1–107). The whole volume runs to 588 pages.)

Other publications:

P. G. Semeria, *I miei quattro papi*, Milan, 1930.

F. Crispolti, *Pio IX, Leone XIII, Pio X, Benedetto XV, Pio XI, Ricordi Personali*, Milan, 1932.

L. Salvatorelli, *La politica della Santa Sede dopo la guerra*, Milan, 1937.

A. Mella di Sant'Elia, *Istantanee inedite degli ultimi quattro papi*, Modena, 1960, III ed.

G. Della Torre, *Memorie*, Milan, 1965.

C. Falconi, *Storia delle Encicliche*, Milan, 1965.

(b) Specialized Bibliography
(including only lesser-known works)

Pius X

For the life of Pius x and bibliography of works on him, especially for sources and for testimonies of contemporaries and collaborators, see the official Life written for the postulation for the cause of canonization by P. G. Dal-Gal, *Il papa Santo, Pio X*, Padua, 1954.

On Leo XIII, mentioned in the early pages of the chapter on Pius x, see Carlo Falconi, 'Leone XIII', in *I Protagonisti*, Milan, C.E.I., 1966, vol. XI, pp. 225–52 ('Giano' edition 1967). Concerning the question of his failure to institute internal reforms in the Church, a plan for reform of the Curia, prepared under him in 1902, has recently come to light in the Archives of the Vicariate of Rome and is to be published shortly.

On Pius x as Bishop of Mantua, see Nello Vian, '*Giuseppe Sarto sula soglia di Mantova*', *L'Osservatore Romano*, 18 July 1965; as Patriarch of Venice, Nello Vian, '*Giorni e opere del patriarca Sarto*', *L'Osservatore Romano*, 10 May 1959, and the same author's *Sulla soglia di Venezia, con lettere del patriarca Giuseppe Sarto all'architetto Pietro Saccardo e due altri saggi*, Rome, 1964.

On the registers kept by Sarto as 'prefect' (p. 23), see Nello Vian, '*Note inedite del chierico Giuseppe Sarto*', *L'Osservatore Romano*, 15–16 May 1961. The registers were discovered by the librarian of the seminary in Padua, Ireneo Daniele, who announced the discovery in *Studia patavina*. He deserves mention for his exhaustive researches on Sarto's years at Padua.

The episode about G. La Piana (p. 41) was mentioned by La Piana himself to the well-known writer on Vatican affairs, Silvio Negri, who told the author about it.

The episode concerning Padre Billot (p. 66) was related by a follower of his, Mgr Luigi Figini, in a lesson on dogmatic theology at which the author was present at the theological faculty of Venegono Inferiore, in the diocese of Milan.

On Pius x and Biblical studies (pp. 69–70), see the collective work issued by the Pontifical Biblical Institute, *San Pio X promotore degli studi biblici, fondatore del Pontificio Istituto Biblico*, Rome, 1965.

On Pius x's reform of the Curia (pp. 27–8), see *Romana Curia a Beato Pio X sapienti consilio reformata*, Rome, 1951 (historical essays). For his reform of seminaries (p. 24), see *L'ordinamento dei seminari da s. Pio X a Pio XII*, Vatican City, 1958 (collected official documents of the various pontificates).

On the relations between Pius x and Mgr Bonomelli, see article by Guido Astori, '*S. Pio X ed il vescovo Geremia Bonomelli (Note storiche con documenti inediti)*', in *Rivista della storia della Chiesa in Italia*, 1956, no. 2, pp. 212–66.

On relations between Pius x and the Catholic movement in Italy, see Roger Aubert, '*Documents relatifs au mouvement catholique italien sous le pontificat de Pie X*', in *Rivista della Storia della Chiesa in Italia*, 1958, no. 2, pp. 202–43, and no. 3, pp. 334–70.

Benedict XV

Of the few existing biographies of Benedict xv, the best known is Francesco Vistalli, *Benedetto XV*, Rome, 1928.

For Austria's attitude to the Conclave of 1914 (p. 91), see Friedrich Engel-Janosi, '*Benedetto XV e l'Austria*', in *Benedetto XV, i cattolici e la prima guerra mondiale, Atti del convegno di studio di Spoleto*, edited by G. Rossini, Rome, 1963, pp. 343–55. This work is also useful for the whole question of Benedict xv and the war.

For the correspondence between Della Chiesa and Menzani (p. 98 ff.), see Lorenzo Bedeschi, '*La questione romana in alcune lettere di Benedetto XV*', in *Rassegna di Politica e di Storia*, no. 119 (1964); also his '*Significato e fine del trust grosoliano*', ibid., June 1964, pp. 7–24, where it is clearly shown that Benedict xv was not a progressive even in the matter of the Catholic press. In his view the question of the Trust's newspapers was 'grossly exaggerated'; their closing down was 'not feared by the Holy See'; they were 'edifices of little value'.

The statements of Stockalper, Serafini, and Canali (pp. 103, 104, 108) are taken from the Proceedings for the beatification of Merry del Val, mentioned above among official sources (pp. 141, 152, and 347–8 respectively).

The episode of the parish priest who captured an eagle (p. 115) is taken from Maricilla Piovanelli, *Un cuore rubato (Benedetto XV)*, Milan, 1959, pp. 101–2. This rather strange biography contains many other stories of Benedict xv, especially of his generosity. Though its method of presentation may be thought dubious, its information is reliable.

On the permission granted by Benedict xv after the war to Heads of State of Catholic countries to visit the King of Italy in the Quirinal (p. 128), which was contained in the encyclical *Pacem Dei munus pulcherrimum* of 31 March 1920, see '*Un documento storico*', by A.B., in *L'Osservatore Romano*, 1 and 2 June 1960.

On Benedict xv's personal charities (pp. 137–8), Mgr Mella di Sant'Elia, speaking of Pius xi in the volume cited in the General Bibliography, repeatedly avers that, when the safe in the pontifical apartment was opened on the day of his election, to his great surprise he found it empty. This was not, of course, the safe of the Vatican, which even in those days had various organizations in charge of its financial administration, but the safe containing the sums placed at the Pope's disposal either by the Vatican administration or the faithful.

The life of Père Lebbe (pp. 145–7) by Jacques Leclercq, *Vie de père Lebbe*, Tournai-Paris, 1955, gives a good picture of the Catholic Church's missionary work in the first quarter of the twentieth century and of Benedict xv's personal role in it.

Pius XI

Of the many biographies of Pius xi, the best for the pre-pontifical period is *Pio XI*, by the Milanese priest Angelo Novelli (Milan, 1922). For Pius xi as Pontiff, *Pio XI visto da vicino*, Turin, 1957, by Carlo Confalonieri, now a cardinal, who was his secretary for eighteen years, is a mine of reliable and original information. For his life as librarian, the writings of his successor at the Ambrosiana, Mgr Giovanni Galbiati, will be found useful. In particular, in his *Papa Pio XI evocato* Galbiati discusses very fully the papers left behind by Ratti. Among them one by Mgr Antonio Ceriani is of especial interest because it contains accounts of the journeys Ratti made in Italy and elsewhere in Europe. The correspondence between Ratti and Mgr Giuseppe Faraoni (twenty-five letters and cards going from 1897 to 1921) is described by Nello Vian in *L'Osservatore Romano* of 31 October and 1 and 6 November 1960 under the title '*Pietà e arguzia in un epistolario minore di Achille Ratti*'. Lastly, as to his speeches: except for official speeches, Pius xi hardly ever wrote his speeches beforehand, nor were they recorded or taken down, but usually summarized without subsequent revision on his part. A collection of the speeches edited by Domenico Bertetto, S.D.B., in three volumes of, respectively, 890, 1105, and 1129 pages, appeared in 1960–1. For his policy, see L. Salvatorelli, *Pio XI e la sua eredità pontificale*, Turin, 1939.

Concerning the Conclave of 1922 and the excommunication incurred by certain of its members (p. 154), the volume of Proceedings for the beatification and canonization of Cardinal Merry del Val contains (pp. 140–6) the deposition of Mgr P. Principi, from which we quote the following passage: 'From Cardinal Gasparri I heard this remark: "Cardinal Merry del Val had boundless ambitions, and during the Conclave that resulted in the election of Pius xi, Cardinal Merry del Val incurred excommunication." I asked Cardinal Gasparri how this could possibly have come about, and the Cardinal told me that when Cardinal De Lai, who was the leader of the group supporting the election of Cardinal Merry del Val, realized that Merry del Val could not be successful, he tried to impose on Cardinal Ratti, who was about to be elected Pope, the condition that he would not choose Cardinal Gasparri as Secretary of State . . .'

On the relations between Ratti and the Milanese aristocracy (pp. 159 ff.), see Tommaso Gallarati Scotti, '*Il prete Achille Ratti*', in *Interpretazioni e Memorie*, Milan, 1960, pp. 137–42.

For Pilsudski see J. Beck, *Dernier rapport: Politique polonaise 1926–1939*, Neuchâtel, 1951, and J. La Roche, *La Pologne de Pilsudski (1926–1935)*, Paris, 1953.

On Ratti's work in Poland and Lithuania (pp. 172 ff.), see Angelo Tamborra, '*Benedetto XV e i problemi nazionali e religiosi dell'Europa orientale*', in G. Rossini ed., *Benedetto XV, i cattolici e la prima guerra mondiale*, 1963, pp. 855–84.

On Pius XI's responsibility in the matter of Hitler's rise to power in Germany (pp. 193 ff.), see J. Nobécourt, '*Le vicaire*' et *l'histoire*, Paris, 1964, pp. 151–6.

On the Concordat of 1933 between the Holy See and the Third Reich (p. 195), see von Papen's *Memoirs* (English edition, London, 1953), and also, for a brief survey, J. Nobécourt, op. cit., pp. 157–62.

On Cardinal Innitzer (p. 215) see Von Papen's *Memoirs* (Italian edition, Milan, pp. 509–11, 423–4).

Of the spiritual change evident in Pius XI during and after his illness (pp. 225 ff.) the Archbishop of Paris, Cardinal Verdier, wrote in a letter to his faithful after an audience he had with the Pope in December 1937. That Pius XI frequently turned at that time to an apocalyptic contemplation of history is also evident from one of his own speeches, made at Castel Gandolfo on 20 October 1938. 'Men and events of all nations,' he said in conclusion, 'thrones and republics; altars set up and dust scattered; wars and peaces that were no peace – they all came together in the course of a few decades to proclaim the incontestable truth that events have not obeyed the sign and hands of men, but the sign and hands of God.'

On the origins of *Mit brennender Sorge* (pp. 228 ff.) see A. Martini, '*Il Cardinal Faulhaber e l'enciclica di Pio XI contro il nazismo*', in *Civiltà Cattolica*, 5 December 1964.

On the last events of Pius XI's pontificate, see A. Martini, '*Gli ultimi giorni di Pio XI*', in *Civiltà Cattolica*, 1959, no. iv, pp. 236–50.

Pius XII

There is as yet no general work of a scholarly kind on Pius XII. Nor are there many testimonies from collaborators. Among these the most notable come from Cardinal Domenico Tardini, who in 1960 brought out an amplified and fully annotated version of an official speech he gave in Rome on Pope Pius XII on 20 October 1959, and from Father Leiber's article in *Stimmen der Zeit*, November 1958. Some interesting details are also given in the book by his physician, Galeazzi-Lisi, *Dans l'ombre et la lumière de Pie XII*, Paris, 1960. E. Buonaiuti's book, *Pio XII* (first edition Rome, 1946, frequently re-issued), unfortunately does not go beyond the end of the Second World War, but even so it does not touch on the subject of his silence concerning Nazi crimes, which gave rise in 1963 to the controversies mentioned in this chapter. Relevant for those controversies, treated in the framework of a broader historical consideration of the question, is J. Nobécourt's *'Le Vicaire' et l'histoire*, already cited. Immediately afterwards a number of volumes based on documents appeared: Saul Friedländer, *Pius XII and the Third Reich* (London, 1965; also in German, French, and Italian editions); C. Falconi, *Il silenzio di Pio XII* (Milan, 1965; also in German, French, and English editions), on relations between the Holy See and Poland and Croatia under the Ustashi régime; and Jenö Levai, *Geheime Reichssache: Papst Pius XII hat nicht geschwiegen* (Cologne, 1965; also in French, *L'Eglise ne s'est pas tue*, Paris, 1966), on relations between the Holy See and Hungary. Also to be mentioned, especially for one particular chapter, is G. Lewy, *The Catholic Church and Nazi Germany*, London, 1964 (also in French and Italian editions). The Holy See, faced with these dangerous revelations, embarked on the publication of the *Actes et documents du Saint Siège relatifs à la seconde guerre mondiale*, of which the only volumes to appear as yet (1966) are *Le Saint Siège et la guerre en Europe: mars 1939–Août 1940* and *Lettres de Pie XII aux évêques allemands, 1939–1944*; but so far these two collections of documents do nothing to controvert the facts given by the aforementioned historians. Previously, the official Catholic theses had been maintained in M. Maccarone, *Il nazionalsocialismo e la Santa Sede*, Rome, 1947, and A. Giovanetti, *Il Vaticano e la guerra (1939–1940)*, Rome, 1960.

The Lourdes episode (p. 240) was related by the editor of the *Journal de la Grotte*, Canon Jourdan, to Thomas Lassagne, on the basis of a confidential note by the auxiliary of the Bishop of Lourdes, Mgr Théas (*L'Italia*, 10 June 1963).

The 'Vatican Pentagon' (pp. 243, 292) is the term used by the present author in a series of articles in *L'Espresso* (nos. 1–10) in 1958, and subsequently in a book (*Il pentagono Vaticano*, Bari, 1958) to describe succinctly the leading group in the Vatican represented by the five Cardinals mentioned.

The Notes of protest from the Holy See to the Reich (p. 252) on the violation of the Concordat (and on that aspect alone), have been the subject of a recent publication: *Der Notenwechsel zwischen dem Heiligen Stuhl und der deutschen Reichsregierung*. T. 1. *Von der Ratifizierung des Reichskonkordats bis zur Enzyklika "Mit brennender Sorge"*, edited by Dieter Albrecht. Mainz, Matthias-Grünewald Verlag, 1965, xxvii + 456 pp.

On the post-war 'propaganda' charity of the Pontificia Opera d'Assistenza (Pontifical Aid Organization) (pp. 274, 302), see Carlo Falconi, *L'Assistenza italiana sotto bandiera pontificia*, Milan, 1957.

On Pius XII's anti-Communism at the end of the Second World War and in the early post-war years, see G. de Rosa, *Pro e contro Mosca*, Milan, 1949.

The 'Sturzo affair' of 1952 (pp. 274–5) has been the subject of recent partial revelations by some contemporary witnesses (e.g. G. Andreotti, in *Concretezza*, August 1965). The Lombardi-De Gasperi episode (p. 275) related by Maria Romana De Gasperi appears in her book, *De Gasperi uomo solo*, Milan, 1964. For Luigi Gedda, see Carlo Falconi, *Luigi Gedda e l'Azione Cattolica*, Florence, 1958.

John XXIII

The biographer who was supplied with the most ample documentation for a life of Pope John XXIII is Leone Algisi, himself from Bergamo; his book, *Giovanni XXIII*, was published in Turin in 1959. As the date suggests, this biography is valuable chiefly for the pre-pontifical period. Roncalli's personal secretary, Mgr Loris Capovilla, has written no full biography for the years of the pontificate, but a series of sketches of varying significance as revealing the man himself and some episodes of his life (e.g. *Giovanni XXIII, Sette Letture*, Rome, 1963).

My chapter on John XXIII includes a reference (p. 361) to some short but felicitous sketches of him by G. de Luca, e.g.

'*Giovanni XXIII*' in *Vita e pensiero*, 1962, no. iv, and '*Qualche linea per un ritratto*', in the centenary number of *L'Osservatore Romano*, July 1961. The best and most thought-provoking interpretation of John XXIII is perhaps E. Balducci's *Papa Giovanni*, Florence, 1964. Of importance is Cardinal Lercaro's lecture, mentioned in the chapter (p. 330), given in Rome on 23 February 1965 under the title '*Indirizzi metodologici per una ricerca sull'opera di papa Giovanni XXIII*', and subsequently published as *Giovanni XXIII. Linee per una ricerca storica*.

But a real knowledge of John XXIII comes above all from his own writings, especially the autobiographical works. Apart from his critical volume, *Atti della visita pastorale di san Carlo*, which does not concern us here, these are: his collected (and rather mediocre) writings on *La propagazione della fede (1921–1925)*, Prato, 1959; *Scritti e discorsi del cardinal A. G. Roncalli*, in three volumes (1953–4, 1955–6, and 1957–8), Rome, 1959; *Souvenirs d'un nonce. Cahiers de France (1944–1953)*, Rome, 1963; and, of course, his speeches and writings as Pope. During the week that he lay dying, and in the days immediately following his death, the *Osservatore Romano* published whole pages of extracts from Pope John's diaries, spiritual and otherwise. The immense interest they aroused suggested the publication of as much as possible of the diaries themselves. This was how the *Giornale dell'anima* saw the light in 1964, and achieved a fantastic success. In the first year 300,000 copies were sold (in England, where it was published as *Journal of a Soul* (The New English Library Limited in association with Geoffrey Chapman Limited, 1965; Four Square Edition, 1966) on 3 March 1965, the first edition of 25,000 copies was sold out in a few hours). By the end of that year it had been translated into nine languages, and Polish, Japanese, Czech, and Slovak editions were in preparation.

Index